My
Life
with
Noël
Coward

Noël by Cecil Beaton. In the background a Coward painting.

My
Life
with
Noël
Coward

Graham
Payn

with
Barry Day

APPLAUSE
NEW YORK • LONDON

An Applause Original

MY LIFE WITH NOËL COWARD
By Graham Payn with Barry Day

Copyright © 1994 by Graham Payn and Barry Day
ISBN 1-55783-247-1 (paper)

Published simultaneously in the U.S. and Great Britain by
Applause Books

Library of Congress Cataloging-in-Publication Data

Payn, Graham.
     My life with Noël Coward / Graham Payn, with Barry Day
          p.   cm.
     "An Applause original" --T.p. verso
     Includes bibliographical references and index.
     ISBN 1-55783-190-4
     1. Coward, Noel, 1899-1973--Biography. 2. Dramatists,
  English--20th century--Biography. 3. Actors--Great Britiain-
  -Biography. 4. Payn, Graham. I. Day, Barry. II. Title
PR6005.085Z84   1995
822'.912--dc20   94-42525
[B]   CIP

British Library Cataloging-in-Publication

A catalogue record for this book is available from the British Library.

APPLAUSE BOOKS   **A&C Black**

211 W. 71st Street   Howard Road, Eaton Socon
New York, NY 10023   Huntington, Cambs PE19 3EZ
Phone: (212) 595-4735   Phone: 0171-242 0946
Fax: (212) 721-2856   Fax: 0171-831 8478

First Applause Paperback Printing: 1996
Distributed in the U.K. and the European Union by A&C Black

THANKS!

Many people went to a great deal of time and trouble to help me put this book together and I'd like to thank each and every one of them. I hope you'll see your contribution in these pages and think the effort worthwhile...

To my Editor and Publisher, Glenn Young, and his wonderful team at APPLAUSE - Kay Radtke, David Cleaver, Bruce G. Bradley, ... and Richard and Audrey Pohlers ... Alan Farley, Joan Hirst, Michael Imison, Richard Mangan, Sheridan Morley, Steve Ross ... my two tireless word processors, Claire Kerrison and Sacha Loder-Symonds ... and for her help and humour every step of this particular way - Lynne Carey...

I would also like to express my appreciation to the following individuals and organisations for permission to reprint material to which they own the rights. In cases where, despite my best efforts, I have been unable to locate the owner of the material - which, in some cases, dates back many years - may I offer my apologies and assure them that proper attribution will be made in any future editions of this book.

I'm grateful to the Alan Melville Estate for permission to reprint his poem, "Envy"; to *The Financial Times* for B.A. Young's poem, "The Noëliad"; to *The Sunday Times* for the "Consider the Public" trilogy of essays; to Mander and Mitchenson for excerpts from Noël's introduction to their book, *Revue;* to Methuen for the excerpt from *The Noël Coward Song Book;* to BBC Enterprises Limited for "The Art of Acting," first published in *The Listener* on October 12, 1961.

BOOK ONE

"PAST FORGETTING"

INTRODUCTION

Chapter One   BEGINNERS, PLEASE...   1

Chapter Two   TOURING DAYS   16

Chapter Three   A COLD SPELL: THE POST-WAR 1940's   30

Chapter Four   SHALL WE JOIN THE LADIES...? (1)   46
       NOËL AND GERTIE

Chapter Five   ANGRY YOUNG ENGLAND: THE 1950's   58

Chapter Six   WORDS AND MUSIC (AND PAINTING)   84

Chapter Seven   BRAVE NEW U.S.A.: THE 1950's   114

Chapter Eight   "GENTLEMEN AND PLAYERS":   130
       GREAT CONTEMPORARIES

Chapter Nine   "DAD'S RENAISSANCE": THE 1960's   160

Chapter Ten   THE ROOMS WITH A VIEW   182

Chapter Eleven   THE FAMILY THAT PLAYS TOGETHER   208

Chapter Twelve   SHALL WE JOIN THE LADIES...? (2)   224
       NOËL AND MARLENE... AND TALLULAH...
       AND BEA... AND VIVIEN... AND...

Chapter Thirteen   "GOODNIGHT, MY DARLINGS": THE 1970's   236

Chapter Fourteen   "VERY 'NOËL COWARD'"   256
       KEEPING A LEGEND ALIVE

BOOK TWO

COWARD ON THEATRE

COWARD ON THEATRE   282

THE UNPUBLISHED PLAYS   314
    A Personal Commentary

"CONSIDER THE PUBLIC"   322
    The Sunday Times Trilogy
    1. A Warning to Pioneers
    2. A Warning to Actors
    3. A Warning to Dramatic Critics

THEATRE ESSAYS   338
    - Stage Fright
    - "How I Wonder What You Are"
    - The Decline of the West End
    - The Art of Acting

ACTING WITH NOËL   356
    Judy Campbell Remembers

NOËL AND JUDY GARLAND   368
    A Conversation

"MERELY PLAYERS..."   376
    Acting Contemporaries

ENVOI   389

BIBLIOGRAPHY   390

INDEX   396

Noël on a visit to Kit Cornell at Snedens Landing, her country home on the Hudson. (1935)

INTRODUCTION

I've never been much of one for writing letters, never mind biographies. For most of my life Noël was nagging me for hardly ever *reading* a book, and here I am trying to *write* one about him. Wherever he is, I'm sure he's having a good laugh.

In any case, Coley wrote the definitive book, *Remembered Laughter*, soon after Noël died. Mine will be more of a memoir: some of the things I felt at the time, some of the pieces of the puzzle that have fallen into place with the passing of twenty years. Most of all, I want to say some of the things to, and about, Noël I should have said at the time.

But as Noël wrote in "Most of Every Day":

> *Time makes a mess of things,*
> *Oh, what a mess of things*
> *Time makes!*
> *Time breaks a lot of things,*
> *Oh, what a lot of things*
> *Time breaks...*

I've been saving up quite a lot to tell him, so here is my letter to bring him up to date:

Dear Noël,

If I say that there hasn't been a day these last twenty years when I haven't missed you, that's going to come out sounding sentimental. But what I've missed most is the fun and the laughter. Wherever we were - you, me and Coley - we laughed. There was an amusing side to just about everything, even when the laugh was on one of us.

When something outrageous has just happened or someone's just uttered something particularly asinine, I often find myself turning to you to hear your clipped verdict. Then I remember I'll have to *imagine* what it might have been. Which I usually can.

People think we lived a grand life, which, of course, we did, but not in the way *they* mean. To this day people say: "Oh, it must have been such a privilege to have met all those amazing people and seen all those wonderful places." It was, and if I didn't say so at the time, which I didn't, "Thanks, chum!"

At the time, it didn't seem like the stuff books were made of: gossip columns or stories, perhaps, but not real books! We just strung one scene on to the next. Somehow, it added up to a life.

It's hard for many people to believe what a *simple* life we led. Some of them don't *want* to believe there was a domestic side to "Noël Coward." Well, that's their problem. For me the very best of times were those quiet moments at weekends, after the show, when the guests had gone, when we'd all sit down, put our feet up and set the world to rights.

We were family. Not your conventional Victorian family, granted, but in many respects something better, more alive. Because we *chose* each other. We got together and stayed together because we wanted to *be* together, and we reaffirmed that choice every day. How many families can say that? It gave us the inner strength to, as you would say, "rise above it." Each of us was vulnerable in our own way, I suppose. We'd had to pick ourselves up early in life and make what we could of the hand we'd been dealt. We sensed that quality in each other; it brought us together and kept us together in a cocoon that kept the world out. After all, who could really hurt us?

And, of course, it helped to be immortal. There was always another place, another face, another song or show or painting. Every day was a new opening night for the rest of our lives.

Then, somewhere near the end of eternity, you decided it was time to go. Your timing had always been impeccable until that exit. It was too soon. And if you thought the party was over, were you wrong about *that?* Not only is it still going on, but you're the guest of honour. Not just here, but all around the world. Not just for the generation you left behind, but for people who weren't even around when we were putting it all together. You're still the topic of conversation. They want to know all about you, what kind of man you really were.

So, if you don't mind, I think the time has come to tell them, at least the way it seemed to me.

I know what you'd say: "If the words are good enough, they'll carry you!"

You see, I *did* listen sometimes!

My love, as always!

"Little Lad"

"Those Were the Days, My Friend..." Noël and I looking unbelievably elegant – well, for 1950-something! I wonder if that style will ever come back? (Jamaica)

Words and Music. *Adelphi Theatre programme cover. (1932)*

CHAPTER ONE

BEGINNERS, PLEASE...

I'll see you again,
Whenever Spring breaks through again;
Time may lie heavy between,
But what has been
Is past forgetting....

("I'll See You Again")

The Scene: A cold and extremely cheerless Adelphi Theatre, London.
The Time: An ungodly hour one winter morning in early 1932.
Dramatis Personae: In the front row of the "audience": several apparently disinterested theatrical executives, including one elegantly poised man. (I remember thinking he was smoking his cigarette in a funny way.) On *our* side of the "footlights": an upright piano with an elderly lady accompanist who'd seen it all before (more than once), and my mother, aggressively swathed in her best and only fur. And me.

I was wearing the *de rigeur* costume for any aspiring male entertainer moving towards puberty: an immaculate Eton suit and a parting in my hair that obeyed all the rules of geometry.

The words my mother had dinned into me before we entered the theatre rang in my ears: "You'd better audition for it, but there can't be much scope for a boy soprano in a show like that...so sing and dance at the same time." The moment the accompanist rattled the keys, I launched into an all-out display of my singing and dancing prowess.

Remembering to do both things more or less together for the next few minutes kept me too busy to notice the audience's absolutely stunned reaction. Undoubtedly these theatrical ladies and gentlemen had been exposed to more than their fair share of child prodigies. But, clearly, never to one singing "Nearer My God to Thee" while doing a tap dance.

Visibly moved, the elegant man got to his feet, turned to his colleagues and declared in clipped tones, "We have to have that kid in the show." Even he, it seemed, had never seen quite such an exhibition! Which is how I came to be booked for *Words and Music*, the new Cochran/Coward revue of 1932, starring John Mills, Joyce Barbour, Doris Hare, Romney Brent (who introduced "Mad Dogs and Englishmen") and Ivy St. Helier, who'd made such a hit in *Bitter Sweet* a couple of years earlier.

And how I first met Noël Coward...

There was not very much for me to do in *Words and Music*. Wearing a white jacket, shorts and top hat, I announced "Mad Dogs." I was also the beggar boy singing to a cinema queue as the lead-in to one of the show's biggest hits, "Mad About the Boy." Never had a young busker given such full value to his audience. I must have come across as a miniature whirling dervish. Pretty impressive stuff, I thought, until after a few rehearsals Noël came up and wagged his finger at me, the first of many thousands of times.

"Graham," he said, "*we* know what a good little artist you are, but this boy, the character you're playing, *he* wouldn't know what you know. He'd stand quite still and just *sing*."

So stand still I did. Like a rock. Never let it be said we pros can't take direction. Unfortunately for me, the part of the stage where I had to stand was just over the brass section of the orchestra. While I was singing my little heart out with the buskers' anthem "I Hear You Calling Me," nobody out front could hear a single plaintive note over the sound of trumpets blasting "Mad About the Boy."

"Mad Dogs and Englishmen" with dapper Master G. Payn in white top hat. The lady with the boa is Ivy St. Helier and the frenetic man on the right is Romney Brent.

"Mad About the Boy." My West End debut was to play the young street urchin entertaining this crowd. Unfortunately, the orchestra played louder than I sang!

My glorious debut was somewhat reduced in scale, which is exactly how a beginner is *supposed* to begin. There was nothing else in the world I'd have been happier doing. I was even paid £5 a week. I'd have paid *them* £5 if I'd had any money!

*   *   *   *

Funny how time comes round in spirals. The Levi's jeans company recently wanted to use "Mad About the Boy" for a television commercial. The Dinah Washington version really does hold up very well, but what would Noël think of his song being used to peddle blue jeans? He'd probably laugh, ask "How much?" and rise above it!

There's often been speculation about who the original "Boy" was. There's a school that puts its money on Rudolph Valentino, even though he'd been dead for a few years by the time the song was written. The lyric compares the "Boy" to Ronald Colman, John Barrymore, Douglas Fairbanks, Jr., Gary Cooper, Ramon Novarro and Richard Dix, so they are all non-starters. Sorry to disappoint the historians, but the "Boy" was just an idealized version of every woman's fantasy, and not based on anyone specific.

In excavating the truth I turned up an extraordinary "lost" verse to the song. It was to have been sung in the 1938 New York revue, *Set to Music* (the US version of *Words and Music*). A dapper businessman in formal black coat and striped trousers is discovered in a smart office setting:

> *Mad about the boy,*
> *I know it's silly,*
> *But I'm mad about the boy,*
> *And even Doctor Freud cannot explain*
> *Those vexing dreams*
> *I've had about the boy.*
> *When I told my wife,*
> *She said:*
> *'I never heard such nonsense in my life!'*
> *Her lack of sympathy*
> *Embarrassed me*
> *And made me frankly* glad *about the boy.*
> *My doctor can't advise me,*
> *He'd help me if he could;*
> *Three times he's tried to psychoanalyse me*
> *But it's just no good.*
> *People I employ*
> *Have the impertinence*
> *To call me Myrna Loy,*
> *I rise above it,*
> *Frankly love it,*
> *'Cos I'm absolutely*
> *MAD ABOUT THE BOY!*

It appears to have been written specifically for the New York production but was cut from the show by the management, who found it too daring. One can see their point. After all, it *was* only 1938!

Attitudes to homosexuality in the arts were light years away from those of today. In England homosexuality was still illegal and remained so until the late Sixties. America took a more lenient social view but in the theatre or on film it was strictly taboo.

The Lord Chamberlain was censor and arbiter of what topics could and could not be addressed on stage. Any suggestion of effeminacy was carefully scrutinised. The only way around it was to avoid specific references on the printed page and "code" it in the performance. "Camp" became the shorthand for "gay." The brittle, verbally bitchy performances of someone like Clifton Webb turned into a stage synonym.

In *The Vortex*, for example, Noël has a character called Pauncefort ("Pawnie") Quentin, who is less than kind to virtually every other character. He refers to one as being "a couple of hundred years too late; she ought to have been a flaunting, intriguing king's mistress, with black page boys and jade baths and things too divine." And to another: "Poor Clare. She eternally labours under the delusion that she really matters." Not vintage Wilde, perhaps, but at the age of twenty-four Noël's *intention* is there.

Of *Semi-Monde* (originally entitled *Ritz Bar*), written in 1926, Noël observed: "It was... on the whole, well-written; its production in London or New York seemed unlikely as some of the characters, owing to lightly suggested abnormalities, would certainly be deleted by the censor."

At that time it was still possible to use the word "gay" in its original sense of "light and cheerful." Ivor Novello's last show was called *Gay's the Word* (1951), and it pulled in the family audience. Many people feel that homosexuality's gain was the English language's loss. We no longer have a word to express that original carefree emotion.

In America, Cole Porter was busily having his own wicked way with words. Noël felt that Porter's lyrics for *Kiss Me, Kate*, though clever, were "too dirty." In the "coded" years, Cole amused himself by pitching his words on two levels, so that the "coach party" audience was content with the obvious, while the "in" group relished the *real* meaning.

Noël was more circumspect. In "Bright Young People," a trio from *Cochran's 1931 Revue*, he offers this observation:

> *Psychology experts we often perplex*
> *And doctors have warned us*
> *We'll end up as wrecks.*
> *They take a degree if they find out our sex.*

Admittedly, he could be more flamboyant. In *Bitter Sweet*, a period piece lampooning Oscar Wilde and Alfred Douglas's floral affectations, surely it was clear he was talking about them then, not *now*? The song was "Green Carnation":

> *Pretty boys, witty boys, you may sneer*
> *At our disintegration,*
> *Haughty boys, naughty boys, dear, dear, dear!*

Swooning with affectation.
Our figures sleek and willowy,
Our lips incarnadine,
May worry the majority a bit.
But matrons rich and billowy
Invite us out to dine,
And revel in our phosphorescent wit,
Faded boys, jaded boys, come what may,
Art is our inspiration,
And as we are the reason for the 'Nineties' being gay,
We all wear a green carnation.

The censor's conventional reflexes were instant. In *Words and Music* John Mills and Joyce Barbour had a lyric that included the lines:

I'd love to know what that stallion thinks
Maybe it's something to do with Spring.

It lasted one night!

The "lost" verse from "Mad About the Boy" was really Noël "trying it on" with no real expectation or intention of seeing it actually performed. There was always an irreverent streak in him that enjoyed taunting the Fates. For instance, very few of the many people who listened to "Mrs. Worthington" on the radio have ever heard the final refrain:

Don't put your daughter on the stage, Mrs. Worthington,
Don't put your daughter on the stage,
One look at her bandy legs should prove
She hasn't got a chance,
In addition to which
The son of a bitch
Can neither sing nor dance,
She's a vile girl and uglier than mortal sin,
One look at her has put me in
A tearing bloody rage,
That sufficed,
Mrs. Worthington,
Christ!
Mrs. Worthington,
Don't put your daughter on the stage.

Most performers feel that Mrs. Worthington got the message without benefit of this verbal *coup de grâce!*

*   *   *   *

I was learning from the best: Charles B. Cochran, London's most impressive impresario, and Noël Coward. They didn't come any bigger than that in the 1930's. If life were a movie, there'd be a montage of train wheels racing, destination boards changing, hands applauding. Through it all my smiling face would emerge. A star overnight. From one Coward success to the next.

In reality, I didn't see Noël again until the war broke out.

Where did this precocious kid first get the taste for the "roar of the greasepaint?" The unlikely provincial try-out was about as far from London as you could get: in Pietermaritzburg, South Africa, where I was born on April 25th, 1918.

My mother, Sybil Graham, was born in South Africa of Scottish middle-class stock. She met and married Philip Francis "Frank" Payn, produced me as the sole offspring and divorced in 1926, though not, she assured me, as cause and effect. My father was an electrical engineer who simply didn't have enough in common with his artistic bride to keep them together. Over the years they saw each other amicably enough from time to time. He never balked at paying my board and school fees but that's as much as I knew of him.

Mother was musical. As a young woman, singing had been her hobby which, luckily, her family could afford to indulge. She decided to have her voice professionally trained, reviewed the merits of the leading European schools, and eventually decided on Germany. There she lived and studied before turning up in London, where she had a small part in a musical. It was there she met Joel Myerson, a tenor who would soon play a supporting role in her career.

As a divorcée with a young son, Mother needed to earn our living; Frank's allowance would go only so far. She decided to take singing seriously. She teamed up with Joel to form Graham and Myerson, with Mother singing the soprano ballads and Joel contributing the more operatic parts. Work in show business in South Africa was sparse, so they set off to tour Australia. All went well until 1929 when the talkies rushed in and their luck ran out. The tour was abruptly cancelled and they were stranded.

Joel took off, but not my indomitable mother. Alone in a strange land, she earned enough money as a barmaid to get back to South Africa, which may not sound much these days, but for a woman in *those* days that kind of independence was quite something. All I knew of this was from the occasional postcard until the day she turned up on the doorstep.

While Mother was on the road, I was boarded out to an endless succession of uncles and aunts. I didn't know anyone was allowed so many. At the tender age of seven my father paid for me to live with Aunt Winnie, his sister, where I was treated with the kindness and warmth accorded a paying guest. As an adult I have often watched young parents playing with their kids and thought, "I never got any affection like that." The closest I ever came to feeling that warmth was from an enthusiastic audience. Then, of course, there was Noël, the first person, other than Mum, who appreciated me for *myself.*

Aunty Winnie and her husband, Uncle Marsy, were busy economising with my father's money, buying all my clothes several sizes too big so that I could grow into them. When Mother returned from a long tour of Australian music halls she was greeted by the spectacle of her son and heir, dressed in the most awful socks and boots and flapping suit. "I've never seen anybody look as terrible as you do," she said. "Out! You're going to stay with your Aunt Jessie in Johannesburg."

Straight from the frying pan into the fire. Aunt Jessie was fond of me, but Uncle George made his feelings clear whenever the ice-cream truck came round on Saturday mornings. He would buy each of his daughters a cone, but I'd have to buy my own. He'd pay the sixpence each for them to go to the swimming baths, but guess who had to find his own sixpence? It was excellent training for Real Life, though I wish the lessons had started a year or two later.

My education, such as it was, was a nomadic affair. I was put into the local school, which was never as grand as those my cousins attended. Even my education was cut-price! I was finally rescued in my eleventh year by Mrs. Davies, a widow who was grateful for my company. The feeling was mutual. I got more genuine attention from her than I'd ever known before.

My luck began to change. Mrs. Cohen, a wonderful piano teacher who lived close by, discovered I could actually carry a tune. She entered me for some local competitions, and, to everyone's surprise, I won. In English *and* Afrikaans!

I also discovered the *Cinema!* Every Saturday morning I'd be off to the "bioscope," as we quaintly called moving pictures in those days. I couldn't get enough of Douglas Fairbanks. I'd go and see him time and again in *The Mark of Zorro* and *The Black Pirate.* I was up there with him, leaping and fencing, and thinking "That's what *I* want to be." So, when Mother next circled back into my orbit, I piped up in my award-winning boy soprano voice, "Mum, I want to go into films." Many kids must have expressed a similar ambition in those days. But *my* mother didn't say what every other mother would have said. *She* said, "Well, come on then, let's go to England. I suppose I can sing there as well as anywhere else."

*   *   *   *

Getting to London was the easy part. What to do once we arrived was a different proposition. The year was 1930. I was twelve.

Like a galleon in full sail, Mother swept into an audition for the BBC, with little me bobbing along in her wake. When she'd finished, Mother, never one to let an opportunity pass unmolested, casually mentioned that her little boy had a beautiful soprano voice. Would they mind if he sang for them? Oh Lord, the looks on their faces! But they listened and I got the job. Mother *didn't*. She left the BBC with a strange look on her face, as if she couldn't decide whether to be upset or proud. Or both.

I immediately started getting work. Mum assumed the full-time rôle of Stage Mother, making the bookings, banking the money, checking the billings, keeping the show on the road. And, of course, coaching me ("Sing out, Graham!"). She used her experience to teach me the tricks of projection in those pre-miked days and how to extend my vocal range.

"Don't take the songs too seriously," she'd say. (She must have had my whirling dervish tendency in mind!) "Don't put in too much expression. Just do them as they're written. The song and your voice will carry you. And in any case, dear, they'll be on your side from the moment you come on."

Boy sopranos weren't exactly thick on the ground, so I did a lot of broadcasting. I suddenly turned into the teenage breadwinner. Boy sopranos are unheard of these days. Somehow it doesn't fit the down and dirty, bare-chested image of pop music. Nonetheless, you often catch rock singers straining for a dramatic high note that I used to reach with no trouble at all. Who was it said something about everything old being new again?

If you had a wind-up victrola and a packet of thorn needles, and certainly if you had the ubiquitous wireless set, you might easily have found yourself listening to Master Graham Payn's rendition of "In An Old Fashioned Town," "I Hear You Calling Me," or that Eric Coates classic, "Bird Songs at Eventide," all of them so sweetly sentimental it was amazing the record didn't melt. I can't claim I was *the* boy soprano of my generation. That title belonged to Master Ernest Lough, whose record of

"O, For the Wings of a Dove" was never off the air waves. But for a while we gave Master Ernest a run for his pocket money.

Around that time, busy little soul that I was, I made three or four Pathé "shorts." In those days you didn't pop into a multi-screen cinema complex just in time to catch the film, miss the adverts and rush off for a quick curry. Today, you see a movie. Then, you went "to the pictures," which meant the main feature, a "B" picture and the newsreel. There'd also be a smiling gentleman bobbing up and down on a Wurlitzer organ that changed colour. If that didn't add up to a full three hours the management would pop in a "short" subject. In each of those five-minute extravaganzas I'd be found singing my little heart out against a variety of recycled backdrops. Production values were not exactly at a premium.

I once sang a number called "Somewhere A Voice Is Calling." Some clever chap crossed out the "o" on the sheet music so that it emerged as "Somewhere A *Vice* is Calling." Everyone *else* found it hugely amusing but, in my innocence, I just wondered: "What on earth can *that* mean?" Ah, the simple pleasures of youth!

I was invited to audition for a Hollywood film. Had I won the part, my life would have turned out very differently: No Noël, no stage career, and probably only a brief flickering moment in the Hollywood firmament. They decided I was too tall for the part, which is how Master Freddie Bartholomew came to be *Little Lord Fauntleroy*.

Some of the bigger cinemas presented full-scale variety shows which ran about fifty-five minutes and featured radio stars such as Tommy Handley, the Western Brothers, and Elsie and Doris Waters. I made my London debut in this extraordinary environment, coming on to sing two or three songs. It was tough going but wonderful training. We'd do three, sometimes five shows a day. I toured the length and breadth of London for several years.

Stardom can be heady stuff! I shudder to recall how I once refused to sing with one band leader on the grounds that he played the songs in strict tempo, while I, as an *artiste*, demanded the freedom to express myself in ballad form. The management didn't seem to care either way and fired the band leader. Luckily, it didn't affect Joe Loss's career too badly as he went on to become England's answer to Glenn Miller.

I played "serious" concerts at all the better venues, including the Wigmore Hall, the Aeolian Hall, and the Queen's Hall. Mother would be there in the front row, willing the paying customers to approve of her son as much as she did.

Education was a continuing problem for a working lad. Mum had put me into Kilburn Grange Council School, which had two advantages: one, it was free, and two, they permitted me to take time off when I had a

"Little Lad" as a little lad singing his little heart out in a Pathé "short." (c. 1933)

Me and Mum!

booking. Fortunately, I was able to repay them in other ways. My outdoor life in South Africa had made me a strong swimmer, and I would win all the cups for them in competition against other schools, which my school seemed to think was a fair exchange.

When bookings became regular, Mother hired a tutor who'd come to the house for a couple of hours a day to try and force the basics into my head. During the long run of a show like *Words and Music* any performer of school age had lessons provided after the matinee, courtesy of the management. There was also the instruction of Miss Italia Conti, a formidable theatrical coach who took no hostages and had managed to keep even precocious students like Noël Coward and Gertie Lawrence in line. My educational record was spotty, to say the least.

I performed as one of the Lost Boys in *Peter Pan.* J.M. Barrie's fantasy play was as much a Christmas tradition as pantomime. Every aspiring young actor and actress dreamed of a rung on Peter Pan's ladder. While only one starstruck Miss could hope to play Wendy, we young Masters had rather better odds; half a dozen Lost Boys were needed to fight the great battles with Captain Hook. In 1931, I was lucky enough to appear as Curly in a cast headed by Jean Forbes-Robertson, whom many people, including Noël, considered to be the definitive Peter Pan.

Peter Pan became a figment of the American imagination too, but the idea could have been conceived only in Britain, where the blurring of the sexes has long been a theatrical tradition. Shakespeare's girls were all played by boys; the pantomime Dame is traditionally a man; and the leading "man" (Dandini, Dick Whittington or whoever), a buxom, thigh-slapping girl. Furthermore, in the children's fiction of E. Nesbit and C.S. Lewis, groups of young boys and girls have all sorts of imaginative adventures without gender ever becoming an issue. Problems, it seems, start with puberty.

Not surprising then, that Peter has come to be played by a girl. Jean Forbes-Robertson was firmly in that great tradition. I wish I could report that she plucked me out of the crowd and said, "We've got to have this kid in the show *every* year or I don't go on." Alas, I don't honestly remember her even patting Curly on his mop of hair, probably because she was too busy whizzing around, courtesy of Kirby's Flying Ballet.

Among the Lost Boys' distinguished alumni was one Master N. Coward, who played Slightly to the great Madge Titheradge's Peter in 1913. Critic Kenneth Tynan joked that "Noël started as Slightly in *Peter Pan* and has been wholly in it ever since!"

In later years Noël and I could communicate privately in public by using Pan shorthand. "That's Nana's bark when she smells danger" could be shortened to "Nana's bark" at a business meeting, meaning "Watch out, they're trying to pull something!" The imaginative Sir James Barrie would surely have approved.

In addition to *Peter Pan*, Noël and I had both played in that other perennial children's Christmas show, *Where the Rainbow Ends*. When I first told Noël that I had made a distinct impression on the audience in the character of The Slacker, he replied that he could well believe it.

In those days there were no stage microphones. If the audience couldn't hear you you'd soon be looking for another job. I can proudly report that *our* generation of Lost Boys, though diminutive of stature, never lost an audience, even in the cavernous Palladium. If we had, Mother would have been the first to pipe up.

The show business mother is quite a phenomenon. Her ambition for her offspring doesn't *create* the talent but it certainly fuels it. I know it did with me. No matter where or when I performed there was always one person in that audience I particularly wanted to impress and to whose performance "notes" I listened with great attention.

I got to know Noël's mother, Violet, in her later years. Frail as she was, you could see the determination that had brooked no impediment to her talented son's progress. Unlike Ivor Novello's "Mam," Violet had no theatrical or musical ambitions of her own. Noël's talent was inherited from his father's side of the family. Even there, there were tales of only modest amateur talent, such as any middle-class family of the period might claim, standing round the upright piano in the parlour while Cousin Vera pounded out "Tales From the Vienna Woods." Noël's parents started going steady after an amateur production of *The Gondoliers*, which may be significant.

Noël often spoke of his father's "sweet tenor voice" and for a while Arthur Coward sold pianos. Aunt Hilda was known for a time as "The Twickenham Nightingale;" Uncle Walter belonged to the Chapel Royal Choir and was instrumental in getting the young Noël into the Chapel Royal School in Clapham for part of his early education. That seems to have been the extent of his family's encouragement. There was definitely no British Beethoven busily composing in the back parlour to inspire the young Noël.

Noël never stopped repaying his debt to his mother every remaining day of her life. For her part, her work done, she could relax and enjoy his success.

In some ways I had more in common with Ivor's situation: We both had a mother whose own ambitions took centre stage in our early years. Ivor wrote of the many "tearful partings and joyful greetings" that I understood so well. He also never forgot the debt he owed to her single-mindedness. Again, he was playing my song.

But that maternal commitment has two sides to it. While it forces to the surface any latent talent the child may have, it creates an isolation. You're out there on your own, cut off from the company of ordinary kids, walking a knife edge. Suppose you fail? In all three of us, Ivor, Noël and me, it bred a kind of social insecurity that we had to find ways to cover up. In our private lives we were gregarious, we liked people around us, we learned to fit in and find a role in the "play," Noël and Ivor as leading actors, I in a supporting role. One way or another, we were always on until we found our "families" and could close the door on the world and relax.

Because of our busy schedule Mother and I didn't go out a great deal, so my memories of the London theatre in the early 1930's are rather vague. I *do* remember the first play she took me to: *Cavalcade* by that theatrical phenomenon, Noël Coward. "Did you enjoy it, Graham?" she asked me afterwards. "Oh yes, it was almost as good as the bioscope!" I piped. Noël's verdict, when I told him years later, was "You stupid little South African (expletive deleted)!" He had a point.

When I was fifteen, Mother thoughtfully said to me: "Your voice ought to be changing. You'd better go and see the doctor." The doctor reported that my voice, in fact, had already broken. "He's using head tones," said the doctor, meaning that, because of the training my mother had given me, I'd learned the technique of singing from the top of my head. All of which might have seemed very clever, if the doctor hadn't then added: "If you go *on* singing like that, you'll strain the voice. You'll never sing again."

So nine weeks' cinema touring work was cancelled. No voice, no job. With all the travelling around, we'd put down no roots, so what was there to keep us in England? Late in 1935 we decided to return to South Africa. I'd like to say that the docks at Southampton were lined with waving crowds, singing "Will Ye No Come Back Again?" but I'd be lying. I don't believe there was a single person to see us off as the *S.S. Watusi* set sail.

Once we arrived, Mother, ever the astute business woman, hit on a scheme to earn our keep. I had been studying tap dancing in England with Buddy Bradley, the dance arranger on *Words and Music.* By the time I left his tutelage, I had picked up Buddy's repertoire of what was then called modern dance. Mother reasoned that it would be a shame to waste all that knowledge. So for the sake of the arts and our pocket books, we sold Buddy's routines to the dance schools in Johannesburg and Durban for twenty-five quid each! I'm sure Buddy would have understood. Though I'm not sure I ever *told* him.

That was the up side. The down side was that there was no theatre world in South Africa in the mid-1930's. With or without a proper voice, there was literally no stage on which to use it. We also discovered that we hated South Africa. If it ever had been our home, it certainly wasn't now. We no longer had any close friends and we'd long since run out of family. We didn't fit in any more. London still beckoned from the backs of our minds.

After three long months of not facing the facts, I said what was on both our minds: "I think we'd better go back to England, don't you, Mum?" "Yes," she agreed. "Let's go home."

A "Very Noël Coward" pose. The way the 1930's saw him.

JULY, 1942   Incorporating PLAY PICTORIAL

THEATRE WORLD

Fine and Dandy *with Dorothy Dickson.* *(Saville Theatre, 1942)*

CHAPTER TWO

TOURING DAYS

I've often wondered if it's possible to recapture
The magic of bygone days.
I feel one couldn't quite resuscitate all the rapture
And joy of a youthful phase.
But still it's nice to remember
The things we used to do
When you were on tour with me, my dear,
And I was on tour with you.

Touring days, touring days,
What ages it seems to be,
Since the landlady at Norwich
Served a mouse up in the porridge
And a beetle in the morning tea.
Touring days, alluring days,
Far back into the past we gaze.
We used to tip the dressers every Friday night
And pass it over lightly when they came in tight,
But somehow to us it all seemed right,
Those wonderful touring days.

(Operette)

On the way back to England I met some chums on the ship who were on their way to the 1936 Berlin Olympics. Mum seemed to feel they were responsible enough for me to join on their holiday, and at seventeen I was more than ready to strike out on my own. No one in our party gave a thought to Adolf Hitler or glorifying the Master Race. We were so keen to go, we hadn't even organized our tickets properly. When we arrived in Hamburg to pick up the events tickets, we discovered they were phony!

One of the girls, called Podgie (we really did give each other ridiculous names in those days!), knew of a charming little island called Heligoland where we could spend the weekend. One evening, during a stroll before dinner, the charm disappeared rather rapidly. We strayed off the path to be greeted by a very loud "Achtung!" and a command to get back on the path. We started noticing all these guns lying around. "How funny," we thought, "that this tiny island should have all those little cannons." But, of course, they weren't cannons; they were anti-aircraft guns and the island was alive with them. I learned later that Heligoland had a very good deep water harbour, a natural home for submarines.

Heaven knows, I was not "politically aware," then or now, but soon even I had a strong instinct that war was coming and that all this talk of disarmament was utterly mad. As my personal attempt to put a dent in Mr. Hitler's plans I joined the Territorial Army in 1938.

It was all a bit like that wonderful Robb Wilton sketch "The Day War Broke Out," exactly the sort of pointless British bravery that Hitler would so gravely underestimate. It was only when the television series, *Dad's Army*, showed how even the least qualified civilians formed themselves into the optimistically-named Home Guard, often without a complete uniform or adequate weapons, that a post-war generation had any concept of the temper of those very strange times. Noël, as ever, caught it in a topical song. "Could You Please Oblige Us With a Bren Gun?" didn't amuse the War Ministry at all!

> *Could you please oblige us with a Bren gun?*
> *Or, failing that, a hand grenade would do.*
> *We've got some ammunition*
> *In a rather damp condition,*
> *And Mayor Huss*
> *Has an arquebus*
> *That was used at Waterloo.*
> *With the Vicar's stirrup pump,*
> *A pitch-fork and a spade*
> *It's rather hard to guard an aerodrome;*
> *So if you can't oblige us with a Bren gun*
> *The Home Guard might as well go home.*

I didn't really have a war, at least not in uniform with epaulettes flashing, despite my early start. I was called up to join the London Irish Rifles on the Friday afternoon before that fateful Sunday, September 3rd, 1939. I heard the news on the radio and I thought, "Before I report to the Duke of York's barracks, I'd better go and collect my pay!" I had a small part in Firth Shephard's revue, *Sitting Pretty*, at the Princes Theatre (now the Shaftesbury). As I was leaving the stage door, six quid in my hot little hand, I overheard a chap say: "Ah, that poor young man. He's off to the wars. We probably won't see *him* again!" Not a very encouraging send-off when you're intent on saving civilization as we know it.

The first order on that balmy September afternoon was to march from the barracks to Olympia. Not exactly Ypres or the Somme, and not even very far as long as you knew the trick, which was: Put all your heavy gear in the truck with your kit bag, and travel light. Muggins here packed his haversack with his rifle and all his worldly goods, humped it onto his back, and set out in the mid-afternoon sun.

Rifleman Payn, G. set out for Olympia, heavy of heart and haversack. Rifleman Payn *arrived* at Olympia plus hernia. An Irish sergeant took pity on me and told me a few facts of service life. "Looks like you'll need an operation for that, lad," he commiserated. "But you don't *have* to have it. According to regulations, you can refuse!" At Millbank Hospital a couple of doctors were literally itching to get their knives into me. I swallowed as hard as the pain would allow and declined the surgery.

"But why?" they gasped. "It's very simple." "Because I'm a professional singer," I replied, "and I've been told it might affect my voice. What *else* can I do to help the war effort?" Apparently I had done quite enough already, because I was promptly given my discharge.

So after all my marching about and all my rifle practice, I wasn't to be allowed to be a defender of the realm. Once again my vocal cords were dictating my life! I stood on the Millbank pavement at something of a loss. With nothing more pressing to do, I hopped on a bus and went back to see if Firth Shephard still had a job for me. Luckily, he had. He later told me that *he* was the pessimistic chap outside the theatre, so perhaps his guilty conscience created the vacancy.

In those immediate pre-war years my dulcet tones were taken from me by Act of God, so I had had to acquire other entertaining skills. There was never anything else I could *possibly* do except appear on stage. So it was back to singing lessons for my "new" voice, back to Buddy Bradley for more tap (with nary a mention of the South African franchises), and to a lady called Joan Davis for "classical" dance.

I began to get occasional bookings. I was in the chorus for a Robert Nesbitt revue called *And On We Go*. Not for long we didn't, because off we came. I was fired a fortnight after joining a revue at the London Casino for not being able to lift a dancer in such manner as to give the impression of a bird in flight. The lady in question was rather solidly built and my arms would soon start to sag. My "soaring bird" became a dying swan. It was all very discouraging.

Then along came television. As a young man dazzled by the lights of Shaftesbury Avenue, I naturally demanded: "Who wants to do television?

Who *watches* it?" Which wasn't quite as stupid a question as it sounds today.

In 1938, the BBC was broadcasting on an experimental basis from Alexandra Palace and some three thousand people were at the other end peering at the rather fuzzy results. Without realizing it, we were genuine pioneers who hadn't the faintest idea of what frontiers we were exploring.

The producers simply picked up the ageless revue format and jammed it lock, stock and barrel inside "the box" on Wednesday and Saturday evenings. You couldn't appear too often or those three thousand captive viewers got sick of the sight of you and you had to be "rested." Of course, we were all given a good long "rest" when the war began.

*　　*　　*　　*

The theatre was in a state of chaos in those early months of the war. Nobody knew whether the theatres would be closed, or who would be available, or for how long, before they were called up. For a lot of theatrical "angels" it was a good time to fold their wings and their tents and silently steal away. Many of them did. Only a few determined producers like Cochran and Firth had the faith, funds and sheer bloodymindedness to keep the show going on.

Shows went on many nights when it was more than a little foolhardy. The stubborn determination of the artistes to dab on a little Leichner No. 5 & 9, rather than cower in an air raid shelter, waiting for the skies to fall, encouraged our audiences to stick it out. Carry on, London!

A small "Notice" in the Saville theatre programme said a lot about those out-of-joint times. It read:

NOTICE

There is accommodation for everyone in the Theatre in the spacious Salon underneath the Orchestra Stalls. It is the most luxurious Air Raid Shelter in London. In case of a warning, an announcement will be made from the Stage, and for those who wish to leave, there is a Public Shelter immediately opposite the front of this Theatre.

DON'T FORGET YOUR GAS-MASK

"C.B." by Max.   Charles B. Cochran, impresario, by Max Beerbohm at the time of Bitter Sweet. *(1929)*

Anyone who didn't live through those times can hardly imagine the surrealistic quality of daily London life. You'd go about your business during the day, then, when night came, you could expect all sorts of hell to fall from the sky. How would the familiar landscape look when you woke next morning? Always supposing you *did* wake next morning.

Mum wasn't worried by any of this, but I was worried about *her*. From our small rented house off Marylebone High Street I moved her into a tiny flat in a safer concrete block in St. John's Wood. Here we camped out for the rest of the war, with Mum in the bedroom and me on the settee.

*   *   *   *

Revue found its true audience in the First World War, as it would again in the second. Light, fast, colourful, undemanding, it was exactly what audiences needed to lift their spirits in those depressing days.

Two distinct styles emerged. André Charlot became associated with the English equivalent of the *revue de grand spectacle*, the expensively dressed, splashy "girls and feathers" production that Ziegfeld was developing on Broadway. "Cockie" (C.B. Cochran) had his own twist on the idea, which eventually came to dominate the form. In the early war years C.B. began to experiment with "intimate revue," his version of the French *revue intime*, a smaller show that relied more on the charm and versatility of a handful of performers than on lavish sets and costumes.

During the 1920's and 1930's Charlot and Cochran were neck and neck when they weren't at each other's throats! They treated each other the way the Shuberts and Nederlanders did in the US, wary but respectful. Douglas Byng, a leading revue artist of the time, summed up the difference between them: "Charlot made stars. Cochran turned them into planets." You had to be very careful if you wanted to be in both sets of good books. Few people managed it; Noël was one who did.

Noël's introduction to Charlot, however, was less than stellar. Bea Lillie brought him in to sing one afternoon and was sternly rebuked by the impresario for wasting his time with "that young composer who played the piano badly and sang worse." Charlot would pay dearly for that remark in the years to come! Noël was later introduced more formally and, precocious boy that he was, suggested he should write an entire revue himself. Charlot diplomatically "forgot" their earlier encounter.

While Charlot liked much of the material Noël offered him, he had the presentiment, later shared by C.B., that a revue couldn't easily be sustained by any one person's point of view. He supplemented Noël's material with other people's and Noël was not then in a strong enough position to argue the point.

London Calling (1923) was the first time Noël saw his name in lights. He was twenty-four. It was also his first West End appearance with Gertrude Lawrence when they sang a duet and danced to "You Were Meant For Me" (which Noël *didn't* write). Although they had known each other as child actors, their careers had travelled along different lines until now. Luckily, Fred Astaire was playing nearby in *Stop Flirting* and Noël, to ensure success, got him to choreograph their dance steps.

The show's success was such that Cochran invited Noël to contribute to a new revue for his management, *On With the Dance*. Staged in 1925, it was the beginning of a decade-long association which saw the production of some of Noël's most important work, including *Private Lives, Cavalcade, Bitter Sweet, Conversation Piece* and, lest we forget, *Words and Music*. Noël characterized C.B. as "a sentimentalist with taste and a cynic with enthusiasm."

Of all their collaborations, Cochran and Noël considered the revues their least successful, brilliant though elements were. The problem lay in the very multiplicity of Noël's talents. *On With the Dance* was followed by *This Year of Grace* (1928), about which Noël was to boast "every word and note was written by me." He could do all of it and so he wanted to do all of it and didn't rest until he had.

When I auditioned for them on that chilly morning at the Adelphi, I had no idea that this was the show where Noël was again about to get his way against C.B.'s better judgement. Fresh from the success of *Private Lives* (1930), Noël proposed a new revue, to be called *Words and Music,* which he had written in its entirety. Gladys Calthrop, his favourite designer, mocked up scenes and costume designs, and Noël had even worked out the running order!

Cochran's theatrical instincts told him this was a dangerous precedent. "The essence of revue," he'd once said, "is variety, rapidity, change of mood and contrast of line and colour!" He was also a great believer in the principle that "homogeneity can lead to monotony." Yet here was a young man, flushed with repeated and recent success, suggesting a one-man show, right down to the black, grey and white colour scheme he'd had Gladys design for him. The businessman in Cochran was subordinated to the showman in Coward.

Despite the billing, audiences did not find themselves at a "Cochran revue" when *Words and Music* (1932) was presented. It met with moderate acclaim but was the last time the two of them collaborated on a show of this kind.

I agreed with C.B. Revue at its best draws on a multiplicity of talents (actors, designers, composers, writers) and is then shaped by a single creative mind. That mind is unlikely to be the writer's unless he can deliberately create diversity, as Noël was to do so dramatically a few years later in *Tonight at 8:30*. Revue requires diversity, which usually turns out to be the prerogative of the producer.

Charlot and Cochran were successful by imposing their own style and focus. When they compromised, they were less so. If Noël was disposed to question Cochran's judgement about *Words and Music*, then a decade later he was to have it proved to him again with *Sigh No More*, and this time with no intermediary to blame.

The revue format kept a performer on his toes in more ways than one. One moment he'd be playing a bit part in a sketch, the next rushing off for a quick change into tails for a romantic number. I was hired almost exclusively for my song and dance talents, but watching the comics taught me about timing. The humour was usually quite broad, the romance chocolate boxy. It didn't require a piercing intellect to get the point. It was simple, harmless fun.

During performances, the producer would be constantly assessing the balance of the show. If a number wasn't getting across, out it would go and a new one would have to be learned for the next performance. More than any other form of entertainment, revue comes into focus during rehearsal, which is why producers like Cochran weren't keen to commit too much money up front on expensive sets and costumes, until they could see what worked and what didn't.

Even when individual numbers seemed to be working, the running order was still the key, another reason Cochran was so sceptical when Noël thought he had it all off pat before *Words and Music* had even been cast, let alone rehearsed. A successful revue that didn't change drastically in rehearsal was unheard of.

The secret of the running order is rhythm. Individually talented as the artistes may be, there must be enough contrast. Two comedy numbers back to back and one is bound to kill the other.

The show must build towards a topper, the big finish that involves all the principals. Most of my revue experience came during a time when austerity was the keynote of our productions. Not for us the big budget spangles and feathers of the lavish pre-war shows. Our "big finishes" were managed with the men in suits as neat as clothing coupons would allow and the girls in suitable frocks.

Noël confessed that he learned the most about running order from Charlot. Charlot would write the names of the acts on cards and then play a game of Patience with them, shuffling them about until he had the order worked out to his satisfaction, which sounds easy enough, except...

Except you can't put two items together because A can't get changed in

Up and Doing. *Patricia Burke and I in a duet to Rodgers & Hart's "This Can't Be Love."* *(Saville Theatre, 1940)*

time to turn up in B's next sketch, or the scene change is too complex to be completed, or...

Even with these caveats, revue was a marvellous breeding ground for new talent. The stars would turn up time and again: Leslie Henson, Sonnie Hale, Douglas Byng, Cyril Ritchard, Stanley Holloway, Bea Lillie. But audiences were always on the lookout for a new face. So the Charlots and Cochrans and their representatives were constantly travelling, checking out variety tours, end-of-pier summer shows, pantomimes, everywhere anyone might be performing in those pre-television days.

This was the world I returned to on Firth Shephard's doorstep that post-demob morning. He immediately put me to work understudying Frank Leighton as the juvenile lead in *Shephard's Pie.* All those years on the road came in handy; it took me no time to learn his routines. This immediately paid dividends when Frank was taken ill a couple of weeks later and I had to go on. Based on that performance, Firth immediately offered me the juvenile lead in his new revue, *Up and Doing,* starring Leslie Henson, just about the biggest revue name of that time. Binnie Hale co-starred with Stanley Holloway and Patricia Burke. I had much smaller billing!

I'd always promised myself and Mum that I'd be in the West End before I was twenty-one. When *Up and Doing* opened at the Saville Theatre on April 17th, 1940, I almost made it. Eight days later I was twenty-two. *Up and Doing* wasn't standard fare. Firth had contrived to acquire the rights to use the score of Rodgers and Hart's *The Boys from Syracuse.*

Binnie Hale delivered "Falling In Love With Love" absolutely beautifully as I was her Troubadour. Pat Burke and I had the duet "This Can't Be Love." Better material did not exist. In what can only be described as an omen, "Falling In Love" was later replaced by Noël's "London Pride."

One night Noël came backstage after the show. I remember being very nervous, not having seen him for the best part of ten years, though I was pleased as punch to be recognised in my own right. Noël could have said "It's beginning to rain" and I wouldn't have known the difference. In fact, he said: "Very good. Splendid." Which, from him, bespoke serious approval.

Noël was not given to the ritual backstage gushing that artistes expect. If he had witnessed a performance that was beyond or, in some cases, beneath criticism, he would pre-empt the "How was I, darling?" with his all-purpose "Un-be-liev-able!" He could extract more syllables from the word than were originally intended.

Noël watched a show with a technician's eye, making his mental comparisons. When he offered a professional criticism (and he usually did), he'd wrap it up in a typical *bon mot* for the recipient to chew over however he liked.

Noël also knew what it was like to be on the receiving end. After a performance of *Private Lives*, he overheard Mrs. Patrick Campbell, in a dressing room full of celebrities, proclaim loudly to Charlie Chaplin: "Oh, I *love* him when he does his little hummings at the piano." Not a word about his *performance.*

He would occasionally be beaten to the punch. Noël had always been rather critical of Ivor Novello's performances ever since his first big musical hit, *Glamorous Night,* at Drury Lane, in 1935. Mary Ellis remembers Noël wagging his finger as he told Ivor all that was wrong with it while Ivor roared with laughter. In 1949, we went to see Ivor in his last appearance, *King's Rhapsody,* and the moment Noël's head peered around the dressing room door Ivor said, "Ah! I *knew* you'd love it!" Noël, knowing he'd been outflanked, just smiled and retreated gracefully in silence.

Sometimes he'd be irritated to the point of asperity. Noël and lifelong friend Joyce Carey once attended a show in which the leading man had given a particularly bilious performance. Backstage they found the "star" pompously holding court, which goaded Noël into snapping: "Look, before you set the world to rights, why don't you stop wearing your wig as though it were a yachting cap?" On the other hand, if the faults were remediable, the wagging finger could accompany stern but constructive criticism.

*   *   *   *

I was now really hitting my stride, which is precisely the time to watch what you're doing. You know enough to get by but not enough to be truly self-critical. I was comfortable enough seeing Noël backstage that I casually sent him a couple of first-night tickets for a revival of *The Lilac Domino*. Noël brought Lornie (Lorn Loraine), his long-time assistant and one of the founding members of the "family." She was a kind woman with a very sharp sense of humour, but that evening she didn't seem terribly amused when she came round with Noël.

Now that I was considered a dancer as well as a singer, I was supposed to help the leading lady, Pat Taylor, who was a singer but very definitely *not* a dancer. I'd lift her up while she waved her skirt about a lot to make it *look* as though she could dance, and we'd both hope we were getting away with it. So did Jack Hylton, who was presenting the show!

Noël stormed into my dressing room that opening night, finger already raised. "I have never seen anybody learn so many bad tricks in so short a time. It's *disgraceful!* We can't bear the show, anyway. So that's it!"

My heart went right down to my tap shoes. I managed to face that steely gaze and mumble something about how that was not the way I *wanted* to behave on stage; I was being *directed* to laugh my head off with a girl on each arm and a glass of champagne in each hand. "Look," I pleaded, "can I sing for you as I *really* sing, not the way I'm forced to by Jack Hylton?" A day or two later, after I did just that, he gave me a small smile and simply said, "That's fine."

Noël's verdict on *Lilac Domino* was perfectly fair. The score was wonderful but the production creaked like an old barn door. It continued to pull in audiences just *because* it was old-fashioned and a million miles away from our own shabby world. I soldiered on, ignoring the crick I developed in my arm from supporting Pat.

There was to be a revival of the musical version of *Alice in Wonderland* at the Palace. Tom Arnold and Ivor Novello were putting it on. Ivor got involved to support his old friend Clemence Dane, who had adapted the story. Richard Addinsell was to compose the music. When I heard a sneak preview of the score and the Mock Turtle's song, "Beautiful Soup," I knew I *had* to get in.

Wonderland in 1944 wasn't without its share of problems. I should have been warned when Ivor confided to me that he thought the show was terrible. How could such a wonderful book not make a wonderful show? My Mock Turtle costume was splendid, my songs even better; and I got to double as Tweedledum *and* Lewis Carroll. Peggy Cummins was an indomitable Alice opposite Sybil Thorndike and Margaret Rutherford, who alternated the part of the Queen of Hearts in their own particular styles.

The major problem was the rather complex scenery, designed by Gladys Calthrop, which had a wicked habit of falling over, particularly when it collided with Kirby's Flying Ballet. It was built mostly on trolleys that were pushed in and out at lightning speed, but unfortunately, Gladys had underestimated the rake of the stage. Various bits of scenery would decide to run down to the footlights, as if to take a bow, often dragging an unwilling member of the cast with them. Peggy nonchalantly acted as though this happened in Wonderland every day of the week. The audience probably believed her.

Alice in Wonderland, like *Peter Pan, Where the Rainbow Ends* and *Toad of Toad Hall* (based on *The Wind in the Willows*), complemented the traditional pantomimes. They were supposedly children's shows but many grown-up kids would bring *their* offspring along to see the spectacle that had delighted them when their hearts were lighter and their eyes wider. Despite the fact that thousands of London children had been evacuated to the safety of the country, in they came but, alas, not in numbers to match their peacetime attendance. We finished our scheduled five-week run and silently stole away.

In my next show, Leslie Henson's *Gaieties* (1945) at the Winter Garden, I got the kind of number I'd been waiting to play all my life, partnering Walter Crisham in "White Tie and Tails." This wasn't written by Irving Berlin but by British composer, Hubert Gregg. No matter. Fred Astaire, eat your heart out! Jack Buchanan, move over! Neither of them was in any real danger, but *I* thought I was elegance personified.

Sadly, Leslie Henson is not as well-remembered as some of his contemporaries. He had a marvellous stage technique which today, I suppose, we'd call "laid back." It was deceptively simple, until you studied it closely, as I had the chance to do in *Up and Doing.* In the number, "The Green Eye of the Little Yellow God," Stanley Holloway, as The Elocutionist, was supposed to recite a poem, while in the box seats two army officers, pukha sahibs played by Leslie and Cyril Ritchard, interrupted him with fatuous questions or comments. It was a typically silly music hall routine where the "serious" character reciting the poem never quite gets to finish. In this case it was a Kiplingesque little verse, which began:

> *There's a little yellow idol*
> *To the south of Katmandu*
> *And a...*

Which is as far as Stanley ever got. The audience broke up as Stanley got more and more irritated and the remarks got more and more bizarre. It's clear those first two lines are all we're *ever* going to hear. At the rehearsal Cyril camped it up like mad, really going over the top, while Leslie seemed to just *sit* there. I remember thinking "Oh Lord, this is terrible. Cyril's going to wipe Leslie off the map."

On the night the effect was startlingly different; I'd clearly underestimated Leslie's technique. He was the still centre for the audience. He underplayed to such a degree that they rather dismissed Cyril for all that ranting and raving. It was Leslie they watched. Talk about less being more. Leslie won hands down.

(Incidentally, that's one of the most misquoted lines in the English language. It's part of every music hall comedy routine. For students of theatre trivia, it's taken from a poem called "The Green Eye of the Yellow God" by one J. Milton Hayes, and the line actually reads:

> *"There's a one-eyed yellow idol*
> *To the north of Katmandu..."*

So now we can all rest easy.)

One night Noël came around as usual, but without the obligatory performance notes. He said: "I'm doing a new revue called *Sigh No More*. And *you* will be in it." And for me, in more ways than one, that was the end of the war.

A Tatler cartoon accompanied their review of Up and Doing, *which said: "Mr. Graham Payn... is apt in dance and pleasant in song." Who was I to argue?*

Pacific 1860 - the show that was to re-open "The Lane" after the war. Noël and Gladys with
Marty Martin and those damned bows! (1946)

CHAPTER THREE

A COLD SPELL:
THE POST-WAR 1940's

This is a changing world, my dear,
New songs are sung, new stars appear...

(*Pacific 1860*)

Sigh No More opened at the Piccadilly Theatre on August 22nd, 1945. It marked the beginning of a personal and professional relationship between Noël and myself that would last until his death. His presence was such that in any given situation I knew exactly what Noël would have said. Often I still seem to hear him saying it.

Not that he always said what you wanted to hear. He'd never compromise his professional standards with his personal feelings. His material had to be performed exactly the way he'd envisioned it. No ifs, no buts about it. I should have remembered that from *Words and Music*, but I'd sung a few songs and danced a few steps since then. I knew what I was doing, or so I thought.

I was struggling with my solo spot in the second half of *Sigh No More*, a number entitled "It Couldn't Matter Less." Frankly, as far as I was concerned, it *couldn't!* I told Noël I didn't think the number was good enough. "Yes it is," he snapped, "it's *very* good!" So I plucked up my courage and challenged him. "All right, then, let's see *you* do it!" There were indrawn breaths from the others at the rehearsal. Would God, let alone The Master, strike me down?

Noël gave me a Look, then took up the gauntlet, which, as an actor/director, he was quite capable of doing. Gladys Cooper once said that when she was rehearsing *Relative Values*, Noël would do all the parts for the cast. "The trouble was, they all sounded like Noël." But she missed the point. Noël was always at pains to say: "This is the gist of it. Play it in your own way. DO NOT IMITATE ME!"

After trying the number a couple of times he conceded, "You're quite right. It *isn't* strong enough. I'll write you another song." "Oh yes, chum,"

I thought, "I've heard *that* one before." I started wondering whether I should have kept my mouth shut. At least I *had* a second half solo. (Noël hadn't written the original song, by the way. His pianist/conductor, Norman Hackforth, had.)

Noël pulled a muscle in his leg and couldn't come to rehearsals for a few days, which turned out to be a lucky break for me! He called to say he'd written a new song. "It's called 'Matelot.' Come around and I'll play it for you." After hearing the first eight bars I knew we had a hit. (Later Noël was to say it was the one thing about the show he couldn't say goodbye to without a pang.)

"MATELOT"

Jean Louis Dominic Pierre Bouchon,
True to the breed that bore him,
Answered the call
That held in thrall
His father's heart before him.
Jean Louis Dominic sailed away
Further than love could find him
Yet through the night
He heard a light
And gentle voice behind him say:

Matelot, Matelot,
Where you go
My thoughts go with you,
Matelot, Matelot,
When you go down to the sea
As you gaze from afar
On the evening star
Wherever you may roam,
You will remember the light
Through the winter night
That guides you safely home.
Though you find
Womankind
To be frail,
One love cannot fail, my son,
Till our days are done,
Matelot, Matelot,
Where you go

My thoughts go with you,
Matelot, Matelot,
When you go down to the sea.

So now we had a powerful emotional number about the way a mother feels for her son. There wouldn't be a dry eye in the house. But Noël had the peculiar notion that I should follow it with a dance!

I just knew in my heart that a dance would kill the moment, but, for some strange reason, Noël couldn't see that. So I deliberately rehearsed the dance very badly. When he saw it at the dress rehearsal, Noël gave me a cryptic look and said, "Cut that bloody thing out and just do the number."

Noël would direct for emotional meaning and he'd use technique as a way to achieve it. With "Matelot" he said, "Don't do very much. Just keep it at a good, reasonable tempo. Don't sentimentalise it." With a song like that, it's a very easy trap to fall into, because it is, after all, a song about the one you love leaving.

I must have been doing something right, because I could still hear the applause as I made my change backstage for the next number. But after a few months, something altered. I had to move faster to make my change in time. "What's happening? Is the orchestra drowning me?" (I remembered "Mad About the Boy!") Naturally it never occurred to me that it might be *my* fault! I asked Peggie Dear, the Stage Director, and she replied, "Well, if you must know, you've added three minutes to the running time of that song!" Three minutes! She was absolutely right; I was doing the one thing Noël had warned me not to do. I was "spreading" it by putting in too much sentiment.

He had given me precisely the same advice as Mum had: "Do it straight, and the song will carry you." I had no intention of compounding that particular felony, so I said, "Tell Mantovani (our conductor) to keep up the tempo to stop me drifting back into that terrible trap." Up went the tempo and the audience reaction came with it. I never made *that* mistake again...though I certainly made many others!

Fortunately, Noël never caught me in my "sentimental mood," or voices and fingers would *certainly* have been raised. He made a point of catching each of his shows on a regular basis for that very reason, to see where socks needed to be pulled up.

He did, however, witness my "improvements" to another number in *Sigh No More*, called "Wait a Bit, Joe." One night he suggested, rather elliptically, "A little charm wouldn't hurt on that number." So next night I put in what I thought was "charm." Noël was round right away. "I said a *little* charm, not *Mary Rose on Ice.*" I was overdoing it again!

Noël's advice was invaluable. On the subject of voice training,

Sigh No More *programme. Cyril Ritchard, Madge Elliott, Mantovani (the Musical Director), Joyce Grenfell and me. (Piccadilly Theatre, 1945)*

however, we differed sharply. I was always practising, trying to strengthen my voice, which drove him mad. After *Pacific 1860* he made me give up singing lessons, saying I worried too much about the voice and not enough about the lyrics. "You're a singer," he'd say. "Just *sing* it!" When I hear the recordings today, I think I was much better in *Pacific 1860* than in later shows. I should have dug my heels in.

We would also differ on the interpretation of material. I took a more "classical" approach, whereas Noël wrote and performed to suit his own limited vocal range. It had been the style of the 1920's, when he had started to sing in public, to pitch orchestrations rather high. Noël's naturally light voice had developed that way. He sometimes referred to it as "thin and feathery." One of his own favourite numbers was "London Pride." Years later he put on an old 78 r.p.m. recording and started complaining about the way the vocalist was singing it in the strict tempo which the band leader, Carroll Gibbons, always favoured. There was a good deal of subdued muttering going on, until I said "What's the matter? Don't you *like* my rendition?" Then the penny dropped. "Oh, so *you're* the little sod who fucked it up, are you?" Exit laughing.

The stars of *Sigh No More* were Cyril Ritchard and Madge Elliott, a well-known Australian husband-and-wife team. Cyril was possessed by his own inner demons. His professional persona was far removed from his casual, amusing off-stage self. Maybe some antipodean inferiority complex was trying to exorcise itself. Once that curtain went up, Cyril went over the top. When he did "Nina (From Argentina)," a marvellously witty number, full of internal rhymes that needed pointing, not pounding, he couldn't control himself.

Noël, who'd started out liking Cyril, became progressively disenchanted as rehearsals went on. Cyril was never satisfied with his material, and was clearly oblivious to the distinct layer of ice forming on the top end of Noël's vocal range when he gave Cyril "notes." There were occasions when Cyril performed with what Noël considered "such raucous vulgarity" that Noël would grip the arms of his seat to prevent himself from leaping up on stage.

Cyril had invented his own version of choreography-by-numbers, a kind of syncopated St. Vitus' dance that totally detracted from the meaning of the song. Noël tried repeatedly to pull him down. "Just do the number. Don't *overdo* the number." But Cyril either couldn't or wouldn't take direction. At the end of one particularly harrowing rehearsal, Cyril took Noël aside (into the hotel bathroom, of all places!) and began to weep. He confessed that he and Madge had been so terrified of Noël that the over-acting developed as some sort of defence mechanism. Noël charitably accepted this form of apology and the show duly went on. It would be heartening to report that Cyril's performance was transformed. Unfortunately, it would also be untrue.

As fate would have it, Cyril lost his voice a few days later and Noël took his place. Unlike Cyril, he didn't cavort about and everything went very much better, but when Cyril returned, so did the gesture-a-word routine. Cyril went on to become quite a big name in the States, although he never appeared in another Coward show. He did co-direct thirty-nine performances of *Look After Lulu* on Broadway in 1959, but "Nina" essentially marked the end of their professional relationship.

Somewhere in the small print of show business, it's written that things rarely work out the way they're originally intended. Noël had written the song "That Is The End Of The News" to be performed by a trio, an arrangement which proved ineffective, so he assigned it to Joyce Grenfell, the show's soubrette. Joyce, who was just achieving recognition for her radio monologues, thought the lyric was a bit strong for her and said: "Oh, no, it would upset my public."

"And what public might that be, my dear?" Noël inquired. "My *radio* public," beamed Joyce, proudly. In no mood to argue, Noël quipped, "Never mind about your radio public, dear. You just learn the lyrics and do the number." So, dressed in a schoolgirl's gym tunic (St. Trinian's waiting in the wings!), she did, and stopped the show. The confidence she gained from extending her range in that number gave her the "edge" she showed in later performances.

Joyce's quality, like her voice, was pure and unaffected. I'd often go to the side of the stage and listen to her sing. Although I worked with her in a couple of wartime troop concerts I never got to know her well. She was a delightful but essentially private person.

Sigh No More ran for two hundred and thirteen performances but was still not considered a huge success. Noël jested that the title "turned out to the best part of the revue." He need not have been so hard on himself; the critics would do that job for him.

Diversity was the essential ingredient in a successful revue. *Sigh No More* was too much a single vision and Noël recognised it. The form was also losing favour, as television caught hold and copied the "variety" format. Certainly he never attempted it again, though he did contribute material to a couple of revues I appeared in during the 1950's, for which I was suitably grateful.

*   *   *   *

In early 1946, while *Sigh No More* was running down to its eventual close, Noël's mind was busily exploring the mythical island of Samolo,

Sigh No More. *"The Burchells of Battersea Rise" number. Cyril Ritchard, Madge Elliott, Joyce Grenfell, and me. (Piccadilly Theatre, 1945)*

Noël either playing with (or threatening!) Wait a Bit, Joe, the poodle named after my other song in Sigh No More. *(Goldenhurst, 1945)*

described in *We Were Dancing* as being "somewhere near Ceylon." Samolo symbolized all that was dear to the heart of a tottering British Empire, a territory that no one cared to possess and few could locate on the map.

Noël used the island as a forum for his humour about spent colonialism, which he mingled with a touch of nostalgia for happier days. It also allowed for the expression of colourful customs, both of the natives and the governors. It was a location he was to use for many years in plays like *South Sea Bubble* and in his one novel, *Pomp and Circumstance*, which shared the same characters.

When a writer invents a place, it becomes as real in fact as it is in imagination. Samolo was an amalgam of the many places Noël had visited on his various Far East trips during the 1920's and '30's.

I remember going down to White Cliffs, Noël's weekend retreat in Kent, to find him and Cole Lesley poring over the "authorised" map of Samolo. They'd already worked out details of climate, topography and a basic historical outline.

For the truly intrepid traveller, here is an extract from the "official" Samolan guidebook that appeared in the programme for *Pacific 1860*. Should you ever find yourself there, please remember to send me a postcard:

Samolo is the principal island of the Samolan archipelago in the South-Western Pacific.
Latitude: 18 degrees North. Longitude: 175 degrees West.
The Samolan group consisting of 34 islands (seven of which are inhabited and a few privately owned) was discovered in 1786 by Captain Evangelous Cobb.
The first English missionaries appeared there in 1814.
Christianity was adopted by the Samolans in 1815 during the reign of King Kefumalani.
The islands became officially a British possession in 1855 during the reign of King Kefumalani II, who wrote personally to Queen Victoria begging her to allow his land to have the privilege of belonging to the British Empire.
The first British Governor-General of Samolo was Sir Douglas Markham, K.C.B., 1855.
In the eighteen-sixties the British population of the islands numbered approximately one thousand four hundred. Sir Lewis Grayshott had succeeded Sir Douglas Markham as Governor-General.
The island of Samolo is of volcanic origin and is 108 miles long and 70 miles wide.

There was much more in this vein, ending with:

This headland is rough and barren with black rocks and a profusion of sea-birds including albatrosses which "indulge much in curious dances two by two." (Extract from *A Guide to Samolo*, published by Ross, Wishart & Sons, 1906)

They weren't quite as deranged as I'm making them sound. Noël had determined that Samolo was to be the setting for *Scarlet Lady*, which was to re-open Drury Lane.

Rather than a musical, *Scarlet Lady* was to be an operette, a French form which Noël always preferred. Immediately he thought of Yvonne Printemps, who'd been wonderful in *Conversation Piece* (1934). The sweetness of Mlle. Printemps' voice, however, was not matched by her English pronunciation, which could be described as a little hit and a lot of miss.

Noël had originally developed this operette with Irene Dunne in mind. Irene is mostly remembered as an aristocratic-looking film star, who played light comedy with Cary Grant (*The Awful Truth*, 1937), or suffered elegantly in some four-hankie weepie. She was also a talented singer in musicals like *Show Boat*, and it was Noël's hope, after he met her in Hollywood, that one day they might work together. Irene, with her rich voice, would have been marvellous as the woman *d'une certaine âge* whose visit to a semi-tropical island leads to an affair with a young man many years her junior. (Played by, guess who?)

Naturally, she tears herself away, but years later she is drawn back to the island, only to find that her lover, assuming his love for her to be hopeless, is to be married that very day. Unseen by him, she watches the festivities. Left alone on stage, she sings a reprise of the show's key song. Curtain. Not a dry handkerchief in the house.

All of this was moot, however, since Irene Dunne's film commitments prevented her from taking the part in *Scarlet Lady*.

So the hunt was on for an alternative choice. Noël had seen a film called *The Great Victor Herbert* (1939) in which Mary Martin adopted a soprano voice instead of her usual punchy delivery associated with numbers like "My Heart Belongs To Daddy." She'd also just enjoyed a huge Broadway success with *One Touch of Venus*. Noël was convinced she could carry the part, but Mary wasn't a true soprano and lacked the necessary range for operetta. Apart from which, she was almost exactly my age, which altered the entire meaning of the book. Instead of a poignant story of love lost between the generations, it became a straightforward romance.

With his decision to offer the part to Mary Martin, Noël had to entirely rewrite the libretto. The rough draft for *Scarlet Lady* was, in my opinion, much better than the eventual Martin-ised version. The show was

Gladys Calthrop and Noël study the costumes Gladys has designed for Pacific 1860. *(1946)*

re-christened *Pacific 1860*, a title, I told Noel, that sounded like a Canadian railroad. He was not amused.

The score featured a very strong solo rhythm number for me, "Fumfumbolo," and two lovely songs for Mary. But something was lacking. I was too inexperienced then to identify the problem, but there's often something in the air that tells you the show's in trouble. People sense it but can't explain it, so they displace their anxiety and pick on trivial issues, details that bear no relation to the real problem.

From the very beginning, Mary was restless. She was supposed to be Madame Eleanor Salvador, an operatic soprano who spoke seven languages. But Mary was a Texas girl who spoke only American English and had never been farther than Tijuana, Mexico. She knew she was miscast, so this sweet lady suddenly became very difficult indeed.

There was, for instance, the matter of Gladys's bows.

Gladys Calthrop had been designing sets and costumes for Noël's shows since *The Vortex* in 1924. She was a determined lady who had very distinct views on what leading ladies in remote British Pacific possessions should wear circa 1860, even if they *did* speak with an American accent.

On this occasion she found herself up against an equally determined lady with distinct views of her own. At her first fitting Mary said to Gladys, "Look, it's wonderful being here and everything, but I must warn you I'm allergic to *bows*. Please, don't give me any bows."

And so, at the first dress rehearsal, there was a gorgeous dress absolutely *covered* with bows. You might say Mary was fit to be tied! Gladys's attitude was not improved when Mary arrived about half an hour late. In Gladys's view, that may be acceptable behaviour in the States, but not in the West End.

That was typical of the ambivalent attitude in the English theatre towards big American names. We wanted to see these legends but we didn't want them lording it over us, a situation which was reversed a few years later when Americans threw up the barriers when they heard the cry: "The British are coming!"

Gladys's bows eventually made a tactful exit. But then Mary's husband began to get on Noël's nerves. Richard Halliday wanted a say in everything, as "Stage Husbands" often do in order to justify their existence.

"Mr. Martin" never stopped complaining, and could only have aggravated Mary's already nervous condition. There were never specific complaints, he simply wanted all these hard-working people to know that his wife was used to better.

Noël once described Mary Martin as "a dream girl, quick and knowledgeable with all the mercurial charm of Gertie at her best with a sweet voice and with more taste!" By the time rehearsals were well under way he would choke on those words. She refused to do a very funny number, "Alice Is At It Again," on the grounds that it was far too vulgar for the Mary Martin image. Was she really too innocent at the time to understand the *double entendre* in "My Heart Belongs to Daddy"?

Mary admitted years later that she should have sung it, that it would probably have stopped the show. We could have used the break.

Watching Noël direct Mary was an object lesson in applied psychology. Realising her technical limitations, he did not apply the kid glove she was used to and expected. He would shock her into instinctive behaviour, to make her "let go" on stage.

In one crucial scene, the temperamental opera star is called upon to lose her temper and hit her manager. Mary just couldn't do it. Noël's ruthless side surfaced. Over the years I saw it happen again and again. He could be as brutal and insulting as was necessary to get through any actor's barrier. He berated Mary in a way she'd never known before. How could she be so *dumb*? Hadn't she learned *anything*? And it worked perfectly. She hit her unfortunate colleague with such a resounding wallop that he couldn't hear straight for days.

Noël laughed and embraced her, as pleased with himself as he was with her. He explained to her that now she knew she had the emotion to express, in future she'd be able to control its expression. She'd broken through the invisible barrier.

On another occasion he taught her to cry on cue, which he demonstrated by doing himself. He turned his back on her for a moment, then spun round, eyes streaming. This, to Noël, was the essence of acting: "You must have the emotion to know it, then you must learn how to use the emotion without suffering it."

He'd learned that the hard way while entertaining wartime troops. He was once so overcome by the sight of all those anxious young men, many of whom would never see home again, that he began to weep. Instead of eliciting a sympathetic reaction, his audience laughed, thinking it was part of the act. From that moment, Noël distrusted *every* emotion on stage and dealt solely in the illusion.

The episode of the bows was followed by the furore over the hat, which, so to speak, capped it all. Mary had never worn a hat on the premise that it made her face too small, and she had absolutely no intention of starting now. Finally Noël insisted, but the episode didn't help a very nervous cast rehearse an extremely complicated show under totally adverse conditions. By opening night, Noël wasn't speaking to Mary and Mary wasn't speaking to *either* of us. On stage we kissed. Off stage we brooded in sulky silence.

Drury Lane should have been the ideal location to open the show. It was the site of Noël's monumental 1931 hit, *Cavalcade*, and the historic venue had deep emotional significance for him. But much had changed in the intervening fifteen years. We were living in a strange new world. Perhaps the Victorian froth we had concocted wouldn't be appropriate, no matter how well done.

Fate, meanwhile, had placed a few other obstacles in our path. The Germans had bombed the Lane in 1940, and there was some very real doubt as to whether the bomb damage would be repaired in time to open in 1946. Noël called in a few personal IOU's to ensure that it would. Rehearsals were frequently interrupted as workmen replaced various sections of the stage around us. You dance a little tentatively when there's an even chance of falling through the floor and breaking your neck! Electricity cuts were such a regular occurrence that the box office got in the habit of selling tickets by candlelight.

Nor is it easy to clasp a girl in your arms, even one as appealing as Mary Martin, and sing with any degree of sincerity,

> *Bright was the day when you came to me,*
> *Someone had whispered your name to me.*
> *Someone had told me how fair you were,*
> *Then at last - there you were.*

Pacific 1860. *With Mary Martin. (Theatre Royal, Drury Lane, 1946)*

especially when the day had been anything but bright. To the prevailing austerity in that unheated, uncompleted theatre, there was added a touch of frost. It was bad enough for the men in their evening dress but I felt many a pang for the girls smiling brightly in their gauzy off-the-shoulder dresses. Noël could have added a new chorus number, orchestrated entirely for chattering teeth!

Audiences had come to expect lavish sets and scene changes on that huge stage. Noël, in *Cavalcade,* and Ivor Novello with his run of musicals, had raised certain expectations. Very little of that could even be contemplated now, and in this post-war shell of a theatre the "Drury Lane show" hopes would be dashed from the moment the curtain went up.

Mary remained an enigma. She was talented but temperamental, in spite of her "adorable" image. Her husband, by comparison, made her seem like sweetness and light. He was a bore and a boor, but he was also a convenient mouthpiece for the things Mary wanted known but didn't have the nerve to actually say.

Mary and I never mixed socially. I believe that our distance showed on the stage: Two perfect strangers singing about the melody in their hearts just doesn't play true. When I was out of the show for a couple of weeks with jaundice, there wasn't even a telephone call, or a "Welcome back" when I returned.

We knew we were in trouble. It was hardly Mary's triumphal conquest of the London stage. Noël was bitterly disappointed, and blamed himself because he was the one who'd cast her. "The voice isn't right, it's too thin," he would mutter. "She's just not right for this."

After *Pacific 1860*, Noël and Mary didn't speak until 1949, when he saw her marvellous New York success in *South Pacific*.

Backstage Noël grabbed her by the shoulders and said firmly, "Let's forget all about that silly nonsense we had in London. We must be friends. I think you're wonderful in the show. It proves the word 'Pacific' in a title is not necessarily the kiss of death!" They became great buddies and later did a 1955 television special for CBS, *Together with Music,* as well as a one-night cabaret appearance at the Café de Paris in 1952 in aid of Noël's Actors' Orphanage.

Noël was distraught over *Pacific 1860*. It should have been a safe bet for his popular post-war return, but the Fates had dealt him a poor hand. Noël's reactions were as clipped and edited as his distinctive speech. Adversity was something he rose above, preferably in private. There was always next time. "No, No, Noël," admonished James Agate in *The Sunday Times;* "Pseudo-Viennese sentimentality in waltz-time, Noël Coward is Lost in the Pacific" was the verdict of the *Evening News;* "Mr. Coward Misses the Pacific Boat," crooned Alan Dent in the *News Chronicle;* "Dead Calm in the Pacific," gloated J.C. Trewin.

His innermost feelings were first completely revealed, even to me, when I read the *Diaries*. His last entry for that Year of Little Grace records: "Home very weary and sick to death of *Pacific 1860* and everything to do with it." He was entitled to say that. After all, he'd written the damned thing. What didn't please him was the verdict of Binkie Beaumont, whose company, H.M. Tennent, had presented the show: "They came to see the theatre, not the show." We had managed to cobble The Lane together again, but the show it housed was a rickety affair.

*   *   *   *

A lot of people have assumed that the *Diaries* were the carefully constructed *bons mots* of the professional writer waiting to be publicly read. Not so. These were his private notes which he would later fashion into *Past Conditional*, the unfinished third volume of his autobiography, intended to pick up where *Present Indicative* (1937) left off and before *Future Indefinite* (1954) began. Once written up, they would have been discarded.

When Sheridan Morley and I edited them, years later, we discovered that the *Diaries* contained such a clearly spontaneous record of Noël's private thoughts and feelings that we didn't dare tamper with them, other than deleting the boring, domestic details. But let me be clear about one thing: No-one ever read a single word of them until after his death.

Much of what he wrote, including what he said about me, was critical, although it was nothing that he hadn't frequently said to my face. But he said it with affection, as he always did to the people he cared most about. He just wanted us to be the best we could be. It wasn't *his* fault if we couldn't always live up to his standards.

*   *   *   *

Two important events occurred in my life about this time. First, I became a British citizen. I'd expected a lot of paperwork and bureaucracy, but it was as simple as filling in a form. Second, I became one of the Coward "family."

During *Sigh No More*, I got to know Coley, Lornie and Gladys very well. Weekends at White Cliffs became the logical progression from working together so closely during the week. There was a spare room, and Noël invited me to move in. Mum wanted her settee back and said she could manage perfectly well on her own, so I couldn't think of a single reason not to. It seemed the most natural thing in the world, especially since Noël and I enjoyed being around each other so much. I somehow never moved out.

Noël and Gertie in "Shadow Play" from Tonight at 8:30. *(Phoenix Theatre, 1936)*

CHAPTER FOUR

SHALL WE JOIN THE LADIES...? (1)
NOËL AND GERTIE

ELYOT: *You're looking very lovely, you know, in this damned moonlight. Your skin is clear and cool, and your eyes are shining, and you're growing lovelier and lovelier every second as I look at you. You don't hold any mystery for me, darling, do you mind?*

*   *   *   *

AMANDA: *Don't say any more, you're making me cry so dreadfully.*

(*Private Lives*)

In the Beginning, and always, there was Gertie. Noël and Gertie.

When Gertie died in 1952, Noël wrote in her obituary in *The Times*: "...no-one I have ever known, however brilliant and however gifted, has contributed quite what she contributed to my work...", a remark which apparently put the joint noses of the Lunts *out* of joint. That was *their* problem. Anybody who saw how Noël and Gertie felt about each other would know precisely what he had meant.

Gertie was "family," part of Noël's intimate circle at all times, to be talked to, to be given a talking-to, to be talked about. "Gertie would hate this" or "I wonder what Gertie would think about that?"

She ricocheted into his life on a train in 1913. Even in their fledgling encounters Gertie managed to shock him with her vulgar streak. He recalled in *Present Indicative*:

> "... a vivacious child with ringlets to whom I took an instant fancy. She wore a black satin coat and a black velvet military hat with a peak, her face was far from pretty, but tremendously alive. She was very *mondaine*, carried a handbag with a powder-puff and frequently dabbed her generously turned-up nose. She confided to me that her name was Gertrude Lawrence, but that I was to call her

Noël and Gertie take time off from rehearsal of Tonight at 8:30 *at Goldenhurst.*
(September 1935)

Noël and Gertie in
Tonight at 8:30.
(1936)

Gert because everybody did, that she was fourteen, just over licensing age, that she had been in *The Miracle* at Olympia and *Fifinella* at the Gaiety, Manchester. She then gave me an orange, and told me a few mildly dirty stories, and I loved her from then onwards."

They were two sides of the same coin and loved each other deeply as truly great friends all their lives. Noël's poem on death, "When I Have Fears," ended with:

How happy they are I cannot know,
But happy am I who loved them so.

None of us doubted that of all the many people he had loved throughout his life, Gertie was undoubtedly first among equals.

There may have been an early attempt on her part to goad Noël into trying "it" purely for the sake of knowing what "it" was all about. She loved to "experiment" and his reaction would have amused her, but Noël forever kept mum on the subject. Their love ultimately transcended sex, and would have been too conventionally defined and confined by a physical relationship. The picture of them standing on the balcony in *Private Lives*, together yet apart, eternally elegant, forever sums them up for anyone who ever saw them.

In the public mind, they were so much a team that few people realised they had only starred together twice in straight plays. This perception of the two of them as professional Siamese twins caused Gertie to remark ruefully, when she was starring in *Susan and God* (1937), "I suppose a lot of people will think that Noël is starring with me in the other rôle!"

Soon after *Pacific 1860* closed, Gertie's remarkable agent, Fanny Holtzmann, suggested a US revival of *Tonight at 8:30*, which they had originated there a decade earlier. Noël was totally opposed to the idea. He'd studiously avoided revivals unless he felt it was absolutely obligatory. ("Never boil your cabbage twice.") Temporary lack of funds could fit the definition of "obligatory," as could an attempt to get back at the critics, like he had in his successful London revival of *Present Laughter* (1947).

Fanny switched strategy. "Why not let Graham play your part? It would only be a summer tour and wouldn't play New York. Besides, Gertie needs the money."

Noël was now in a genuine quandary. On the one hand, he was keen to build my career. On the other, he dreaded the prospect of my doing an American tour opposite Gertrude Lawrence. I'd met her only once and been instantly enslaved. Without having to think, I exclaimed, "That would be wonderful!"

But Noël was increasingly convinced that it would be an ill-advised career move: "They'll attack you on this one. Don't do it." Noël and Fanny batted me back and forth like a shuttlecock. Finally, with fingers firmly crossed, it was settled. Jack Wilson, Noël's longtime manager and friend, was signed up to direct.

It was the issue of Gertie's finances which finally tipped the balance for Noël. She had absolutely no concept of money and would spend it in spectacular fashion, in the abiding belief that there would always be more. In 1936, during rehearsals for the original production of *Tonight*, there wasn't, and she was declared bankrupt. Fanny ensured there would be no recurrence by designating herself as guardian of Gertie's income. Gertie would proudly open her purse and show me the "spending money" Fanny allowed her.

I'd heard so much about Gertie from Noël that I loved her before I met her. Gertie was a life force, constantly re-inventing herself and the world around her. But those same charming qualities could also prove intensely frustrating. Recalling their two most famous collaborations, *Private Lives* and *Tonight at 8:30*, Noël would fume: "She never plays a damn part the same way twice. You never know which of her you're going to get." Because matinées were staggered during the week, Gertie would go to see a play in the afternoon and play her part that evening in the style of whatever play she'd seen. Sometimes she'd take pity on her disconcerted colleagues and help them through this "new" play she'd thrown them into. But she wasn't always in the mood.

My self-confidence was shaken when Noël told me Gertie would occasionally get muddled on which parts she was playing. She once came on in *Still Life*, using the voice she'd used in *Hands Across the Sea*. Noël said, "I stopped and said: 'Dear, what are you *at?*' Then, using a line from *Shadow Play*, I said: 'Stick to the *script!*' She broke up. We continued the play rather convulsively, but it was better!"

Gertie was as different from the chilly Miss Martin as it was possible to be. I was in awe of her. This must have come across because a couple of weeks into the tour, she took me aside after *Red Peppers* and said: "Listen, *you're* supposed to be in charge of this act, so *take* charge. If you don't, I'm going to act you off the stage. Now, come on, *you* be the bossy one!" All my previous experience had been as a straight juvenile lead, but I was so scared of Gertie's wrath I took charge, knowing that if I didn't she'd be as good as her word and annihilate me.

We were shameless. We pinched other people's gags. The British comedian, Tommy Trinder, had a famous catch phrase, "You Lucky People!", which we threw in with every terrible joke we could think of. Because we were playing third-rate British music hall comedians we should

Noël directs Gertie for the 1948 tour of Tonight at 8:30 *and enjoys re-creating an original bit of stage "business"!*

have been fine, but our American audiences knew nothing about the tradition we were sending up. They just thought the jokes weren't very funny, so out they had to come!

Off-stage, Gertie was nothing like the madcap I'd heard so much about. She was the quietly-married Mrs. Richard Aldrich who avoided the parties that were thrown wherever we went, preferring to stay in her hotel and have an early night. We would have an occasional meal together, and she would be quiet and subdued until she had to turn it on. Then, on cue, the old Gertie would emerge.

I've often wondered whether this was the beginning of the illness that finally took her from us. The more likely explanation is, that she was approaching fifty, and had to manage her physical resources carefully if she was to get through those varied and taxing parts Noël had written for her. Professionally and personally, I've always been of a nervous disposition, so I'd always arrive early at the theatre to limber up. Gertie would always be there before me.

The twenty-year age difference began to worry me after a while, so at one performance I decided to remedy it. Gertie spotted it immediately. "Why have you greyed up your hair? And what's that silly moustache?" Hurriedly covering my embarrassment, I said, "I thought it made me look more distinguished." Her withering look put a swift end to *that* notion.

Noël and Gertie with Ivy St. Helier. She introduced the haunting "If Love Were All" in Bitter Sweet. *(1929) He wrote the show for Gertie but her vocal range couldn't sustain the lead rôle.*

In 1948, an influenza microbe achieved what the great Fanny Holtzmann could not. Noël and Gertie were re-united for a few performances in San Francisco when I came down with a rather bad cold. Noël and Gertie clearly loved it as much as the audience. The years melted away as they invented those familiar lines all over again.

Gertie was very much the Broadway star, making only occasional visits to England. Noël was still the quintessential Englishman, though he had an amazing adaptability to any surroundings. For them to meet again on stage would have taken significant rearranging of their lives. It was never to happen. That coda in San Francisco became their farewell performance.

Playing opposite Gertie made me aware not only of her mercurial and unpredictable quality, but also of her competitive spirit. She was perfectly capable of walking zombie-like through the part if the mood took her and the audience didn't. But if she felt challenged, she'd fight for every laugh and milk every last piece of business. She was, Noël always maintained, an "intuitive" actress, definitely "not a thinking reed."

(He'd originally written the starring role in *Bitter Sweet* for her.

Cochran was to produce but, nervous about her vocal range, he wanted a clause in the contract that insisted on three months of singing lessons. Gertie preferred instead to go to Hollywood and make a movie for quick money.)

There were times during *Private Lives* when the devil would take her over and she'd go hell-bent for the laughs. ("You had to hit her over the head occasionally.") One evening, after she'd over-acted outrageously, a few choice words were being exchanged backstage. Into the dressing room rushed Everley Gregg, who played the maid, hairbrush in hand, prepared to separate the contestants. "Don't! Don't!" she cried plaintively. "I love you both!" "That," snapped Noël, "is entirely irrelevant and you are fired!" Everley left in tears. Gertie broke up in tears of an entirely different kind and Noël, pleased by his one-liner, went off to reinstate Everley.

Amanda in *Private Lives* was based in part on Doris Delvigne, a glamorous figure of 1920's society, who was publicly pursued by, and briefly married to, Lord Castlerosse. Their married bliss, or lack of it, fascinated Noël and made the characters in the play all the more real to most people who saw them. There were notable exceptions. Lady Kenmore came to the dressing room on the first night to congratulate Noël and Gertie, but had one concern: "Those quarrels and rolling round on the floor, all that seemed quite unreal. Surely no couple could possibly quarrel like that in real life?" Noël shot back: "You obviously don't know the Castlerosses!"

There's a famous story of Gertie when she was starring in *Nymph Errant* (1933). On opening night, the young Elisabeth Welch stopped the show cold with her rendition of "Solomon (Who Had a Thousand Wives)." Gertie's friends had knots in their stomachs. Was the show being hi-jacked in front of their eyes?

Backstage the Lawrence loins were being girded. On sailed Gertie to put across "The Physician (But He Never Said He Loved Me)" as even its creator, Cole Porter, had never envisaged. Game, set and match to Miss Lawrence. She obviously enjoyed the experience, because she went on to do precisely the same thing to Danny Kaye in *Lady in the Dark* (1941).

Gertie never once compared my performance to Noël's, though the temptation must often have been great, and she would never take a press interview without including me.

There were, however, two unfortunate aspects about *Tonight at 8:30*. The first was Jack Wilson. Jack was an American who had been closest to Noël during the late 1920's and 1930's. He'd been to see *The Vortex* countless times and managed to introduce himself to Noël. Things went merrily on from there and, for a while, they were inseparable. In more recent times, he'd been Noël's main professional and financial

Tonight at 8:30. *With Gertie in "Ways and Means." (New York, 1948)*

representative in the States, a function he'd similarly performed for Gertie and Cole Porter. At some point he decided he could direct, so Noël indulged him until he realised that Jack was putting several of Noël's valuable properties at risk by his slapdash treatments. It also became increasingly clear that Jack was, shall we say, maximising his legitimate share of the "take" on touring productions of *Blithe Spirit*, among others. Noël was finally forced to let the scales fall from his eyes and see Jack for who he really was.

This painful process of revelation was going on as we were putting the show together, so the auspices for my US debut were not the brightest.

Jack Wilson loathed me.   In simple terms, he was jealous of the relationship I now had with Noël. He saw me as a younger version of himself, though I was not aware of this. Here was a successful Broadway impresario, happily married (so I thought) to the beautiful Natasha Paley, a Romanov Princess. Why should he pick on *me*? Even at our first read-through, he couldn't resist making dirty cracks at me, raising his eyebrows as if to say, "What are we going to do with *this* one?"

It became patently clear to the New York management that there was going to be trouble. By the time I got back to my apartment, the producers were already there, stating their case to Noël. "You can't leave Jack to direct Graham. He'll crucify him up on that stage. You must direct the show yourself, at least until we open in Baltimore!"

Fortunately for me, Noël did. You can imagine how much Jack liked

Tonight at 8:30. *With Gertie as "The Red Peppers". (New York, 1948)*

me for *that*. I don't think we ever exchanged more than the merest civilities until he died in 1961. By that time Noël had finally cut him out of the "family." I don't think I've ever known someone waste more talent, or sour more relationships with the people who genuinely loved him, as Jack. God knows what demons drove him. It took a lot for Noël to turn against an old friend, but Jack finally managed the trick.

The second unfortunate aspect was New York. Noël had reluctantly agreed to the tour only because there was absolutely no question of it coming into town. Because of our big success in Los Angeles, he softened. When a theatre came available in New York, Fanny coaxed us into it, against Noël's better judgement.

And they *killed* us! One review read: "Payn is his name and that's what he is." It was the fate I'd dreaded most, but when it actually happened, I found myself laughing about it. The critics were genuinely hysterical. No matter what I'd done, I wasn't Noël Coward and they weren't about to forgive me for that. It didn't occur to them that they were being inconsistent. When Noël had performed with Gertie, the critics had savaged the *plays*. They were dubbed "light rubbish," and only the stars could carry them through. Twelve years later, the plays were absolutely wonderful and *I* was the light rubbish!

Gertie was furious and called the critics unladylike names, while Noël was not at all pleased to have been proved right. As the audiences dwindled, Gertie became almost childishly petulant. "This theatre is far too empty," she said. "I shall insist that the management remove three or four rows of stalls." We eked out four weeks at the National Theatre before finally putting up the notices.

As sympathetic as Noël was about the Broadway reaction, he knew all too well how it felt to be a flop. He comforted me with "Don't worry. In a few weeks it will all be forgotten. This is only funny old New York. The rest of the world couldn't care less."

His next suggestion cheered me up immediately: "Why don't we go to Jamaica?"

*   *   *   *

Noël and Gertie kept in touch, of course, and saw each other from time to time but their lives had polarised. New York was her town. London was his.

Their last professional link was a US tour of *Blithe Spirit*, with Gertie as Elvira. They nearly appeared together in *The King and I*, but Noël turned down the role which made Yul Brynner a huge star.

During the run of *The King and I*, Gertie's performance deteriorated to the point that the patrons were complaining. She'd been known to sing off-key in the past but this was something more serious. Gertie knew something was wrong but refused to leave the cast. She felt she was going through a "bad patch," as all actors did, and it would pass.

Oscar Hammerstein and Dick Rodgers came to Noël for help. Couldn't he, wouldn't he write the play he'd been promising Gertie and lure her out of *The King and I?* Noël toyed with the idea, but no inspiration came, probably because he felt it would be too devious a way to deal with someone who was herself so direct. If Gertie said it would all come good, then she must be trusted to know best.

Noël often talked of writing something new for the two of them, but it was unlikely they could surpass what they'd already achieved. Perhaps he wanted to preserve the memory of how they were at their peak, reaching out to each other in *Shadow Play*, fearful of losing that precious moment. Those few "accidental" performances in San Francisco had been their going back. They probably felt they should leave it at that.

*   *   *   *

That twelve-month period of 1951-52 was devastating for Noël on a personal level. Cochran drowned in his bath in a stupid domestic accident and Ivor died from a sudden heart attack, neither of which Noël could have anticipated. But Gertie? Shouldn't he have seen the signs? Couldn't he have done something? This was not exactly the stable emotional basis on which to rebuild a career.

Noël in cabaret at the Café de Paris with Norman Hackforth at the piano. (1951)

CHAPTER FIVE

ANGRY YOUNG ENGLAND: THE 1950's

There are bad times just around the corner,
There are dark clouds hurtling through the sky
And it's no good whining
About a silver lining
For we know from experience that they won't roll by...

(*The Globe Revue*)

Viewed in retrospect, every decade seems to take on a character of its own. Once it's packaged as the Roaring Twenties or the Swinging Sixties, that's it. Fixed forever. The 1950's will probably not go down as a vintage decade for society in general, but in the theatre, at least, some important corners were turned.

For Noël and me, it was the worst of times and the best of times. Noël set sail from British shores in search of a more responsive chord. He promptly found it in the American television studios of CBS, and a Las Vegas night club unknown in Britain.

He'd always liked the States: the no-nonsense *speed* of the place, the way things got *done* instead of endlessly *discussed*. He'd learned the secret of pace on stage from all the Broadway shows he'd devoured on his pre-war visits. On the English stage, lines were carefully and clearly enunciated, all very formal. On Broadway, actors had developed the technique of "stepping on" each other's lines, giving a sense of urgency, modernity and reality. Noël tried to see *everything*. On his first trip in 1921, he caught *Nice People* (with Tallulah Bankhead and Katharine Cornell in supporting roles), *Sally* (with Marilyn Miller), Maugham's *The Circle* (with Estelle Winwood), and *The Love Letter* (with the Astaires). He also took in one of the first black revues, *Shuffle Along*, and the current *Ziegfeld Follies* (starring, among others, Fanny Brice). Not bad for a twenty-one year old man down on his uppers! He religiously applied what he learned to his own work. If truth be told, he relished the unique image he created for himself in that out-of-town town.

For the rest of his life, New York was a second theatrical home, full of friends like the Lunts, Kit Cornell and her husband, Guthrie McClintic, and Radie Harris, who was, Noël said, "the only gossip columnist who knew when not to gossip." His personal phone book rivalled that of Manhattan.

He committed his abiding affection to song in *Ace of Clubs:*

> *But I like America,*
> *Its Society*
> *Offers infinite variety*
> *And come what may*
> *I shall return some day*
> *To the good old U.S.A.*

> *But I like America,*
> *Every scrap of it,*
> *All the sentimental crap of it...*

The rather convoluted birth of this show should have warned Noël that this was not to be the instant fully-fledged, self-composing success he'd enjoyed before.

After *Pacific 1860,* he was anxious to demonstrate to his critics that he wasn't an outdated fuddy-duddy composing sentimental operetta. Obviously he must write a contemporary subject. There were several false starts. He broke new ground with *Peace in our Time* (formerly *Might Have Been*), which speculated on life in Britain under Nazi occupation. It was unenthusiastically received by critics and public alike, who considered it "not exactly Noël Coward." He just couldn't win. Eventually he wrote a gangster story set in a seedy London night club.

The heroine was Pinkie (Pat Kirkwood), star of the cabaret, and the owner's mistress. A sailor, Harry Hornby (played by Guess Who?), falls in love with her but finally must give her up. Noël's theory was that any numbers that would not fit into the club milieu could be shoe-horned into the floor show within the production.

There was supposed to be an edge of social commentary. Hardly the traditional Boy Meets Girl romance, it was even a little sordid, like the New Britain it depicted. To prevent the audience from becoming too uncomfortable, it was softened by a comic touch. The two principals should have been played by comedy actors, but Pat and I were directed to play it as straight juvenile leads. It didn't work.

Noël had convinced himself that it would work because he *wanted* it to work. He desperately needed a success, but he was basically writing from

Ace of Clubs. *As Harry Hornby with Pat Kirkwood as Pinkie Leroy. (Cambridge Theatre, 1950)*

his head. Noël had no first-hand knowledge of the seedy world of *Ace of Clubs* and he felt no sympathy for it. It was put together from abstract knowledge and stage craftsmanship. He didn't realise that the underside of society could only be portrayed properly if it's affectionate and satirical, as Frank Loesser and Damon Runyon did in *Guys and Dolls* (1950), or tragic, as Leonard Bernstein and Stephen Sondheim did with *West Side Story* (1957). When we saw the Broadway production of *Guys and Dolls* in 1951, Noël found it "absolutely wonderful and brilliantly staged." It must have galled him to design and launch his own little ship, only to watch helplessly as this sleek ocean liner went steaming past. Typically, his only comment was to commend the superb professionalism of the 46th Street Theatre production that night.

"I Like America," was lyrically marvellous, but I was worried about having to carry a comedy song, something I'd never had to do before. Noël agreed to end the number with the girls and me dancing our way off, which worked, but we didn't stop the show.

We were never sure what was wrong with the construction of that number, it just seemed to go on too long. A couple of years later, Noël appeared at the Café de Paris. "Do you want to hear how the song *should* be sung?" he challenged me. "I'm putting it in the act." I'd always been convinced it was my fault that it hadn't worked, but after three performances in cabaret Noël knew it was wrong and he cut the number. He never re-wrote it, but he did sing it brilliantly on the *New York* album. Perhaps it was Peter Matz's clever arrangement that transformed it.

"Sail Away" was my other song in *Ace of Clubs*, but there was something awkward about the placing of it, which is a critical factor in any musical show. Perhaps the song never really belonged in that show, but it was clearly too good to be allowed to die, so Noël adopted it as the title song for a far more successful enterprise eleven years later.

Ace wasn't the debilitating running battle that *Pacific 1860* had been. Pat Kirkwood wasn't in the same league as Mary Martin, though she could be quite the prima donna. Once again the leading lady's wardrobe became a bone of contention. In one fierce finger-wagging confrontation, Noël told Pat that her own clothes had become a byword for horror. "Didn't you know," Pat snapped back, "that striped shirts are out of fashion? All you need is a straw hat and a banjo!"

We weren't holding a winning hand as far as the critics were concerned. "This Ace is No Trumps," quipped the *Sunday Graphic*. "Ace is Not a Master Card" (*The Daily Mail*). There's a lesson in theatrical nomenclature here: Never give your show a title that allows sub-editors to make obvious puns at your expense!

Before we move on down the theatrical Yellow Brick Road, let's make a short detour to the world of film. When producer Sydney Box signed me up in 1949 to a one-year contract at £4,000, it looked like a star would be born. As luck, or lack, would have it, that was one of many "fallow" years for the British film industry. Sydney couldn't replicate the Hollywood studio system single-handedly. In any case, he was beholden for distribution to the good offices of J. Arthur Rank, who had plenty of other producers at his beck and call.

Britain had long been able to compete technically with Hollywood, but the "product" wasn't taken seriously on the world market, where Tinseltown still reigned supreme. Rank had made his money from flour-milling, and saw it as his God-given mission to be Britain's Warner or Mayer. J. Arthur's conservative religious convictions, however, heavily influenced the subject matter he was prepared to back, and certainly diluted its treatment. That pervasive influence made a critical difference to the frequently bland pictures he produced.

As I was about to break into big time movie-making, I found myself sitting idly on a studio bench with the other "employees," waiting to be allocated a film.   The net result of my contract year was an appearance in an adaptation of William Douglas Home's play, *Boys in Brown*, a story of Borstal life. (Borstal was the prison to which young offenders were sent.)   It seemed that everybody else in the British film industry who could run, walk or be carried to the studio was in that very boring film!   When my year was up, I felt as if I'd *served* time.

Most significantly from that period was the screen test I did with Noël in preparation for *The Astonished Heart*, an adaptation of a short play from *Tonight at 8:30*.   Michael Redgrave had been signed to play Christian Faber, a tortured psychiatrist, opposite Margaret Leighton and Celia Johnson.   But it was evident from early test filming that Michael was embarrassed by the raw emotion he was required to express, so Noël stepped in and played the part himself. I played his assistant, Tim Verney.

The Astonished Heart (1950) was an emotionally draining experience for audiences.   By no stretch of the imagination could the film, which ended with the hero's suicide, be described as upbeat.   It certainly depressed the critics and confirmed Noël's feeling that he was better off sticking to acting on the stage.   He would occasionally turn up on screen in a juicy character rôle, but he never seriously entertained subsequent offers to star in films.

His judgement was unduly clouded by the reaction to *The Astonished Heart*.   Not for the first time, he had written the best parts for the two leading ladies.   The hero was an emotional punching bag, and *no-one* could have scored in the rôle.   Noël hadn't even enjoyed the experience on stage in the first place: "I hated playing Faber. It depressed me."   On stage, for forty-five minutes, it doesn't much matter.   On the big screen, stretched to feature-film length, the structural defect is all too obvious.   On top of that, Noël Coward wasn't being "Noël Coward."

The critics were completely underwhelmed.   *Punch* dubbed it a "Piece of High-Class Heartbreak," while Milton Shulman in the *Evening Standard* fumed "This Noël Coward Film is Incredible."   He *didn't* mean incredibly good.   *The Observer* considered it "Shallow Analysis."   It was to have a peculiar kind of after-life, however.

The Astonished Heart is now a cult film in Paris art houses.   Noël would undoubtedly have said: "I told you so."   But the French, of course, also adore Jerry Lewis!

*   *   *   *

After *Ace of Clubs*, I gratefully returned to the safe haven of revue. 1951 was Festival of Britain year, a celebration of all that was best and

The Lyric Revue. *My "Lucky Day" number written by Kay Thompson. (Globe Theatre, 1952)*

British. It was a rather bizarre event in light of how little, in those dreary post-war years, there really was to celebrate. The whole point of the Festival was, of course, to raise morale and scrape together a few blessings to count.

In May, I went into *The Lyric Revue*, which was scheduled to run for six weeks during the Festival at the Lyric, Hammersmith. We were blessed with wonderful comedy material by Arthur Macrae. I was playing beside Dora Bryan, Joan Heal and Ian Carmichael, all of them at the top of their form. Dora, by the way, had been re-christened by Noël, who decreed that her real name, Dora Broadbent, was "*most* unsuitable for the West End."

Kay Thompson, one of Noël's oldest friends and soon to become one of mine, saw the show out of town. She immediately grabbed Coley and said, "How can we get Graham out of this terrible show? It's going to be the biggest flop!" We were getting the same vibrations up on stage. Many of the topical references weren't coming across. Audience response was polite but uninvolved, and they left the theatre looking slightly bemused. We were giving it our all but it looked like it wasn't going to be nearly enough.

On opening night at the Lyric, however, everything suddenly ignited. Norman Hackforth struck up the orchestra, and the roof came off! It was such an enormous success that the six-week engagement was indefinitely extended. "It's a Grand Lark," chortled one critic, "A Banquet of Wit," enthused another. "West London, Not West End Has Festival's Best Revue." One reviewer even claimed we were "Brighter Than Coward." We diplomatically ignored that one. We eventually moved to the Globe Theatre in the West End proper, where we ran for two years. We had learned an invaluable lesson: Never try out a West End revue in the provinces!

Kay Thompson. Entertainer, my mentor...and friend to all of us.

Kay Thompson, perhaps out of a sense of guilt, wrote a strong number for me, called "Lucky Day," about a gambler who loses on every race he bets on. It was very much in Kay's distinctive "never-stop-singing-for-a-second-and-while-you're-singing-keep-moving" style.

Kay is best-remembered by British audiences for her appearance with Fred Astaire in the film version of *Funny Face* (1957). (Remember the opening "Think Pink" number where she's the editor of a *Vogue*-type magazine?) In MGM's golden years she'd been a vocal coach to Judy Garland and Lena Horne. When coaching me to sing "All I Do the Whole Day Through is Dream of You," she'd start off, "All I do is *what?*"... "Dream of you"... *"When?"*... "The whole day through." She used every little trick to make you think of the meaning of the words, not simply the sound.

Whenever Kay visited us, she and Noël would make a beeline for the twin grand pianos that were always a part of our furnishings. Kay would strike a few strange chords, Noël would respond and, before you knew it, they'd be extemporising brilliantly. I kick myself that we never taped any of these sessions, but taping in those days was not as easy as it is now. We lost a marvellous musical treasure by missing those demented duets.

Noël's contributions to *The Lyric Revue* included a song about the Festival, which, because of its topicality, is hardly ever revived today. It captured the slightly embarrassed, endearingly British quality of taking pleasures, if not seriously, then at least lugubriously:

> *Don't make fun of the Festival,*
> *Don't make fun of the fair.*
> *We down-trodden British*
> *Must learn to be skittish*
> *And give an impression of devil-may-care...*

That ironic vein was a very fruitful one for Noël, who considered the Festival to be "the last word in squalor and completely ungay." He had a great verbal knack for satirizing what he appeared to be praising. During the war there was "Don't Let's Be Beastly to the Germans," which caused high indignation among those who took the sentiment seriously. He followed that with "Could You Please Oblige Us With a Bren Gun (The Home Guard Might As Well Go Home)." And later there was "What's Going to Happen to the Children (When There Aren't Any More Grown-Ups?)."

To his audience, this irreverence was the icing on the cake. When *The Lyric Revue* became *The Globe Revue*, he composed that marvellous quartet number "Bad Times Are Just Around the Corner," which Joan Heal,

The Globe Revue. *"Bad Times are Just Around the Corner" for Dora Bryan, Joan Heal, Ian Carmichael - not to mention yours truly. (1952)*

Dora Bryan, Ian Carmichael and I had the distinct honour to sing. The sentiment in that song never seemed truer than it does right now!

> *There are bad times just around the corner,*
> *There are dark clouds hurtling through the sky*
> *And it's no good whining*
> *About a silver lining*
> *For we know from experience that they won't roll by...*

There was an amusing post script to *The Lyric Revue*, penned by satirist Alan Melville. In the programme, the designer had accidentally omitted the two "dots" from Noël's name, a punctuation device grammarians call *dieresis*, indicating that the vowels must be pronounced separately. Melville wrote the following verse:

"ENVY"

On the bills of The Lyric Revue
The contributors number a score:

Composers, designers,
And other top-liners,
And authors of sketches galore.
Yet something is missing from view
In that lengthy contributing gang:
They've omitted - the clots -
Those two little dots
Which have caused me an envious pang...

I want a small dieresis like Noël Coward's got.
I feel it adds distinction to one's name.
The moment he adopted it I envied him a lot:
I'd give anything to have one just the same.
Though for fifty years he's managed
With an ordinary "e"
(He was born, the records say, in '99)
How astute of him to realise
That, dotty, though it be,
A dieresis is simply too divine.

I long for a dieresis like Noël Coward has.
It makes a vowel seem really much more chic.
Terry-Thomas has his hyphen;
That's quite common now, whereas
A dieresis is terribly unique.
I can't think how he got it:
It just suddenly appeared:
One day his vowel was normal; then - sensation!...
The daintiest dieresis Jamaica ever reared
Was added to delight the British nation.

I yearn for a dieresis like Noël's little dots.
Alas, it can't be done: my vowels won't function.
Although it looks as though one's name
Was coming out in spots,
I'd change my own without the least compunction.
The French describe diereses as
Toujours comme il faut:
Australians call the little things fair dinkum.
I wish I'd one like Mr. Coward, the lucky so-and-so-
Or failing his dieresis, his income.

Many people think Noël added the dieresis as an affectation, but that was not so. Others were inconsistent in their use of it, probably because they couldn't decide whether the dots went over the "o" or the "e"! "I didn't put them there," he used to say. "The language did. Otherwise it's not Noël but Nool!"

While I was busily engaged in revue, Noël had written and staged *Relative Values* (1951), starring Gladys Cooper, Angela Baddeley and Judy Campbell. It earned his best reviews since the war, even though Gladys had some trouble with her lines. It was vintage Coward and ran at the Savoy for a very respectable four hundred and seventy-seven performances.

At the time, the play seemed like a last-ditch defence of the social system. The heir to a stately home is determined to marry "unsuitably," i.e. "beneath" him, contrary to the wishes of his mother, the Countess of Marshwood (Gladys Cooper). (Guess whose side Coward takes?) Crestwell, the omniscient butler, acts as a laconic Shakespearean Chorus. When it was revived recently, the piece hadn't dated worth a damn, suggesting that not much has changed in our fragile social fabric.

Noël's most important single decision that year was to perform in cabaret again at the Café de Paris. It was unlikely that many of the current patrons would remember his first appearance there, and Noël certainly wasn't about to remind them.

In 1916, when it was called the Elysée Restaurant, he'd been hired as part of a song-and-dance act with a young lady called Eileen Denis for the princely sum of £2 a week *each*. The patrons were offered a waltz, a tango, a "rather untidy one-step" and something the Management referred to as a "Pierrot fantasia," which may have been the inspiration for a later Coward couplet:

> *Parisian Pierrot,*
> *Your spirit's at zero...*

Eager to enlarge his professional power base, Noël decided to throw in a solo number, during which he totally forgot the words. Substituting a spirited rendering of "La-la-la," he made a less than triumphant exit.

Noël wasn't exactly an amateur at the game. He'd been singing for years at parties, concerts and "social" gatherings; much of it had been recorded. But when the Café de Paris approached him, he pretended to be surprised before agreeing to the, then, enormous sum of £750 a week.

He expressed private concerns about putting his singing voice to such a severe test: "It's a composer's voice. It has considerable range but no tone, little music, but lots of *meaning*." Noël now had the chance to practice

Noël's booking at the Café de Paris wasn't exactly his cabaret debut. That had taken place at 15 and he'd forgotten his words. He didn't make that mistake in 1951...

what he preached about performing. "Don't move about too much! Let the words do the work! Gestures with the hands must be above the waist!"

All of which he did superbly. Opening night he appeared at the top of a sweeping staircase, waiting until he had the audience exactly where he wanted them before even taking a step down. He then proceeded, in his thin, feathery voice, to "tear the place up."

Ken Tynan described his performance thus: "The head tilts back, the eyes narrow confidingly. Amused by his own frolicsomeness, he sways from side to side, occasionally wagging a finger if your attention looks like wandering.... Baring his teeth as if unveiling some grotesque monument and cooing like a baritone dove, he displays his own two weapons, wit and sentimentality."

Noël's successes at the Café between 1951 and 1954 gave him the confidence to tackle Las Vegas. He'd had little chance to develop a cabaret technique for an audience that owed him nothing for times past, but it was undoubtedly his Vegas exposure that repositioned him as a relevant artist in the United States. It would also give him the financial stability that had so long eluded him.

*   *   *   *

Before Vegas, though, there was *After the Ball.* Just as I had regained my professional confidence by taking refuge in revue, Noël retreated into period operetta. *Bitter Sweet* (1929), *Conversation Piece* (1934) and, to a lesser extent, *Operette* (1938) had placed him firmly in the mainstream of musical theatre. Only Ivor had surpassed his rate of success with his own magnificent string of Drury Lane hits: *Glamorous Night* (1935), *Careless Rapture* (1936), *The Dancing Years* (1939), *Perchance to Dream* (1945) and finally, *King's Rhapsody* (1949). To carry on the tradition, Noël was determined to come up with *Bitter Sweet 2.*

Noël never fully understood or accepted the full measure of what Ivor had achieved. Whereas Noël was firmly in the "Viennese" tradition of composers like Franz Lehar, Rudolf Friml and Sigmund Romberg, Ivor had created a unique form which was described as "part opera, part melodrama, part operetta, part musical comedy." Noël found it vulgar; audiences couldn't get enough of it.

Noël needed to ask himself whether such a tradition was worth continuing in the mid-1950's. In an age when rock 'n' roll was noisily tuning up, did people still want, in Ivor's immortal words, to gather lilacs in the Spring again?

After the Ball was an adaptation of Oscar Wilde's play, *Lady Windermere's Fan,* a story of social disgrace that had shocked Victorian sensibilities in 1892. Noël could be forgiven for thinking that this was the surefire, sophisticated formula he had been searching for: Wilde's wit mixed with Novello's sentiment and coated with Coward's music. Belt was added to braces by casting Novello "repertory" players like Vanessa Lee, Peter Graves and Mary Ellis. They had never failed Ivor, how could they fail Noël?

"Mary" must be an ill-fated name for Noël since he twice made the same mistake with it. He persuaded himself that Mary Martin had the vocal range to carry *Pacific 1860* when she did not. Now he cast Mary Ellis on her assurance that she could manage the very demanding operatic rôle of Mrs. Erlynne. Once again, he was woefully wrong. We had saddled ourselves with successive Marys who proved to be quite contrary.

Miss Ellis had been a great American musical star for many years, creating the lead rôle in *Rose Marie.* Ivor brought her to London in 1935 to star in *Glamorous Night.* Noël was immensely fond of her, and had been told that she had sung comparable roles. Nonetheless, in light of the experience of *Pacific 1860,* it was unprofessional of him not to have personally checked out such an important element in his comeback strategy. This atypical behaviour proved fatal. The sustained critical

After After the Ball...*Noël with his leading ladies, Vanessa Lee and Mary Ellis. That smile was one of his finest performances. (Globe Theatre, 1954)*

battering he'd been taking affected his confidence much more than he would ever admit, even to his closest friends. The old Noël would have sounded out other professionals and invited their opinions, as he had for many years with effective results. An embattled Noël didn't have the freedom to take counsel. He felt he had to be impervious to uninformed criticism. But, not surprisingly, he was privately scared that the critics were right. Suppose he *had* lost his touch?

Mary Ellis's voice, like so many other singers' before her, had started to go with age. She simply couldn't sing such a demanding rôle, but she wasn't prepared to admit it. Noël was too solicitous to ask her to audition, so she was given the rôle on the nod.

As rehearsals went on, the truth became clear. Even so, Noël missed an opportunity to replace her, which he would have done with regret, and instead, he tinkered with the show in order to save Mary's feelings. Her entrance music was cut, as was her big duet with Vanessa Lee, who did have a powerful voice. The scale of the show was dwindling, along with Mary's singing rôle. She still had star billing, so something had to be done.

Noël gave her funny dialogue, but Mary was no comedienne and never claimed to be. At rehearsal she spoke the words, but Noël never even cracked a smile. Noël came as close to losing his careful cool as I have ever seen. He grumbled bitterly to director Bobbie Helpmann, "She couldn't get a laugh if she pulled a kipper out of her - (and he named an orifice specific to the female gender)!" The uncharacteristic crudeness of the remark told me all I needed to know about the deep frustration he was suffering.

The sad thing is that audiences missed two very beautiful numbers which, sung as written, could have steered the show firmly towards operetta.

Here are the lyrics to those "missing" songs, the first of which would have "keyed" the show:

"MRS. ERLYNNE'S ENTRANCE"
(Act 1)

MRS. ERLYNNE:

> *Good evening, Lady Windermere,*
> *How gracious of you to receive a stranger*
> *Who for many a year*
> *Has been away.*
> *It's really so delightful here,*
> *Forgive me if I sound naive*
> *But having been abroad so much*
> *And, frankly, being bored so much*
> *With foreign ways and alien skies*
> *I find, to my immense surprise,*
> *The London that I used to despise*
> *Is really gay.*

ALL:

> *What there was in London that she used to despise,*
> *She is really not prepared to say.*

MRS. ERLYNNE:

> *This city really can't compare*
> *With any other that I know*
> *From Lincoln's Inn to Grosvenor Square*
> *It's quite unique.*
> *Saint Petersburg, of course, has flair*
> *But can be dull without the snow,*
> *Berlin is much too polyglot*
> *And Rome in Summer dreadfully hot,*
> *Vienna makes one ill at ease*

With all those vocal Viennese,
And Athens with its ruins and fleas,
Is far too Greek.

ALL:

Though we know that Athens
Has a great many fleas.
It is certainly a Greek antique.
Who is this fabulous lady
Who lives abroad
Can there be anything shady
About her past?
And makes no secret of the fact.
That she is bored
With half the cities of the world?
Can she afford
To be so blasé *and selective*
And to take up such a tone?
It would perhaps be more effective
To be rather less high-flown.
We disagree
With such excessive jeu d'esprit...

MRS. ERLYNNE:

It's such a pleasure to be
Home again at last
Your wife looks radiant tonight.
I'm quite aghast
At all these formidable glances.
Worse than croupiers at Nice,
Their eyes are piercing me like lances
And they're cackling like geese.
Don't turn away
And leave me utterly at bay.

ALL:

Who can she be?
Lord Windermere looks thoroughly at sea
Her gown is bold,
Her eyes are cold,
Her manner seems a trifle too controlled.

MRS. ERLYNNE:

Ah, Lord Augustus, how d' you do?
How shamefully you've neglected me!

I haven't heard a word from you
Since yesterday at three.
LORD AUGUSTUS:
Missis Erlynne, pray let me explain to you.
MRS. ERLYNNE:
No, that I cannot do
It's such a bore.
I simply loathe explanations,
I cannot bear expressions of regret.
They upset all my vibrations,
And my vibrations mustn't be upset.
Forgive me, please,
Forgive me, please
And set my heart a little bit at ease.
Just hold my fan, you foolish man.
I promise to forgive you if I can.
But do not speak of hearts to me,
For hearts are only for the young
And songs of love, at forty-three,
Have long ago been sung.

SEGUE: *"Light is the Heart"*

For the first act finale, Mrs. Erlynne soliloquises about her situation in what could have been a full-blown operatic aria:

"MRS. ERLYNNE'S ARIA"
(Act 1 Finale)

MRS. ERLYNNE:
What can it mean, this desolate sense of dread?
I who have been so sure that the past was dead
Why, when at last I thought I had paid in full
With suffering and shame
Should life defeat me, cheat me?
How much can one mad moment of passion cost?
How little joy is gained and how much is lost?
How can I save my child from the same despair,
The same humiliating fate
Before it is too late?
I cannot ever let her know
The lonely anguish that

The sight of her awakes in me
For I renounced long ago
The right to hold her close to me,
Lovingly and tenderly.
She must not hear the secret words
My empty heart is sighing, crying
Now I must plead with her alone
This is the punishment that Destiny has held for me
This is my chance to atone
For all those bitter years ago
When my love failed her so
No matter what the Gods decide,
I shall at least, at least, have tried.

After the Ball provided a few light moments.

Bobbie Helpmann was an Australian choreographer, best known as the lead "character" dancer in Powell and Pressburger films like *The Red Shoes* (1948) and *Tales of Hoffman* (1951). His background was in ballet, where the essence of drama is the gesture of mime. Bobbie broke Rule One in the Coward Book of Acting by adding a gesture to virtually every word we spoke. It all became a blur of movement which killed the meaning of the lyrics.

Instead of exploding, Noël made a joke of it. "This shouldn't be called *After the Ball*, it should be called *St. Vitus' Dance!*" Bobbie laughingly admitted his error of excess, so we then went through even *more* hell, retraining every impulse, so we could get rid of all the gestures we had just finished learning.

There were also problems with the basic construction of the piece. The libretto of a successful operetta is a soufflé, whose main purpose is to get you painlessly from one musical number to the next. Noël's problem was, how to shoehorn the music into Wilde's beautifully-crafted play without stopping it cold? Nobody had thought to encourage Oscar to keep things simple, in the event that his play would one day be turned into a musical.

There was also the question of style. Because of his quick verbal wit, Noël was often compared to Wilde, but comparable isn't identical. There's an underlying affection in Noël's wit that's lacking in Wilde's, though Noël certainly felt the desire to compete, as his *Diaries* reveal: "I am forced to admit that the more Coward we can get into the script and the more Wilde we can eliminate, the happier we shall be." Oscar, Noël felt, was a "tiresome, affected sod... a silly, conceited, inadequate creature...." It was "odd that such brilliant wit should be allied to no humour at all." The problem with *After the Ball*, however, was not Oscar Wilde.

Bobbie Helpmann was uniquely placed to assess the essential weakness of the whole enterprise. "There was no way it could ever work," he accurately observed. "Everything that Noël sent up, Wilde was sentimental about, and everything that Wilde sent up Noël was sentimental about.... It was like having *two* funny people at a dinner party."

For Noël it was another disappointment. In all, he cut about a third of the score ("It is now, subtly, a bit lopsided") in his bid to rearrange it around Mary. It's unlikely that the original show would have caught the temper of the times, for the same reason that it's practically impossible to revive a Novello show today. The book is irrelevant to a modern audience, and its period isn't distant enough in time to have true historical interest. It wasn't *Bitter Sweet 2*. Instead, it left a sour taste. The critics were unanimous: "What a Couple of Victorians," groaned Beverley Baxter in the *Sunday Express;* "Sigh No More - it's the Same Coward," Alan Dent in the *News Chronicle;* "I was Glad when the Ball was Over," *Tribune.*

When you're used to a diet of success and acclaim, everything else tastes like ashes. Since the war, a lot of Noël's ventures had a distinctly charred flavour.

After the Ball. *With Patricia Cree and Irene Browne. (1954)*

He was also ambitious for me, and his *Diaries* bring his belief in my talent poignantly to life. Every time something of his faltered, he felt as badly for me as he did for himself. As ambitious as I was, the blazing success Noël envisaged, the kind that he was used to with *Bitter Sweet* or *Cavalcade*, never was quite re-ignited. I knew he felt responsible, though of course, he wasn't. Tastes in entertainment had changed by the mid-1950's, and there was only so far Noël was prepared to go to adapt.

*   *   *   *

1956 was the year of John Osborne's *Look Back in Anger*, a play which left Noël with mixed feelings about the "Kitchen Sink" school. He had forgotten how Gerald du Maurier had detested *The Vortex* and talked about "the younger generation... knocking at the dustbin." Noël confided to his *Diaries*, in words that would never have passed his lips, "I cannot understand why the younger generation, instead of knocking at the door, should bash the fuck out of it." He didn't discount their technical writing skills, but their subversive pattern of motivation worried him. Many critics perceived his antipathy as an "attack on Youth." Noël responded that "Youth is a wonderful thing in the theatre and I have no intention of attacking it. I do attack certain 'propaganda' plays, which I find bad art. I don't like propaganda in art - which is why I attack either very right- or left-wing plays. They smell of propaganda, which is why I slightly resent them."

When pressed to be more specific, he admitted that he didn't "care for the plays of Mr. Brecht," which, though he was sure they were "immensely sincere," he found "dull to look at." In Noël's view, this was the cardinal theatrical sin. "I like being *entertained* in the theatre. The moment you go on a tub and start thumping it," he opined, "art goes out of the window."

Of the new crop of playwrights, he much admired Harold Pinter ("an extraordinary writer and remarkable theatre man"), whose use of language was not "derivative." Kenneth Tynan always claimed that Pinter's style owed much to Noël's influence. Early in his career, Harold had contributed to revue, which may account for some of the concision in his writing. Tynan quotes, as an example, one of Gertie's speeches in *Shadow Play* (1935): "Small talk, a lot of small talk with other thoughts going on behind." Pinter, twenty years early!

Noël distrusted Osborne's achievement as essentially superficial. "Destructive vituperation is too easy. I cannot believe that this writer, the first of the 'angry young men,' was ever really angry at all. Dissatisfied, perhaps, and certainly envious and, to a degree, talented, but no more than that. No leader of thought or ideas, a conceited, calculating young man blowing a little trumpet!" He wrote those words in 1959 and little happened to change his mind over the years. "...talented, shrewd, calculating fake.... What is even more vulgar is Osborne's misuse of the English language." *That* was unforgiveable! Comparing himself and Osborne as playwrights, Noël judged that "We both wrote about what we saw and didn't like. Mine was a more circumscribed dislike. *Everything* bothers him."

Noël felt some sympathy for Arnold Wesker, whose work had not sustained its early popularity. Wesker's fatal flaws (in Noël's view) were his lack of construction and his sociological preoccupations: "What does he show? Lentils boiling in a pot while six men march up and down. Is that entertainment...?" "He devotes far too much time to a perfectly sincere but slightly misguided sense of fighting for a cause. I think he has a rich and wonderful talent and he should write about *people*, not about causes. Because for the causes he writes about, the battle has already been won."

At his own invitation, Wesker once visited us in Switzerland, and earnestly implored Noël to contribute to a scheme for a Workers' Theatre project, Centre 42. Though it wasn't quite his cup of tea, Noël was touched by Wesker's obvious sincerity. To show there was no ill feeling, he later agreed to spend "...unnecessarily... four hours at the Old Vic in wig, eyebrows and moustache" doing a five-line walk-on in a performance of *The Kitchen* to honour the Royal Court's late director, George Devine.

Noël assessed that group of writers by saying, "I have nothing but admiration and praise for the younger playwrights who really mind about the theatre. The thing that irritates me is minding about a political or a personal cause more than the theatre."

Against his protestations, attacks on Noël as the Dark Destroyer of Youth escalated to the point where he felt compelled to publish a three-part "manifesto" of his feelings in *The Sunday Times*, under the heading "Consider the Public." (These essays are reprinted in Book Two.) Many of the windmills at which he was tilting managed to blow themselves out with no further assistance from him.

Far from assuaging the situation, Noël's remarks raised the stakes. Whatever causes the new playwrights and critics espoused individually, they now had a common cause in attacking Noël. After *Relative Values*, nothing he offered met with their approval. *Quadrille* (1952), an Edwardian soufflé written for the Lunts as the promised successor to *Design for Living*, limped along for a while, though the consensus was that the pace was too leisurely for post-war tastes. "*Quadrille* is rehash of *Private Lives*," attested the *News Chronicle*. "Coward Says It All Twice Over," was Kenneth Tynan's verdict in the *Evening Standard*. Cecil Beaton had valiantly attempted a picture-postcard design, but it wasn't enough. The American production fared a little better, where Lynn and Alfred determinedly squeezed every last drop out of one hundred and fifty painful performances. For the hard-bitten audiences of the 1950's, the unconsummated peccadilloes of Marquesses and Marchionesses offered little in the way of a thrill.

Nude with Violin (1956) did slightly better, largely on the strength of John Gielgud in the lead, but it was casually dismissed as another of Noël's fuddy-duddy attacks on another contemporary form he clearly misunderstood, in this case modern art. The plot centred on a famous artist who informs his family in his will that all his "masterpieces" were fakes. Little did the critics realise that, at the time he wrote the play, Noël was an accomplished artist in his own right, and had a very clear understanding of his subject! *Nude* was a smash hit with the public and ran for eighteen months, in spite of the critics: "Coward serves a non-fizzer" (John Barber in the *Daily Express*); "So Very Trivial, Mr. Coward," (*News Chronicle*); "A Problem Canvas," (*Tatler*).

Noël established a protocol to circumvent the press: Put a big star in the leading role to attract the punters, and damn the critics. The Lunts and

"Nude with Violin". *Binkie chose my version over Noël's and Coley's to use in the production — but audiences found my nude too rude! (Goldenhurst, 1956)*

Johnny G. had done it in their vehicles; now it was Vivien Leigh's turn in *South Sea Bubble* (1956).

The play had started life as *Home and Colonial*, a trifle set in Samolo with a leading lady based on a cross between Diana Cooper and Edwina Mountbatten. Noël wrote it with Gertie in mind, but she wasn't very enthusiastic about it. After a lengthy gestation period, the play, now called *Island Fling*, was staged in 1951 at the Westport Playhouse in Connecticut (run by the infamous Jack Wilson). The lead was played by Claudette Colbert, so a certain amount of Americanisation necessarily took place, and much of the colonial humour was dissipated. It was modestly successful, but nobody seriously discussed Broadway.

When it resurfaced in the UK in 1956, as *South Sea Bubble*, Vivien's character was closer to Noël's original "colonial" conception. Vivien's name pulled in the paying customers, though a review like "Coward up the Creek" (*Tribune*) was sadly typical.

Viv's success offered some much-needed stability to her own life, too. When her late, unsuccessful pregnancy finally took her out of the show, it would be only a matter of time before the notices went up. But for a respectable period, Samolo was on the theatrical map. (The principal characters would turn up later in Noël's only novel, *Pomp and Circumstance*.)

Vivien returned in Noël's adaptation of a Feydeau farce, *Occupe-toi d'Amélie*, which was re-christened *Look After Lulu* (1959). During this period, projects were forever stopping and starting. If Vivien couldn't do it, Noël would have to turn to Dora Bryan ("...who, if carefully watched, will be brilliant...she has more warmth and is a much better comedienne").

Noël's principal concern was Vivien's state of mind. ("...I have a clear feeling that all she wants is a month or two, *réclame*, lovely notices and then something else! Great big glamorous stars can be very tiresome.")

He need not have wasted his worries; the play opened in August and closed by year-end. ("We probably inserted too many Coward jokes for Feydeau's good.") Bernard Levin, in the *Daily Express*, warned that "Lulu Isn't the Lady to Do Coward Any Good," and was even inspired to doggerel:

> But oh, my dears,
> It confirmed my horridest fears
> Mr. Coward simply cannot be French Without Tears

"A Tepid Run Around the Beds," yawned the *Daily Mail*, while Richard Findlater, in the *Sunday Dispatch*, minced no words: "Oh Chuck It In, Mr. Coward."

Viv was in great distress. Larry had gone to America without her, and she had no credible reason for not joining him, except that he didn't want her to. Noël and I took her to Switzerland for Christmas, where tears and tantrums were the order of the day. Viv desperately needed reassuring that everything would be alright with Larry, that he would come back to her. We wanted to say "No," but, of course, didn't. It was not the holiday any of us wanted, but it was not entirely unexpected. Noël determinedly kept the press at bay by pretending they were there to see *him*, and waxing lyrical about his next projects.

*   *   *   *

The second half of the 1950's was also a pretty mixed bag for me. I did a spell in cabaret at the Café de Paris. In his *Diaries*, Noël paid me a huge compliment, saying that I sang five songs and did three dances "gently and without forcing." In person, "Not bad at all," was as much as I got. I was paid £150 a week, as opposed to Noël's £750, so if anyone asks you the price of stardom in 1955 it was precisely six hundred quid a week!

I joined the third incarnation of the cast of *Nude with Violin*, starring Bobbie Helpmann. Most of the fizz had left with Johnny G. but it was still a highly enjoyable evening. Bobbie, as Sebastian, was the third actor in that rôle, Johnny G. having been followed by Michael Wilding. Michael's limited acting ability was compensated by his considerable star quality. During his stint it was Standing Room Only. To maintain his boyish figure, however, Michael was not eating in the proper way, with the unfortunate side effect that his throat seized up and he couldn't speak properly. Noël tackled this bad case of thespian arrest by sending a steak to Michael's dressing room every night, with the strict instruction that he eat it before he went on. I'd heard of feeding an actor his lines, but this was indeed a unique approach.

My next West End experience looked good on the surface, but it was not one I'd willingly relive. Peter Sellers opened to decent reviews in *Brouhaha* in 1959. The other lead, American actor, Jules Munshin, had just been recalled to the States. Naturally, I was delighted to get a part with nary a song or dance in sight. This would extend my range and showcase my talent to producers.

George Tabori's play was a slight enough piece about a Sultan who tries to attract financial investment in his tiny kingdom by deliberately causing disturbances which will encourage the superpowers to subsidise his "neutrality." If that plot bears more than a passing resemblance to Sellers's film, *The Mouse That Roared*, I accept no responsibility.

Though the Management clearly wanted me, Peter Sellers, for reasons of his own, did not. To this day, I don't know why. He refused to rehearse with me; at the dress rehearsal he sulked, waffled, and wouldn't give cue lines. It was a disaster!

Director Peter Hall took me aside and said, "Graham, you're doing fine. But I can't stay, because if I lose my temper with Peter, he'll walk out and close the play!" Exit Director, Stage Left.

I approached Sellers with what I thought was a reasonable request: Since I knew only my part and not the whole show, could he please stick to the script for the first couple of performances, until I could find my feet? He glared at me and said nothing. On the first night, however, he said a great deal, very little of it from the play! On my first entrance he launched into a monologue about my clothes, wanting to know where I bought them. New York? Brooks Brothers?

Rather than making me nervous, his attitude made me angry. I was determined not to be beaten by this unpleasant little man. Somehow I got through it, though what few laughs were in my part to begin with, he managed to kill with some nonsensical bit of business.

I thought I'd try a different tack. I went to his dressing room and said, "Pete, I need your help. I'm really just a straight 'juvenile' and this is a comedy part. Can you please help me get those laughs, because you do it so much better than I do?" I got that silent glare again, but I also started getting the feed lines.

Showing who was boss was one of Sellers' endearing little traits. Because of his threats to walk off and close the show, he was not a popular performer with theatre managements. He'd abandon the script to talk to the audience, as if to remind them that it was Peter Sellers they had paid to see. Audiences loved him, but this wasn't how I'd wanted to make my West End debut in a straight rôle, I can tell you!

The 1950's in Britain was a time of social ferment, artistic torment and general upheaval. In our respective ways, Noël and I were caught up in it. We were part of a society that was struggling to come to terms with its new rôle, without knowing exactly how to define what that rôle would be.

A few thousand miles away, though, things looked very different.

Noël with one of his own paintings - an imaginary Italian landscape - before a charity auction. (1953)

CHAPTER SIX

WORDS AND MUSIC
(AND PAINTING)

"Our nation's songs are its pride and its grace
Evermore and after,
Though the shape of the world may alter,
In our songs the laughter
Blends the tears.
From the past we hear
The echo of the songs that proved us free,
They are bequeathed to you and me
For ever and ever."

("There Have Been Songs in England")

Everything seemed to come effortlessly to Noël. It amused him to play with his carefully crafted image: the clipped speech, the appraising look, the theatrical pause before delivering a polished phrase. A psychologist might wish to analyze the complex forces that drove the private man, but the public persona was entirely Noël's own creation.

Later in life he was unwilling to admit to his artifice. To interviewer Hunter Davies, he claimed that he affected nothing, not even his accent: "I always talked as I talk now and always liked to wear nice clothes. I like being chic. The young enchanters of today may have talent but why must they look so grubby...? I've always had a feeling for being an attractive public figure. I would do nothing to spoil it. Being witty was also part of the image, but I haven't minded having to be that. I am." Even that performance was part of his act, as I knew from personal experience.

Noël loved to be admired, although his manner created distance between himself and those who would approach him. Anyone invading his personal space uninvited would find themselves impaled on a sharp look or a barbed phrase. Because of my early hand-to-mouth existence, I longed to be accepted, to be part of the group. Noël preferred to remain apart until he decided it was worthwhile to join. There were notable exceptions. As a young man he'd been "discovered" and lionised by certain sections of the nobility, and he never lost his taste for the country weekend. Society became a theatre in which he could practice and polish his act. In the early 1920's, it was fascinating to observe him filing away information for future reference. At a weekend house party he would notice the difference in dress codes:

> "... the returning game-players were so much, much more suitably attired for the country than I. Their shirts and flannels were yellow and well used, against which mine seemed too newly white, too immaculately moulded from musical comedy. Their socks, thick and carelessly wrinkled round their ankles, so unlike mine of too thin silk, caught up by intricate suspenders."
>
> (*Present Indicative*)

That *milieu* faded with the changing years, but Noël's public persona remained crystalline and intact. Privately, though, he was self-deprecating. He could send himself up, and those around him, something rotten. That was also part of the performance, but it was his performance. No-one ribbed him who hadn't been granted a licence.

His image became a double-edged sword, wielded against him in a sustained onslaught during wartime and the post-war years. What was Noël Coward doing issuing orders to the Secret Service in Paris? Why was he in the U.S.A. when he should be fighting with the rest of us? What was he doing making a film about the Navy? Why was he leaving England? The list of his supposed "sins" was a mile long.

From the day he became a well-known artiste, a celebrity, the Press couldn't seem to leave him alone. There was something about his cool, effortless personality that got under their collective skin. His apparently impervious attitude fascinated and irritated them. They perpetuated the image while simultaneously trying to undermine it. The more untouched he appeared, which was far from the truth, the more they frothed and foamed. Neither side would give ground. In *Future Indefinite*, written in 1954, Noël reflected on the phenomenon:

> "... in the case of a celebrity, the label has been fixed and the clichés set for years. Sometime in the past, when they stepped into contemporary fame for the first time, some reporter coined a phrase, some interviewer emphasised a peculiarity, some incident occurred that stamped their personalities indelibly onto the journalistic mind..."

Noël's image was created in 1924 when he played Nicky Lancaster in *The Vortex*.

> "All that was important for monotonous future reference was the created image - the talented, neurotic, sophisticated playboy... It still exists today with the slight modification that I am now an ageing playboy, still witty, still brittle and still sophisticated, although the sophistication is, alas, no longer up-to-date, no longer valid."

Although he didn't realise it then, there would be another twenty years of it still to come.

Some of Noël's jabs could be very sharp indeed, even to members of the "family." Although important things never bothered him, he was a particularly intolerant man over small things. "*Must* we have this Alpine tornado raging through the room?" (if a door was left ajar); "Has this whisky enjoyed more than a tentative flirtation with soda?" (if his drink wasn't just to his taste). There'd be a huge, theatrical outburst and then, like a summer storm, it would pass, with no grudges and probably a good laugh to follow.

He rarely admitted to error. If he dropped the subject, that was your pay-off. You couldn't have everything! We didn't mind the cracks because, though they might sting, there was no malice behind them. That was just Noël being himself, an actor who wrote his own parts, a writer used to getting the last word.

Once, in Jamaica, Noël, Coley and I were messing around by the swimming pool at Firefly, Noël's hill-top haven. I was feeling very pleased with life, so I performed an impromptu song-and-dance routine. This gave rise to some crack from Noël about my singing, so in mock indignation, I drew myself up and blustered: "I'll have you know, people have paid good money to see me sing and dance." Noël shot back, "Yes, but not very many and not for very long!" Thoroughly pleased with himself, he plunged into the pool. I wanted to say, "Well, it was mostly your material, chum," but I didn't. He'd devised his exit line and I had to let him keep it.

*   *   *   *

Noël had the nesting instinct, the need for a specific spot to settle himself down to work, like a dog which turns around and around until he's found the perfect position. Maugham had a little house in the garden that was sacrosanct. Noël was just like that. And once he'd marked out his terrain, keep off! At White Cliffs, it was the guest house opening onto the beach; at Gerald Road, a corner of the sitting room; at Goldenhurst, his bedroom overlooking the moors; at Firefly, it was the corner window, where his view of the Spanish Main was guaranteed to unlock writer's block. A small bell was always at hand to summon sustenance for the body, while the mind kept working.

Once he had decided to work, he was totally single-minded. He followed his routine religiously, and accepted no social engagement until the job was done:

> "I have an absolutely routine, disciplined mind. When I'm writing, I'm at my desk and hope that by lunchtime something will have appeared. Sometimes it doesn't until about ten to one. Sometimes it flows from the word go. You can't tell. But you can only do it by doing it regularly... My advice to aspiring writers is to *write*, and try where possible in doing so to use a little critical faculty."

His routine never varied: an early morning start, followed by a light breakfast, with no interruptions but a cup of coffee until lunchtime. In the afternoon he might revise the morning's work, and, if the mood was right, he'd keep going. If not, he'd put the work aside and do some painting.

His devotion to painting began as a simple diversion for his hyperactive mind. You could almost *hear* his mind bubbling away, ideas straining to be released onto paper or canvas. "I am less easily pleased with my work than I used to be," he told an interviewer in 1960. "I am always working on something, because, if I don't, I get irritable and impatient. If I haven't a job to do, I paint or write verses or play the piano or learn Italian." Aside from French, in which he was reasonably fluent, he taught himself enough Italian and Spanish to create an impression, though he never truly mastered American!

His ideas had a life of their own. They would hover in his mind just before he went to sleep, and next morning, something good was ready to happen. He believed that ideas would always turn up if you were ready to embrace them.

When the ideas arrived, it was usually in a torrent, as with *Blithe Spirit*. In *Future Indefinite* he wrote: "For some time past an idea for light comedy had been rattling at the door of my mind and I thought the time had come to let it in and show it a little courtesy." "It fell into my mind and on to the manuscript." He wrote it in six days, working on a strict schedule from eight-forty to one, and from two to seven, "...while Joyce [Carey] was struggling with Keats and Fanny Brawne, the subject of *her* play." He was a literary Madame Arcati, letting the words flow through. He was further motivated by the knowledge that Georges Simenon had written a Maigret book in just eleven days employing an identical daily routine.

Private Lives was rattled off in four days with an Eversharp pencil and a foolscap-sized writing block, which were his constant companions in the 1920's and '30's. He remarked, rather smugly, "Shakespeare never wrote anything so quickly. Not even *Twelfth Night* or *Macbeth*." (Both of which were supposed to have taken ten days from writing to first performance.) His personal best was "good old *Hay Fever*... written and conceived in about three days in that little cottage in Dockenfield in 1924. What a profitable weekend *that* was."

Noël cultivated the playwright-as-medium image as part of the Coward legend. ("It is a truly wonderful gift, my natural and trained gift for dialogue.") He explained to Cecil Beaton in 1942: "If I type easily, then I know the stuff is good....*Blithe Spirit* is a bloody good play, and *Private Lives* will always be revived and will go into the history of comedy like a play by Congreve or Wilde." It would be twenty years before that prophecy was fulfilled.

His Muse could take him in remarkable ways. Once, when stuck on a song for *Conversation Piece*, he went to turn off the light, and instead composed "I'll Follow My Secret Heart" straight off. *Cavalcade* was complete except for the final "Toast to the Future" speech, but after a good night's sleep, he woke up to write it down exactly as it was later performed. It was never the Hollywood cliché of Cole Porter composing "Night and Day" as the grandfather clock ticked away. No sitting bolt upright in bed with shouts of "Eureka!" He simply kept a pad and pencil by the bedside to jot down his ideas when he awoke.

His inspiration was largely due to preparation. The mind had already been working in overdrive in readiness for that mysterious moment when Noël would go into one of his famous creative "trances."

Noël's original idea for *Blithe Spirit* was to have ghosts from different ages meet in an old house in Paris. The comedy would be sparked by their conflict of attitudes, but he could never get that concept to work in his mind. The ghosts, however, would not leave him, and finally manifested themselves in a domestic "black" comedy. The play was criticised for its morbid subject matter at a time when the world was still very much in the grip of death. But Noël was adamant: "There's no question of that, because there's no *heart* in the play. You can't sympathise with *any* of them. If there *was* a heart, it would be a sad story." He was right. It was a comedy with no deep emotional meaning, and enough people seemed to agree with Noël; it ran for nearly two thousand performances.

Many writers jot down every little thought, every *bon mot*, in endless notebooks and journals, but Noël trusted his mind to be his filing system. He could beckon ideas at will, and if they came out untidily, he'd simply ditch them and turn his attention elsewhere. He was never afraid to start afresh.

Noël was subject to a few professional "superstitions." He admitted in a late interview:

> "I used to write straight onto the typewriter in a very dashing way. But that's a bit dangerous, because once it's typed, a play looks as if it's finished. And sometimes it isn't. So now, I've taken to writing longhand, and revising it as I go along. I write straight the way through from the beginning. 'Act One, Scene One. The curtain rises...' My danger is in writing too easily. Too much facility...

> "I always construct first. In my early days I didn't. I just pressed on and hoped for the best. But experience taught me you've got to have a strong structure under you, to give room for irrelevancies and the light dialogue. The *bones* of the play. It was Gilbert Miller who told me that a play depended, like a house, on the architecture. The dialogue was the interior decoration. But however good the interior decoration was, it wouldn't be much good if the walls fell down."

Watching him at work, I often wondered where on earth all the words came from. He wasn't a traditionally well-educated man, yet he possessed the most subtle and sophisticated vocabulary of anyone I'd ever known. Noël soaked up information like a sponge. He could reduce the dinner table to a hush by conducting a conversation on the intricacies of a kidney stone operation, or the ecology of wetlands, or Polynesian circumcision rites. Sharing knowledge was one of his great joys.

He was a voracious reader, particularly of the classics, which he would re-read again and again. Trollope and Dickens were his special favourites. They intrigued him as much for sheer technique as for the storyline or the characters. Every nuance of plot was carefully filed away: the way a Dickens phrase brought a character to life, or the subtleties of Trollope's social universe.

There was great excitement the day a huge consignment of the complete Modern Library arrived in Switzerland. It took up an entire wall, and Noël now felt he was ready for anything! He devoured anything that demonstrated imagination, or explored the human heart, and was especially fascinated by writers who dealt sympathetically with children. He maintained that E. Nesbit had no peer in that regard: "She, of all the writers I have ever read, has given me over the years the most complete satisfaction." When Noël died, her book, *The Enchanted Castle*, was on his bedside table.

Noël was almost childlike in his enthusiasm. The spirit of Peter Pan never really left him. Everything became an "adventure," whether it was a book, a car, or the ingredients for some new culinary concoction. When writing to his friends, he used a patented version of baby talk ("Toley," "Doycie"), which was both sincere and satirical. In the harsh realities of the world, a retreat to childhood gave him a sense of security.

In later years, he became more concerned that he should read "good writing." As a self-educated person, Noël was consciously steering his choice of reading matter toward what he felt he *should* read. There may be reason to think that this self-editing had an intellectual influence, which made his own writing worse.

He was a Renaissance man stranded in the twentieth century, blessed with the additional talents of determination and discipline. A typical entry in the *Diaries* reads: "Now my intention is to relax for a little, rewrite the small bits that have to be rewritten in *Nude with Violin*, have a desultory jab at my neglected novel, polish up some lyrics for Las Vegas, paint some pictures and read a book." Yes, Noël, but what are you going to do *after* lunch?

Every word had its appointed place, and he couldn't tolerate actors and actresses who paraphrased. He agreed with Shakespeare's advice to the Players in *Hamlet:* "Speak the speech...," though he occasionally found himself "hoist with his own petard." Such was the case when he played King Magnus in George Bernard Shaw's *The Apple Cart* during Coronation Year (1953). He was faced with one of the most demanding rôles in contemporary theatre. The actor in him felt that the part needed some cutting, but the playwright in him was forced to admit: "It's absolutely impossible to cut Shaw. It's so beautifully constructed that if you take out one *line*, you ruin the balance of the whole paragraph and the speech." He kept every word. He would practise on the beach in Jamaica, and claimed that the seagulls knew the rôle better than he did! He later expressed the wish that Shaw could have seen him perform: "Not that he'd have approved. I sentimentalised it a bit." Then he quickly added: "But it's a jolly good play!"

Noël needed peace and quiet to write, but he didn't much care for solitude. He always made sure he had company, whether on his long, exotic trips to the Far East and South America, or while relaxing with the "family" at White Cliffs and Goldenhurst, or surrounding himself with hot-and-cold running house guests in Jamaica and Switzerland. Everyone was wined, dined, and entertained, but always with the requirement that they be available whenever Noël needed company.

After finishing his morning's work, he'd join us for a drink, and we knew immediately by his face whether his Muse had dropped by for tea that morning. If he was particularly pleased with something, he might read it to us, but he was very sensitive to criticism, particularly when the offering was still warm. We discovered that a careless word might send him off in the wrong direction, and none of us wanted *that* responsibility.

Noël did not adhere too rigidly to Somerset Maugham's rule of thumb, to write from seven to one o'clock and never go back in the afternoon, even if you're tempted to. But, as the years went by, the morning stint usually wrapped it up for the day. He developed the habit of breaking off in the middle of a sentence, but when he returned to work, he could easily complete it and pick up the momentum again.

*   *   *   *

Lyric writing was something he tackled in a more intermittent fashion, occasionally returning to polish the words until he was satisfied. Sometimes they'd arrive complete and in a rush; more often, they'd be pieced together like a crossword puzzle, with the same sense of delight when the last clue was locked in place:

> "Being a natural musician, I found it easier to write tunes jangling in my head than to devote myself to mastering iambics, trochees, anapæsts, or dactyls. If a tune came first, I would set them to music at the piano. This latter process almost invariably necessitated changing the verse to fit the tune. If you happen to be born with a built-in sense of rhythm, any verse is apt to fall into a set pattern and remain within its set pattern until it is completed. This is perfectly satisfactory from the point of view of reading or reciting, but when you attempt to set the pattern to a tune, either the tune gives in and allows itself to be inhibited by the rigidity of your original scansion, or it rebels, refuses to be dominated and displays some ideas of its own, usually in the form of unequal lines and

unexpected accents. This is why I seldom write a lyric first and set it to music later. I think that the best lyrics I have written are those which have developed more or less at the same time as the music."

The ideas could materialise quite out of context, though Noël said that one of the few songs which had the decency to arrive appropriately was "Mad Dogs," which he conceived while driving from Hanoi to Tonkin. "True, the only white people to be seen were French, but one can't have everything." He added, "I sang it triumphantly and unaccompanied to my travelling companion on the verandah of a small jungle guest house. Not only Jeffery, but the gekko lizards and the tree frogs gave every vocal indication of enthusiasm."

As with so many of his activities, Noël started early. He recalled his apprenticeship during the First World War:

> "Through the influence of Max Darewski, I signed a three-year contract with his brother, Herman, who at that time had a publishing firm in the Charing Cross Road. The contract was for lyrics only, and I was to be paid fifty pounds for the first year, seventy-five for the second, and one hundred pounds for the third year. I appeared dutifully every week or so for the first few months, armed with verses, and ideas for songs. I waited for many hours in the outer office, but seldom, if ever, clapped eyes on Herman Darewski, and nobody seemed at all interested in my lyrics....Some while after this, the Herman Darewski publishing firm went bust, a fact that has never altogether astonished me."
>
> (Present Indicative)

Noël talked of filling notebooks with his juvenilia, but there's little chance of their turning up. There do survive, however, his early collaborations with Herman's brother Max. The lyrics catch the feelings of those fragile years, when war still held a touch of tortured romance. Ivor had already published the war's theme song, "Keep the Home Fires Burning," a fact which was not lost on the eighteen-year old Noël when he and Max wrote "When You Come Home on Leave":

> *Dear one, I want you just to know*
> *That I am carrying on*
> *Tho' life's at best a dreary show*

Now that you have gone.
I'd like you just to realise
That tho' we're far apart
Where 'ere you go on land or sea
You have with you my heart.
Tho' days for me are dull and drear
You need not have the slightest fear
For
When you come home on leave
I'll still be waiting
Waiting to greet you with a smile
To charm away your pain
And make you feel again
That life is going to be worthwhile.
I love you so my heart is simply yearning
And this is what I want you to believe
That tho' sorrows there may be
There'll be one glad day for me
On the day you come home on leave.

I dream of you the whole night through
I think of you all day
I'm weary for the sight of you
You've been so long away.
The weeks for me are very sad
And happy days are few
Remember when you're feeling bad
That I am lonely too.
But as I gaze across the sea
I know that you'll return to me
And
When you come home on leave...etc.

At the bottom of the manuscript, Noël had scribbled, "Good old pot-boiling words." He need not have been so apologetic: Vera Lynn sang similar sentiments to great acclaim during World War II, over twenty years later. In this, as in everything, he was the perfectionist: "Bad rhyming sets my teeth on edge."

Noël wrote at least one other song with Max's partner, Doris Joel, aptly titled "Peter Pan." It appeared in André Charlot's 1918 revue, *Tails Up:*

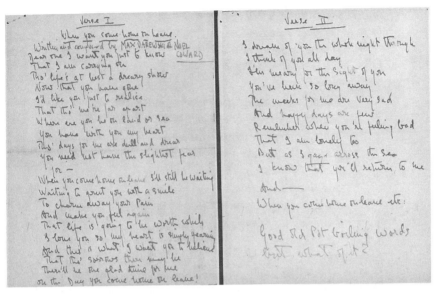

The 18-year old Noël's answer to Ivor's "Keep the Home Fires Burning." He referred to it as "pot-boiling words" but a war later Vera Lynn would probably have turned it into a hit!

If you believe in Fairies, they say,
All thro' your lifetime happy you'll be,
Peter and Wendy both know the way,
That's why they're always children, you see,
Even the Fairies, so I've been told,
Follow the fashions too,
Once they get started, nothing can hold
Them back from a dance that is new.

    Peter Pan has learned to do the latest dance,
    Wendy too, thought she would like to take a chance,
    Captain Hook was really most disgusted,
    Smee and Starky seemed to look quite flustered,
    And pretty Tinker Bell,
    Said to Peter Pan,
    "Clap your hands if you believe in Fairies,
    And come and dance as well!"

Even the mermaids in the lagoon,
Tho' they had only tails to wag,
Danced with the pirates under the moon,
Each time they heard that wonderful Rag,

Sometimes at night when ev'rything's still,
They try to sleep in vain,
Peter comes tripping up the hill,
Then off they go dancing again

Peter Pan has learnt to do the latest dance,
Wendy too, thought she would like to take a chance
J.M. Barrie fainted when he knew it,
Cried, "You really must not do it," Peter Pan,
Said, "If it's wrong for boys to dance
It is most unkind,
And although I said I'd never grow up,
I think I'll change my mind."

The only other surviving fragment from that time seems unlikely to have ever been set to music. Here is the short saga of "Annabel":

Annabel Devigne
Had a flat in Golders Green,
And her ways were really most endearing.
She desired to learn a bit
And she thought she'd make a hit
If she did a little auctioneering.
On a box she'd take her stand
With a hammer in her hand
And a firm resolve to keep from skidding.
But don't think that she fell,
She went most awfully well
With the men who came to do her bidding.
Anna was an auctioneer
Though what she sold is not quite clear.
And as a business woman she
May never quite have shone.
She discovered young men's choice was
To hear how nice her voice was -
Going, going, gone.

Although Annabel was not fated to survive in the Coward canon, she was surely a distant relative of the infamous "Alice (Who Was At It Again)."

*   *   *   *

Noël's approach to music was a different matter altogether. He had no formal training, other than a few casual lessons in harmony and composition at the Guildhall School of Music. He never learned to read or write music. "I have played the piano since I was seven and compose by improvising, with a tape-recorder running...my music...is purely inspirational." In the early 1920's, he wrote:

> "I just go on with the business of living, like other people do, until something occurs to me....If I am anywhere near a piano, I fly to it and play the tune with one hand. That 'fixes' it, as a photographer would say, and I can proceed with the rest in a more leisurely way.

> "The next step is to get the harmony exactly as I want it, playing it over and over again if necessary. After that my task is practically ended. I play it to a trained musician, who writes the notes down and then repeats the piece to me so that I can make quite sure that he has reproduced it correctly... particularly the harmonics.

> "One does not need a deep knowledge of the mysteries of theory and musical form in order to compose light songs of the revue and musical comedy type. What is necessary is a perfect ear for pleasant sounds. When I think of what seems to me to be a good tune, the most suitable harmony suggests itself at the same time - in a rough form, at any rate. I don't know whether I'm breaking conventional rules of theory, and care less. The sound's the thing...

> "I don't even know how I got my musical talent, unless it has been handed down from a grandfather who was an organist for many years at the Crystal Palace.

> "But I wonder if it is fair to his memory to say so?"

Actually, there was always a strong love of music in Noël's family. His father sang in a choir, which is where he met Noël's mother, and for a while sold pianos and published music. A Coward family tradition was to sing songs round the parlour piano in the evening, with even the lodgers joining in. Noël was happily exposed to most of the popular musical gems of the late-Victorian era.

Noël's musical education may have been limited, but his ear was not.

Noël at Goldenhurst. (1935)

Gladys captures Noël at the piano. Pencil and water-colour. (1930's)

He could listen to an orchestra play one of his scores and detect a single instrument, even a single note or harmony, which was being played incorrectly. It was an uncanny ability.

He rarely had a problem coming up with a melody ("Suddenly a new and lovely tune appeared") and was often able to compose something straight through, as he had with "I'll Follow My Secret Heart." His problem was recalling it! With no tape recorder, and no way of writing it down, he had to play "Secret Heart" for hours on end to be sure of remembering it the next day. So it was that Noël employed one Elsie April. She was a "small, sharp-eyed woman, whose mastery of musical technique was miraculous. She could transfer melody and harmony onto paper with the swiftness of an expert shorthand stenographer." Noël's extraordinary ear would instantly detect if she'd transcribed a single wrong chord.

His memory for other people's music, however, was amazing. After we'd seen a musical, he could accurately play on his studio piano two-thirds of the score we'd heard an hour before. He was, remarkably, a self-taught pianist, who never took lessons to improve his technique, because he felt he might lose his spontaneity in all the theory. He required an immediate audience for any new composition: "Come and listen to this. It's the best thing I've ever written!"

With the romantic songs, the melody invariably came first and he'd find the lyrics to fit. With the comedy or "point" songs, he'd fix a metre, write a draft lyric and worry about the music later, much in the way that Cole Porter did.

While on vacation in Haiti, Noël was thrilled to hear that Irving Berlin was a guest at the same resort. Berlin fascinated Noël, who knew *all* his music. One of the few songs Noël ever used that he didn't write himself was Berlin's "Always," which the psychic maid employed to conjure up the ghost of Elvira in *Blithe Spirit*.

One evening, Noël plucked up his courage and performed from memory a medley of Berlin songs on the hotel piano. Berlin was so impressed that he asked Noël who'd written a particular tune he was playing. "Why, *you* did, sir," replied a bewildered Noël. The tune was "White Christmas."

By 1955, Berlin's reputation was in decline, his glory days of *Annie Get Your Gun* (1946) and *Call Me Madam* (1950) behind him. He seemed, said Noël, like "a little old man who was feeling very, very sad." Noël's tribute and the reception of the other resort guests seemed to cheer him up. One self-taught genius encouraging another.

After Elsie April's departure, Robb Stewart and Norman Hackforth acted as Noël's musical amanuenses as well as his accompanists. Noël was so prolific, he'd forget what he'd composed, and there's no question that without them important work would have been lost.

After Noël's death, Norman Hackforth discovered an unfinished song which Noël had probably intended to use in his next musical after the war. Noël seemed to have forgotten about it, but Norman had an instinctive feeling that he'd better commit it to paper. The song (from around 1944) was called "There Will Always Be," but without Norman it never would have! Musicologists may trace the stylistic influences from elsewhere in the Coward canon, but the lyrics certainly echo Noël's basic philosophy of life:

"THERE WILL ALWAYS BE"

There will always be
Enough in the world for me -
Moonlight and stars and sea,
These there will always be.

I shall always find,
If Destiny's only kind,
Something that's new
And good and true
To calm my questing mind.

Though dark days may grieve me,
Though the fates deceive me,
I'll always know
Deep down inside me
Love will be there to guide me.

There will always be
This personal thing
To set my spirit free
This there will always be -
This there will always be.

*   *   *   *

Noël and I met Cole Porter in New York in 1949. Porter was still resisting the necessary amputations he had dreaded for so long and he looked very tired. "How on earth he manages to summon up that joy of spirit in his songs when he's hurting like hell every minute of the day, I'll never know," marvelled Noël, who was no stranger to health problems himself. It made him feel humble.

Noël and Cole agree to Let's Do It *in the Chichester Festival production anthologising their songs. (1994)*

Noël's presence clearly brought Cole to life. They had known each other since "the merry years" of the 1920's, and in the second-act musical sequence of *Private Lives*, Noël had briefly interpolated Cole's song, "I Never Realized." Indeed, their careers had numerous parallels, including their struggles against post-war critics who insisted on writing them off.

I'd have to say Cole won their bloodless competition on points. The success of *Kiss Me, Kate* certainly exceeded anything Noël produced in those years, though Noël had mixed feelings about the show when he saw it in 1949. He loved the score, but he found the lyrics "brilliant but too dirty." He took a more liberal view of it later. His initial reaction was probably tinged with the realisation that he was watching a truly major work, and it wasn't his.

A stylistic trait they shared was verbal acuity: rhymes within rhymes upon rhymes. Most songwriters are grateful to end the line with their scansion intact. Only Lorenz Hart matched their sophistication, though Alan Jay Lerner and Stephen Sondheim could also be added to what must be a very short list.

References to each other's work became teasing tributes which they defied the rest of us to spot. In 1930, Noël wrote about the way "Englishmen detest a siesta." In 1940, in *Panama Hattie*, Cole exclaimed "We detest a Fiesta!" Imagine waiting ten years to find a suitable rhyme!

There were other uncanny echoes. In 1938, Cole wrote a show called *Leave It To Me*. Noël agreed. How could he not, when he'd written *I'll Leave It To You* in 1920!

It was extremely, and typically, generous of Cole to give Noël permission to parody one of his biggest hits, "Let's Do It," for his Las Vegas act. Noël-after-Cole, in Noël's favourite phrase, "tore the place up":

> *Mr. Irving Berlin*
> *Often emphasizes sin*
> *In a charming way.*
> *Mr. Coward we know*
> *Wrote a song or two to show*
> *Sex was here to stay.*
> *Richard Rodgers it's true*
> *Takes a more romantic view*
> *Of that sly biological urge.*
> *But it really was Cole*
> *Who contrived to make the whole*
> *Thing merge.*

The affectionate mutual ribbing continued. Cole parodied Noël in *The Man Who Came to Dinner* and *Jubilee*. Noël returned the dig at Cole in "Nina":

> *She declined to begin the Beguine*
> *Though they besought her to*
> *And in language profane and obscene*
> *She cursed the man who taught her to,*
> *She cursed Cole Porter too!*

Their sophisticated audiences delighted in picking up the references, but Noël reserved his more wicked parodies for the "in" set. One of Cole's most wistful melodies was a song called "Weren't We Fools?":

> *Weren't we fools to lose each other...*
> *Though we knew we loved each other*
> *You chose another, so did I....*

It was a personal favourite which he sang at private parties, until Noël substituted an alternative last line:

You chose your brother, so did I....

I walked into the living room at White Cliffs one Sunday afternoon in November, 1945, to find Noël playing Jerome Kern melodies. It gave us an eerie feeling later, to realise that this impromptu concert had been taking place at almost exactly the same time as Kern was dying. He'd collapsed on a New York street and had been taken anonymously to a charity hospital. Through his ASCAP card, he was identified by Oscar Hammerstein, and was soon removed to a private hospital, where he died six days later. This was a tragic end for someone whose music brought joy into so many lives all around the world.

It is not widely known that Noël and Jerry actually collaborated back in the early 1920's. Jerry was a frequent visitor to London in those years, and we can well imagine them at a cocktail party discussing the possibility of a joint effort. But whereas Kern was a constant collaborator (he wrote songs with seventy-five separate lyricists), Noël was not.

So it came as a huge surprise when, in 1982, two Kern/Coward songs were discovered in sheet music form in a derelict Warner Bros. Music warehouse in Secaucus, New Jersey. Among the treasure trove were also "lost" numbers by Porter, the Gershwins and many others, which had been cut from films or shows and consigned to oblivion. The two unpublished Kern/Coward songs, a gypsy ballad called "Tamarind" and a duet called "Morganatic Wife," were written about 1923. There is no documentation of why they were written, nor any evidence that a full-scale partnership was planned.

The significance of the duet is not the quality of the song itself (it's a typical minor song of the period), but the fact that Noël never mentioned writing it. You'd hardly forget a collaboration with Jerome Kern.

American lyricist Howard Dietz was invited by Kern to collaborate on *Dear Sir* (1924), and when he arrived at Kern's house, the great man thrust a manuscript at him with the instruction to "do a twist on these lyrics." The name at the top of the sheet was "Noël Coward" and, for the title, Jerry had scribbled "If You Will Be My Morganatic Wife." Dietz duly returned with the lyric "If We Could Lead a Merry Mormon Life," which "delighted Kern." Neither the show nor the song excited much attention, though there is much interest now in authenticating Noël's *original* song.

"Morganatic," by the way, describes the marriage of a person of high rank (like the King in the song) to someone of lower rank, wherein neither the spouse nor her children have any claim on his title or possessions.

"MORGANATIC WIFE"

KING: *Any King*
               May have his fling
               But when it comes to love
               A bitter sacrifice
               He always has to make...
MISTRESS: *Royalties*
               Have loyalties,
               Which have to be considered
               When the morale
               Of the country is at stake.
KING: *I'd like to take you for my own*
               And plant you firmly on the throne
               But, as I'm King,
               You'll understand
               We'll have to be
               More underhand...
BOTH: *We'll have a spree,*
               Morganatically
MISTRESS: *For we agree*
               Love is free,
               Most emphatically.
KING: *We'll manage things*
               Diplomatically...
MISTRESS: *And as we can't be good,*
               We'll lead a careful life.
KING: *If you will only be*
               My morganatic wife.
MISTRESS: *I shall pit*
               My polished wit
               Against the bold ambassadors
               Who've tried to win my heart
               And been refused..
KING: *Any bloke*
               Who'll make a joke
               Against your reputation
               I shall quell by saying -
               'We are not *amused!'*
MISTRESS: *And when I have to meet the Queen,*
KING: *(Oh, dear!)*
MISTRESS: *There'll be a most dramatic scene*

	She'll cloak her hate beneath a sneer
	And I shall say -
	'Look here, old dear...'
BOTH:	*We'll have a spree,*
	Morganatically
MISTRESS:	*I've got the King*
	On a string,
	Systematically.
	I rule the roost
	Automatically.
KING:	*And we will lead them all*
	The devil of a life
	When you're my cosy little
	Morganatic wife.
BOTH:	*And we will lead them all*
	The devil of a life
KING:	*When you're my*
MISTRESS:	*When I'm your*
BOTH:	*Cosy little*
	Morganatic wife!

I met Dick Rodgers and Oscar Hammerstein, and just about everyone else Noël knew, on my first trip to New York in August, 1947. Edna Ferber threw a typical New York party that first weekend, which had a guest list you could have sold tickets for. It was a relaxed atmosphere, however, in which friends felt free to leave their public personas at the door.

Noël flew to the nearest piano like a homing pigeon to sing and play his own songs. Not to be outdone, Dick performed a medley from the incredible repertoire he'd created with Larry Hart and Oscar Hammerstein. A composer is ever anxious to preview his current work, so we were treated to some numbers from *Allegro*, a charming show that had not yet reached London.

I even plucked up the courage to sing "Matelot," which went down well enough, so I gave them "Sigh No More." Flushed with success, I mentioned to Dick that I'd sung one of his songs, "This Can't Be Love," in a London show. He looked puzzled, probably wondering how the boys and girls in London had got to meet *The Boys from Syracuse* without his knowledge. I immediately let the matter drop, but I bet his agent got a call the next day.

On a later visit to London, Dick and Oscar informed Noël that they were turning *Anna and the King of Siam*, the hit 1946 film with Rex Harrison and Irene Dunne, into a musical. (This was the movie which had made Irene unavailable for *Scarlet Lady*.) The combination of a romantic story and an exotic setting would make a terrific Broadway vehicle for Gertie. Would Noël direct? Would Noël direct *and* play the King? How could Noël refuse? But he did. At least one reason he turned down a fat paycheck and a virtually guaranteed smash hit, was his well-known aversion to long runs.

Another may have been that Noël's mental computer had started beeping to alert him that it was time to write. ("I know that this is a moment in my life when I must really be careful. I have earned time to think and I am going to have it.") It became his immediate priority to write his way above all of the recent criticism, and to "get into the swim of the period."

Because of their great friendship, though, Noël was anxious to help Dick, so he reminded him about a young man we'd heard singing and playing guitar at a party in New York. He was the offspring of a Romanov gypsy and a Mongolian father, with a strong Slovak face and a mesmerising presence. Noël remarked at the time that, "To have a background like that is like living with a woman who always wears red."

Dick promised to audition the young Yul Brynner and...need I continue? Yul, quite coincidentally, later became a neighbour of ours in Switzerland. The last time I saw him was backstage at the Palladium after a revival of the show that *became* his later career. Always the "King," he had commandeered the two main dressing rooms, leaving lesser mortals to scurry around changing in the rafters. A far cry from the thin young man taking his plaintive guitar to a party, in the hope that someone would ask him to play.

Noël, it seemed, was making a second career out of refusal. He refused to play Harry Lime in Korda's *The Third Man* because of personal differences with Graham Greene; he refused to adapt *Pygmalion* as a musical for Mary Martin; he refused Professor Higgins in *My Fair Lady* on the grounds that Michael Redgrave had been offered it first! Nor would he play Colonel Nicholson in *The Bridge On the River Kwai* (1957). ("What put me off was that everybody seemed to spend so much time under water.") He changed his tune when Alec Guinness won an Oscar: "I rather wish now that I had done it." He even passed up Humbert Humbert in *Lolita* (1962). ("At my time of life the film story would be logical if the twelve-year-old heroine was a sweet, little old lady.") Had he accepted these, and other rôles, his later years might have been made much easier. But his Muse dictated otherwise.

*   *   *   *

Noël was constantly concerned about artistic excess, though he didn't always avoid it himself. In the *Diaries,* he refers to a particular first draft as being "well written, except for the usual splurge of qualifying adjectives and adverbs... redo on typewriter." Reading the first draft of a short story, *Pretty Polly Barlow* (later *Pretty Polly*), he finds "far too many adverbs and qualifying adjectives - I have been fairly, greatly, firmly, winsomely, rather, almost, very, briskly ruthless!"

Noël never felt he'd "perfected" a style: he was always learning. In the late '50's he took to writing verse and, as often happened, the form took him over. After completing a long narrative verse called *P and O 1930* (1957), he confided: "This writing of free verse, which I am enjoying so very much, is wonderful exercise for my mind and vocabulary....My sense of words, a natural gift, is becoming more trained and selective and I suspect, when I next sit down to write a play, things may happen that have not happened before."

*   *   *   *

The more the critics picked apart his reputation in the '50's and '60's, the more Noël retreated into his painting. This was a distinctly private activity, with only himself to please. With one exception for charity in 1955, he refused to exhibit. ("Some of them are bound to be bought, if not from genuine artistic appraisal, at least for celebrity snobbism.") He thought of himself as a Sunday afternoon painter who practised whenever he felt like it, and most people agree he was a rather talented amateur. But he knew only too well that, if he did formally exhibit, the critics would slaughter him, so he kept it for himself. His paintings became gifts to friends on birthdays, Christmas or first nights, personal tokens, nothing more.

It was the influence of Winston Churchill which got him started. Before the war, Noël dabbled in water colours, starting with a study of Nell Gwynne when he was only ten. When Churchill saw Noël's work, he rightly said, "No, no, no, you must paint with *oils.* That way you can paint out all your mistakes." Oils embolden the artist by removing the fear of mistakes.

Each new work would be held up for our admiration: "This is my masterpiece!" His infectious enthusiasm spurred Coley and me to the canvas. We became three painting fools. Noël insisted it had to be oils, for which his bold colour sense was supremely adapted. We were intensely competitive, always sneaking a look at each others' work, or dashing back to add a last private dab to achieve perfection.

When the frenzy seized him, Noël would abandon his afternoon tea

One of Noël's many Jamaican
studies. Almost all of them
were painted in the studio
from memory.

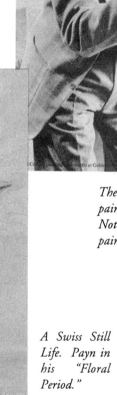

The Master masters a new skill. No[...]
painting in the studio at Goldenhur[...]
Note the gloves. Noël was allergic to [...]
paint.

A Swiss Still
Life. Payn in
his "Floral
Period."

Market Scene
by Noël.
Jamaica.

and sacrifice his beloved pre-dinner drink. He was even known to sneak back after dinner. ("We all paint violently every afternoon. I have inaugurated a new 'period.' Masses of figures scampering about all over the canvases.") The figures reminded me of L.S. Lowry's stick people transported to an unexpected tropical paradise. But, although he greatly admired the French Impressionists, Noël wasn't influenced by any one painter.

He was adamant that his work could not be fully appreciated unless properly framed, so he picked up nondescript Victorian pictures in junk shops solely for the sake of their frames; then he'd happily paint over them. It's entirely possible that someone somewhere has a Corot under his Coward.

We seldom painted outdoors. Noël disliked the nuisance of the wind blowing or the flies settling on his canvas. Most of those colourful Jamaican primitives were done in the studio. Even there he'd wear thin gloves, as he was allergic to turpentine. In the end he gave up pure oils for gouache.

Noël's canvases came from what he remembered of certain parts of the island, a "fantastical impression of Jamaica," so quality of light was never a factor. His imagination flourished equally well under electric and natural light.

Because painting was a game, something for which he was accountable to no one but himself, he could boast, "I'm still at the stage where I break rules without having *learned* them." He was not, however, above making a few rules of his own!

Once he'd suborned Coley, and I lost my last canasta partner, it was inevitable I'd paint too. Five minutes after I started, Noël was loftily advising me: "You put the green paint at the bottom of the canvas and the blue at the top. That's what you call a 'landscape'." To Coley, who was enjoying a neo-Impressionist phase: "Monet, Monet, Monet, that's all you can think of!"

We'd go to a Matthew Smith exhibition and he'd rush back and start using huge splashes of colour everywhere. "Behold, Touch and Gauguin!" He was forever inventing "new styles." Joking apart, I can think of only one other painter who captured the indolent heat of the tropics as well as Noël, and that was Gauguin.

In painting, as in everything, Noël's sense of humour shone through. He had done a small painting which, at first glance, seemed to depict two nuns sitting on a bench with their rosaries. On the small sunny street behind them is an arch, through which a priest is disappearing. Closer inspection reveals a naked young man sitting next to them, enjoying the noonday sun. You then look at those nuns with new eyes. What are they thinking? And what are they telling their *beads?*

Noël was quite the *connoisseur* of painting. When he'd done something out of the ordinary, he'd often settle for a small sketch or painting instead of money. For his cameo appearance in *Around the World in Eighty Days*, for instance, Mike Todd gave Noël a Bonnard costing £4,500 in lieu of salary. For performing two extra weeks at the Café de Paris in 1951, he was given a Boudin seascape, and when Binkie wanted to recognise his consistent contribution to the H.M. Tennent coffers, Noël chose a Sickert painting of *Trelawny of the Wells.*

By the time he left England, he had quite an impressive art collection. Not by Getty standards, certainly, but something that reflected his personal taste: Vlaminck, Brianchon, Nash and many others. The tragedy is that when he moved, his tax accountants insisted he sell up lock, stock and barrel. Any possessions he maintained might suggest to the Inland Revenue an intention to return in the future. The property at Gerald Road and Goldenhurst clearly had to go, but he could have simply shipped the paintings abroad. He never entirely recovered from his mistake. Each painting represented a memory which he had to leave behind.

Nude with Violin (1956) expressed his ambivalent feelings about the phoney attitudes that afflicted modern art. Painting seemed enjoyable and easy if you had only yourself to please. In the *Diaries* he records, "It is astonishing how easy modern painting is....I should think Braque could do a picture a day without turning a camel-hair."

Binkie Beaumont was presenting *Nude with Violin*, Noël's painterly satire. Binkie knew about the three artistic musketeers, so he proposed that we each paint a picture for the play and, without signing them, send him the three paintings. So Noël, Coley and I each painted our version of "Nude with Violin" and, to my amazement, Binkie chose mine! The victory was short-lived. The painting was removed immediately after the Dublin opening because it was considered to be too vulgar! Binkie kept all three originals. Unless he did what Lady Churchill did to Graham Sutherland's portrait of Winston, somewhere there's a large, indecorous "Nude by Noël." What would that fetch at Christie's?

Noël painted for relaxation and inspiration. When he had a brush in his hand, it wasn't necessarily the painting that was receiving his undivided attention. The peace of a studio allowed him the mental space to work out other problems. Without his painting, his playwriting and songwriting might not have progressed so smoothly.

In 1988, there was an amazing conclusion to all this artistic endeavour. Among the personal possessions that were still in Firefly when I donated it to the Jamaican National Trust, were many of Noël's paintings. Friends who visited the house (I didn't have the heart to return myself) told me that the climate was having a horrific effect on the canvasses. The Jamaican government had the foresight to remove and catalogue them, which made me think that, until there's a permanent Coward Museum or a Noël Coward Theatre (which is long overdue), it might be better to let a few people enjoy them, rather than store them in a basement gathering dust.

I called Christie's for an auction evaluation. They quoted a low reserve figure, "...because," they sniffed, "he wasn't a painter, you know." "Neither was Winston Churchill," I retorted. On February 18th, 1988, the sale realised roughly three times the reserve, which would have pleased Noël immensely, because every last penny went to the Actors Charitable Trust for Denville Hall, a home for retired actors.

For a brief time, one of Noël's preoccupations was sculpture, though he would never have Henry Moore reaching for a posthumous chisel. During the war, Noël enjoyed painting with his long-time and multi-talented friend, Winifred Ashton (a.k.a. Clemence Dane), in her ramshackle Covent Garden flat. Nobody ever *taught* Noël anything, but he certainly learned from her.

Winifred was also an accomplished amateur sculptress. Her bust of Noël later adorned the National Portrait Gallery, which could have

Winifred Ashton (Clemence Dane) by Low. She dropped enough verbal bricks to build a sizeable villa but never uttered a dull word.

prompted one of her infamous malapropisms: "Noël, dear, do take my bust and hang it in the National Gallery, where everyone can see it!"

She tried briefly to interest Noël in sculpture, but her initial instructions are probably what made him stick to painting: "Always keep your tool clean," she advised him, "then *ram* it in and when you withdraw, wiggle-waggle, wiggle-waggle it out very gently." With words like that ringing in your ears, it's hard to aspire to Rodin status.

*   *   *   *

Another of Noël's creative forays was into the culinary arts. He was convinced he was an Escoffier-in-waiting, though his friends were sceptical. When he cooked, which wasn't often, he attacked a humble omelette with the same frenzy that would produce a three-act play: "I spent thirty-six hours trying to make my first puff pastry, during which I had to cancel all engagements and lost a night's sleep into the bargain!"

Whatever was on the menu would always involve a multitude of ingredients. Shopping would be a production in itself, involving detailed lists, expeditions to the local stores, return visits to get the things we'd forgotten the first time, with endless recriminations. The whole process resembled the preparations for childbirth. The ingredients were then carefully coded in Coward's Cookery Cupboard. (Try saying *that* in a hurry!) There would be liberal applications of herbs and spices, despite my protestations that the *bravura* of one cancelled the *finesse* of another. Father knew best and whatever he produced was, in his humble opinion, the best he'd ever tasted!

Mother, Noël said, had been a good plain cook, with the accent on "plain." Son was determined to make improvements. The love of spices must have originated on those early oriental journeys, though he would never attempt *authentic* Chinese or Indian dishes. Instead, there were many ordinary dishes that happened to be, shall we say, highly flavoured? None of it was actually life-threatening. Noël *was* good at flaky pastry, so there was lots of that! His own assessment of his expertise is charmingly accurate: "I am inclined to put in far too much flavouring, as in painting I put in far too much colour, but I am learning restraint. I am also learning to be fearless with eggs and undismayed by deep fat and flour and bread crumbs. It all comes under the heading of living dangerously and maybe the day will come when I can cook a joint, stuff a chicken's arse with butter, and make pastry so light that it flies away at a touch."

The most remarkable episode in "Cooking With Coward" occurred one evening in Bermuda, in one of our sporadic attempts to entertain the locals. The meal was to begin with "Huîtres Surprises à la Noël," so he bought a tin of Japanese oysters. We should have been warned! Each of these luckless creatures was entombed in mashed potato and plunged into boiling fat. The idea was that they would be presented as crispy little morsels, which you bit into and *voilà!*

Dinner passed, nobody said a word. The guests departed looking a little listless, even furtive. Noël was, frankly, rather hurt. He'd hoped for more from the oysters and certainly from the guests. Admittedly, he hadn't expected the grey colour to seep through quite so much, but they were, without doubt, the best fried oysters he'd ever tasted.

As we tidied up, all was revealed. In every plant pot, behind every piece of furniture, was a grey virgin *huître*. Not a single one had been eaten. Which, on the whole, was probably just as well.

Escoffier was laughing so hard he couldn't speak!

Cover of the best-selling record of Noël's American cabaret debut. He was frequently asked to repeat the pose for publicity photos. (1955)

CHAPTER SEVEN

BRAVE NEW U.S.A.: THE 1950's

I like America,
I have played around
Every slappy-happy hunting ground
But I find America, okay.
I've been about a bit
But I must admit
That I didn't know the half of it
Till I hit the U.S.A.

(Ace of Clubs)

In 1949, Noël viewed Americans "...as a race spiritually impoverished. Their vulgarity," he said, "is much worse than it used to be....The dollar as a god is even more enervating than the Holy Trinity." By 1959, America would have enriched him with those same dollars for the high value they attached to his *lack* of vulgarity. Noël became America's true definition of a "class act."

Noël never worked in Los Angeles, but it became one of his more successful stopovers. He had once said of Hollywood that he'd "prefer a cup of cocoa," but now embraced its peculiarly perverse lack of culture. He was resigned to the fact that any topic was reduced to $$$ signs, and that an individual's worth was measured by what his last picture grossed. It saddened him to see promising writers, like playwright Ronnie Millar, attracted like moths to the tinsel flame. Noël had felt the lure himself. Ronnie recalls the finger wag he received one evening on the boat to New York just after the war, as Noël insisted on knowing why he, Ronnie, was wasting his talent? Monetary reasons were not enough. Since Ronnie later wrote speeches for another famous finger-wagger, Margaret Thatcher, the Hollywood experience was presumably invaluable.

If I'd had my autograph book handy at our friendly reunions, it would have been full of such names as Joan Crawford, Ronald Colman, Kate Hepburn, Judy Garland, Gene Kelly, Bette Davis, Irene Dunne (where was she when we needed her?), Doug Fairbanks, Jr. and Charlie Chaplin.

*Noël with
Clifton Webb.*

Clifton Webb had been part of the Broadway and Hollywood scene for years, and he was now achieving popular success with his rather acerbic personality in films such as *Laura* (1944) and *Sitting Pretty* (1948).

Noël had known him since the 1920's. Clifton introduced *Blithe Spirit* to Broadway in 1941, but his 1947 revival of *Present Laughter* met with rather disappointing results. He'd played Garry Essendine in a dismissive, chilly manner that killed the essential charm of the character. The box office was equally cold. Clifton started as a Broadway song-and-dance man in the Astaire mould, and was now a respected Hollywood character actor. His rôle as Mr. Belvedere, the intellectual babysitter in *Sitting Pretty* and its sequels, brought him near stardom. His clipped, waspish personality amused Noël, though in later years it became increasingly irritating to him. Clifton's manner was an attempt at an American "Noël Coward," which may explain Noël's ambivalent feelings. He saw his mirror image, and there were days when he wasn't in the mood to face it! Certainly, Noël and his ambience fascinated Clifton and he was extremely hospitable to all of us.

Clifton once invited me to stay with him and his old mum, a legendary character of extreme years. She was renowned for her own special version of the can-can, which she'd perform at the least provocation. Mabelle Webb provided one of my more humbling experiences. The guest loo was right next to her bedroom, so she knew exactly who was doing what and when. I was in there one day and I'd taken the newspaper with me. She knocked on the door and asked if I was all right. I replied that I was reading the paper. She must have misunderstood, because within moments she had returned, opened the door, and handed me a roll of toilet paper! There is, I told Clifton, a limit to hospitality.

Over the years, Clifton's love for his mother became almost an obsession. They gave the appearance of an oddly-matched husband and wife. When she died, at the grand age of ninety-four, Clifton cabled us in Jamaica to break the news. He later phoned with the minute details, and was so overcome that he tied up the line for an eternity with wordless sobs. Noël threatened to reverse the charge. As soon as normal service had been resumed, Noël remarked sadly, "You realise this makes Clifton the oldest orphan in the world?" Clifton was cast as the perpetual son of a mother who refused to accept age. They weren't apart for long. Mabelle's death desolated him, and he couldn't see the point in starting over again, so he didn't. As Noël said, "Age defeated him."

*   *   *   *

Most of Noël's plays eventually appeared on Broadway, but the seismic shift in his professional and economic fortunes was to occur in a desert far from Times Square. In late 1954, after a performance at the Café de Paris, a gentleman named Joe Glaser paid Noël what seemed a perfunctory visit. In the matter-of-fact tone of someone discussing the weather, he offered Noël $35,000 a week to appear at Wilbur Clark's Desert Inn in Las Vegas. None of us could have put Las Vegas on the map with any degree of accuracy, but we had no difficulty at all in pinpointing the money!

Noël had the presence of mind not to kiss the hand he shook, but the urge must have been tremendous. Mr. Glaser couldn't have known how empty the piggy bank was at that moment. Noël was nearly £20,000 in overdraft, a situation he could see no way to remedy in a hurry, and ever at his back he could hear the snapping fingers of the UK tax man. He had no way of knowing that the deal he signed with Joe Glaser the next day at Gerald Road would effectively seal his decision to move abroad.

Abroad was where he could make the money he needed. A move might attract more adverse publicity, but Noël learned that he could not avoid attention; he was the lightning conductor for feelings of jealousy from those who had neither his talent nor his choices. Still, he couldn't help justifying himself: "I've hardly ever lived in England since 1920. I've always been travelling. As I've never lived here, why should I pay English tax? And to a government I didn't vote for. An Englishman is the highest example of a human being who is a free man. As an Englishman I have a right to live where I like."

Our instant friend Joe departed, having dropped salvation in our lap, leaving behind a delighted but befuddled group. What would all those middle-aged American gamblers make of Noël? Noël declared himself unconcerned. A man who could sing "Mad Dogs" while the guns of battle roared could easily withstand a hail of beer bottles. The audiences actually turned out to be so mild-mannered and willing to please that he dubbed them the "Nescafé Society."

When she heard the news, Marlene Dietrich recommended Noël to a wonderful pianist she'd been working with, called Peter Matz. In truth, Noël hadn't given much thought to adapting the Café de Paris act. He supposed that he and Norman Hackforth would take it lock, stock and barrel, but it transpired that Norman couldn't obtain an American work visa. Enter Pete.

He took one look at Noël's orchestrations and said, "You're not going to use *these*, are you?" Noël was quick enough to say, "Oh no, I want *you* to re-orchestrate all the songs," which he did. The songs Noël performed at the Café de Paris are unrecognizable on the Las Vegas album. Pete modernized the material, changing tempos, making the sound fuller without drowning Noël out. By comparison, the Café de Paris arrangements sounded like an English tea-lounge trio, complete with a singer whose high notes might break at any moment. Noël not only had Pete Matz's arrangements, he had Pete as his accompanist, too. Pete was a great "follower." When Noël did "Mad Dogs" in a very fast tempo, he'd instruct Pete, "You just keep going. *I'll* catch up with *you!*"

There was one more important "make-over" to be accomplished before opening night in Vegas. On the insistent advice of Mary Martin and Kate Hepburn, Noël put himself in the hands of America's well-known vocal coach, Alfred Dixon. Noël certainly knew how to put a number across, but the dry Nevada air is notorious for its adverse effects on singers. Noël's rather thin, breathy voice had to be brought down, a feat which Mr. Dixon achieved with a distinctive technique: "Imagine you're a cow, only moo with your mouth shut. Then imagine the cow is a long way away, so you moo quietly. Now it's getting closer, louder, now it's going away again, softly, softly."

This technique might not endear you to your neighbours, but it extended Noël's vocal range considerably. Because of his training as an actor, Noël had also developed the habit of "reaching," trying to take too much in one breath. But dialogue falls where you choose; lyrics fall where

Frank   Sinatra visits Noël backstage at The Desert Inn during Noël's cabaret engagement in Las Vegas. (1955)

they must. "Use the smallest amount of breath possible," Dixon advised, "and sip in a little more when you need to. Don't be so aware of the physical aspects of singing."

Coley and I would break up whenever we heard Noël bellowing his bovine version of the "Indian Love Call" from *Rose Marie*. "Here comes the silly old moo," we'd say to each other, though never when Noël was in earshot.

"The Land of the Free" certainly gave Noël the freedom to re-invent himself. In Las Vegas, he presented himself in a radical way that would have incensed the London press. Not only did the customers not throw beer bottles, the Desert Inn crowd lavished their spontaneous affection upon him night after night. Without the influence of the critics telling them what they were supposed to think, they responded instinctively to the phenomenon that was Noël Coward.

"Las Vegas, Flipping, Shouts 'More!' as Noël Coward Wows 'Em in Café Town," trumpeted *Variety* in its typically understated fashion. Noël reciprocated his audience's enthusiasm. He loved the "plush and honky-tonk" and told a reporter: "I love being the modern day Jenny Lind. All those top notes!" Though he'd visited the States many times, nothing had prepared him for the larger-than-life Las Vegas:

> "If I want chops for my secretary and myself, I order one portion and share them with him. If I say I want absolutely nothing else on the plate - none of the refinements - they say 'Yes,' and four waiters arrive laden with plates on which there is a surfeit of chops, haricots, potatoes, peas and some bright pink sauce laughingly called French Dressing. I conceal an extra plate in the suite on which I pile everything and send it back. It only takes a minute if you're organised. The waiters are very sweet about it. They pay no attention."

The stars swooped down from the Hollywood Hills. Frank Sinatra brought a plane-load and then went on radio to tell the world: "If you want to hear how songs *should* be sung, get the hell over to the Desert Inn!" Sammy Davis, Jr., playing across the Strip, ended his act with the instruction: "Now, cross the street and see The Master at work." Every night the front seats looked like an MGM publicity photo: "More stars than there are in Heaven."

Four weeks later, and a great deal richer, Noël packed his bags feeling that he'd been to a marvellous party: "I couldn't have liked it more!" What he liked even better was that the LP recordings of his performance became best-sellers, and they have never been out of print since.

*   *   *   *

Two months later, Noël and Mary Martin were sitting by the pool at Firefly. After burying the hatchet of *Pacific 1860*, they were not merely friends; they were collaborating on a live ninety-minute television special, *Together with Music*. "The TV Spectacular I am going to do with Mary Martin," Noël told a reporter, "will be completely spontaneous. The kind of spontaneity I like best, the kind that comes after five weeks' rehearsal!"

A two-person show of that duration is rarely seen today because, as one of Noël's songs for the show pointed out, "Ninety Minutes is a Long, Long Time." Noël soon began to appreciate the built-in complexities of this new medium. Could two people, however talented, hold an audience of millions for that long?

Together Again. Noël and Mary Martin patched up their differences after Pacific 1860 *with a 90-minute live TV spectacular in 1955 for CBS and Ford -* Together with Music.

His Las Vegas fame was parlayed into a deal with Bill Paley at CBS for a three-show contract, sponsored by Ford. The schedule of the three broadcasts would consist of the opening "special," followed by two one-and-a-half hour adaptations of Coward plays. He was to be paid the extraordinary sum of $450,000 by CBS and Ford. General Motors and Chrysler made higher bids (Chrysler went as high as $600,000), but it was Ford's link to CBS that clinched it for Noël. He thought CBS had the better organisation to produce the shows he had in mind, a judgement he would later have cause to question.

With Pete Matz at work on the arrangements, Noël and Mary had a fine time putting the show together, though they first had to get past the problem of the title song. Mary didn't like Noël's first attempt, finding it too cold and clever. Noël decided to grit his teeth and rewrite a softer, more romantic version that was more suited to the show. Mary's instincts had been right after all.

Mary was no coloratura soprano-in-waiting but, within her range, she was an honest, natural performer. Noël wrote of her: "She is a great artist within her limited scope and this scope is only limited by her general naïveté." Her husband, Richard, continued to be a pain ("Neurotic, hysterical, noisy and a bad drinker," Noël had concluded). Mary had apparently come to that realisation, too, and she'd turn on him whenever he made his asinine interruptions.

At the CBS studio, in mid-October, Noël was still coming to grips with the realities of live production. Before the invention of videotape, performance was still judged by the same standards as stage production. To complicate matters, this was CBS's first live colour production! In the midst of rehearsal for that daunting "first" night, Noël discovered it was common studio practice to kinescope the actual production for archival purposes. Noël ingenuously suggested, couldn't they kinescope a *rehearsal*, so that we could learn from our mistakes? This wonderful idea was enthusiastically received. In viewing the result, even a neophyte like Noël knew enough about camera technique to see that the production was sloppy; the sound balance was frequently off, most of it was in long shot, and the "point" numbers were made pointless. It was terrible!

With disaster looming, Noël firmly took control. He re-blocked the entire show to ensure that the majority of it was seen in close-up. "It's no

Friends Again! Charlie Chaplin joins Noël's reunion with Mary Martin as they put Pacific 1860 *firmly in the past.*

MARY MARTIN

NOEL COWARD

"*Together with Music*"

An archive recording of
the entire brilliant television
event made during the
actual television broadcast.

"Ninety Minutes is a Long, Long Time" warned the opening number. It didn't seem it... (1955)

use my trying to sing witty lyrics, if they can't see my eyes." He marked the script in precise detail, instructing cameramen on which line to use close-up for a particular point. He learned invaluable lessons on how to use less facial expression, how to curb distracting body language, how to avoid "clever" camera movements, so that the performers kept audience attention. Such active involvement in the process did a lot to calm his nerves as a performer.

His meticulous attention to detail duly paid off. The critic of *The New York Post* praised Mary's performance: "A single camera held her head and shoulders in close-up from the beginning to the end of the song. She sang with her voice, with every muscle in her face and with all the magnetism of her thrilling personality."

None of the critics observed what Noël most certainly did: In her nervousness, Mary missed an important cue. "I had to think very quickly, scan the script in my mind - which, fortunately, I could do, since I had written it - cut to a page or so later and pick up the flow. I don't think anyone, except the poor dear continuity girl, noticed, but if I hadn't had that detailed run-through first, Mary and I could easily have found ourselves looking at one another like a couple of goldfish."

During one rehearsal an executive from Ford, the sponsor of the show, demanded that Noël cut some of the lyrics in "Nina." When Noël asked why, he was told, "In that song you sing about her 'forever wriggling her guts' and we consider that vulgar." Noël snapped back, "Well, you ought to know about vulgarity, because I've just seen the commercial for your new Ford." Exit Ford party, pursued by inscrutable Coward smile.

Noël could never resist the temptation to "cap" a remark. It was the little boy in him showing off and waiting for the audience reaction. He actually considered the Ford commercial to be very good, but his reflex action in the irritation of the moment was to strike with wit. Nina remained *virgo intacta*. His comment was to cost him in the long run, however, when relations soured between himself, Ford and CBS.

The reviews were glowing. "Coward's Debut Stylishly Magnificent," beamed the *New York Journal-American*. "Channel 2 Rings Out With Song, Talent," cheered the *New York Times*'s Jack Gould. The ratings, however, were not so grand.

Two of the three commitments were yet to be fulfilled. The first, *Blithe Spirit*, immediately presented the problem of length. The play had to be cut down to under an hour and a half to allow for commercials. When something fits together like a precision watch, that's neither an easy nor a pleasant task, but the influence of dollar signs allowed the scalpel to replace the pen.

The show was to be produced live in Hollywood. Noël would reprise his rôle as Charles Condomine and Lauren Bacall would play Elvira. Noël already knew the Bogarts socially. They'd been among his faithful followers at the Desert Inn, so he was doubly delighted to have Betty in the production. She appeared on the set the first day word-perfect, even though she had finished working on a film only the night before.

We spent a day Chez Bogart where I met the most dangerous man in Hollywood. He certainly didn't look dangerous. Quietly spoken, smaller than I'd imagined, he clearly adored his beautiful young wife. Only the distinctive voice and side-of-the-mouth smile to remind you of his screen self. The most dangerous member of the Bogart family that day turned out to be Bogie's small son, Steve. In a gesture undoubtedly intended to make me feel one of the family, he suddenly hit me over the head with a tin tray! Only then did I catch a flash of the Bogart expression. He didn't actually say, "That's my boy!", but he was clearly thinking it. Whenever I'm asked,

"How did Bogart strike you?", I answer (in my best Noël Coward impersonation), "With a tin tray!"

Bogie later phoned Noël and said, "Please be gentle with Betty. She's much more nervous than you think." He needn't have worried. Betty was a real pro in every respect: word-perfect, good-natured, full of thoughtful suggestions which she offered tentatively and which Noël happily considered. Her co-operative attitude was in marked contrast to the third member of the trio.

Claudette Colbert was to play Ruth, who provides much of the comedy by not realising that Elvira has materialised in her own home. Like so many of Noël's post-war leading ladies, the enchanting Claudette was a personal friend and a professional pain. Where Betty Bacall had assiduously learned her lines, Claudette was a graduate of the Gladys Cooper school, which did not subscribe to the same philosophy. The part should be "shaped" as rehearsals progressed; "feel" the rôle and somehow, sometime, the words would come. Claudette's real problem, though, was her limited stage experience. She'd premiered Noël's first draft of *South Sea Bubble* (as *Island Fling*) a few years earlier, but she was first and foremost a film actress. She understood neither the complexity nor the expense of camera set-ups and rehearsal time in terms of the available budget, so she wasted both for everyone else.

She was so concerned to preserve her "correct" profile that the first run-through had to be completely re-blocked. It consisted entirely of close-ups of Noël, which flattered his personal vanity but not his professional sense. Incidentally, whenever Claudette visited us in Jamaica or Switzerland, we tried every trick in the book to snap the "other" profile but, when the pictures were developed, there was always an hibiscus or someone's ear in the way. I'm not entirely convinced Claudette *has* another profile.

What worried Noël more than Miss Colbert's peccadilloes was the *way* she wanted to play Ruth. Like so many "nice" lady stars, Claudette was worried about her film image. She was determined, Noël said, to play Ruth as "...a mixture of Mary Rose and Rebecca of Sunnybrook Farm - and very, very slowly." Ruth must be straight, direct, no-nonsense and tolerant of others to a very limited degree. She must give the hyperactive Charles and Elvira something to play against. A "sweet" Ruth makes the whole thing seem like an incestuous *ménage à trois*.

Noël's verdict in the *Diaries* sums it up: "God preserve me in future from female stars. I don't suppose He will...." It must be noted, however, that Claudette finally gave an exquisite performance.

In the third and final production for *Ford Star Jubilee* (*This Happy Breed*), the leading lady was West End stage star Edna Best, an old friend of

Noël's who knew better than to push her luck. *Present Laughter* was originally intended to end the sequence, with Noël reprising Garry Essendine. Casting was well under way when CBS chairman Bill Paley suddenly pulled the plug. His argument was that the Bible Belt of Middle America would slip a notch. ("He fears angry letters sitting in the mail box, written by outraged Methodists in Omaha.") To judge from the viewing figures of the first two shows, those of a religious turn of mind wouldn't watch Noël Coward in *anything*. Mr. Paley was unable or unwilling to articulate just what there was in the play to offend.

Noël suspected that the Vulgar Majority at Ford were behind the move. There had been comments about the language in *Blithe Spirit*, to which Noël had responded: "People who object to the profanity in *Blithe Spirit* are crackpots and Mr. Ford should be happy if even one of them doesn't buy his car. They would be a menace on the highway!" It's doubtful Mr. Ford shared the sentiment! The likeliest explanation is that Paley simply didn't care for the play (or for Noël, either), and the rest was so much blowing of smoke.

Noël refused to face the reality of the situation: "I intend to do it whether they like it or not. It is a wonderful part for me and I shall not be too dependent on fractious leading ladies." But Paley was the American equivalent of Binkie Beaumont; his authority was total. Consequently, in May, 1956, Noël and Edna played Frank and Ethel Gibbons in *This Happy Breed*.

Edna had recently suffered a nervous breakdown, which caused some early concern. She turned out to be very much like the unflappably British character she played. Comparing her behaviour with some of the female irrationality he'd been experiencing lately, Noël was relieved to find himself opposite a leading lady who wasn't attempting to give *him* a breakdown!

Noël was fairly satisfied with the way the piece turned out. He didn't consider it a patch on the 1944 David Lean film, but even Lean hadn't quite caught the play's elusive quality. Nonetheless, considering the combined problems of an abbreviated text and the mechanical constraints of live television, Noël felt some degree of success. He was particularly pleased to have Paley call to tell him it was "the greatest thing he had ever seen on television."

Frankly, the British working-class subject held little appeal for American audiences. In many ways it was a postscript to *Cavalcade*, another celebration of the cosy British conviction that adversity brings out the best in them. *Cavalcade* had shown Britain taking it from the Boer War through the Great War to End All Wars. *This Happy Breed* picked up the theme in the inter-war years and carried it up to World War II. It was essentially another theatrical saga, with the characters ageing and developing with time.

Broadway welcomes Noël on his 1958 return in Nude with Violin.

Frank and Ethel Gibbons watch their kids grow up in their Clapham Common "semi": A son joins the services, a headstrong daughter leaves home but finally settles for the boy next door, the next generation is born, and the circle turns. It's a play of observation and attitude rather than incident and it depends on a steady pace. But there's a limit to how much saga can be crammed into ninety minutes minus commercials! Noël used linking narration to bridge the huge gaps created by his editing of the text. What had been subtly suggested by dialogue and body language was now weighed down by lengthy exposition.

The biggest problem was the lack of a true dramatic ending. In the original, Frank (now a grandfather) delivers a patriotic speech over the pram of his new grandchild, a symbol of Britain's future. It's really another version of the toast at the end of *Cavalcade*, but to lose this peroration means to lose the point of the family's, and their country's, history. It was deemed too "wordy" for a television audience, so out it went, and with it the point of the play.

Even if the adaptation had worked better, it still wouldn't have pleased an American audience that expected Noël "Anyone For Tennis" Coward. Ironically, what he felt so deeply, they perceived as lower class affectation. They saw him as patronising the people he deeply loved. His good intentions came across as Noël Coward wearing a funny moustache and parodying an ordinary suburban man. The cultural gap was just too wide.

Noël was too close to the process to be objective about the result. All his friends told him the show was an unqualified success. He did, however, derive at least one benefit, which came as a result of the sheer mechanics of adapting both plays: "This cutting of my plays for television is certainly a salutary experience and I believe that the next time I embark on a full length play for the theatre, I shall find I have profited by this. I shall have learned, for instance, to dispense with amusing irrelevancies that have no direct bearing on the story and to get back to my original method of saying what I have to say in as few lines as possible with the minimum of atmosphere padding and linguistic flourishes." All very true, but if he'd originally scripted *This Happy Breed* for television, it would have been significantly and dramatically different from the cut-and-paste job he ended up doing.

The greatest disappointment of that season was that Noël didn't film *Present Laughter*. There seemed plenty of time to do it later, but it didn't turn out that way. There is, sadly, no record of one of his definitive performances.

Those three live television shows, together with his Las Vegas success, represented the culmination of the 1950's for Noël. They had posed a series of technical challenges in new and different media and, as always, he proved he could rise above it. ("Oh, the cleverness of me!" said Peter Pan.) The post-war lesson seemed to be that Noël should keep moving forward, trying new endeavours, and not allowing the past to hold him back.

When America and Noël Coward discovered each other, a whole succession of doors swung open. If they'd opened immediately after the war, when he was in his forties, he might have relaunched himself in the UK. As it was, he had to wait until the 1960's for the UK to rediscover the original Noël Coward, when the game was almost over.

It's easy to see that now. At the time, we were scuttling from one thing to the next with no thought of a pattern to our lives. Even the most illustrious of shuttlecocks has little sense of direction while the game is actually in progress.

Winston Churchill. (1940) "Noël and Winston were like two dogs sniffing around each other..."

CHAPTER EIGHT

"GENTLEMEN AND PLAYERS": GREAT CONTEMPORARIES

We represent those carefree days
That still retained a bland hypocrisy
And looked upon Democracy
As quaint.
A certain transitory phase
Which every accurate historian
Has blamed upon Victorian
Restraint.
Our life was gay,
Champagne adorning it,
It passed away
And left us mourning it.
We've run our race
Time can't replace
These years of grace.

(Prologue from *Operette*)

WINSTON CHURCHILL

"Deeply as I revere and admire him, I could never have loved him."

Noël and Winston were like two dogs sniffing around each other, anxiously protecting their turf. They were both proud of their verbal skills, and frequently matched wits.

It was Churchill who personally insisted that Noël's war effort be confined to singing "Mad Dogs" to the troops, which he did several hundred times. There was a postscript to that which did not please Noël immensely. In August, 1941, Roosevelt and Churchill met on *H.M.S. Prince Of Wales* to draft the Atlantic Charter. The one serious difference of opinion, as Noël delighted to recount, was a "fairly sharp altercation"

Entertaining the troops in World War II with Leslie Henson (right).

concerning the second refrain of "Mad Dogs." Churchill's affection for the song, Noël often said, "bordered on the pathological." The argument stemmed from the question of whether the lines:

> *In Bangkok*
> *At twelve o'clock*
> *They foam at the mouth and run*

come at the end of the first refrain, or the second? Noël later pointed out, on a live television broadcast in 1964, that Roosevelt had been right and Churchill wrong. When this was relayed to the Old Man in private, he reportedly muttered, "Britain can take it!"

And now we come to a small *crise*.

The actual second refrain in the *Lyrics* reads:

> *Mad dogs and Englishmen*
> *Go out in the midday sun.*
> *The toughest Burmese bandit*
> *Can never understand it.*

In Rangoon the heat of noon
Is just what the natives shun.
They put their Scotch or Rye down
And lie down.
In a jungle town
Where the sun beats down
To the rage of man and beast
The English garb
Of the English sahib
Merely gets a bit more creased.
In Bangkok
At twelve o'clock
They foam at the mouth and run,
But mad dogs and Englishmen
Go out in the midday sun.

Having wagged an affectionate finger at "Sir," Noël proceeded to sing that contentious second refrain, except that he sang:

Mad dogs and Englishmen
Go out in the midday sun.
The smallest Malay rabbit
Deplores this stupid habit.
In Hong Kong
They strike a gong
And fire off a noonday gun
To reprimand each inmate
Who's in late.
In a jungle town
Where the sun beats down
To the rage of man and beast
The English garb
Of the English sahib
Merely gets a bit more creased.
In Bangkok
At twelve o'clock
They foam at the mouth and run,
But mad dogs and Englishmen
Go out in the midday sun.

According to the published lyrics, Noël confused and combined refrains two and three. An author can put his words anywhere he damn well wants, but there is a case for saying that, when they are published, the public is entitled to assume that that is that. Perhaps Churchill was right after all. He should have demanded a recount!

The occasion of that telecast was the BBC's tribute to Winston on his ninetieth birthday, a *pot-pourri* of song, dance and sentiment called "Ninety Years On." Noël hosted on camera from a script by Terence Rattigan.

Even that harmless appearance did not pass uncriticised. Throughout the evening Noël addressed Winston as "Sir," and the next day's newspaper reviews lambasted him for sycophancy. If only they'd heard some of the exchanges between the two over the years! Noël simply felt, as did many, "that if anyone deserved due respect for all he'd done, this man did and, by God, he was going to get it."

Another of Noël's songs that engaged Churchill's attention was a satirical wartime ditty entitled "Don't Let's Be Beastly to the Germans." Churchill, by the way, was quite capable of missing the point of a song like this. Although he was adept at making mordant remarks, a sense of humour was not among his major attributes. But Churchill made Noël sing that song no less than *seven* times in one evening!

Winston's enthusiasm was not shared by Lord Reith's BBC (who refused to broadcast it) or HMV (who declined to issue the record). Both organisations claimed it could be perceived as unpatriotic and subversive to the war effort!

Noël couldn't believe it! As he said, if a line like

> *"Let's help the dirty swine again
> To occupy the Rhine again"*

was to be taken at face value, his next booking would surely have been the Tower of London.

During the awkward "Would he?/Wouldn't he?" romance between Edward VIII and his "friend," Mrs. Simpson, the country feasted on every little hint and hushed whisper. Only very recently has the Royal menu caused such salivation in the popular media. In 1937 it was the highest of High Drama, the subject of every dinner party conversation.

At one such dinner The Topic came up and Winston, probably to be deliberately argumentative, proclaimed, "Well, I don't see why he shouldn't marry his little cutie." Noël snapped back, "Because England does not *want* a Queen Cutie!" An awkward pause ensued, during which Churchill probably silently condemned Noël to several hundred more renderings of "Mad Dogs" for the troops, when the moment arrived!

There was a strong mutual respect between Winston and Noël, but not much genuine affection. Noël's "gnawing suspicion" about Winston's true disposition towards him began with his abortive attempt to enlist. He later confided to his *Diaries* that he agreed with a recently-published biography, which, "...in spite of his intrinsic greatness...," portrayed Churchill as "...a spoiled, petulant, gaga old sod, which is no surprise to me." On another occasion he wrote that Churchill was "a great man with more Achilles heels than are usual in a bi-ped, one of which is a remarkable capacity for self-deception and another a strong vein of cheapness." Who ever said greatness had to be lovable?

THE WINDSORS

The Windsors were not exactly joy unconfined, although the Duchess was a lot quicker and wittier than her husband. The Duke, to be honest, was an extremely dull man. Noël said he even danced a boring Charleston, which is no mean feat. There was the occasion when he rather boorishly insisted Noël play the piano to accompany him on the ukulele. Noël's verdict was that the Duke was "no George Formby" (the popular entertainer of the period). The next day Windsor cut Noël dead in a West End store. Perhaps he thought Noël was "no Charlie Kunz."

One evening at dinner, Wallis turned to Noël in coy bewilderment. "You know, I don't understand why the British dislike me so much." There was a breathless pause before Noël, with fingers crossed, informed her, "Well, because you stole their Prince Charming." She rather liked that.

On social occasions Windsor rarely spoke, not because his mind was preoccupied with lofty thoughts, but because he simply had nothing to say. He had, in Noël's estimation, "the charm of the world with nothing whatever to back it up."

One evening, after an elaborate dinner party, Noël and I put on an impromptu cabaret for the guests. Later, Windsor came over as if to introduce himself, and asked, "What sort of plane did you come over on?" I thought he'd lost his mind, until I remembered they'd invited six fighter pilots as guests. He had mistaken me for one of them, even though he'd seen me on stage a few minutes earlier and had been chatting to me at dinner.

Noël had an aversion to people who were slow on the uptake, and had never taken to Windsor, although it's doubtful the Duke was sensitive enough to notice. Why did Noël bother? Where Royalty was concerned, Noël was a snob: "There is no sense having a constitutional monarchy and not being a cosy royal snob." He genuinely liked many of them, and their company never ceased to impress him. What was the boy from Teddington doing in this exalted company? After an evening with the Windsors in

1956, which immediately followed an evening with Loel and Gloria Guinness, Noël "reflected wryly on the way home that I had spent two meals in one week sucking up to two people who had been steadfastly against me since I was in my twenties. It seemed a pity that Max Beaverbrook was missing."

Noël genuinely adored the Yorks, whom he visited quite often, much to the irritation of Mary, who was then the Queen Mother. She felt Windsor, her eldest, was being upstaged, which bothered Noël not one bit. The friendship he established with the Duchess of York (who later became Queen and then Queen Mother) lasted until the day he died. She was truly amused by his company and her genuine laughter proved it. Of all the Royals the Queen Mother was by far his favourite, and there was genuine affection on both sides.

In 1965, when the Queen Mum was touring Jamaica, Noël invited her to lunch, never thinking for a moment that she'd be allowed to accept.

The Duke and Duchess of Windsor. (Paris, 1937)

"The Day the Queen Mum Dropped In..." Noël with Lynn Fontanne, Alfred Lunt and Blanche Blackwell. (Firefly, February 28, 1965)

He'd reckoned without the Royal will.   Schedules were frantically rearranged. Her Majesty would be delighted....

There followed much hair-tearing and frenzy on our part. What do you serve a Queen Mother when she drops in for a bite of lunch? Noël decided he would prepare the meal himself. There would be curry in coconuts, fish mousse and rum cream pie.

Down to the local village for the ingredients.   Every item was as carefully hand-picked as if he were casting his next show, which, in a way, he was. Many a fish was rejected as unfit to set before a queen. No surgeon ever prepared his implements more carefully; no chef ever wore an apron so spotless.

Typically, the fish mousse gave up the ghost just before The Guest was due, taking on a texture which Noël described as akin to "an ordinary Slazenger tennis ball." Rising above it, which was not difficult in view of its refusal to stand up and be counted, Noël whipped up an iced soup, just as the entourage crossed the threshold. *Crème de Queen Mum* undoubtedly saved the day, though God knows what went into it!

SOMERSET MAUGHAM

In the 1920's and early '30's, one name regularly bracketed with Noël's in any analysis of English playwrights was Somerset Maugham. When I met Willie, he was permanently ensconced in his villa on Cap Ferrat with his secretary/companion, Alan Searle.

Noël had long been a fan of the "lovely, lucid simplicity" of Maugham's prose: "He never overwrites. He has never, since his very early youth, become besotted with words, drunk on the Oxford Dictionary." He was a pretty cold fish, though, and as he got older, his behaviour became increasingly eccentric and cantankerous. Noël nicknamed him the "Lizard of Oz."

Noël's affection for Maugham dwindled with the 1962 publication of his autobiography, *Looking Back*. Willie raked up a lot of old stuff about his ex-wife, Syrie, who had remained a chum of Noël's. Though it was all so long ago that nobody cared any more, it clearly still rankled with Willie, so out poured the venom again.

Noël wrote in his *Diaries* that the book showed "streaks of profound vulgarity, much malice and no heart." That was also a fair summation of what Willie had become in his later years. Noël thought it went deeper than just senile irritability. Willie, he thought, suffered from "inherent vulgarity - not of words but emotion."

As playwrights they trod parallel paths. Both were fascinated by the ebb and flow of personal relationships, both besotted with the affectations and complications of the English class system. Critic Harold Hobson considered that Noël, "with his contemptuous admiration, joined Maugham in destroying the reputation of the well-born, the well-to-do and the well-educated." Soon after Noël established his reputation in the West End, Maugham's prolific theatrical output ceased altogether. Critics like Desmond MacCarthy said that Willie couldn't compete with Noël's style. When Willie's *The Breadwinner* and Noël's *Private Lives* were simultaneously running in the West End in 1930, MacCarthy wrote that, "Maugham is not so deft at catching life-rhythms in dialogue." Willie described himself as having been "put firmly on the shelf."

Maugham's plays don't revive well because he stuck too closely to the specific idiom of the period. Most of Noël's dialogue, on the other hand, holds up because, like P.G. Wodehouse, he made his people talk like people talk in a Noël Coward play!

Towards the end, their relationship became forced. What started as lively banter between well-matched sparring partners had degenerated into a rigid politesse. The last time Noël saw him, Maugham was in his late eighties. Willie knew his mind had vacated the premises and was just waiting for the rest of him to go. As Noël poignantly said, "There's such a thing as *too* old."

We used to laugh over one of Willie's regular tricks. After lunch he'd say, "I'm going to take you for a walk around the garden." When he reached the front door, he'd exclaim, "Oh, here's your car."

The conclusion of their relationship was documented in *A Song at Twilight* (1966), the last section of *Suite in Three Keys*, in which Noël appeared.

Noël had witnessed Willie's vitriolic attacks on Syrie long after their "marriage" was over, his abortive attempt to disinherit his biological daughter in favour of his live-in lover, Gerald Haxton, and a continuous stream of barbed remarks he aimed at everyone we knew. No doubt we became targets too. Well into his anecdotage Willie liked to play the part of the world-weary philosopher. He would boast that he had no illusions about his fellow men, which prompted Noël to remark: "He had just one illusion about them and that was they were no good." Now he would get his comeuppance, albeit posthumously. Everyone who read *Song* before it was put on, substituted Willie for Sir Hugo Latymer, the lead character. The resemblance was such (*The Times* review said it was "beyond question") that there was some initial concern about libel suits. Willie graciously avoided any legal unpleasantness by finally cashing in his chips.

Noël later played the aged author himself, a man confronted by his (for the times) scandalous homosexual past. Noël insisted Sir Hugo was a composite of several people, including Maugham and Max Beerbohm. When the play appeared, nobody made any fuss at all. It was just good commercial theatre and, in any case, society's attitude was changing. Who cared? In the battle of words, Noël had the last shot.

IVOR NOVELLO

Noël once observed that, "The two most beautiful things in the world are Ivor's profile and my mind."

The media enjoyed building up a fierce rivalry between Noël and Ivor Novello which never actually materialised. They'd known each other all their professional lives, and maintained a distant but genuine friendship throughout. In 1937, Noël could write about "a friendship which has lasted hilariously until now, and shows every indication of enduring through any worlds which may lie beyond us."

Their respective lives bore many similarities. They both had adoring mothers whose extremely powerful influences remained until they died; they both travelled with an entourage, or "family." Each group had its core members, though there was "The Overlap Gang," fully paid-up members of both: Joycie Carey and her mother, Lilian Braithwaite, Gladys Cooper and Edna Best. Noël and Ivor didn't meet very often, but there were plenty of links to keep each informed about the other's doings. Ivor would stay with us at White Cliffs; we'd go to Redroofs, his house near Maidenhead. They both owned property in Jamaica.

What function did these "families" perform for them? They offered emotional protection, certainly; a ready audience they could return to after the Muse had called them apart. But there was something more. Each of them was, so to speak, afraid of the dark, and no individual could adequately provide the reassurance they needed.

We'd often take that creaking lift to Ivor's famous "flat" above Covent Garden for one of his soirées:

> "The Flat" sat ... on the very top of the Strand Theatre, and in order to reach it, a perilous ascent was made in a small, self-worked lift. Ivor's guests crushed themselves timorously together in this frightening little box, someone pulled a rope, there was a sharp grinding noise, a scream from some less hardy member of the party; then, swaying and rattling, the box ascended. Upon reaching the top, it would hit the roof with a crash and, more often than not, creak all the way down again. Many people preferred to toil up seven long flights of stairs rather than face the lift....The big room of the flat had a raised dais running across one end. Upon this, there were sometimes two, at other times no grand pianos, sometimes a gramophone, and nearly always Viola Tree...."
>
> (*Present Indicative*)

Ivor ("The Guv") had his table at The Ivy Restaurant. Noël ("The Master") had his. Ivor wrote the popular song of World War One ("Keep the Home Fires Burning"). Noël did the same for World War Two ("London Pride"). Patriotic as well as theatrical competitors.

Ivor, at Noël's specific request, played the lead in one of Noël's early plays, *Sirocco* (1927), though the compliment was never returned. The brittle Coward presence would not have been an easy fit in a romantic

Novello play. *Sirocco* was such a colossal flop that the director, Basil Dean, claimed the word entered theatrical jargon. "How did the show go tonight?" "Oh, it was a Sirocco, old boy!" Noël and Ivor both made one film each for D.W. Griffith. Neither was a success.

Ivor and Noël finally came face to face on the musical stage as twin custodians of the operetta form. Noël had the first and most enduring success with *Bitter Sweet,* but Ivor enjoyed an unbroken run of hits from the mid-1930's until his early death in 1951, at the age of fifty-eight. Noël

Ivor Novello and Dame Lilian Braithwaite (Joycie's mother) at Ivor's country home, Redroofs. (1936)

admired Ivor's gift for composing such beautiful melodies, although he found the shows themselves somewhat turgid. The general public did not agree. Hit followed Novello hit. It's hard to describe Ivor's style for a modern audience. It was lush in the Viennese tradition, filled with heart-on-sleeve emotionalism. Not a dry eye in the house.

Sandy Wilson summed up the difference between the two men as: "Noël's wit sprang from his intellect" (hence the aphorisms and *bons mots*) "Ivor relied on a chance concentration of time, place and personality." Ivor's humour was spontaneous, of the moment, and didn't travel. But each of them made the other laugh continuously.

The common opinion that they were both old-style Romantics wasn't strictly accurate. Ivor was a true Romantic. He believed in the sentiments he evoked, which is why he dealt with them so wholeheartedly. It is not disparaging to say that he had a Barbara Cartland quality.

Noël had a Romantic streak which occasionally ran through his work. He lacked the pure blind faith, the emotional naïveté that Ivor's work showed on stage. The cool Mr. Coward couldn't easily allow that for himself. Theatre historian W. Macqueen Pope put them in perspective when he compared Noël as Sheridan to Ivor as Cervantes. Ivor summed up a "Novello Show" best to one of his regular stars, Vanessa Lee; *King's Rhapsody* came after the war and an unexpectedly long period of austerity. "We haven't seen any beautiful things. I think I'm going to do the last of Ruritania and we can have the lot: Kings and Queens, Princes and Princesses, church music, everything."

Noël had written successful romantic operettas but, Pope concluded, his emotional grounding was in the reality of a *Cavalcade*:

> "Noël Coward has infinite appeal to the smart sophisticates of the time, which he understood and which he always gave the appearance of belonging to himself, though my private belief is that he laughed at it behind its back. The sharp, staccato style, the quick gleam, the stiletto point of his plays was his own and his sense of humour, if somewhat sardonic at times, was and is immense....Coward, in short, represents modernity, while Ivor represents a firm belief in the past."

In Ivor's obituary, Noël mused that "there is a small measure of consolation in the thought that Ivor died at the height of his triumphant career and will never know the weariness of age nor the sadness of decline." When he wrote those words, he was still making comparisons. He was only fifty-one, but already he had been forced to dine on decline, and the *Diaries* were beginning to indicate the early signs of an obsession with age. Ivor's theatrical instincts helped him pick the perfect time to make his exit. Noël hoped that his would, too.

BINKIE BEAUMONT

Hugh (Binkie) Beaumont was known throughout the West End as "The Boss." Born in Wales in 1908 as Hughes Griffiths Morgan, he became Beaumont when his divorced mother remarried. At the ludicrously early age of seventeen, Binkie insinuated himself into theatrical management in his home town of Cardiff. People who knew him as a young man said he had the looks and confident bearing of a matinee idol. When I first met him, during the war, he was still a handsome man. Everything about him was carefully manicured and groomed, his manners impeccable; he was what used to be called "dapper."

As I got to know him better, observing him around people in the business, I began to see him in a "frame within a frame." Wasn't he *too* calculating? Was there any real feeling at the heart of all that careful control? Or was control the point?

Binkie Beaumont *was* H.M. Tennent, and for three robust decades, H.M. Tennent *was* West End theatre. Its dominance was so marked that the company became the subject of a Government enquiry. Binkie fervently argued that there were really two companies: H.M. Tennent, the commercial arm, occasionally made a small profit, but the main company, Tennent Productions, was a non-profit organisation engaged in producing works of cultural merit, and thus entitled to privileged tax status. He got away with it!

Other managements were left scrabbling for whatever Binkie turned down. Luckily for them, and for British theatre, he wasn't infallible and there were areas he preferred to leave alone. "Experimental" theatre was not his choice. He preferred gilt-edged investments. Lavishly-mounted plays (often revivals) with all-star casts, shows with proven success, preferably on Broadway, these were the hallmarks of an "H.M. Tennent Production." Final decisions were Binkie's, and his alone. The Shuberts or David Merrick on Broadway had comparable power, but in recent British theatrical history Binkie was unique.

He and Noël were constant cronies, perpetually on the phone to each other. Noël would rush around to Binkie's townhouse in Lord North Street the moment he got back to London, to catch up on the latest gossip. They'd also been business partners since Noël wrote *Operette* at Binkie's suggestion in 1937, and from 1939 onwards Binkie took over the presentation of all Noël's work in the UK. Nearly two thousand

Noël and Binkie. (June 1937)

performances of *Blithe Spirit* alone helped to swell the Tennent coffers, but Noël could proudly write of his business associate: "I love him for his personal loyalty to me."

A well-known actor, who owed much of his early success to Noël, was heard criticising Noël in particularly personal terms. When word got to Binkie, he literally sent for the actor and declared, "If I hear any more of this, you'll never work in the West End again." The abrupt cessation of the stories speaks volumes about the immense power Binkie wielded. (I can't name names because the eminent actor concerned is still with us.)

Noël set a great deal of store by loyalty, and took a very personal approach to his business relationships. "Binkie at bedrock is entirely to be trusted," he wrote as late as 1959, but went on to qualify his verdict: "...on other strata he is apt to be devious and tricky." (Peter Hall's assessment was not so generous; he once described Binkie as "secret as a snake.") Sad to say, Noël was frequently misguided in his loyalties, and was always chastened by the realisation. Jack Wilson was the classic example; incidentally, he also acted as Binkie's US representative for many years.

Binkie either changed markedly as the years went by, or the real Binkie began to emerge. In his formative years as a producer, his passion shaped his savvy; his genius took instructions from his heart. By the mid-1950's his power was unchallenged, but his passion for the theatre was dying. Noël perceived, at the end of 1954, a "curious feeling of sadness about him. There is no concrete reason for this but an inner instinct tells me that he is due for unhappiness."

One reason for Binkie's abstraction was the new and potentially valuable toy of commercial television. He became a leading figure in a consortium, ATV (Associated Television), which provided regional programme material.   His fellow impresario, Prince Littler, was a co-director.   Behind their backs there was talk of "Binkie-Vision."   A real friend, knowing Noël's shaky financial situation in the mid-1950's, might have encouraged Noël to invest in the enterprise, as, no doubt, Noël would have.   But the word never came.   The "licence to print money" (the unfortunate phrase that media baron, Lord Thomson, coined to describe commercial television) fell into other hands.   By then Noël was so substantially in debt that he was forced to leave the country to alleviate his tax burden.

The "sadness" Noël sensed was actually headed in his direction. The word "hit" hadn't loomed large over his post-war shows, and the critics had their brickbats stockpiled.   Noël Coward was no longer "box office." Binkie rapidly re-evaluated his professional position: A Coward property would henceforth be "considered," rather than automatically scheduled.

Noël was oblivious to Binkie's increasingly pragmatic vision. In 1957 he observed that Binkie "...has changed, too. His 'theatre' energy seems to have diminished....I don't think he really minds as much as he used to." Binkie had "minded" enough to turn down *Ace of Clubs* in 1950 on the grounds that he didn't do musicals. They were expensive and he really didn't understand the form. In fact, he *did* do musicals, provided that they'd proved themselves elsewhere. He turned down *Pacific 1860*, but he accepted *Oklahoma!* and *My Fair Lady*. He just didn't like *Ace of Clubs*, and on this occasion, at least, his instincts didn't let him down.

It was the continued reluctance to support his projects that began to bother Noël.   There were unexpected delays and hesitations with both *Nude with Violin* and *South Sea Bubble*, little irritations that had never surfaced in the "golden days." Was modern art really a suitable subject? Was Vivien Leigh the right casting? Noël refused to see what was becoming increasingly obvious. In the past, Binkie had cheerfully handed out *carte blanche* on matters like these. Now he couldn't deal with Noël in the direct, often brutal, way he could with other people who lost his favour.

The first visible sign of a falling-out came over Vivien's pregnancy. When *South Sea Bubble* (1956), after a mouthful of teething troubles, had finally settled into a solid commercial hit, Binkie informed Noël that his star was several months pregnant and about to leave the show. He claimed to have been sworn to secrecy by Larry and Viv. What Noël found particularly hurtful was not so much the fact of their cabal, but that by telling him so late in the day, they had prevented him from casting an effective replacement in one of the few genuine hits he'd enjoyed since the war. He saw it as a betrayal on all their parts, but particularly on the part of Binkie and Viv, who were directly involved in the production. He records in his *Diaries* that one October evening he "...had the satisfaction of saying [to Binkie] what has been fomenting in my mind for a long time." When he returned home later, the anger had softened to sorrow: "How could they do this, after all I've done for *all* of them? I can't believe they'd *do* this."

Noël was assuming that he had the ultimate say in the relationship. He no longer had. Binkie was the piper.

Noël had every expectation that Binkie would produce *Waiting in the Wings*, but he was proved wrong. Noël had written it with Gladys Cooper in mind, because, in spite of her difficulty in learning her lines for *Relative Values*, she was true box office. Binkie reported back to Noël that Gladys didn't like the play, and that Edith Evans "loathed it." Gladys later chided Noël for never having written her a sequel to *Relative Values*. If he was putting on a play about elderly actresses, surely there was a part for her? Binkie, of course, had never even shown her the script. It was very hard for Noël to accept that he was now receiving the kind of treatment Binkie was notorious for dishing out to lesser mortals. He confided sadly to his *Diaries:* "In the old days he used to... allow himself to be gently advised by John G., me, Joycie, etc. - now his advisers are John Perry, Prince Littler and Irene Selznick and the change is *not* for the better." He concluded: "Too much power and too much concentration on money grubbing...I suddenly saw all the pallid little wheels whizzing round: the fear of me, the lack of moral courage, the preoccupation with money, etc., and there was, clearly and unmistakably, the end of a long friendship."

Noël obviously found it easier to write about his feelings than to act upon them. As with Jack Wilson, he would constantly raise his own Sword of Damocles without ever bringing it down. When Binkie and Noël would meet, as they inevitably and frequently did on Shaftesbury Avenue, the bonhomie appeared intact, the jokes and mock insults were still traded. But the exchanges were hollow, the friendliness a little forced.

There was one final collaboration which, to some extent, wiped the slate clean. In 1966, Binkie produced *Suite in Three Keys*, Noël's successful farewell to the West End. It was probably inspired by his desire to make amends, tempered with his commercial instinct that people would come to see Noël on stage for what might well be the last time.

But let me go back a year...

For some time I'd been trying to break out of musicals and into straight plays, but nobody would give me the opportunity. A rising tide lifts all boats, so presumably an ebb-tide sinks them. My friendship with Noël, which had undoubtedly helped me in the past, had now become a liability. Binkie saw me as part of the Coward "package." With Noël at the height of his fame, Binkie had had no option but to agree, but now he could get back at Noël through me.

When casting the 1965 revival of *Present Laughter*, Noël requested that I be given a minor role. Binkie demurred. Noël insisted. "What does it matter? It's a very small part and Graham wants to show that he can *talk* on stage." Grudgingly, Binkie allowed me to play Morris, a character based loosely on Jack Wilson. There's irony for you!

In my previous West End appearance for Binkie, *After the Ball*, I'd had star billing above the title. Now I was accorded the smallest print at the bottom of the bill, along with three actors who'd never appeared on the West End stage in their lives! To add insult to injury, I was assigned a dressing room at the top of the house. Binkie was trying to render me present but invisible, and he succeeded.

After a period of failing health, Binkie died in his sleep shortly before Noël. During Noël's last days in Jamaica, the most difficult task Coley and I had was to distract Noël from the fact of Binkie's death. "I can't get Binkie out of my mind," would be his first words to us as we came up to Firefly for our evening drink. The insincerities of the later years melted away and he recalled only the jokes and the gossip of forty years.

Binkie had become tragically tired of the life that provided his power and fame. With all his economic influence, he was himself controlled by alcohol. At his own parties in later years he would have a couple of young men waiting in the wings. When he was too drunk to stand, they would pick him up from his chair and cart him off to bed. On more than one occasion I saw him pass out cold. My last sight of him was being carried unconscious from a society party.

Whatever demons Binkie had, he fought them alone. The fact that Noël never really knew what Furies pursued his old friend was perhaps, after all, an act of friendship on Binkie's part.

LORD BEAVERBROOK

When Max, Lord Beaverbrook, died, Noël's reaction was uncharacteristically harsh: "Max Beaverbrook died on Friday (July 12th,

1964). This long - too long - delayed occurrence requires no comment. God is still presumably in his heaven unless he has been forced to move over." Their paths and their swords had crossed many times over the years, with the interruption of an occasional wary truce. Their relationship would best be characterised as largely adversarial. Max grudgingly recognised that Noël was his own invention, who had cleverly played the Press to become one of the first media-made "celebrities."

But the media, according to the Beaverbrook Bible, should be the ones who pull the strings. Public figures with contrary views became personal enemies. How dare the puppets have a life of their own? Max made it a mission to cut Noël down to size, just as he tried with Mountbatten and others. Perhaps he took that little device of the Crusader breaking free from his chains seriously when he put it on the masthead of his *Daily Express*. Where the Beaverbrook press led, the rest of Fleet Street blindly followed. It was open season for Noël-baiting.

Many of this century's most powerful media figures in Britain have come from the old colonies: Max Beaverbrook, Roy Thomson and Conrad Black were all Canadians, Rupert Murdoch an Australian. Perhaps they had something to prove and this was the quickest way to impress themselves on the public and be taken seriously. The term "press baron" became part of the language during Beaverbrook's "reign." Long before he was given his actual title he certainly acted like a robber baron!

By 1955, Noël had reason to neither like nor admire the Press. He could write in the *Diaries:* "There really is something sinister about journalism, it has an insidious effect on character and distorts viewpoint. I am convinced that the reason I distrust and dislike journalists as a general rule is that after a while, like politicians, they become subtly corrupted by their job. They develop a facile cynicism based on superficial observation, and the real truths below the surface of people and events evade them. Max Beaverbrook is their god - dynamic, saturated with power, autocratic, charming when he pleases, in mortal fear of death, and spiritually one of the greatest vulgarians that have ever lived."

It's hard to appreciate now just how much real power Beaverbrook had. Not only did he possess the power to attack someone in print, Max also had the ear of the great and the good. During the war he was a member of Churchill's cabinet, charged with the task of organising aircraft production. No one will ever know just what contribution he made, though to hear Max tell it, he'd done it alone.

Noël was an early victim of Max's régime. A wartime job that he had been promised was summarily cancelled on the grounds that Noël Coward would be too "visible" when "complete secrecy is the foundation of our work." Noël could never prove it, but he always believed, based on his own

Beaverbrook by Low.

investigation, that Beaverbrook and Churchill were behind the sabotage. (Similar stratagems aborted the move to knight Noël.) Both of them were clever enough to cover their tracks, but the question remains: Who briefed the saboteurs? Was Noël's homosexuality a factor? To be homosexual in those days was to be *persona* distinctly *non grata*, but if public offices had been purged, the ship of state would have steered a somewhat uncertain course!

In later years, Noël would say that "all that was settled in 1942," a reference to the technical currency offence for which he'd been routinely fined, but which predictably caught the media eye. Whatever the cause, it was something else for him to rise above.

Noël was naturally wary of Beaverbrook, a tortured little man who devoted the last part of his life trying to recapture the omnipotence he'd once known. In so doing, he managed to turn himself into a caricature, a spectacle on which the rest of the media greedily feasted.

Something of a *rapprochement* was achieved aboard the *Queen Elizabeth* in 1949, when both of them were held captive in the same society for several days. This enabled a number of mutual friends, such as Loelia Westminster, Coco Chanel and Evelyn Waugh, to keep the drinks flowing and the chatter inconsequential, a fairly infallible recipe for social thawing. Noël's *Diaries* record the dénouement: "Max very amiable and asked me to stay with him at Montego"..."Drinks after dinner with Max. Long talk about the past, a polite duel which on the whole I won." What started at sea was later consummated over lunch on dry land in Jamaica.

"On the whole" was the operative phrase. Noël had "won" from Max a promise to call off the snipers for a year. Max was as good as his word, and as literal. One year later to the day, the campaign re-started in the Beaverbrook press, but the viciousness had evaporated and the vendetta became something of a joke. Max lost interest in keeping score. Noël had been inclined to refer to him grudgingly as a "witty old bastard," never less than a worthy adversary. Surprisingly, Max never turned up as a character in one of the later plays. Noël probably felt he'd starred on his own stage long enough.

LOUIS MOUNTBATTEN

Noël's snobbery about royalty was readily extended to *neo*-Royalty. He revered the social function and was genuinely fond of many of the accidental incumbents, to the point where he would happily bend his own rules. Against his better judgement, he would suffer titled fools reasonably gladly, as he did with Windsor.

The Royals genuinely liked Noël, and did not merely patronize him as a celebrity, to be considered quaint and then put back in his box. They were loyal personal friends, who stood by him during his post-war wanderings in the critical wilderness. Their support sustained his morale when the press was taking him to task over one trivial issue after another: the building permits for Goldenhurst, his tax problems. There was always something. A visit to the Palace or a noisy evening with Princess Margaret and Lord Snowdon would soon cheer him up. As support systems go, it went a long way!

Louis Mountbatten wasn't, strictly speaking, Royalty, though he had all of the trappings. On occasion, his manner was more "regal" than Royal, and for Noël he also exuded the additional aura of his connection with the Navy.

Noël had a love of the sea for as long as he could remember. ("God knows why," he'd say, "since our part of Teddington was somewhat land-locked.") During the visit to Shanghai in 1929 that also gave birth to *Private Lives*, he was invited to make a short trip on the Royal Navy cruiser, *H.M.S. Suffolk*. The combination of the sea itself and the orderliness of naval life attracted him and he wrote: "The secret of naval good manners is hard to define; perhaps discipline has a lot to do with it and prolonged contact with the sea; perhaps a permanent background of such dignity makes for simplicity of mind." Noël believed that even an apparently free activity, such as the theatre, should have its own set of disciplines. In his own life he applied them rigorously, so there was for him a kind of Theatre of the Sea.

Before the public spotlight fixed them forever, the Mountbattens had all the appearance of a "Noël Coward couple." Noël openly based the characters of Piggie and Peter Gilpin in *Hands Across the Sea* (1935) on them. He recalled they "used to give cocktail parties and people used to arrive that nobody had ever heard of and sit about and go away again; somebody Dickie had met somewhere, or somebody Edwina had met - and nobody knew who they were. We all talked among ourselves."

In the play, the Gilpins receive some unexpected visitors from overseas. Piggie tries to persuade Peter to take them off her hands:

PETER: *You know perfectly well I don't have time to take mothers and fathers and daughters with bad legs around the dockyard -*
PIGGIE: *It wouldn't take a minute, they took (Maud and me) all over their rubber plantation.*
PETER: *It probably served you right.*
PIGGIE: *You're so disobliging, darling, you really should try and conquer it - it's something to do with being English, I think - as a race I'm ashamed of us - no sense of hospitality - the least we can do when people are kind to us in far-off places is to be a little gracious in return.*
PETER: *They weren't kind to me in far-off places.*
PIGGIE: *You know, there's a certain grudging, sullen streak in your character - I've been very worried about it lately - it's spreading like a forest fire...*

The Mountbattens were distinctly not amused, until their friends pointed out what a compliment it was and expressed an envious wish that somebody would write a play about *them*. After that, Louis and Edwina liked to give the impression they'd been in on the joke from the beginning.

Edwina was what we'd now call "feisty." Just how feisty we only found out rather later, when the details of her *amours* became public knowledge. Louis also was much more relaxed in those years before he took on the *gravitas* of his later "position."

Noël's personal friendship with the Mountbattens developed into an informal working relationship as the '30's edged nervously towards war. It began with a project, instigated by Mountbatten, to equip the fleet with

Noël and Edwina Mountbatten leave the first night of the film of As You Like It. *Noël didn't agree with its claim to be "the gayest comedy ever written." (1936)*

Louis Mountbatten at the time of In Which We Serve. *(1942)*

film projectors to entertain the men at sea. Noël set up a liaison procedure with the film industry that soon accomplished the task. His research also taught him something about popular taste. The film stars the men wanted to see most were George Formby, Jack Hulbert, Cicely Courtneidge and Jessie Matthews, all local stars with not a Hollywood name among them. It was a salutary lesson: To appeal to a broadly-based audience, as opposed to the sophisticates of the West End theatre, it was better to concentrate on fundamental feelings, simply and humorously expressed. People wanted the security of seeing idealised versions of themselves up on that screen.

Noël had been greatly upset when Churchill dismissed his offer to serve in the war. He was determined to find another solution. Troop concerts were all very well but Noël's patriotism, not to mention his egotism, yearned to make a more significant contribution. If they wouldn't issue him a sword, nobody could stop Noël Coward from picking up his pen. Perhaps he could provide a play, a song, even a film that would help people during these difficult days?

The artist is often the conduit for the work. What emerges isn't always what is expected. The *play* was *Blithe Spirit*, and it arrived in 1941. It had nothing whatsoever to do with the war, but it did distract and entertain audiences for the duration.

Then came the *song*. "London Pride" was in many ways the anthem of World War Two. It didn't have the defiant, even militant, emotion of Ivor's "Keep the Home Fires Burning," but "London Pride" captured the quiet determination of a people who stolidly went about the daily task of living under the Blitz. Its banked-down emotion precisely caught the mood of the nation.

What remained to complete Noël's trinity was the *film*. His relationship with Mountbatten came back into the frame again. The story of Mountbatten's own command, *H.M.S. Kelly*, sunk in 1941 with considerable loss of life, became the basis of a powerful patriotic film. The Navy was immediately supportive and permission was given for Mountbatten to become Noël's close collaborator. ("He is really profoundly enthusiastic about the whole idea. He told me many touching incidents of the *Kelly*.") The draft script for *White Ensign*, which became *In Which We Serve*, was quickly completed.

That proved to be the easy part. There was a great deal of opposition, at both the official and the popular press level, to the idea of Noël Coward, lightweight entertainer, playing a naval captain. It was again Mountbatten who steered the project through those heavy seas, obtained the necessary permissions and helped Noël and co-director, David Lean, produce one of the most effective war films, or rather, *anti*-war films, ever made.

Noël insisted that he had been careful not to model his hero too closely on Mountbatten: "My Captain ['D' Kinross] is quite ordinary, with an income of about £800 a year, a small country house near Plymouth, a reasonably nice-looking wife (Mrs., not Lady), two children and a cocker spaniel." Noël was kidding himself. In the early drafts of the script, several of the Captain's speeches were provided verbatim by Mountbatten.

Louis continued to express misgivings about something which clearly pleased him greatly. "You may not realise it," he wrote to Noël later, "but I have been greatly criticised for being a party to the making of a film designed to boost me personally." He asked if the film could not be changed somehow to suggest that "my co-operation over this film was based on the understanding that it was not to be recognisable as the story of my own ship and certainly not as my own story?" The question was clearly rhetorical.

Noël's homework paid off and his love of the Navy showed through. As a tribute it was both affectionate and accurate. To this day, the film is shown to Naval recruits as a primer on naval conduct.

Although Churchill had vigorously opposed the concept, he cheerfully applauded the execution. He saw it several times and admitted that it brought tears to his eyes. The fact that the film was made at all was entirely due to Mountbatten's perseverance, a fact which caused Noël to write: "I am more and more convinced that he is a great man."

The film's critical and propaganda success came at a particularly low point in the war, and reignited speculation about a knighthood for Noël. Mountbatten suggested it to King George, who supposedly gave it his blessing. Others, presumably Churchill and Beaverbrook, counselled otherwise. For nearly thirty years, it remained a *cause célèbre* for "Dickie," which only Noël could call him. He undoubtedly had a manicured hand in Queen Elizabeth's final decision.

There was one unfortunate side effect of the film. Mountbatten was convinced that Beaverbrook's vendetta was triggered by a shot in the film in which a copy of the *Daily Express*, dated September 1st, 1939, bore the headline: "There Will Be No War This Year." The paper was shown sinking into the sea.

At a dinner party hosted by Averill Harriman in October, 1942, Beaverbrook confronted Mountbatten, accusing him of self-glorification and colluding in an underhand attack on the Beaverbrook press: "You and Coward have gone out of your way to insult me and try to hold up the *Daily Express* to ridicule!" he screamed. Mountbatten protested that he had asked Noël to cut the scene from the finished film, but Beaverbrook was dismissive: "I shall never forgive you for this piece of disloyalty. From now on, you watch out. You will live to regret the day that you took part in such a vile attack on me!" Although he spoke specifically to Louis, his threat rang true for both men.

It's become fashionable lately to deconstruct Mountbatten, to depict him as a poseur, someone who parlayed his fringe position in the Royal circle into a hand full of aces. He was, it's true, physically vain and socially garrulous, but so was Noël. It was a childlike affectation in both of them, a form of reassurance for the deserved good fortunes which befell them. Almost all of Noël's closest celebrity friends (the Lunts, Marlene, even Churchill) were self-constructed, echoing one or another aspect of Noël's multi-faceted character. Each saw themselves reflected in the other.

All of them wanted to be famous and loved. All of them were always "on stage," trying out this mannerism, that look, the other phrase. If it "played," it became part of the "act." If it didn't, it was ruthlessly discarded. They became a collection of behavioural mannerisms which could, and, in the case of Dietrich, finally did, obscure the real person within. Insecurity demands the reassurance of public approval.

Mountbatten became a willing victim of the media, assuming the image they'd created for him. His act developed into a public refuge from the private pain which intensified with Edwina's increasingly erratic sexual behaviour. How ironic that men who pride themselves on their manhood can be so undermined by their women. The golden couple had been acting out a charade for years. Even when they see what is happening, the closest friends can say only so much.

Noël's relationship with the Mountbattens was typical of those he most desperately wanted to succeed; an initial period of euphoria, followed by a gradual and grudging disenchantment. In 1957 he would write: "They have both changed beyond recognition. No more humour and an overwhelming pomposity. It is a shame but there is obviously nothing to be done. *Tout lasse, tout passe, tout casse.* Life goes on and little bits of us get lost."

Mountbatten aged rapidly after Edwina's death in 1960, but seemed to rediscover something of his old self, much to Noël's relief. In 1966 a minor event cemented the pieces back together. Noël was invited to attend a reunion of the remaining crew of the *Kelly* and was inducted as an honorary member of the ship's company. He confided to his *Diaries:* "It was so unimportant and so very, very important." What was just as important was that he'd rededicated the foundations of his relationship with "Dickie" Mountbatten.

CECIL BEATON

Noël had long been acquainted with Cecil Beaton before they got to know each other well on a ship bound for New York in 1930.

In the 1920's, social life on both sides of the Atlantic was a ritual dance with everyone constantly changing partners. By the late '20's, Noël's fame was at its height and the younger Beaton, as he later confessed, was frankly jealous.

After seeing Noël at a New York party, Cecil wrote in his diary: "He didn't succeed in saying anything amusing or clever. He was extremely badly dressed in trousers too short...." His verdict on *Fallen Angels* in 1925 was, "I do think the play will help to ruin old Coward. It is quite definite that he won't live long. People will get so tired of him!" Noël was unaware of these gadfly stings at first, but once he was, retaliation was swift. In the lyric of "Marvellous Party" he chortles:

> *Dear Cecil arrived wearing armour,*
> *Some shells and a black feather boa...*

It was all good, if not particularly clean, fun.

The meeting at sea struck a mutual alliance between two men who had many shared sensibilities. After this meeting Cecil was honest enough to admit: "I admire everything about his work: his homesick, sadly melodious tunes, his revues, his witty plays, his astringent acting!"

Noël was quick to respond to the olive branch. He'd criticised Cecil for being "floppy, flabby and affected" with an "undulating" walk and "exaggerated" clothes, but Noël had endured many of the problems of personal presentation that now bedevilled Cecil. He freely rendered constructive advice about the way he'd carefully pieced together "Noël Coward," down to the detail of the way he dressed: "I take ruthless stock of myself in the mirror before going out."

That honesty created a lasting, if fragile, bond. They didn't meet with any regularity for several years, so the ice would re-form and the occasional ill-considered remark would break through. As late as the mid-'40's Cecil was referring to Noël as "the Artful Dodger of society," which, I suppose, might just be taken as a compliment!

The turning point in their friendship came early in 1941. Cecil visited the set of *In Which We Serve*, and in the course of conversation he complained that Noël clearly didn't appreciate his talent. Noël was forced to admit that he had been jealous, because he was convinced that Cecil's contribution to the war effort was more significant than his own. ("It just shows how utterly wrong I've been. You've been yourself always and how right you've been.") That may not have been true, but after his abortive efforts to enlist and with the success of *In Which We Serve* yet to come, it's easy to see why Noël thought so. It was Noël's conviction that "people like us should be friends rather than enemies because we really have so much in

The Jamaican Gang: Noël, Ian Fleming, Ann Rothermere, Natasha Wilson and Cecil Beaton, who managed to take the picture and be in it. (Goldeneye, 1960's)

common - powers of observation, wit, industriousness and professionalism!"

It was that professionalism which ultimately cemented their friendship when, in 1952, Noël invited Cecil to design the sets and costumes for *Quadrille*, the new play he'd written for the Lunts. This was the first time since *The Vortex* in 1924 that Gladys Calthrop hadn't automatically been assigned the task on a Coward play. There was no ill will between them, but it became increasingly obvious that Gladys's enthusiasm was waning and Noël was increasingly disenchanted with her work. The break was mutually acceptable and did nothing to hurt their personal friendship.

Quadrille presented many of the same practical problems we encountered with *Pacific 1860*. Britain was still in its austerity phase and most basic materials for producing the period clothes were difficult to obtain. One of Lynn's dresses was multi-layered and used several different materials. It proved particularly difficult and had to be hand-painted when the loom broke down. A lot of midnight oil was burned in producing it on time. At the run-through, Noël turned to Cecil and said, "I'm afraid we

Noël by Cecil.

don't like it." Cecil looked at the dress quizzically, pursed his lips and said, "Neither do I. It's too fussy. Let's give it to Marian Spencer" (one of the supporting actresses). The production proceeded smoothly and Marian looked delightful in the dress, fussy or not.

Cecil confessed that his professional admiration for Noël grew markedly as he watched him in action. The Lunts were old and dear friends, but on stage they were transformed into competitive autocrats. Cecil had never seen such behaviour and he asked Noël, "Doesn't it make you want to tear your hair out?" Noël replied thoughtfully, "Not really. It doesn't do you any good and it's bad for the hair."

Complete harmony never reigned between them because each saw too many similarities to himself in the other. Noël thought Cecil verged on the precious; Cecil saw a pedestrian, suburban side to Noël. He wrote in his own *Diaries* (1979), after his first visit to Switzerland in 1972, that the house "might have been brought from Eastbourne." He went on, "It is true the house suits Noël perfectly. It has no real character, is ugly, is decorated in the typical theatre-folk style, but it is warm and comfortable and it works."

Quadrille was their principal collaboration, though Cecil designed sets and costumes for *Look After Lulu* in 1959. Working together broke the ice once and for all and they maintained close contact until Noël's death. Cecil was a frequent visitor to Firefly. He would pose us for photographic posterity on the verandah, then dash back to be in the picture as we were all frozen in time by the insistent little "click" of the camera.

Nothing Noël said or wrote about Cecil came close to Cecil's considered verdict on Noël, which he published in his book, *The Face of the World* (1957): "He is a crystallized phenomenon, the wonder of the decade (no matter which decade), a cocktail of Mayfair and madness, the hair of the dog that bit us."

THE ALGONQUIN ROUND TABLE

Noël frequently criss-crossed the Atlantic, keeping in touch with friends in New York. He was awarded an honorary membership of the Algonquin Round Table, courtesy of Alexander Woollcott, who referred to him as "destiny's tot." Noël was obliged to occupy a probationary pew until those legends in their own lunchtime had seen what he was made of.

Noël's recollection of that time was *nostalgie du temps perdu*. The club satisfied Noël's appetite for approval, but he preferred centre stage and couldn't sit there comfortably for long while the legendary game of "pass the *bon mot*" went interminably on.

Arriving for lunch one day, Noël spied the diminutive figure of novelist Edna Ferber seated next to the walrus-like Woollcott. Edna, a lifelong spinster of that parish, was wearing a tailored man's suit then fashionable among "smart" women. Slightly taken aback by this early example of cross-dressing, Noël said brightly, "Edna, why it's you. You look almost like a man." Came back Miss Ferber's chilly riposte, "So do you."

Edna became a close confidante of Noël's and was the prevailing voice of sanity when he was receiving contradictory advice. When Hollywood beckoned, it was Edna who advised against it. "It will ruin your writing," she warned him. "If you're short of money, I'll help you, but please don't go!" Noël heeded her, thus avoiding the fate of other famous writers like Scott Fitzgerald. He was always grateful to Edna for making him see sense and for talking to him (though he never put it this way!) man to man.

Noël with Lilli Palmer in "Come Into the Garden, Maud," one of the plays from Suite in Three Keys. *(Apollo Theatre, 1966)*

CHAPTER NINE

"DAD'S RENAISSANCE": THE 1960's

"Who would have thought the landmarks of the Sixties would include...the emergence of Noël Coward as the grand old man of British drama? There he was one morning flipping verbal tiddlywinks with reporters about 'Dad's Renaissance'...the next, he was there again,...slightly older than the century on which he sits, his eyelids wearier than ever, hanging beside Forster, Eliot and the O.M.s, demonstrably the greatest living English playwright."

Ronald Bryden
New Statesman

If Noël had been told at the end of the decade that the Swinging Sixties had swung for him, he would have delivered The Look and a brisk riposte. Noël was now most definitely a tax exile, and the decade started with his domestic relocation from Bermuda to Switzerland. From there he shuttled between Jamaica, New York and, on a carefully tax-rationed basis, the UK.

Until the mid-'60's, the decade was a professional see-saw, with Noël's reputation going up here and there with the public, only to be tipped back down by the heavy hands of the critics.

It was a prolific period which encompassed plays and musicals, short stories, verse, his one and only novel, and his final stage performances. Noël packed more into those few years than most people achieve in a lifetime. All of his work, however, had to be done against a back-drop of the public's unrealistic expectations; "Noël Coward" was a creature who, by now, had largely become a figment of the collective imagination.

*   *   *   *

Noël inaugurated the decade on stage with *Waiting in the Wings* (1960). This was one of his most enduring and least appreciated accomplishments. The subject centred on a group of retired actresses

Waiting in the Wings. *One of the guests of The Wings nursing home has said her last lines. Sybil Thorndike and a cast of London "senior" leading ladies. (Duke of York Theatre, 1960)*

playing out the last act of their lives in an old people's home. It sounds like a rather depressing saga, but Noël made it gently amusing by conceiving the ladies as pure theatrical "characters." Life was a continuous performance and they were forever "on." Sybil Thorndike, Mary Clare and Marie Lohr, among others, had the time of their "senior" lives.

The major obstacle in staging the piece was Binkie's dislike of it. Perhaps he heard echoes of time's wingèd chariot racing up to his own back. Only later did we learn about the game-playing that had gone on between Binkie, Gladys Cooper and Edith Evans.

Eventually, Michael Redgrave braved the theatrical elements and produced a modestly successful run of nine months. It was a solid production, but it couldn't compare with the beautifully packaged Fortnum & Mason version that Binkie and Tennent could have given us.

The ladies were troupers in perfect harmony, not a scratched eye in the cast. They were all aware of the problems Noël had encountered and knew that this was not the time for upstaging. Margaret Webster directed with great sensitivity to the play's humour and pathos.

Sybil was known to be difficult, routinely insisting on a part for her husband, Lewis Casson, whether or not there was anything suitable in the script. We saw none of this behaviour. Sybil was a tower of strength who was word-perfect for the first rehearsal, took direction, and even spurred on the other ladies to greater efforts. She would prompt them discreetly when they faltered, without any attempt to score points. Her example as a team player shamed anyone who might have been tempted to throw a temper tantrum. She was particularly kind to some of the very senior ladies, who spent more time in their own world than in the one we were trying to create.

During the run of *Waiting in the Wings*, my mother was terminally ill in Westminster Hospital.

From the time I moved in with the Coward "family," Mum had lived with a lady companion in her own flat. I saw her regularly, and she shared my "ups" and sympathised with my "downs." Our relationship was very similar to that of Noël and *his* mother. Our mothers became friends and confidantes, and we had no need to pretend around them. But there was no one we wanted to please more.

Both women, by closely involving themselves in their sons' careers, stayed young at heart, but in the end the clock caught up with them. Mum had remained her active and independent self, and visited America to see the sights and old friends. For a while she acted as *concierge* to Noël's house in Bermuda, but at the end of the 1950's she began to ail. Cancer was diagnosed and it was only a question of time. She was taken ill on the 'plane back from Bermuda and whisked straight into hospital. I'd visit her on the way to the theatre and phone immediately after the show. As always she wanted to know every detail of how it had gone.

On December 2nd, I instinctively knew I was seeing her for the last time. I wanted to stay with her, but I could almost hear her telling me: "Get off with you, you've got a show to do. I'll be fine!" When I came off stage, I was handed the message I'd been dreading. Mum had died while I was on stage.

In *Wings*, I played Perry Lascoe, the Secretary to The Wings Fund that organised the home, as good a supporting role as can be expected for a man in a woman's play. I also sang a haunting melody called, "Come the Wild, Wild Weather." It hadn't been written for the show and was clearly unrelated to the plot, but as a "turn" in the party scene it seemed to fit nicely. Noël couldn't have known the personal poignancy those last lines would have:

> *Come the wild, wild weather,*
> *Come the wind and the rain,*
> *Come the little white flakes of snow,*

Come the joy, come the pain,
We shall still be together
When our life's journey ends,
For wherever we chance to go
We shall always be friends....

Come the wild, wild weather,
If we've lost or we've won,
We'll remember these words we say
Till our story is done.

The critics' reaction to *Waiting in the Wings* was worse than I could ever have anticipated. Noël reports in the *Diaries:* "With the exception of *The Times* (guarded), *Telegraph* (kindly), *Chronicle* (good) and *Herald* (fair), I have never read such abuse in my life. The *Mail...*, *Express...*, and *Standard...*were vile and the *Evening News* violently vituperative. I was accused of tastelessness, vulgarity, sentimentality, etc. To read them was like being repeatedly slashed in the face."

The *Express* called it "A Play About Nothing At All" and the *Mail:* "Just Timeless Rootless Prattle." The *Manchester Mail* took a little longer to come to a similar conclusion: "Mr. Coward's Weak Tea Is Oh, So Bitter Sweet!" Someone had been waiting years to use that one!

When the reviews had had time to sink in, Noël saw that, yet again, something he cared about was not going to fulfill its promise. He was forced to admit: "Perhaps, after all, those bastards of critics did some damage." "...there is quite an accumulation of bitterness in my heart for those mean, ungenerous, envious, ignorant little critics."

Those mean-spirited people apparently hadn't watched the same show that deeply moved audiences night after night. We should have been used to it, but we weren't. *Ace of Clubs* might have misconstrued a new world; *After the Ball* might have treated the past indecisively. Neither had been the show Noël originally conceived. But *Waiting in the Wings* was very much the show he intended, portraying with dignity and humour a subject he intimately understood. The play deserved serious attention, but it failed to move critics whose meritorious heads were now firmly wedged in the kitchen sink. Noël's effrontery in writing about something as obsolete as death and dying apparently offended them.

Ironically, the *film* critics in those very same newspapers were praising Noël for having "stolen" his latest film, *Surprise Package*, from under the noses of stars Yul Brynner and Mitzi Gaynor. This was the second such triumph in a row. A few months earlier, the critics took a similar view of his *succès d'estime*, not to mention *d'argent*, in *Our Man in Havana* with

Alec Guinness. "Don't act with dogs, babies or Noël Coward" was becoming a movie motto.

To keep himself from falling into a rut, Noël produced The Novel. *Pomp and Circumstance* was a Samolan Soufflé which Noël described to his American publishers as being "so light that you will have trouble capturing it between covers." The pages, however, were captured, as was the attention of the American public who kept it on *The New York Times* best-seller list for six months. Fortunately, Noël's bow had many strings.

*   *   *   *

Noël spent much of early 1961 in Jamaica, writing a musical about travel, a subject he really knew well. The *mores* of travel and travellers had always fascinated him. From the '20's on, whenever he was tired, depressed or generally bored, Noël would go to some exotic spot where the sun beat down. ("Settling down anywhere for long is not for me.") Inspiration would invariably strike in his new surroundings, and the intended fallow period would become extremely productive. The plot of *Private Lives* was hatched in the Imperial Hotel, Tokyo. "The moment I switched out the lights, Gertie appeared in a white Molyneux dress on a terrace in the South of France and refused to go again until four a.m." She actually refused to leave until he'd committed her story to paper a few days later in the Cathay hotel in Shanghai.

The new project started life in 1956 as a film script, "...a brittle, stylized, sophisticated, insignificant comedy with music...*Later Than Spring*." It was to have starred Noël and Marlene, supported by Van Johnson, Betsy Drake, Marti Stevens and me.

The movies were never really Noël's *métier* as an author. When he wrote a play he could expect to see it produced in the way that he'd envisaged. Putting together a film involved the egos and whims of so many other people that he rapidly lost interest. When his choice of stars was endlessly debated or they weren't available, "Sod it!" he'd say, and either drop the project or adapt it for a more comfortable medium.

By 1960 he'd recast *Later Than Spring* as a musical called *Sail Away*, and which gave a home to a song which had been looking for one ever since I'd introduced it in *Ace of Clubs*.

The new show would feature the immortal character of Mrs. Wentworth-Brewster, the bibulous lady of the "bar on the Piccola Marina," to be played by Ethel Merman, then either Rosalind Russell or Judy Holliday.

Roz Russell felt her elegant image was unsuited to the British suburban excesses of Mrs. W-B, so the dear lady was laid to rest and replaced by

Bonard Productions
in association with Charles Russell *presents*

Noël Coward's

new musical comedy

Sail Away

starring

Elaine Stritch   **Jean Fenn**

with

James Hurst   Margalo Gillmore   Alice Pearce   Patricia Harty   Grover Dale
Carroll McComas   William Hutt   Charles Braswell   Betty Jane Watson   Evelyn Russell

Production Designed by OLIVER SMITH
Costumes Designed by HELENE PONS *and* OLIVER SMITH
Lighting by Peggy Clark
Musical Direction and Dance Arrangements by Peter Matz
Orchestrations by Irwin Kostal   *Vocal Arrangements by* Fred Werner

Musical Numbers and Dances Staged by JOE LAYTON
Book, Music, Lyrics and Direction by NOËL COWARD

COLONIAL THEATRE MATS. WED. & SAT. BOSTON   **WED. AUG. 9** THRU **SAT. SEPT. 2**

Printed by Artcraft Litho. & Ptg. Co., Inc. N. Y. C.   191

In addition to performing all the other chores in the show, Noël even designed the poster...

Mimi Paragon, the social hostess on a British cruise ship sailing between New York and the Mediterranean. Kay Thompson would have been ideal for Mimi but, like so many of Noël's first choices, she wasn't available.

Noël put more into *Sail Away* than into any other project to date; he was determined to succeed. His professional enthusiasm summoned up the full range of his many talents. He wrote the book, music and lyrics, designed the poster, and even recorded the voice of Captain Wilberforce, which is heard over the ship's tannoy.

Then came the changes. He had, he said, "never done an original American musical with expert choreographers, expert orchestrators, expert lighting, etc. I have always had to fight the dear old English *laissez-aller* which at the moment seems more indestructible than ever."

It's not uncommon for a show to go through a number of incarnations before being born in the form by which the world knows it. The finished product often surpasses, and even makes redundant, the original property. Everyone's seen *Casablanca,* but few saw the original play, *Everyone Comes to Rick's.* No-one reads Michener's *Tales of the South Pacific,* when they can see a revival of Rodgers and Hammerstein's *South Pacific.* These are successful examples. All too often, however, the sum of the parts adds up to *less* than the original. Such was the case with *Sail Away.*

Adaptation can be a painful process, especially if the fit isn't there to begin with. It's also a very public process if you're producing a play (particularly a musical play) and the show is already on the road. The novelist, essayist or poet can cut and paste to his heart's content in private; the playwright performs his surgery in the glare of the media spotlight under constant threat from those "Show-in-Trouble" headlines that spell box-office poison. The inevitable decision must be made: Change or leave alone?

Noël learned from his painful post-war experiences to trust his theatrical instincts. He was prepared to do what had to be done and risk the temporary consequences; a few years earlier he would have tried to justify a flawed original.

During the Boston and Philadelphia tryouts he realised that the focus of the piece was divided. Elaine Stritch, as the hostess, had the comedy material; but Jean Fenn, as an unhappily married woman, bore the burden of the plot's romance. She flirts with a younger man, attempts suicide and finally goes back to her husband. It wasn't exactly upbeat and it certainly slowed things down.

Audiences were inclined to sit on their hands until Stritch was on stage. Noël faced facts and cut the sub-plot. Jean had played a difficult part well, but her personality had begun to grate on Noël's nerves. She demanded to wear her own choice of costume. If she'd heard Noël muttering, "Why

The song version of one of Noël's poems. It was cut from Sail Away (1961) *and never performed. For some reason it varied from the original, which read "I Am No Good."*

does she insist on wearing that linen iron lung?" she might have read the danger signals. With some creative juggling of the score, Stritch became romantic *and* comedy lead.

There was a bitter-sweet aspect to the love story which Noël hoped to salvage. Two numbers, "This Is A Changing World" and "This Is A Night For Lovers" from *Pacific 1860*, were worthy of wider exposure, but by no stretch would they fit Stritch, so out they went. A musical setting of one of Noël's poems, "I Am No Good At Love," was another victim of the cuts.

The show entirely lost its "European" quality and became one hundred per cent Broadway brassy. The extensively revised version headed for New York, New York, for better or for worse. Noël's money was on the former. Things started ominously well. It was the first of his musicals to have an

American, rather than a London, opening.   Boston and Philadelphia lapped it up. House records. Standing Room Only. Elaine Stritch became an overnight star.

"Stritchie" was (and is) a big, blonde broad, and that is meant entirely as a compliment. She could belt out a number like a *sotto* (but not too *sotto*) *voce* Ethel Merman, but then bring surprising tenderness to an emotional ballad. She also had great legs! She was in the tradition of the great leading ladies but with a new face. Audiences loved her! Noël loved her, too.   He cherished her similarities with Gertie: her verve, her irreverence, her infectious vulgarity. From that moment on, she was a "chum."

When *Sail Away* opened in New York, a horribly familiar pattern emerged. Tremendous first night reception. Huge advance ($1.5 million).

Sail Away. *Noël rehearses Elaine Stritch. (1961)*

Great word of mouth. Mixed reviews. Then came the famous "Noël Coward musical nosedive." The advance dropped off; the word began to speak out of the side of the mouth; some of the critics began to have second thoughts: What were they doing, liking an old-fashioned Noël Coward show? What had been "light" was now "slight." The "boys" in the show were all fags and the girls weren't pretty enough. The bandwagon began to roll backwards.

After its early success, Noël returned to New York at Thanksgiving and, finding things in trouble, called a Friday rehearsal. "The rehearsal started with me giving a three-quarters of an hour homily on the art of acting truly, disregarding dull audiences, not coming out and begging for laughs, and *not* interpolating lines and business without the permission of the author-director." When the hoopla finally died down, the general feeling was that in 1936 it would have been the best musical of the year. In 1961 it ran for five months.

Noël was bitterly hurt. He'd hoped this show would be his "banker," the financial cushion for an "old age" he now spoke of with more rather than less irony. He didn't openly express himself, but his *Diaries* (as ever) told the whole story. He speculated about the nature of modern theatre audiences:

> "In the old days, when there were no organized [theatre party] audiences...the public paid box-office prices, and if they liked a show it was a success and if they didn't it was a failure. In those happier days a certain number of theatre devotees read the notices but the large majority judged for themselves, nor were their opinions prejudiced in advance by radio and television comments."

He went on to ponder whether there might not, after all, be something missing in the material he was producing:

> "Another fact that I must face is that I am rising sixty-two, whether I like it or not, and it is perfectly possible that I am out of touch with the times. I don't care for the present trends either in literature or the theatre. Pornography bores me. Squalor disgusts me. Garishness, vulgarity and commonness of mind offend me....Subtlety, discretion, restraint, finesse, charm, intelligence, good manners, talent and glamour still enchant me....Am I falling into the famous trap of *nostalgie du temps perdu*? Have I really, or at least nearly, reached the crucial moment when I should retire from the fray and spend my remaining years sorting out my

memories and sentimentalizing the past at the expense of the present?"

Sail Away docked in London some months later under Harold Fielding's management at the Savoy. Elaine Stritch was made available by the Broadway closing. The London story was a carbon copy. A successful provincial tour, an effusive opening night audience, grudging reviews. An encouraging start and an abrupt falling away of audience interest.

Noël concluded that the book had let the show down. He'd "...deliberately kept the 'book' down to a minimum, in the belief that the public would be relieved at not having to sit through acres of dialogue between numbers. In fact I have used a revue formula with a mere thread of story running through it. Presumably I was wrong!"

Noël Coward's name on the marquee brought in audiences who expected, if not acres, then at least a few densely-wooded square yards of vintage Coward dialogue. They felt short-changed at not getting it. Noël was obliged to accept an unpleasant and unexpected reality: "I have already risen up and twitched my mantle blue."

*   *   *   *

Herman Levin was a Broadway producer who possessed one extremely persuasive credential: *My Fair Lady.* He had hired Hollywood screenwriter Harry Kurnitz to turn Terence Rattigan's *The Sleeping Prince* (1953) into a musical libretto, and wanted Noël to write the score and lyrics.

Noël weighed the pros and cons. On the plus side, Terry's well-crafted story was unlikely to suffer significant damage from Kurnitz's dubious Hollywood skills. It was "period" and that always held a fatal fascination for Noël. He also harboured a superstitious feeling about having turned down both previous incarnations of *My Fair Lady.* Perhaps Herman was unwittingly offering him an opportunity to make it "Third time's a charm."

On the minus side, it was yet another adaptation, and not even of his own work. Would Rattigan prove as intractable as Wilde and Feydeau? One small straw in the prevailing wind might have been a hint. When he told Vivien Leigh (who had been in the original play) about his plan, Viv ingenuously chirped, "How thrilling! You must get Dick Addinsell to write the music." Noël, for once, was silent.

The bottom line won and Noël accepted Levin's offer. Events ran their predictable course. Noël's initial enthusiasm for Harry Kurnitz's book was rapidly followed by Noël's diminishing enthusiasm for Kurnitz's book; his admiration for Joe Layton's direction swiftly turned to frustration reminiscent of Bobbie Helpmann and *After the Ball* ("*Why* have choreographers no respect for dialogue or lyrics?"). By this time the "book" had changed its gender. *The Sleeping Prince* became *The Girl Who Came to Supper*, but even here Noël was frustrated. He had proposed the punny title *Passing Fancy*, but was over-ruled by the producer. (The movie version of the play, with Olivier and Monroe, went by yet another title, *The Prince and the Showgirl*.)

Someday our Prince would come, but who would he be? Rex Harrison listened to the score, liked the key song, "I Remember Her," but regretfully...Christopher Plummer gave it careful consideration but... Keith Michell was signed...then José Ferrer auditioned and Keith Michell was promptly *un*signed.

These vicissitudes are not uncommon but they were crowding in on Noël's recent activities. He found them unsettling. The Boston previews were "rapturous," yet within weeks, Noël was "...getting sick (of) the frustration of not being able to put things right for myself. I suppose it's good for my soul."

First indications in New York were that we had a smash hit. Once again, Noël continued to hear inner voices of doubt. Jo Ferrer was a name, but not attractive enough, and Noël thought neither he nor Florence Henderson (the "Girl") had "star-quality."

In Noël's considered opinion, "a musical smash" on Broadway was a successful amalgamation of imponderables. "It is only rarely, as in the case of *Oklahoma!* or *West Side Story*, that a big show can succeed without a star name." His second thoughts, unfortunately, came in first. *The Girl Who Came to Supper* stayed for only three months and never did show up in London.

None of the numerous changes along the way had helped. Terry's story had been set in London to coincide with the coronation of George V. Mary, a chorus girl from Milwaukee, meets the Prince Regent of Carpathia who, with the worst of intentions, invites her to dinner at the embassy. By the end of the play, of course, he's genuinely in love with her. The fact of his pre-existing marriage would have to be dealt with after the curtain came down.

As the script evolved, the adulterous Prince became a widower, a slender storyline was stretched thin and finally snapped under the weight of becoming a great big musical, in which there were shows within shows.

The *Girl's* biggest problem was that she wanted to be *My Fair Lady*, the sweet soprano from the wrong side of the tracks who gets the non-singing older man. There the comparison ended. Besides, there were new girls in town, *Dolly* and *Funny Girl*, who proved to be more congenial company.

One footnote for the historical, rather than the theatrical, archives.

One of Jo Ferrer's songs had to be pulled in Philadelphia. It was called "Long Live the King (If He Can)!":

> Long live the King, if he can,
> And if he can, it takes a most remarkable man
> To remain undismayed
> When a hand-made grenade
> Makes a loud explosion
> Every time the national anthem's played.
> When launching a ship
> With a stiff upper lip
> Or opening a Church bazaar
> He longs for the calm
> And the gracious charm
> Of a heavily armoured car.
> Every procession of state
> May, or may not, be lightly shot at
> As it leaves the palace gate,
> If the Monarch's bodyguard is twenty seconds late,
> He'll be as dead as Queen Anne,
> Long live the King, if he can.

That was the week President Kennedy was assassinated.

*   *   *   *

Meanwhile, back in London, the clouds were lifting, though we were too engrossed in what was happening on Broadway to notice. James Roose-Evans was reviving *Private Lives* at the Hampstead Theatre Club. The production did well enough to transfer to the Duke of York's, where it was respectfully reviewed and ran for the remainder of 1963. It was not hailed as the start of a Coward "revival," but that, essentially, is when the momentum began to build up.

*   *   *   *

We allowed ourselves a cautious excitement over the Broadway production of *High Spirits*, a musical adaptation of *Blithe Spirit* by Hugh Martin and Timothy Gray; cautious because we'd heard it all before. Leonard Bernstein had asked Noël for permission to turn *Brief Encounter* into a musical, and since he hadn't done such a bad job with *Romeo and Juliet*, it seemed a reasonable request. Noël never heard another word.

Hugh Martin had similar thoughts about *Hay Fever*. Again, nothing. Why should *Blithe Spirit* be any different?

But it was to prove very different. Martin and Gray brought the score to Jamaica and played it to Noël in early 1963. "...quite brilliant," said Noël. "The music is melodic and delightful, the lyrics really witty, and they have done a complete book outline keeping to my original play and yet making it effective as a musical." He liked it enough to begin mental casting: Gwen Verdon as Elvira, Celeste Holm as Ruth, Keith Michell (to compensate for *The Girl Who Came to Supper*) as Charles, and Kay Thompson as Madame Arcati. Needless to say, none of the above appeared in the final Broadway production, nor was Bob Fosse available to direct. Noël finally did that himself with some later help from Gower Champion.

One shouldn't look a gift horse in the mouth, and *High Spirits* (which was known briefly as *Faster Than Sound*) was a commercial success that turned Noël a reasonable profit. Today, it doesn't sound like a great score, not very blithe, and never really catching the spirit. The black humour and irony get lost in songs that flatly express the literal content of the lines and the action. It did, however, suggest enough about both in the Broadway production to work for an audience who hadn't seen the original play.

What the production had, specifically, were those "imponderables" of Noël's. It finished up with two star names: Beatrice Lillie and Tammy Grimes. Tammy was nimbly scaling the Broadway ladder at the time, having scored a recent success in a peculiarly American show called *The Unsinkable Molly Brown* (1960). Any show Bea Lillie decided to grace with her presence always threatened to become *An Evening with Beatrice Lillie*. Noël had experience of working with Beattie (as he always called her), so presumably he could handle that proclivity. A Bea Lillie performance, particularly in her later years, would be like the curate's egg, but the *good* parts could still carry a show.

(Perhaps I should explain that phrase, "the curate's egg," for my American readers. In an 1895 *Punch* cartoon, a nervous young curate is taking breakfast with a senior churchman, and he finds that the boiled egg he has been given is rotten. "I'm afraid you've got a bad egg, Mr. Jones," observes the Bishop. Terminally anxious to please, Mr. Jones stutters nervously, "Oh, no, my Lord, I assure you! Parts of it are excellent!" I've always thought show business was a bit like that....)

Three Broadway musicals in as many years looks, at first glance, like a major triumph. Noël's name was plastered over all of them, yet only *Sail Away* was wholly his creation. The frustration of not being in control of the others was pulling him down. Wherever he turned and whatever he tried, he seemed unable to hit the target cleanly. As he approached his mid-sixties, Noël was finally beginning to lose heart.

During the latter half of 1963 his energies were too dissipated; consequently nothing was done exceptionally. Writing material for *The Girl* and simultaneously trying to cast *High Spirits* left Noël involved in both, but with a decisive voice in neither.

High Spirits was qualified chaos from beginning to end. My full-time job consisted of rushing around trying to put out brush fires before they raged into forest fires. The quirky Tammy was being intermittently fey. Beattie was trying to come to grips with the first scripted part she'd had in years. In the middle of it all was Edward Woodward, wondering whether his role as leading man was more frenzied when the curtain was up or down. Noël would cast a doleful expression my way that started out by asking, "Why?", then resolved itself into, "The money!"

There was a quality of desperation about Noël as the year ended. *The Girl* had come to supper and looked set to stay for breakfast, but she clearly wasn't moving in. Noël needed a genuine, twenty-four-carat diamond-studded success. If it wasn't to be *The Girl*, it *had* to be *High Spirits*. ("We shall see. Oh, indeed, we shall see, and alarmingly soon.") By the following March, with *High Spirits* due to open in early April, Noël was exhausted. Even he could recognise that fatigue might temporarily cloud his judgement. In his heart he knew Ferrer and Henderson lacked the spark to ignite Broadway audiences. He should have insisted on more casting. Instead, he had settled, and now he was stuck. ("I am really very tired indeed. I took on far too much.")

*   *   *   *

His diary entry of March 23, 1964, largely devoted to his frustration over the last two Broadway musicals, contains this curious entry: "My next assignment is *Hay Fever* for the new National Theatre in London, and I intend to worm my way out of it."

The unexpected success of the Hampstead revival of *Private Lives* sparked it, but what really set the notion on fire was Larry Olivier's decision, as Artistic Director, to ask Noël to direct the revival himself after his own calendar became too full. It would be the first presentation of a work by a living playwright at the National. "Dad's Renaissance" was under way.

Technically the decision had been Larry's, but the idea originated from Kenneth Tynan. That most literate and acerbic of critics was now Literary Manager at the National. Larry, thoroughly irritated by Tynan's continuously barbed attentions, had decided that it was more desirable to have Kenneth inside the tent looking out, on the principle that "If you can't beat them, have them join you."

The National Theatre's 1964 revival of Hay Fever *turns the tide. Edith Evans and "A Cast That Could Play the Albanian Telephone Directory."*

For the first time in years, Noël found himself working with a hand-picked cast ("They could play the Albanian telephone directory"). He had Edith Evans as Judith Bliss, Maggie Smith, Robert Stephens, Lynn Redgrave, Sarah Miles, Derek Jacobi and, waiting in the wings as his assistant director, John Dexter. To make doubly certain that London wouldn't miss Dad's return to the West End, *Hay Fever* was scheduled to open on the very same night in early November as *High Spirits*. By another coincidence of booking, both productions would also play in Manchester the week before. Somebody Up There was having a fine old time pulling the strings!

*   *   *   *

We were greedy with *High Spirits*. The sniff of a (qualified) Broadway success was enough to make us want to bring the show over while it was still warm. We clearly couldn't disturb the American company, even though our best chance would have been to wait for Bea Lillie to come available. British audiences still loved her for her post-war successes in *An Evening with Beatrice Lillie* (1954) and *Auntie Mame* (1958). More to the point, she deserved the chance to do it if she wanted to. Without her we'd have had to retitle the thing *Medium-Low Spirits*.

Noël, by now, was "sick to death of the damned thing." A request from Japan for an "all-girl" production put the lid on it. He felt the whole thing was drifting steadily into the realm of the absurd ("I can't wait to see a large-hipped geisha as Dr. Bradman").

I was deputed to co-direct in London with Timothy Gray. I'd never directed before, though I'd seen enough directors in action to have a pretty fair idea of the basics. Perhaps if only one of us had done the job, things might have worked, but while I was trying to keep the production faithful to Noël's original Broadway concept, Tim saw this as a chance to steer the show *his* way. He wanted to broaden it. As custodian of the Coward version, I should have dug my heels in more and insisted. If that didn't work, I should have walked away from the whole thing and explained my reasons, as an experienced director would have done. My inexperience led to too many compromises, and in the end it was no one's show.

On paper everything seemed fine. Our cast included Cicely Courtneidge, Denis Quilley, Fenella Fielding (later replaced by Marti Stevens) and Jan Waters, but it went downhill from there.

Noël couldn't believe his luck in securing Cis ("In the first place, she is a thorough professional and can act. In the second place, she can sing and dance. In the third place, she is quick-witted, intelligent and hilariously funny....") But in the fourth place, she had no intention of playing Madame Arcati as anyone other than Cis Courtneidge! She was also, it turned out, jealous of Beattie for reasons shrouded in the mists of time. Neither was she about to take direction. "If that woman can play Beatrice Lillie in the part, I can play Cis Courtneidge." When Noël, who'd had quite enough of Miss Lillie, got into the act and gave her a Grade One Finger Wag, the whole thing deteriorated further. She complained that Noël was "cruel" to her. Their friendship was never the same high-spirited affair after *High Spirits*.

We still awaited the verdict of the London critics, but the news was that Dad, shaking his head at the irony of it all, was back with a vengeance. Noël stood in front of the television cameras at the Midland Hotel, Manchester, at a cocktail reception for both companies. He fielded questions from youthful interviewers who, until recently, had probably thought Noël Coward was dead. Their inadequate questions betrayed a hurried briefing:

Q.:"Mr. Coward, for some ten years after the war you were almost written off as a 'has-been' in terms of the theatre. Now, quite suddenly, every play that you've written is being chased after by agents. You're now almost the biggest box office in the country. Can you explain this phenomenon?"

A.:"Well, in the first place, nobody of particular importance *wrote me off. And in the second place, I didn't notice it..."*

A flash of his alligator grin would follow. It was a part of the façade he'd carefully maintained throughout those years "in the wilderness." It just didn't happen to be the way he really felt.

The world is supposed to end with a whimper. We began with one. The whole cast of *High Spirits* seemed to know they were beaten from the start. Cis, not being allowed to play Cis, didn't know what else to do except (in Noël's phrase) "vulgarize Madame Arcati." The first night audience, as they so often do, cheered the show they'd *hoped* to see. The next day reality set in. Barely two months later the notices went up.

*   *   *   *

Hay Fever was a totally different story. With a brilliant cast in what may well be Noël's best play, everything came together at just the right moment.

Edith continued to mumble and fumble her way through the part of Judith Bliss, but that old "star quality" came to her aid. The threat of "the Smith gal," word-perfect in the wings, kept her on her toes. Even so, Noël said, she took her curtain calls "as though she had just been un-nailed from the cross." Celia Johnson took over after a while and gave a quite different reading of the part. She was more charming but lacked the comic "attack" the part needs and which Edith, whatever her other shortcomings, was capable of finding.

When Noël's work, confidently written to please no one but himself, is played with respect for the way the words were written, it burns with a clear flame. Compared with a series of collaborations, adaptations and general tinkering to suit a customer, the result is salutary. It was only when you saw what *Hay Fever* could be that you realised what *Blithe Spirit* had become, tricked out in Broadway tinsel.

"Dad's Renaissance didn't come a moment too soon." Of all its positive effects on the legend, not to mention the bank balance, there was one I particularly welcomed: Noel was determined to write for *himself* in future.

There was to be one last hurrah. A year or so earlier Noël had declared his intention to "search for or write a play for myself to do in London next year as a sort of swan-song. I would like to act once more before I fold my bedraggled wings." His first concept was "a series of short plays, two a night, under the collective title of *Neutral Territory;* each play, separate in itself, will take place in a hotel suite in Switzerland."

In the Spring of 1965 Noël started work on the trilogy, *Suite in Three Keys*. The first play, *A Song at Twilight*, had come to mind when he was reading David Cecil's biography of Max Beerbohm. The incident that caught his imagination was when Max, in elegant retirement in Rapallo, was visited by Constance Collier, his mistress from many decades earlier. ("My play is more sinister, and there is Maugham in it as well as Max.") The new wave of popular and critical success he was enjoying liberated him. The dialogue flowed so freely that he talked of "rationing" himself, so that he wouldn't finish it too soon.

Binkie arranged to stage the sequence the following Spring, giving Noël plenty of time to cast the two important female parts. He would, of course, play the three male leads himself. It was to be *Tonight at 8:30* revisited. Nemesis, our familiar neighbour, was waiting in the wings.

There wasn't a single post-war Coward show that didn't suffer on the distaff side. Noël had written the new plays with Irene Worth and Margaret Leighton in mind. Irene duly appeared. Maggie was something else altogether. Ever since they had appeared together in the rather forgettable film of *The Astonished Heart* (1949), Noël had been a devotee. Playing opposite her on stage in *The Apple Cart* (1953) had increased his admiration. By August, we were beginning to see the familiar symptoms of grande dame-ery; the principal difference was that constant exposure to the virus had left Noël immune to patience. Phone call followed frenzied phone call from Maggie. She was dying to do the plays, but she couldn't possibly come to England without her husband, Michael Wilding. But, of course, we'd pay for him, wouldn't we?

Noël and Binkie barked as one that they most certainly would *not*, and Noël acerbically added that Leighton had obviously "gone Hollywood" and gone out of the rest of what passed for her mind. "Forget the whole thing. I'm not having any more of this from anyone!"

Lilli Palmer was our neighbour in Switzerland and Noël had often read excerpts from the trilogy to her as he was writing it. When she heard Noël's decision on Maggie, Lilli exclaimed, "Oh, I'd give anything to play those parts, absolutely *anything!*" So Noël said, "Yours!" I mention this detail mainly to record the way time rearranges memory. In her autobiography, *Change Lobsters and Dance* (1976), Lilli recalls the way Noël drove dramatically to her house to read the parts to her hoping she would consent to play them.

In fact, he read those first two plays to her on the settee in his own house and the decision was made there with me to witness it. Later visits to her with Binkie were after the event.

Ironically, one of Noël's main reasons for pulling the plug on further discussion with Maggie was the Spouse Syndrome. ("I have had enough of stars' husbands and lovers!") To his horror, he discovered that he'd simply exchanged Maggie's Michael Wilding for Lilli's Carlos Thompson, a second-grade star for a third.

It wasn't long before the termites were at work. Glen Byam Shaw, a jewel in the established theatre's crown, was set to direct. Then, with all the agony of a Wolfit death scene, he withdrew on the grounds that Noël would interfere too much. By way of an exit line, he recommended that Noël ditch one of the plays and write a thriller. Vivian Matalon took over.

Lilli hadn't acted on stage in more than ten years and had trouble unlearning her film technique. Noël caustically remarked that she was acting like something out of the German silent cinema: "She has a gesture for every word!"

Carlos loomed up and, bearding Noël in his own dressing room, made the apparently serious suggestion that *he* should direct, since he understood the plays better than either Noël or Vivian and could bring "music" to them. Noël's answer was commendably brief: "It's not a musical. So get out!" Noël had cut his teeth on Richard Halliday, so Carlos was easily seen off. It was just one more hassle he didn't need as he faced one of the biggest battles of his professional career.

Lilli wasn't the only one who had trouble with her lines. An Italian actor, Carlo Palmucci, had been cast in the small part of Felix, the waiter who appears in all three plays. Carlo's grasp of certain English pronunciation was not the surest. He insisted on referring to Sir Hugo's "tastes" as Sir Hugo's "testes." Noël quipped, "I know this play is about homosexuality but that is going *too* far!"

Writing the parts was no problem. The words still flowed. The gift for dialogue was unimpaired. Noël's current problem was *remembering* the lines he'd written. During the run of *Suite in Three Keys* he began to suffer from what every actor most dreads: drying on stage. For someone who had always insisted on word perfection in others, it was abject humiliation, made worse by the fact that he was forgetting words he'd written himself.

Lilli, who had been tiresome since the Carlos episode, came through in the crisis and prompted him gently. Audiences were never aware of the fluffs. In a way, Noël's reputation helped, because if an audience can't conceive of something, they're unlikely to actually see it. On this occasion, at least, the theory worked in practice.

Noël makes no reference to the episode in his *Diaries*, but it was clear to all of us that he knew this particular game was up. His health had been suspect for some time: circulation problems, stomach problems. People who live on their nerves seem more susceptible to illness, and Noël had never quite recovered from the amœbic dysentery he suffered in the Seychelles the previous year. There was a real doubt whether he'd even be able to perform *Suite* in London after the Dublin opening was cancelled. He'd lived at such a pace for so long, he had literally worn himself out.

All was forgotten in the triumph the plays turned out to be. Even the critics forgot to dip their pens in vitriol, and most of the media decided that it was now fashionable to praise Cæsar instead of burying him: "Coward Triumphant As of Old," W.A. Darlington (*Daily Telegraph*); "Noël Coward's Hat Trick;" "Brilliant Coward At His Zenith," Herbert Kretzmer (*Daily Express*).

It was Renaissance Time, and Dad was loving every minute!

Noël with Lilli Palmer and her husband Carlos Thompson. Noël became progressively disenchanted with theatrical spouses - of either gender. (Switzerland, 1972)

come to Jamaica — it's no place like home

Think of the most beautiful place you've yet seen in the world. Jamaica is more so, *outrageously* so. Jamaica's the place to get away *with* it and/or get away *from* it. An (enthused) international "Who's Who" — *not a word* flocks here to do as it pleases. The sun shines all the time. In Jamaica — *never at night* you can find perfect (peace.) Yet the island pulses with theatrical — *peace, peace, perfect peace... and one's loved ones far away* contrasts between new and old, civilized and primitive. If you hanker to see the world, better do that first. Because once here, Jamaica will bewitch you — and may become all of the world you'll ever care to see.

Jamaica, for me, is the loveliest island in the world Noël Coward

only 2 hours away!

come to Jamaica — it's not far from home

"Dear Boy, I never go anywhere without my tea cup!" (1959)

CHAPTER TEN

THE ROOMS WITH A VIEW

A room with a view, and you,
With no one to worry us,
No one to hurry us, through
This dream we've found,
We'll gaze at the sky, and try
To guess what it's all about,
Then we will figure out, why
The world is round.

(*This Year of Grace*)

"I have never liked living anywhere all the year round."

People don't think of Noël as being a homebody but his domestic environment was always important to him. So too was the "family," which included not only his mother and Auntie Vida, but also Gladys, Lornie, Joyce, Coley and myself. Lornie later brought in Joan Hirst. We didn't all live together, though in the London days we were close neighbours. We were a travelling troupe of friends who enjoyed working together, all of us thriving on each other's company.

At the hub of his personal *Cavalcade*, enjoying it most of all, was Noël. Many of us turned up as a character in some play or another, but perhaps I'd rather not know.

When Noël and I met again in the early part of the war, he was living at No. 17 Gerald Road, Pimlico, in what was usually referred to as "The Studio." This was the upper part of a sizeable house near Eaton Square, described by Kenneth Tynan as though it might belong to a landscape painter with a rich Italian mistress. Set back from the road, it was approachable by what *Vogue* termed a "garden passage," but what Gladys preferred to call a "tunnelly thing."

Noël bought No. 1 Burton Mews, which backed onto No. 17 Gerald Road, and knocked the two into one dwelling. Lornie's office was in No.

The famous flat in Gerald Road where so much of Noël's early work was written. (1930's)

1 and there was a bedroom above, which was Coley's. During the war, before Coley's return, it was briefly Noël's, when a German bomb made a shambles of No. 17.

The Studio, with its determinedly *art deco* look, was his London base until he was obliged to sell it as part of his tax "retreat" in the mid-'50's. Its bohemian atmosphere was the inspiration for the many early successes he conceived here. This was before the critics made him the focus of everything they found wrong with that era.

Certainly, the glory years came flooding back as he contemplated leaving it:

> "It is none the less horrid to feel that I shall never live there again, never have relish in the magic power of walking briskly up the alleyway, bounding up the stairs, leaving a 'To be called' note on the round table and retiring to my cosy little bedroom where, let's face it, a *great deal* has happened during the last twenty-six years. The myriad 'somethings on a tray,' the mornings after opening nights, the interminable telephone conversations, the morning séances with Lorn, the ideas conceived and the plans made

and above all the jokes, the rich, wonderful jokes with Lorn and Cole and Little Lad roaring with laughter and me hopping out of bed in the middle of all the hilarity and rushing down to the loo."

When he had the petrol, and could get away at the weekend, he'd motor down to White Cliffs in St. Margaret's Bay, Kent, a house he'd rented in 1945 until he could reclaim Goldenhurst from its Army of Occupation.

During the war it was a criminal offence to use more than your "ration" of petrol for private purposes. Ivor Novello found this out the hard way. The authorities decided to make an example of someone famous in order to make their seriousness well known to the general public. Ivor, who was an innocent in all things practical, was arrested, charged and put in prison for four weeks. Many of his friends were convinced that the experience broke his health and hastened his premature death in 1951 at the age of fifty-eight.

Noël had no intention of risking that fate, but he did rush for the peace and quiet of White Cliffs as often as he could, taking Coley with him. I'd join them on a Saturday evening after my last show. That short break, with

Noël's painting of the White Cliffs that brooded over his first post-war home, White Cliffs.

its rounds of croquet, canasta, singing and general tomfoolery, replenished rather than depleted our energies. The Monday morning return to town was quite definitely the low point of the week.

White Cliffs was rented because the Army had requisitioned Noël's home at Goldenhurst. Its size made it a highly suitable officers' hostel. When we were finally able to reclaim it, after fighting tooth and nail for the inevitable permits, there were media mutterings about favoured treatment. Noël was sick of it. "If giving the Army free board and lodging for the duration of the war isn't contributing to the War Effort," he moaned, "I don't know what is." He conveniently overlooked the fact that the "gift" had been involuntary!

Noël's war wasn't fictional, but it should have been! Contrary to the repeated contentions of the press, Noël desperately wanted to get right into the heart of things. He could see himself quite clearly in an heroic role but nobody would take him seriously. How could Noël Coward be in the front line? That was the general reaction, starting with Churchill, who said: "Go and sing to them when the guns are firing, that's your job!" Noël felt like retorting, "What earthly good is *that* going to do, if they can't hear the lyrics for the sound of the guns?"

Eventually, he was signed up for a secret service job to be based in Paris, and he took a flat in the Place Vendôme. Noël's responsibilities were a secret even to him, so he improvised. He'd be a "creative" spy:

> "There was a saying, much quoted in the war years, that if
> an Englishman told you he was a secret agent it was a lie,
> and that if an American told you the same, it was true."
> (*Future Indefinite*)

When the Royal Air Force started bombing Berlin, the German propaganda machine went into full blown denial. There *were* no attacks, it was all a Great British Lie. God knows who the poor German civilians thought was bombing the hell out of them night after night.

Noël suggested that we drop huge bundles of confetti over Berlin, sticky on one side, with "We're British" and the Union Jack printed on them. His theory was that they would adhere to the pavements, so the authorities couldn't pick them up fast enough to prevent the general public from reading them. They'd also look pretty stupid trying. The high command gave him a funny look and said they'd think about this somewhat unorthodox proposal. After that, things went from bad to worse.

Nothing he suggested seemed to please them. At one point he sent a memo To Whom It Might Possibly Concern: "If the policy of His

Majesty's Government is to *bore* the Germans to death, I don't think we have time." He once tried to put through a coded telephone call to the War Department. He would get confused and the Department kept demanding, "What the hell are you talking about?" Finally, in frustration, he spelled out the code on the phone ("L for Lion," etc.) and buggered up the whole thing. Soon after that it was suggested that Noël should spend some time in the States, trying to "sell" the neutral Americans on the idea of joining the war. The Press naturally erupted with more stories about Noël running away from the war. He just couldn't win. It was only the enormous number of front line troop concerts he gave later that shut them up.

The Press were not alone in their misconception of Noël's temporary status; his friends were also concerned. Adrianne Allen, the original Sybil in *Private Lives*, immediately contacted him and implored him to persuade Prime Minister Neville Chamberlain, and Monsieur Daladier, the French equivalent, to obtain the help of President Roosevelt. Noël replied, "Though internationally bossy, I am not yet internationally authoritative. I fear the gentlemen you mention might conceivably resent my telling them how to read their lines."

One good thing that came from Noël's Paris stint was the Place Vendôme apartment, which we used after the liberation and during those strange post-war years. Noël loved the place and dearly wanted to keep it. It later came up for sale for the French equivalent of £7,000, a paltry sum, but it was illegal to take money out of the UK at that time. Noël asked his old friend, the designer Edward Molyneux, to lend him the money. Since he lived in Paris, that should have been easy enough, but Edward turned out to be frugal with a franc and made the excuse that all his currency was tied up in stocks and bonds. That didn't, however, deter Edward from accepting a good deal more than £7,000 worth of hospitality in Jamaica a few years later.

Paris was always special to Noël and he was very despondent about leaving the Place Vendôme to the tender mercies of the Nazis. He would lament that now we'd never see the Paris he'd known.

He was deeply touched when Jerome Kern dedicated "The Last Time I Saw Paris" to him. It is not widely appreciated that when Noël recorded it, he sang it in Kern's original upbeat tempo. Most interpreters render it as a ballad, about half the tempo that Noël adopted. Far be it from me to argue with the combined talents of Messrs. Kern and Coward, but I think that exquisite song is better done slower, and yes, I *can* feel a finger wagging somewhere.

*   *   *   *

From the day in 1945 when Noël bought the lease from socialite Kay Norton over lunch at the Caprice, White Cliffs was our home for the next six years. It was a dramatic little spot, to say the least. Noël had always loved the sea and the house nestled at the end of a beach with the famous cliffs looming above.

The sea actually lapped or, according to its mood, pounded against the wall of Noël's own room, something he found either intensely romantic or "bloody irritating," according to his own mood. As a place to work, it had its limitations. Noël reflected later: "...I have never worked really well here - there is something curiously distracting about it; someone crunches by on the beach or a big ship passes and one's concentration snaps."

It was, because of its strategic position, requisitioned by the military "for security reasons." We Brits had a fixation for standing on the Kentish cliffs and peering in the general direction of Abroad, trying to spot Adolf's Armada approaching. Just what we'd do if they did turn up was never entirely clear. Give them a good talking to, beat them round the head with broomsticks and send them packing, probably. Many shoreline houses suffered an English Army of Occupation that left their temporary quarters in a state of dilapidation. Mr. Hitler could scarcely have inflicted worse.

White Cliffs did not escape this treatment, but Noël persevered. He and Coley, with a little help from Gladys and local friends, restored most of it with their own hands. My impeccable sense of timing, helped by my appearance in *Sigh No More*, ensured that I didn't move in until the backbreaking work was safely over. Even then, it was, as Noël remarked, "no Blenheim." There was no electricity and some of the windows were missing, but we managed. Five years of war has to prepare you for *something*.

Noël had the idea of annexing three other small houses nearby to form a sort of private "colony." This was very much against the spirit of the times. If "N. Coward" had appeared on all the rent books, we could have expected another barrage of bad publicity, but "C. Lesley" and "L. Loraine" drew no one's attention. The Eric Amblers moved in, as did Noël's Mum and Auntie Vida, and with Gladys literally overhead, it really became a family affair.

As soon as we were shipshape, the weekend guests began arriving, usually driven down after the Saturday evening show by Joycie and myself: Gertie, Daphne du Maurier, Ian Fleming and his future wife, Ann (who eventually acquired the house from Noël), the Lunts, the Joseph Cottens, Rebecca West, and Winifred Ashton, who immortalised our latest craze by painting us all playing canasta.

Noël would stay as many days in his refuge as he could manage. Much of *Pacific 1860* and *Ace of Clubs* was written there. I'd often find Noël and Coley labouring away. Coley was developing his skills on translations, and helping Noël with research.

The serious drawback at White Cliffs, other than the occasionally cruel sea, was the presence of those damn "white cliffs," which are a lot less threatening in song than when they are brooding overhead. Noël was forced to have one section wired up for safety, and long after we'd all moved on, it finally fell, crushing the room which had been Noël's. The unfortunate tenants were, fortunately, away.

Noël was basically a simple domestic person. Not that he was forever rushing round doing household jobs. Anything mechanical, he'd throw up his hands and walk away, but he enjoyed his creature comforts as well as the next man. Visitors to Firefly since his death comment on how "ordinary" it is, presumably meaning that they expect extraordinary people to live in extraordinary settings. But why should they?

Noël was also a great pet lover. Soon after I moved in, a friend of my mother's gave him a little grey poodle called Matelot, in memory of the song. Since Matelot was frequently home alone, I bought another one called Wait a Bit, Joe (also in memory of *Sigh No More*). To save the poor dog from becoming neurotic, we shortened his name to Joe.

Matelot, like all members of the Coward household, turned out to be quite the entertainer. Whenever a Deanna Durbin record was on, Matelot would put his paws on the gramophone and give his canine rendition. Only Deanna Durbin would set him off, which says something about his musical taste, though I'm not sure what. "I'll Follow My Secret Heart" would probably have won him more brownie points from Noël.

*   *   *   *

Noël considered Goldenhurst his true home in England. He'd discovered the farm in 1927, when he and Jack Wilson returned from a trip to America.

> "There was the house proper which was lop-sided and had a Victorian air; jammed up against this was the 'new wing,' a square edifice wearing perkily a pink corrugated tin roof and looking as though it had just dropped in on the way to the races. There was a muddy yard enclosed by thatched barns which were falling to pieces, there were two small ponds, five poplars, a ramshackle garden consisting almost entirely of hedges, and an ancient, deeply green orchard with thick grass and low-growing apple-

trees....The house itself was indeed poky and quite hideous, made up into dark little rooms and passages, but there was a certain atmosphere about the place that felt soothing and somehow right...."

(Present Indicative)

Because of its shabby appearance, the owners had it on the market at a knock-down price. It turned out to be a seventeenth-century farmhouse with its original oak beams intact under flaking plaster, which Noël and Jack rapidly removed. Noël also added private quarters for Mrs. Coward and Auntie Vida. He brought in Syrie Maugham, ex-wife of Willie and one of London's top interior decorators, to "gentrify" the place.

By the time it was finished, it possessed all the elements of a country house in a Noël Coward play. If you'd walked through those French windows in *Hay Fever*, you'd have been disappointed not to see a tree-lined walk, a croquet lawn, and a duck pond into which a recklessly-driven sports car might plunge (and occasionally did). The guest list at Goldenhurst was the pre-war social, political and theatrical *Who's Who*, supplemented by "family" members like Gladys, who had a small mill house close by.

Goldenhurst. *The Library. The books behind the wire netting were part of Noël's collection of first editions.*

Jack Wilson, Anthony Eden and Noël. (Goldenhurst, 1938)

The outbreak of war abruptly altered that.

What was particularly upsetting later, was the casual way the Army hung on to the place, long after they'd finished with it, without even letting us know. It was 1951 before we staged *The Return to Goldenhurst.* Noël confided to his *Diaries:* "...I decided that I am going to... go back to Goldenhurst....I shall miss the sea and the ships, but I shall have the marsh and the trees, the orchard and the croquet lawn."

Permits to renovate presented the first big problem. In those early post-war years it seemed you needed a permit to get a permit. On Noël's fifty-second birthday, after his last night of cabaret at the Café de Paris, we moved into Goldenhurst. ("Probably the nicest birthday I have ever had...the house and land seemed to envelop me in a warm and lovely welcome.")

How Goldenhurst II compared with the original I'm not qualified to say. Less hectic, I imagine, less of a golden summer haze and more in keeping with the kind of life post-war Britain dictated. To me it felt fine. There were weekends of idle conversation and laughter with the "family" and a steady flow of visitors like the Lunts, Larry and Viv, and Kay.

On Friday evening or Saturday morning, the guests arrived. Noël allocated the bedrooms according to a system known only to himself. The prize was the Four-Poster Room. Quite a few famous bodies spent the night in that bed, including Garbo, Dietrich and Hepburn, though not all at the same time, I hasten to add. After settling in, the guests would congregate in the Sitting Room for drinks and conversation. On one of England's occasional Summer days, we'd rush to sit out on the terrace.

The events were entirely spontaneous: a walk down the lanes, a drive off to do some shopping, a game of croquet on the lawn. It was important to avoid playing against Noël; he wielded a mean mallet and wasn't above "debating" the rules.

In the evenings there'd be a gathering of the Canasta Clan, while that infuriating game held its spell; a little impromptu piano playing, which inevitably ended with Noël being dragged to the piano and, later, having to be almost forcibly removed *from* it.

Mostly, there was talk. There was no formal Madame de Sévigné-like *salon*, just an irrepressible flood of ideas, opinions and prejudices from some of the most articulate people of the time. Not for them the carefully polished *bons mots* of the Algonquin Round Table, slipped into a vest pocket, ready to be dropped. These were the unedited outpourings of genuine friends who enjoyed the cut-and-thrust of informal badinage at each other's expense. They would not, like the Round Tablers, claim to be "Wits," but the Goldenhurst Group had more genuine fun.

On Monday morning the caravans, with their captains and kings, would depart, and peace would be restored to the Kent countryside. Until the next Friday.

The time eventually came to move on. Noël was disenchanted with England. The personal vindictiveness of the press, which went far beyond critical rejection, would have been reason enough, but financial considerations played an important rôle.

Most of Noël's considerable earnings had vanished straight into the tax man's pocket. When his accountant adroitly pointed out that Noël could look forward to being old, famous and poor, there was really no alternative. Noël was forced to sell his UK "residence," which meant sacrificing the home in Gerald Road for £11,000, then Goldenhurst for a measly £5,750!

In 1956, he made the mistake of moving to Bermuda. Because of its tax status, but for no other reason, Bermuda made logical sense, but it had no individual ethos, though many of the people were charming to us. They were thrilled to have a celebrity in their midst, but the incessant social invitations impinged on the private space Noël always craved. The solitary life he maintained at White Cliffs or Goldenhurst was totally eroded in this island version of suburbia. There was literally nowhere to go that didn't involve swimming! It didn't take long to realise we'd yet to reach our safe harbour.

For a while the South of France offered possibilities. Noël had always enjoyed its pre-war ambiance: eating out of doors, the beaches, a little light gambling, a few chums always somewhere down the road. We would go to Edward's place near Antibes until there was the falling-out over money, but Noël was seeing the Côte d'Azur through memory's rose-tinted eye. It was no longer the hazy, lazy days of endless summer with Maxine Elliott and her group. The reality of the 1950's was a whole lot grittier.

Noël's financial advisers were leaning heavily towards Switzerland. Coley was deputed to lead the search and, through an ad in the *Daily Telegraph*, located a chalet in the Vaud canton, high above Montreux on Lake Geneva. He and Noël went to see it and immediately realised its potential. Noël complained about the "ugly 1900 chalet quality of the house," but after a brief conversation with the owners, Colonel and Mrs. Petrie (and £12,000 later), Noël was the reasonably proud owner of several rooms with a view.

Except that there was none. The house was dark, sheltered by a stand of huge fir trees. One of Noël's first acts as owner, in "ignorance" of local law, was to remove the trees. The Petries were horrified until they saw for

The living room in Switzerland. Drawing by Joe Layton.

Noël in Switzerland with Louis Mountbatten, Oona Chaplin, Lynn, Alfred, and Charlie Chaplin. (September 1971)

themselves. Mrs. Petrie murmured, sadly and quietly, "I'd *forgotten* the view." There, on a clear day, you could not see Marlowe, but the whole spread of Lake Geneva.

Our second stroke of luck was Jean-René. Noël was suffering from circulatory problems in his legs, but was lazy about taking any form of exercise beyond reaching for a cigarette. When he made the move to Switzerland in 1959, several friends recommended various exclusive health centres, one of the country's leading industries. Noël was less than enthusiastic until someone recommended the alternative of a masseur who'd make house visits. Through another ad we found a young blond giant of a man, Jean-René. From his qualifications, it became clear that he was only incidentally a masseur. His forte was as a chef.

All these years later, Jean-René is still the chef, major domo and general driving force within the Coward household. Now a proud husband and father, he does everything from answering the phone to building a conservatory, and anything he doesn't do, his wife, Gladys, does.

For purely practical reasons the house will remain anonymous. Fans think they *own* the object of their admiration. Day after day, they'll ring the doorbell or simply stroll round the garden. "So *this* is where he lived!"

They seem to regard the house's occupants as the intruders. It's almost a quarter of a century since Noël died, and their numbers don't diminish. The interest is flattering but you can't live that way. So we prefer to live *Chez No Name.*

It was Goldenhurst *sur-les-Alpes.* Once we were established, we discovered that many of our neighbours were friends. The Charlie Chaplins were *down* the hill, the David Nivens were *up* the hill. Joan Sutherland and her husband stayed with us while *they* were house-hunting. Joan, looking at the house next door, mused plaintively, "I don't suppose *that's* for sale?" "We won't know until we ask," said Noël grandly, naturally leaving someone else to do the asking.

Enquiries turned up the fact that our Unknown Neighbour was a Brit who was pining away among the pines for lack of English television! Joan picked up the place for a song, without ever having to open her mouth.

Noël was particularly fond of Audrey Hepburn and would have been devastated to see her die so young. That fawn-like little face brightened many an Alpine gathering.

It became our Boxing Day ritual to visit David and Hjordis Niven. We would take the small local train, exchange presents, drink numerous Bloody Marys, make lots of noise and eventually stagger back onto the

Yul and Doris Brynner, Noël, Audrey Hepburn and her husband, Mel Ferrer. (Switzerland, 1965)

A Swiss Christmas. *Noël accompanies our neighbour, Joan Sutherland...* *(1967)*

train home. All very pointless, but very enjoyable. As inevitably as Boxing Day follows Christmas Day, this ritual went on as long as Noël was alive. Then, nothing. No Noël, no Niven Boxing Day. Lynn and Alfred, Kit Cornell, Liz Taylor and many others met Coley and me through Noël, but over the years we'd become chums in our own right. David and Hjordis were the only ones who defined their friendship for us quite so narrowly.

*   *   *   *

Jamaica was everything that Bermuda wasn't. The only thing they had in common was that they were both surrounded by sea! Jamaica had hot sun and wild rain. Bermuda just had rain. It reminded Noël of Eastbourne, except he couldn't catch a train up to town.

In 1954, in *Future Indefinite*, Noël recorded his first glimpse of the island:

> "My first view of Jamaica was from an altitude of about eight thousand feet. The morning was cloudless and the island was discernible from many miles away. Now, remembering that moment...my mind becomes choked with clichés. 'Had I but known then...' 'Little did I dream...' 'If only I could have foreseen...', but of course I didn't know or dream or foresee how familiar that particular sight would become, how many times in the

future I was destined to see these green hills and blue mountains rising out of the sea."

My first sight of Jamaica was after the New York reception to *Tonight at 8:30*. Adrianne Allen assured Noël it was the perfect place for him, so he accepted an invitation to use Ian Fleming's house there. Ian called it Goldeneye, but if that evokes some grand hacienda *à la* James Bond, disabuse yourself of the idea. "Sparse" would be a generous description. Noël immediately rechristened it "Golden Eye, Nose and Throat," in keeping with its clinical appointments. The food was so abominable that Noël would cross himself before taking a mouthful. Ian would later have a few choice words of his own about Noël's domestic arrangements: "Noël's 'firefly' house is a near disaster....The rain pours into it from every angle and even through the stone walls, so that the rooms are running with damp."

Who cared about a house, when you had that sun and those beaches, in the halcyon days before tourists discovered Jamaica and before the Jamaicans themselves had spoiled what they had?

During one of our exploratory drives, a cardboard "For Sale" sign nailed to a palm tree led us to a parcel of land that was to become the site

Jamaica. *A swim at Blue Harbour. Only later did we find sharks inside the netting...*

of "Blue Harbour." The land was on the side of a very steep hill going down to the beach. We spent hours playing amateur architects, deciding how the house would be built on different layers like steps, a Jamaican version of the Hanging Gardens of Babylon. Very grand. A guaranteed centre spread in *Architectural Digest*.

A year later, we returned to find that the local architect had totally ignored our instructions. He'd cut down all the wonderful trees and built the house straight up in a single structure. "Oh my God," gasped Noël. "It looks bloody awful. It's just like the Flatiron Building in New York. Get some trees and plant them quickly!" Blue Harbour, beautiful as it was in its own right, would never live up to our dreams for it. Sharks discovered cruising inside the safety area didn't help, either!

Noël wrote a verse which summed up the conflicting charms of his chosen island:

> *Jamaica's an island surrounded by sea*
> *(Like Alderney, Guernsey and Sark are)*
> *It's wise not to dive with exuberant glee*
> *Where large barracuda and shark are.*
> *The reefs are entrancing; the water is clear,*
> *The colouring couldn't be dreamier*
> *But one coral scratch and you may spend a year*
> *In bed with acute septicemia.*

Jamaica could legitimately lay claim to being an island paradise in those days. The house could be left with the shutters open and the door unlocked. Sadly, it wasn't long before bolts, bars and, later, a security guard had to be installed. Still, we did enjoy a brief moment in Paradise.

We knew that Jamaica could be only our holiday home. We were city people. Living forever on an island couldn't ultimately satisfy Noël. He would always need his regular fix of London, New York and beyond. But Jamaica became a vital part of his life, a place to take refuge, to sort out ideas and impressions and transform them into colourful creations. Most of his later writing was done in Jamaica.

Ian Fleming was a fascinating man. He and Noël enjoyed a camaraderie based on teasing each other with word games and general wit-upmanship. Ian wrote all the early Bond books at Goldeneye and would present them to Noël to read before they were published. Noël, recognizing they were quite outside his own range, thought they were terrific. Never was the wagging finger raised. Noël's portrait of the MI5

In tropical times there are certain times of day… Jamaica 1960's

operative in the film of *Our Man in Havana* (1959) was his own satirical comment on Ian's work (which was a satire in its own right).

In spite of the success of the Bond novels, no television offer was forthcoming, so Ian persuaded me to take *Casino Royale* to the BBC. It would have made a wonderful series because each chapter was written as a complete episode. They politely declined on the grounds that shooting on location would be far too expensive. This was probably the best favour I ever did Ian. If I'd been a more persuasive salesman, he'd have got BBC scale fees instead of the big film series that came along later. He lived long enough to enjoy at least the start of that success.

Ironically, when the first Bond feature was made in 1962, Noël was offered the part of Dr. No himself! He would have been marvellous, but he turned it down in a telegram that read, "No, no, no, a 1,000 times No!" Joseph Wiseman, who eventually played the part, looked every bit like Noël's description of himself in an early celebrity photo: "Sitting up in an over-elaborate bed looking like a heavily-doped Chinese Illusionist."

For a while, there was a story going around Jamaica that Ian, tongue firmly in cheek, had based the character of Pussy Galore in *Goldfinger* on Blanche Blackwell, the lady who'd sold land to both of them, and who is a wonderful friend to this very day. Blanche was always, shall we say, colourful, and if she *wasn't* the original Miss Galore she *should* have been!

Ian's literary intrigues were matched only by his own personal dramas. Ian had never married, but at last he fell in love with Ann, the Lady Rothermere. She contrived against all odds to sneak off and stay with Ian at Goldeneye. Noël would conspire in protecting their privacy. Whenever Beaverbrook was on the island, for instance, I would rush over to smuggle Annie back to Blue Harbour, where she was *supposed* to be staying. Max's papers would have had a field day with the story. Later, of course, it all came into the open. She and Ian had a child, married and settled down, but for a while there, I was scuttling about like $003\frac{1}{2}$! Licensed to spill the beans. Fortunately, I never did!

Noël went to great pains to protect their *liaison*, despite his friendship with Rothermere. If the Rothermere press had combined with Beaverbrook against him, it would have done irreparable damage, but for Noël friendship came first.

He was guided by his affection for Ian. Ann he took on trust, as we all did, but at the back of our minds was the lingering suspicion that she was using Ian. Ann's first husband had already left her "comfortable" when she married Esmond, Lord Rothermere, who was not exactly impecunious or lacking the odd stately home. Ian was the forbidden fruit which she made very little obvious effort to resist. When she became pregnant, she refused an abortion and duly became Ann Fleming in 1952.

In happy endings, friends are supposed to fall on each other's shoulders, but once she had snared Ian, Ann's "old friends" rapidly became dispensable.   The publication of her letters in 1985 clarified her methodology.   It was clear that she never really liked Noël at all.   "The answer to Noël is that he 'should be used as a cabaret and not as a guest, he does not understand the give and take of talk and the deserts of pomposity between the oases of wit are too vast.'"   "It is ungrateful of me to be catty," but while 'he continues to pose as intimate friend of the royal family' it is irresistible."

Her "ingratitude" did not begin and end with Noël.   Elsewhere in her letters are irritating anti-Semitic diminutives, supposedly affectionate but revealing an underlying patronisation.   Binkie is referred to as "Binkelstein," Cecil Beaton as "Beatnik" and Graham Greene's then mistress, Catherine Walston, as "Mrs. Wolfstein."

Noël was very sensitive to Ann's social body language: "...when surrounded by her own set...she changes completely and becomes shrill and strident, like one of those doomed Michael Arlen characters of the Twenties.   I am really surprised that Ian doesn't sock her in the chops and tell her to shut up."

By the late 1950's, it was clear that the gilt had tarnished on Goldeneye. Ann was anxiously reassuring her true inner circle that she hadn't sold out to these "terrible people."   What she didn't know was that many of those terrible people had suffered her and her tedious dinner parties purely for Ian's sake.   At heart she was the worst kind of pseudo-intellectual and the dish most often on her social menu was sour grapes.   It's too bad that, on one of my mercy missions, the car didn't "accidentally" break down in front of Max Beaverbrook's house.   It might have saved us all a lot of aggravation.

*   *   *   *

We'd been in Blue Harbour for only a matter of weeks when we made another fortuitous discovery.   While out driving, we found ourselves on a little plateau with a breathtaking view of the Spanish Main.   The place was called "Look Out," so named by Captain Henry Morgan, the sometime Governor of Jamaica, who had used it in his pirate days for just that purpose: a place from where he could spot likely prey.   All that remained was a stone ruin, but Noël put a new roof on it and made it into a couple of guest suites.   No-one was destined to stay there, however, because as "Firefly Hill" it became his personal haven.

He bought the five-acre plot at £10 an acre from Blanche, and built a very simple, unpretentious little place with only one bedroom.   Noël described it as a "tiny, ungrand house."   Anyone was welcome to visit him and spend the day there, but after evening drinks guests were firmly dispatched down to the house on Blue Harbour.

Even before the house was completed, we'd go up there for our evening drinks and take in that incredible view. Noël had his favourite spot, which is where he's now buried. As dusk fell over the Spanish Main, the fireflies would come out like enormous jewels and flit around us. It was a magical moment of spontaneous theatre. What else could he call it but "Firefly"?

The world and his wife, or in some cases, someone else's wife, started to come to the island, and many of Noël's friends bought houses there.

Ivor had a very small back-to-back kind of house in Montego Bay. Perhaps it reminded him of Wales. Noël loathed it. Gladys bought a house there. Noël and Ivor *both* loathed it. Max Beaverbrook's house was anything but suburban. Edward Molyneux, who made a hobby of building houses all over the place (which is presumably why he couldn't lend Noël the £7,000 for Place Vendôme), had his latest acquisition decorated entirely in yellow with yellow flowers. Noël and Ian promptly christened it "Jaundice House."

Edward, frankly, was a pain. He was talented and great fun, but after the second martini his whole personality would change. He'd had an eye operation and Noël invited him to come to Jamaica to recuperate, but as soon as he saw that Blue Harbour was built on a steep hill, Edward was off on a blue streak. He complained of vertigo; he was afraid he would fall over the edge; he didn't like sunbathing; he didn't like fresh fruit. Noël calmly suggested that he move on. Next thing we knew he was over in Montego Bay, complaining to some other friends. Mr. Molyneux and Noël had been friends for many years and had happily quarrelled for most of them.

"Creative quarrelling" was a fashion in the '30's. People would insult each other one moment and be best buddies the next. The Algonquin Round Table group was the shining example, but it was common in Europe too, at least in Noël's social circle.

I learned this etiquette the hard way. In my naïveté, I thought that friends were supposed to be polite to each other. A weekend with Jack and Natasha Wilson shattered that illusion. Natasha ran an *haute couture* shop which designed the dresses for a revival of *Private Lives*. Noël thought the dresses were terrible and said so very plainly. Natasha snapped back at him and a real row blew up. When it started looking serious, I attempted to intervene. George Cukor pulled me aside, shaking his head, and said, "Hey, Little Lad, don't be Pollyanna. It's the usual jargon with this lot. Forget it!" He was quite right. Five minutes later they were all laughing and playing croquet.

Alec Guinness came to stay just before he and Noël began shooting *Our Man in Havana*, a film which many people felt Noël "stole" and which later caused a certain *froideur* on Alec's part. Things were never quite the same after Alec was promised the part of King Magnus in Shaw's *The Apple Cart* during Coronation Year, after Noël had finished his contracted three-month run. Alec refused.

I remember driving Maggie Smith up that pock-marked track from Blue Harbour to Firefly for the ritual evening cocktail hour. Looking at the smiling faces of the locals as we passed by, she enquired in her distinctive creaking voice: "What strange religious ceremony do the natives believe we come here to observe?"

Noël adored Maggie. He awarded the ultimate accolade of describing her as being "almost as vulgar as Gertie." The halo would occasionally slip. For a while she was playing *Private Lives* virtually non-stop on both sides of the Atlantic. When she gets used to a part, Maggie is inclined to "highlight" it, so after watching her once, Noël had to resort to the dressing room Finger Wag. "Not *Kenneth Williams on Ice*, if you don't mind, dear!" Her performance immediately straightened out.

She was particularly over the top in Chicago, playing opposite John Standing. Then, something happened that affected her more than any direction from Noël. Someone sent her a copy of the original text, and she was so moved by reading it that she completely revised her performance for the New York opening. "How long did it last?" Noël asked John, later. "A few...weeks?" John responded tactfully.

Maggie was one of the more "energetic" guests at Firefly, frequently standing on her head on the lawn out of sheer exuberance. You can't say *that* about your average Dame.

Graham Greene visited more than once. He and Noël had kept a polite distance in earlier years. Greene had been critically dismissive of much of Noël's work, calling *Blithe Spirit*, for instance, "a weary exhibition of bad taste." When they finally met in 1949, there was a wary thawing.

Three or four years later he stayed at Blue Harbour for the first time, having taken great pains to assure himself that we had "enough double beds." He and his friend, Mrs. Walston, duly arrived and we heard no complaints about the facilities. On subsequent visits the accommodation stayed the same, even though the "friend" might vary. He clearly believed you should sup with sin before you write about it. He later told Noël that he had been wrong about *Blithe Spirit* and that it was really a very good play. Perhaps the realisation came to him on one of those comfortable Jamaican mattresses.

Kate Hepburn came with Irene Selznick and left us a souvenir of a tree painted on bark. I simply thought of it as a charmingly original idea until

*Mad dogs, Englishmen and – apparently – Noël Coward go out in the midday sun...
(1937)*

I saw her interviewed on *The Barbara Walters Show*. She said she'd like to *be* a tree. Perhaps the idea came to her in Jamaica!

When the Lunts came, Noël took Lynn, who had never been to Jamaica before, to enjoy one of his favourite views of the island. They climbed a mountain track with precipitous drops on either side, until breathlessly they reached the top. Noël showed her, with great pride, the terraces, the forest, the distant beach, the sparkling Caribbean. What, he enquired, did she think? Lynn's one-track mind instinctively adjudged, "It looks like a bad matinée with rows and rows of empty seats."

One of my duties was to drive guests from Blue Harbour up to Firefly to spend the day with Noël. The track was almost non-existent, but I became adept at weaving my way round the potholes at quite a speed. A glimpse of white knuckles would make me realise that this was not exactly the excitement our guests anticipated, but I'd put the more nervous at their ease by pointing out that the Queen Mother had navigated this very same track in a Rolls-Royce!

Noël would be sitting at the open window, enjoying the view and a cigarette in equal measure, waiting to hold court. In later years it took a lot of persuasion to evict him from his favourite spot.

On hot days, when the pool looked particularly inviting, I'd try to coax Noël in for a swim. He needed to stimulate his faulty circulation, but getting him to take exercise was the very devil. He was like a child inventing excuses to miss school. A gust of wind and it would be blowing a hurricane. A patch of cloud and he had no intention of going out when a storm was clearly imminent. It was a contest he won more often than not.

When he could be persuaded to swim, he'd invariably go naked. When diving became too much for him, he'd jump in at the deep end, holding his nose like a young boy skinny-dipping at the local pond.

He wasn't playing the piano much any more, partly because they were soon out of tune in that damp climate. He still liked to sing and, as the years went by, he returned with total recall to the songs of his youth: old music hall songs by artistes like Albert Chevalier, Gilbert and Sullivan, snatches of long-forgotten operettas; less and less his own material.

In the evenings, before we were banished to Blue Harbour, we'd watch the sun go down while Miguel, as barman, served us his version of "cocktails." You never knew quite what to expect; you could only be sure it wouldn't taste the same way twice.

Of the many evenings we spent like that, one sticks in my mind. About a year before Noël died, the cocktail group included Joan Sutherland and her husband, Richard Bonynge. We'd been enjoying an impromptu singalong, when Joan tenderly took Noël's hand and sang to him "I'll See You Again." That pure voice against the dark velvet sky was one of the most moving experiences of my life. When she'd finished, there was complete silence. Noël broke it with, "Goodnight, my darlings," his ritual farewell. It was too dark to see if there was a tear in Noël's eye, but I know there was one in mine.

After Noël's death the property at Firefly came to me. In 1978, I gave it to the Jamaican National Trust to be turned into a national monument. I never had the heart to use it again and I hoped it might bring pleasure to Noël's devotees.

I began receiving reports from friends and other visitors to the island, telling me that lack of attention and the punitive climate were causing serious damage to Firefly's fragile structure. The terrible state of the Jamaican economy meant that there were no funds for what they surely considered a "luxury" project. There was also a very real fear on my part that any money donated by friends would not find its way to the project. The result was an unsatisfying stalemate.

Many visitors were struck by Firefly's simple domesticity: the clothes left on the shelf, the spectacles by the bed. Others were angry at the decay of the place: the ivory piano keys falling off the Bechstein and the Chappell grand pianos, the rain blowing in on the murals. What sort of memorial was this for one of England's finest? They couldn't know that I no longer had any say in things, but still it hurt.

Occasionally there'd be a wry smile. A lady from the Trust wrote to tell me that Mr. Coward's "old books," many of them first editions, were rotting on the shelves. But I was not to worry, as they were being replaced by paperbacks "in much prettier colours"! The "old books" probably went straight in the bin. They should never have been exposed to that climate in the first place.

In the late '80's, thanks to the efforts of a number of devoted admirers, the place was restored to reasonable order and even became a top tourist attraction. But disaster struck in 1989 when Hurricane Gilbert tore off most of the roof. It really looked as though we weren't *meant* to win, until along came our White Knight in the shape of Chris Blackwell, founder of Island Records and son of the legendary Blanche. The Blackwells are an old Jamaican family and the land on which Firefly was built used to belong to them. In a way, they'd come home.

Chris took out a twenty-five year lease on the property, as well as on Ian Fleming's Goldeneye, and totally restored it. At the official reopening in December, 1993, I saw it again with a strange mixture of feelings. It was wonderful to see the old place looking crisp and clean with its newly painted face and fresh plantings, but somehow it wasn't the place I'd known, slightly shabby and very much lived in. The voices had gone. It looked like Firefly, but it wasn't Firefly. I could leave now, once and for all.

Excusing myself from the other guests, I took one more quiet walk around the garden, ending up by Noël's grave. The protective railings had been removed, as if to give him an uninterrupted view of the vista he loved so much. The laughter of the guests and the tinkling of their glasses seemed to fade into the sound of three old friends talking endlessly about nothing much all those years ago, as they waited to see who could spot the first of the evening's fireflies starting to glow.

Raising my glass, I made a silent toast: "You know, I do believe we've risen above it."

Firefly then and now. Though the house is happily restored, the pool has been filled in.

We Three...*With Joycie and Coley. (Switzerland, 1969)*

CHAPTER ELEVEN

THE FAMILY THAT PLAYS TOGETHER

When I have fears, as Keats had fears,
Of the moment I'll cease to be
I console myself with vanished years
Remembered laughter, remembered tears,
And the peace of the changing sea.

When I feel sad, as Keats felt sad,
That my life is so nearly done
It gives me comfort to dwell upon
Remembered friends who are dead and gone
And the jokes we had and the fun.

How happy they are I cannot know,
But happy am I who loved them so.

("When I Have Fears")

"I have many friends who I love dearly but all my life I've been able to count the ones who matter the most on the fingers of one hand."

A troupe of characters parades through the *Diaries* like the cast of one of Noël's plays. He referred to them as the "Family," a slightly less frenetic household version of a Kaufman and Hart comedy, where everyone is larger than life and no one notices! We were more light-hearted than screwball, although there were moments.

Scene: The Studio, No. 17 Gerald Road.
Time: Anytime from the early 1930's to the mid-50's.
The upper part of a large house; along one wall is a large dais with an enormous window above it, forming an impromptu stage with a piano at each end. Here The Master indulges his whim to duet with the great, the good and the merely adequate.

A woman enters from stage left. Handsome, neat but not particularly chic. There is humour in the way she emerges from her office in the mews behind the Studio, where a door has been knocked through. She carries a shoe box full of letters and magazines to The Master, who waits in his bed to begin the inviolate morning ritual:

> "We had two letter files, known as 'Poppy' and 'Queen Anne' respectively, and a sinister cardboard-box labelled 'Shortly,' into which we put all the letters we felt incapable of answering at the moment. About once in every month or so it overflowed and we had to concentrate, finding, to our delight, that lapse of time had made unnecessary to answer at all at least three-quarters of its contents."
>
> (*Present Indicative*)

If this scene seems familiar, it's because it appeared in *Present Laughter;* Noël played Garry Essendine and his secretary, Monica, was Lorn Loraine.

As the play opens, Daphne, latest victim of Garry Essendine's much-practised charm, emerges from the spare room, where she has spent the night. Monica enters with the mail and Daphne tries to pump her for information:

DAPHNE: *Have you been with him for a long while?*

MONICA: *Just on seventeen years.*

DAPHNE: (enthusiastically) *How wonderful! I expect you know him better than anybody.*

MONICA: *Less intimately than some, better than most.*

DAPHNE: *Is he happy, do you think? I mean really happy?*

MONICA: *I don't believe I've ever asked him.*

DAPHNE: *He has a sad look in his eyes every now and then.*

MONICA: *Oh, you noticed that, did you?*

DAPHNE: *We talked for hours last night. He told me all about his early struggles.*

MONICA: *Did he by any chance mention that Life was passing him by?*

DAPHNE: *I think he did say something like that.*

. . .

DAPHNE: *You've no idea how I envy you, working for him, but then I expect everybody does. It must be absolute heaven.*

MONICA: *It's certainly not dull.*

DAPHNE: *I hope you don't think it's awful me staying here for the night - I mean it does look rather bad, doesn't it?*

MONICA: *Well, really, Miss - Miss - ?*

DAPHNE: *Stillington. Daphne Stillington.*
MONICA: *Miss Stillington - it's hardly my business, is it?*
DAPHNE: *No, I suppose not, but I wouldn't like you to think -*
MONICA: *Seventeen years is a long time, Miss Stillington. I gave up that sort of thinking in the Spring of Nineteen Twenty Two.*
DAPHNE: *Oh, I see.*

FRED comes out of the service door with a tray of orange juice, coffee and toast.

FRED: *Will you 'ave it in here, Miss, or in the bedroom?*
DAPHNE: *Here, please.*
MONICA: *I think it would really be more comfortable for you in the bedroom. The studio becomes rather active round about eleven. People call, you know, and the telephone rings...*

Not only would Noël have been disinclined to compromise a young lady in that way, it's equally unlikely that the *real* Lorn would exchange polished badinage with *anyone* who could not state his or her business clearly and concisely. She possessed the vocabulary and the attitude, but certainly lacked the patience. She did not suffer fools gladly, and even fame was no automatic open sesame to the inner sanctum. She never really trusted Binkie, for instance, and the claws were loosely sheathed whenever he appeared.

LORN LORAINE (née Macnaughtan), known affectionately as Lornie, was described when she was young as fair with pale hair, eyes and skin. They must have been the only pale things about her!

Lornie never needed Monica's strong-arm tactics to get what she wanted. Her well-bred accent and infectious laugh would do the trick. Knowing where all the bodies were buried didn't hurt! Although she could clear a room with a brisk "Get out!" in that cut-glass South Kensington voice, she also had the knack of disappearing into the woodwork when necessary. Like the rest of us, Lornie's bond to the Coward "family" was laughter. Reverence was *de trop*, self-mockery *de rigeur*.

No-one ever treated Lornie like a servant, even on first meeting. She was an immensely efficient woman whose personal system, nevertheless, did not include a facility with the typewriter. She did, however, (as did Coley) possess a remarkable talent for copying Noël's handwriting! Many who treasured a signed Coward photo were the proud possessors of a genuine Lorn or Coley!

Lornie had once nursed theatrical ambitions of her own. She had been a dancer in the chorus of *Irene* at the Empire, and was still apt to break into

The ever-watchful Lornie keeps an eye on enthusiastic fans at a Variety Club lunch.

an occasional routine at festive moments. She also laid claim to fame when Noël published his collection of poetic parodies, *A Withered Nosegay*, in 1922. The artistic credit read, "With illustrations from Old Masters by Lorn Macnaughtan."

The rather severe lady coming in now, clutching a sheaf of drawings and smoking a determined cigarette, is GLADYS CALTHROP. Noël once quipped that "her judgement has been faulty ever since Munich." Unlike Lornie, Gladys was a woman of private means, concerning whose source we discreetly did not care to enquire. Gladys was a genuine snob, though a charmingly absent-minded one. She once forgot a new serving-girl's nationality, but with a little lateral thought she arrived at an answer: "What's the Queen's husband called? Philip? Yes, that's it; the girl's *Filipino.*"

Gladys, though not traditionally beautiful, was a striking looking woman. Prolonged exposure to the sun in her youth had left "laughter lines" on her face, which one didn't notice on a daily basis. Other women were not always so discreet.

One evening, Gladys and I were dining at a fashionable new spot with Ina Claire, the famous American comedienne. Ina, clearly exercised, indicated that the lighting in the room was terrible. "We must *do* something! The British will never learn, will they?'" I reassured her with all the suavity at my disposal that she looked lovely, whatever the lighting. "Yes, I know," she replied, "but look at Gladys!"

Gladys's ability with costume surpassed her talent with sets. Mary Martin notwithstanding, she was always right about the period dresses in *Pacific 1860,* but her sets were heavy and oppressive and did little to catch

Stanley Hall (who made all Noël's theatrical wigs), Joan Hirst (successor to Lornie and right hand to the Coward Estate), Gladys Calthrop and Geoffrey Johnson, Noël's American representative from the 1960's on. (1972)

the atmosphere of a sun-drenched Pacific island.   Her professional relationship with Noël was interrupted by mutual consent when *Quadrille* (1952) was designed by Cecil Beaton. His elegant work on that production was his greatest period triumph until *My Fair Lady* four years later.

Gladys, who died in 1980, remained the best of friends with Noël.

If Noël was the "father" of the family, then Coley, as Noël's general right-hand man and quiet voice of reason, was the "uncle."

When I met him in 1945, at the time of *Sigh No More*, we already had the humiliation of the hernia in common, which eventually resulted in an operation for me, but Coley had had four! As far as I could discern during the next thirty-five years, that was his only weakness. He could write, type, cook, organise, and was sickeningly bright. In addition to which, he was a wonderful and loyal friend. I never met anyone who had a bad word to say about Coley, which makes it particularly hard to describe him.

Coley's competence and loyalty served as an invaluable buffer, allowing Noël to get on with what he had to do without interference. He might easily have resented me as the newcomer, since I had no particular "duties" and no appointed place in the scheme of things. But, to the surprise of many, we liked each other at first sight. Jack Wilson was typically blunt: "You must hate Graham moving in on you like that?" Coley casually replied: "No, I like Graham very much." That didn't please Jack one bit. Today we would describe Coley's manner as "laid-back." He was far from unemotional; he'd simply learned to present a calm, controlled surface, which reassured everyone around him.

LEONARD (Coley) COLE, son of a Kent grocer, had come a long way since he'd joined Noël as his dresser in 1936 at the Phoenix. He gradually became so indispensable that Noël renamed him Cole Lesley and made him his "Secretary" in 1950, promoting Lornie to be his "Representative." Entries in the *Diaries* reflect Noël's growing dependence on him. "Whatever should I do without him?" he wrote in 1966. "He has the capacity for devotion which, as the years close in on me, I shall certainly need."

Devotion was only a small part of what Noël saw in Coley and me. We were a reflection of an essential part of his own persona. We all hailed from unpromising backgrounds, but we burned with a driving ambition to "make something" of ourselves. We accepted each other for who we were, becoming, if you like, conspirators in a harmless plot.

So Leonard Cole begat Cole Lesley who became the urbane Coley, sleek of hair, quiet of voice, polished in manner, Noël's Jeeves. When the guests had gone, though, Coley would shred their affectations amid gales of laughter with the rest of us.

As early as *Pacific 1860,* Coley demonstrated his writing skills by helping Noël create Samolan folklore. Coley and I, in a bid to become Britain's answer to Rodgers and Hammerstein, wrote one song, "This Seems To Be The Moment," which was performed in 1951 in *The Lyric Revue:*

"THIS SEEMS TO BE THE MOMENT"

This seems to be the moment,
The hour, the place, the night.
The setting is romantic,
The atmosphere is right.
The breeze provides a tune for us,
They've even lit the moon for us
So let's make the most of our chances
And hold on tight.
So many stars are shining,
We couldn't ask for more
This seems to be the moment in Time
We've waited for.

The fate of our first attempt at a complete musical, however, was aptly reflected by its title, *Ghost of a Chance.* The story involved a theatrical company who lose their leading man as their revue is about to make them all stars. By a cunning twist, a ghost is recruited to take his place.

The plot has more than a hint of *Blithe Spirit* and *Topper* about it, I must admit, but it did give us the opportunity openings for such witty exchanges as:

- *I can't have a ghost in the lead. It would upset the company terribly.*
- *No one need know.*
- *But of course they'd know. They'd see through him in a flash!*

I've paid good money to sit through much worse!

Coley was responsible for much of the preliminary work in adapting *Lady Windermere's Fan* as *After the Ball.* He blocked out scenes, edited dialogue, and produced most of the first draft. He also translated Jean-Pierre Aumont's comedy *L'Ile Heureuse* into English. It was to have been the stage debut of Aumont's wife, Maria Montez, but the poor lady was tragically drowned in her bath and the play was never put on. Coley's fluency in French was instrumental in helping Noël translate Feydeau's *Occupe-toi d'Amélie* into *Look After Lulu*, which was no picnic. (Feydeau, said Noël, was an "untidy" playwright, frequently leaving characters unaccounted for. Such Gallic *sang froid* upset Noël's meticulous mind.)

The real proof of Coley the Writer came much later with his very thorough and witty biography of Noël, *Remembered Laughter*. It remains the definitive account, combining recorded history with Coley's firsthand observations.

JOHN C. (Jack) WILSON was a good-looking, lively young man whom even the cynical Lornie thought witty and good company, but by the time I came along, the ranks of the "family" were being closed against him.

For many years he had been an important figure in Noël's emotional life, though they had parted amicably many years before I met Noël. In 1937, Jack married Princess Natasha Paley, a supposed descendant of the Romanovs. They were living in Connecticut at the time I first met them, and as far as Jack was concerned, it was jealousy at first sight. He saw in me a younger version of himself, a notion which threatened to cut through the protective skin he'd built up over the years.

Jack was an emotionally self-destructive man, against whom Noël had no protection. Noël was only trustingly capable of seeing the witty companion of youth, not the embittered, ageing alcoholic Jack had become. His sorry saga of degeneration is detailed in the *Diaries*, but, in each case, Noël's anger is tempered by a verbal finger wag. "Positively Jack's Last Chance" became a recurring theme.

Jack became very petty towards Noël in ways that he had to know would be discovered. For instance, he had tried to talk Mary Martin out of accepting the lead in *Pacific 1860*, saying that the part was not right for her. As it turned out, his judgement was correct, but his motives certainly were not.

The professional relationship eventually turned as sour as the personal one. Jack saw himself as a theatrical all-rounder, agent, producer, director. Noël begged to differ, citing Jack's 1946 production of *Present Laughter* with Clifton Webb, which demonstrated a distinct "lack of taste and imagination."

Jack even tried to sabotage *Tonight at 8:30* by telling Noël that it would be impossible for me to get a work permit, even though Fanny Holtzmann had already arranged it, a fact Jack must have known we'd discover. Writing of that incident, Noël glumly confided to his *Diaries*, "I feel this is the end of the friendship between Jack and me....It is a bitter revelation that I can no longer trust him."

It became increasingly obvious that Jack was padding his share of the box office of *Tonight*. Noël tolerated the various follies of his friends, but dishonesty he could not condone.   He determined to sever their professional ties for good.

The personal knot, though, proved harder to cut. In the end it was left to Jack to end their theatrical association in mid-1951. Noël notes in the *Diaries*: "This is a relief, as I think little of him as a theatre man," though as late as 1955 he still considered involving Jack in the US version of *Nude with Violin*. He attempted to explain this apparent inconsistency with, "I suppose there is a core of deep, sentimental pride in me that refuses to let him rot... I am so very responsible for his career, such as it has been."

For the next few years Jack and Natasha would turn up like characters in a badly-written play, delivering the odd line without advancing the plot. At each successive appearance we were shocked by the deterioration in their physical state. Booze destroyed Jack before the Great Producer finally stepped in, but unfortunately, along the way, he had persuaded Natasha to keep him alcoholic company. It made Noël desperately sad, and when Jack finally died in 1961, he wrote: "I am almost sure he was aware of his inadequacy. I believe, in his heart, he knew he couldn't direct well and that all he did know about it was second-hand....To me he died years ago."

Natasha and Jack Wilson. (Goldenhurst, 1936)

Ironically, the year Jack died was the same year that Geoffrey Johnson came into our lives. An actor turned stage manager (and later a casting agent), Geoffrey played a leading part in helping steer a straight course when we were having trouble bringing *Sail Away* to a safe harbour in New York. It was such a relief to have someone in America whom we could trust, and Geoffrey was signed on for the duration. He became Noël's US representative, a position he holds for the Estate to this day.

Although she was never a major star, JOYCE CAREY's familiar face graced the stage, the screen and television for seventy years. Among her many memorable characterizations was Myrtle, the feisty manageress of the railway-station buffet in *Brief Encounter*. Joycie could and did play everything from genuine nobility to "refined" lower-middle class gentility. Serenely patrician in appearance, there was a touch of devilment that would pop out every now and then, especially from her mouth.

On a particularly bumpy flight from New York with Noël and Eva Gabor, Joycie shrieked, "Oh, I *hate* this fucking plane!", whereupon Eva fell on her neck and embraced her warmly. Joycie looked to Noël for

Joycie with head by Winifred. Unfortunately, it fell victim to its critical sculptor's hammer. (1938)

enlightenment on this curious behaviour. "She was afraid that you were a Great Lady," Noël calmly explained from beneath a raised eyebrow.

Noël and Joycie became good companions from the time when Joycie's mother, Lilian Braithwaite, played the lead opposite Noël in his first major success, *The Vortex* (1924). Joycie never married, although there were one or two "special relationships," perhaps because the "family" was too much competition. Whatever the reason, Joycie was one of our own.

She was also an accomplished writer and had at least one very successful play, *Sweet Aloes* (1937), produced in London and New York. Joycie was determined to find a quiet spot to write her next play, which was to be about Keats, so she and Noël settled on the Welsh village of Portmeirion, later made famous as the setting for *The Prisoner*. By the time they left, Noël had finished *Blithe Spirit;* I don't know if Joycie *ever* finished hers.

She was a cornucopia of Noël stories. After a tedious dinner at some pretentious person's flat, Joycie tried to salvage something from the evening by referring to the host's picture collection: "There was a beautiful Sargent in the bedroom." Noël shot back, "I am not at all surprised."

After her appearance in a short-lived production of *As You Like It,* she received, as we all did from time to time, a Noël verse:

> *To pretty, witty winsome Joyce,*
> *The Queen of old revivals,*
> *Confronted by the awful choice*
> *Of hunger or* The Rivals,
> *Le Maître qui vous adore si bien*
> *Hopes for the love of Mike it*
> *Will not amount so soon to rien*
> *As poor old* As You Like It.

When Joycie was in *Nude with Violin,* Michael Wilding, who had just given his first tentative performance, insisted that she accompany him to a party at Winifred's (Clemence Dane's) flat. Michael admired one of Winifred's paintings and asked her how she'd achieved a particular effect. "Oh, you take your tool and dip it in hot wax." When Joycie relayed this answer to Noël, he observed thoughtfully: "That's what Michael must have done before the performance."

Joycie was particularly good at The Game, an exercise in linguistics that the "family" played, and which was, in essence, a version of the game the guests are forced to play in *Hay Fever.* The basic rule was simple: Make a fool of yourself. After that, it became more complicated. The luckless player was given a phrase to act out in mime, which was relatively straightforward with a phrase like "Little Bo-peep has lost her sheep." With Noël as the prime mover, though, things were rarely that easy for the visiting team. He was particularly mischievous with the more elegant younger actresses.

After watching Margaret Lockwood contort herself to no avail in an unseemly manner, my incredulous expression triggered off her combustible temper. "Well," she blustered, "what would *you* do with 'Up shit creek without a paddle'?" To be honest, offhand I couldn't think.

Joycie and Noël had a telepathic communion that could have earned them a career in music hall. They'd worked out an infallible private code which worked even when they were in separate rooms. Anybody up against Noël and Joycie discovered to their chagrin what the poor souls in *Hay Fever* must have gone through. If Noël had taken the trouble to work that damned code out in 1940, the war would have been a good deal shorter and some of our evenings might have ended more amicably!

Greta Garbo declined to take part. "I don't play games," she demurred. "You will here!" insisted Noël. When she saw how much fun everyone else was having, she threw herself into an impersonation of Margot Fonteyn, with Geoffrey Johnson as Nureyev, even though she was no longer young. It made me wish that we'd been allowed to see the prima ballerina she played in *Grand Hotel* (1932) actually perform ("Garbo Dances!").

WINIFRED ASHTON was a polymath; a playwright, painter, sculptor and dropper of verbal bricks. Noël would upset party guests by arguing, half-seriously, that Winifred's place in posterity would be more secure than that of, say, Cyril Connolly, who was then the intellectual blue-eyed boy. He may ultimately be proven right but, in truth, they were both fairly marginal characters. Winifred, though, was infinitely nicer.

She acquired her pen name in her typically full-frontal approach to life. A friend told her that "Winifred Ashton" was not a bold enough name for literary greatness, and that she should use "something inescapable, like 'Westminster Abbey'." Winifred was pondering this very thought when she passed an edifice that just happened to be St. Clement Dane's!

As Clemence Dane she wrote a number of successful plays, including *Will Shakespeare, Come Of Age* and *A Bill of Divorcement*, and novels such as *Broome Stages* and *The Flower Girls*. Winifred was constantly engrossed in a project full of learning and high moral tone. Her thought process, however, passed from brain to tongue with no intervening filter, and it was not unusual to find yourself up against the mental ropes with Winifred bearing down in remorseless fashion. She irritated Noël to the point where he'd completely fabricate literary references to seriously debate with her.

Clemence Dane. Blue Harbour, Jamaica. (1971)

When she would realize what was happening, he'd receive a roguish and incapacitating dig in the ribs for his pains.

To quote Noël's admonishment to "Mrs. Worthington," Winifred was a "big girl," built along the lines of Masefield's "stately Spanish galleon," although she was fiercely and patriotically British. At her crowded flat in Tavistock Street, the air of British history could be cut with a knife. A mutual friend once remarked that she reminded him "in wholesome vigour of the entire hockey team of a good girls' school."

Winifred was the inspiration for Madame Arcati in *Blithe Spirit*. She could have played it to perfection for precisely the same reason that Margaret Rutherford eventually did: Neither of them ever realized that what they did was funny.

Just like Johnny G., Winifred had acquired a justifiable and charming reputation for dropping verbal bricks. There's probably some perfectly logical explanation for this brand of "aural dyslexia" but, since it's not life-threatening and is most definitely life-enhancing, who cares?

There was the time she took Joycie to intellectual task in the crowded foyer of the Old Vic, as she boomed: "Oh, but Joyce, it's *well known* that Shakespeare sucked Bacon dry!" On another occasion, Joycie enquired over the fate of some goldfish Winifred had in a pool where the sun beat down to the rage of man, beast and fish. She was reassured: "Oh they're all right now! They've got a vast erection covered with everlasting pea!"

There was the morning she came down to breakfast at Binkie's country place and dazzled the assembled breakfast guests with: "Ah, the pleasure of waking up to see a row of tits outside your window!" On another morning at the same venue, she arrived at breakfast to find the assembled Messrs. Beaumont, Perry, Gielgud, Rattigan, Beaton and Coward. She blithely greeted them with: "Oh, it's simply too lovely, it's just like fairyland!"

She once reminisced fondly to the Governor of Jamaica about a mutual acquaintance: "Do you remember the night we all had Dick on toast?" Winifred had quite a thing about our feathered friends. She once phoned Noël to invite him to lunch. With typical enthusiasm, she bellowed down the line: "Do come! I've got such a lovely cock!" Noël replied mildly: "I *do* wish you'd call it a *hen*, dear."

The verbal tinsel shouldn't obscure the fact that Winifred was in every sense a rock to her friends. From the time Noël first met her, he never published any major work without first sharpening it on that fine mind. Or, as Winifred might have said, "Oh, Noël always likes to bring it round to my place and give it a good seeing to!"

I was the latest adoptee into the family. Noël had various epithets for me, of which "illiterate little sod" is one of the few that is printable. I was christened with my nickname one day in Gerald Road when I interrupted Noël and Lornie in the middle of a high-level business discussion. I pressed on with my prattling until Lornie shot an admonitory "Hey, dear little lad!" This was a reference to a song lyric from "Willy" in *Sigh No More*, about a little boy who'd died and gone to heaven:

> *Dear little lad unheeding,*
> *Pray give a thought to your immortal soul.*

In other words, "Watch it!" From that moment on, I was Little Lad.

*   *   *   *

On the subject of pseudonyms, people often ask how Noël came to be called "The Master," for which John Mills has an explanation. Johnnie's association with Noël went back as far as his juvenile lead in *Words and Music* in the '30's. John was a supporting actor in the films *This Happy Breed* and *In Which We Serve*, and was one of the players Noël trusted.

In 1930, Noël found himself in Singapore at the same time as a touring theatrical company, The Quaints. They were staging a revival of R.C.

Sheriff's famous war play, *Journey's End*. The part of Raleigh was being undertaken by one J. Mills, but the actor playing the demanding lead part of Stanhope was taken ill. Noël offered to help the company out.

They were suitably overawed and rehearsals proceeded. Since he was simply a guest actor, Noël was diffident in his suggestions for improving the performance. In an attempt to relax the young Mills, he suggested they call each other by their Christian names, a notion that actually increased Johnnie's nervousness. He informed Noël that he really didn't think he could do that just yet. "Somehow it just doesn't seem right. After all, you are, well, I mean...well, you're The Master."

It's a good, and possibly even a true story, though the origin might have been more prosaic. Lornie was in the habit of addressing Noël as "Master," with the merest hint of irony in her inflection. In later years, Noël would vary his answer to suit his mood. He told one interviewer, "Oh, you know, Jack of All Trades, Master of None."

"The Master" it was. And The Master he was.

*   *   *   *

Neither Coley nor I ever had a real family. Gladys and Lornie were widows, and Joycie never married. Noël's "family" provided our support system, though the saddest thing for me, as the "junior member," was to watch it dwindle as the years took their toll. First Winifred in 1965, followed by Lornie in 1967, then Noël, then Coley and Gladys in the same year, and quite recently Joycie. It's the kind of curtain call one can do without.

To quote Noël's last poem:

> *How happy they are I cannot know,*
> *But happy am I who loved them so.*

On one memorable occasion we were actually mistaken for a family. We'd been visiting friends just outside Antibes and went down to the nearby beach to bathe on a blistering day. The pebbles were so hot that we were skipping around as gingerly as the proverbial cat on a hot tin roof.

Noël, particularly, hopped around like a cross between Dudley Moore in *10* and Monsieur Hulot. The humour was not lost on a small French child, who turned to me, clearly thinking I was the son, and chuckled: "*Oh, comme il est drôle, le Papa!*" If he had heard, Noël would certainly have gone back over those sands of fire and simplified his performance.

Noël and Marlene. (1940)

CHAPTER TWELVE

SHALL WE JOIN THE LADIES...? (2) NOËL AND MARLENE... AND TALLULAH... AND BEA...AND VIVIEN...AND...

Sigh no more, sigh no more...
Sweet and beguiling ladies, sigh no more.

(*Sigh No More*)

"Poor darling glamorous stars everywhere, their lives are so lonely and wretched and frustrated. Nothing but applause, flowers, Rolls-Royces, expensive hotel suites, constant adulation. It's too pathetic and wrings the heart."

(*Diaries*)

The concept of stardom is changing, and not for the better. Norma Desmond hit the mark in *Sunset Boulevard,* when she snapped, "We had *faces!*" From the 1920's on, Noël worked with some of the most fabulous female faces on both sides of the Atlantic. Many of them became close personal friends, though their introductions were often a little unorthodox.

MARLENE DIETRICH

Not everyone started a life-long love affair with Marlene Dietrich by hanging up on her. Marlene had seen Noël in his first American film, *The Scoundrel* (1935), and called to congratulate him. Noël, convinced it was a gag, promptly hung up! Marlene never let him forget the incident and what it said about the state of his self-confidence.

Whatever else may be said about her, Marlene was generous to a fault, particularly with other people's money. It was Marlene's phone bills after a visit to us in Switzerland that caused Noël to have the phones removed from the guest rooms. "Doesn't the dear girl know *anybody* who doesn't live eight thousand miles away?"

Noël was instrumental in starting Marlene's cabaret career. He encouraged her to try her luck at the Café de Paris, where her success was such that, in later years, it created a twinge of jealousy among even the most seasoned cabaret performers.

In everything she attempted, Marlene knew precisely what she wanted. Nothing and no-one was allowed to stand in her way. During her 1954 season at the Café, Noël teased her about the arrangements she'd insisted on for her appearance: "For Marlene it's cloth of gold on the walls and purple marmosets swinging from the chandeliers. But for me, sweet fuck all!" During one of his own performances there, he couldn't resist a little dig at his friendly competitor. He swept down the stairs, snuggled up to the piano, kicked aside the train of an imaginary dress, and whispered a husky "Hello" into the mike. The audience immediately picked up the reference and loved it.

When he first introduced Marlene at the Café, Noël prepared one of his tongue-in-cheek verses, as he often did for his favourite people:

> We know God made the trees
> And the birds and the bees
> And the sea for the fishes to swim in.
> We are also aware
> That he has quite a flair
> For creating exceptional women.

I had also performed in cabaret at the Café de Paris and was contemplating taking the act to New York. An agent who specialised in US cabaret bookings was coming to see me rehearse, so I asked Marlene to come and see me run through my stuff. She knew I was nervous about this high-powered lady, so she agreed. At the end of the rehearsal she said, "Darling, I'm going to be perfectly frank with you. In America there are lots of good-looking men who can sing and dance and who have far better choreography than you do. Do not do this act for this woman because she'll *kill* you, and you will never, *never* get a job in cabaret in America."

It wasn't the easiest thing to say, or to hear, but she came right out with it and I respected her for it. She confirmed what I already felt, that cabaret wasn't my niche, so I scrapped the act. After my experience with *Tonight at 8:30*, I didn't need the aggravation.

Noël and Marlene were founding members of the Self-Invention

Society. Each of them had worked out every detail of how they wanted their public to perceive them; dress, speech, deportment, all scrupulously tailored to fit the image. Anything that didn't was ruthlessly eliminated. Each of them admired the elegant machinery at work in the other.

The difference between them was that Noël never took himself too seriously. Self-mockery was never far away. Marlene could laugh and enjoy herself, but she didn't have much of a sense of humour in English, though, for all I know, she might have been hilarious in German. Noël dubbed her and Lilli Palmer his "two Prussian cows." Conversation with Marlene was almost exclusively *about* Marlene. So self-absorbed was she that once, she so deeply displeased Coley that he "cut" her for two years, and she didn't even notice!

One evening, when we were in her suite at the Dorchester (Noël, Vivien Leigh, myself and a few others), Marlene suddenly jumped up and said, "I've got a record I want you to hear!"

Marlene by Wada.

We naturally thought it was her latest album, but it was a record of different kinds of applause. Marlene started polling us on which sort of applause should follow which song? We were astonished. Vivien thought Marlene was stark, raving, bloody mad! An applause track on an album was unheard of in those days, though it's commonplace enough now.

If she organized her applause, you can imagine what her dresser drawers looked like. Noël once invited her to a black-tie gala event, complete with the works. Unfortunately, the lady hadn't brought "the works" with her on the trip, so the next thing we heard was that husky voice on the phone, briefing her maid back in New York. Marlene had her entire wardrobe catalogued and stored in six-foot-high cabin trunks that would hold a dress uncreased. "Trunk 5, Drawer 3..." The works arrived on cue.

Marlene and Katharine Hepburn were with us on that marvellous train, the Twentieth Century, taking *Tonight at 8:30* into New York for that ill-starred opening. We all met up in Noël's little drawing room. When Katie left, Marlene brought out her jewel case and started exhibiting her incredible collection. She knew the history of every piece, which she proceeded to recount to us in painful detail. Gertie was getting thoroughly fed up with this monologue and could contain herself no longer. Finally, she said sweetly, "Oh, Marlene, dear, they're absolutely beautiful. I only got yachts." Marlene, at least on that occasion, was speechless. (Gertie wasn't entirely making it up. Somebody actually did give her a yacht once.)

TALLULAH BANKHEAD

Tallulah Bankhead had much in common with Gertie, except that Tallulah's decibel level was higher and her taste a good deal lower.

The first time I saw Tallulah was in a revival of *Private Lives* in Chicago in 1947. The Lunts joined us, as curious as we were to see if Amanda could survive Tallulah. *Private Lives* is a piece of finely balanced, precision engineering for two equal players, but Tallulah managed to turn it into a one-woman show. She strutted onto that stage and shook the audience by the scruff of its collective neck. She enjoyed herself enormously, and so did the paying public. Her leading man was...forget it! This was one leading man who was being led.

Lynn and Alfred were absolutely flabbergasted at her performance, which had absolutely *nothing* to do with *Private Lives*. I was wondering what the hell Noël was going to say, but, not for the first time, he surprised us all. He marched into the leading man's dressing room and said, "Don't worry about it. Just take the money on Friday nights and enjoy yourself!"

Meanwhile, I went with the Lunts to Tallulah's dressing room, and Lynn, putting on a brave face, said all she could think to say. "Oh darling, we thought you were absolutely *wonderful*." Tallulah, always inclined to an unorthodox turn of phrase, bleated, "I don't give a fuck what *you* think. Where's my author?" Realising that this wasn't quite the language Lynn was used to, she tried to change the subject. "Oh, by the way, Lynnie," she breezed on, "Estelle Winwood and I were talking about you the other day and saying, 'Where would Lynn be without Alfred?'" Next day, in the car on the way back from Chicago, Lynn tapped me on the shoulder and said ruefully, "I *should* have said, 'Playing *Private Lives*, dear.'"

None of us could understand what had possessed Noël to let Tallulah do the play in the first place. *Private Lives* was turning into *Public Exhibition*. A short tour for the money seemed to be the only explanation. The dear girl was always running out of *that*, but then he let her bring the show into New York.

Tallulah was very grateful to Noël for her success in the show. "Thank

Tallulah Bankhead.

you, darling," she crooned, "it's meant a lot to me. Well, it's meant a new swimming pool, to be precise!"   She later sent him a present, an unattractive, though obviously quite expensive, Augustus John painting of a young man. Noël didn't like it very much, which was just as well, because about two years later she sent him a snippy letter, saying, "You've had the picture long enough. Will you please send it back?" It wasn't a gift at all, it was a loan! He was only too delighted to return it.

Tallulah was too broad a "broad" to be a typical "Coward actress." What she'd done to *Private Lives* she'd already inflicted on *Fallen Angels*, with comparable success.

Tallulah was...Tallulah.   Her absurd generosity meant she was perennially broke. She insisted on paying our entire hotel bill in Chicago, since during the immediate post-war period we weren't permitted to take money out of Britain. When she invited us to go out on the town, we had no option but to accept. Noël absolutely adored her but he found her a bit of a bore after too many drinks and too many night clubs. That night we had had both, but we didn't like to say so and spoil her evening.

We eventually got back to the hotel where Tallulah's sister was also staying. Noël and I got out of the elevator first, while Tallulah went up to another floor to drop off her sister. We were horrified to find ourselves face-to-face with a man clutching a fire axe, wildly muttering, "Where's the Bankhead apartment? Where's the Bankhead apartment?" Noël quickly assessed the situation and calmly informed the man he had the wrong hotel. It didn't take a genius to see that the fellow had no charitable intentions towards Tallulah with that hatchet! So, while Noël improvised on his theme of mistaken accommodation, I summoned the police, who duly removed the maniac. We never found out for sure just what had upset him so much, but we assumed he must have played opposite her in *Private Lives!* We never told Tallulah because she would probably have gone down to the jail, insisted on bailing him out and invited him back for a drink.

BEA LILLIE

This may sound sexist but I don't know many funny women. Peculiar, certainly, but not funny. Gertie could be. Bea Lillie was. It has nothing to do with intelligence or technique. It's an attitude, an irreverent way of looking at life.

Bea was an anarchist. She loved throwing things off balance. In the middle of a scene, she'd get bored, throw in a bit of business, get tangled up in a feather boa, totally divert the audience's attention. It could be disconcerting to be constantly wondering whether, or from where, your leading lady would make her next entrance. In a long run of *High Spirits*, she took to coming in through the fireplace to relieve the tedium. Audiences, sensing theatrical danger, loved it!

Noël had known her for years and never called her anything but "Beattie." He always insisted that she had "star quality, moments of genius and little...acting talent." What she did have was a great talent for satirizing her material even as she was playing it. She'd been one of the big transatlantic names, along with Gertie, since the 1920's and had appeared with Noël in *This Year of Grace* (1928). She starred in the Broadway version of *Words and Music,* called *Set to Music* (1938), in which she introduced "Mad About the Boy" to America, as well as a song Noël wrote specially for her, "I've Been to a Marvellous Party."

I first met her doing wartime entertainment for the forces. I had heard so much about her, and I loved to watch her from the wings. The pattern of the performance was almost predictable. She'd do her first couple of numbers to polite applause, the boys in uniform naturally grateful to her for having taken the trouble. They'd never heard of Bea Lillie, but it gradually dawned on them that she was a very funny lady and they wouldn't let her go. It never failed. She never pushed, but had the confidence to know that, if she gave it time, her particular kind of magic would work its spell.

I got to know her better when we were in New York for *High Spirits* in 1964. It didn't start auspiciously, because, like many ladies of a certain age, Bea had trouble learning her lines. Noël expected actors to come to

Words and Music *reaches America as* Set to Music *(1938). Noël takes a bow with its Broadway star, Bea Lillie.*

rehearsal knowing their lines, just as he himself did, but Bea adroitly pointed out to him, "It's all right for you, darling, you wrote the bloody thing!"

Gladys Cooper had similar problems with *Relative Values* and was still carrying her script around at dress rehearsal, until Noël finally tore it out of her hand. It's just as well, because Gladys would inform anyone who would listen, "I never had the book out of my hand for Gerald [du Maurier] and I'm damned if I'm going to start for *him*." It's unlikely that she ever actually *said* it to "him."

Edith Evans suffered similarly in the revival of *Hay Fever* at the National. Noël wondered whether she'd *ever* get it right, although she'd played the part on television only a year earlier with no trouble at all. It was Noël's view that the actor should deliver the line exactly as the author wrote it, and not some reasonable approximation thereof. Edith was to look out of the French windows and say, "On a clear day you can see Marlowe." For some unknown reason, she insisted on saying, "On a *really* clear day you can see Marlowe." Exasperated beyond belief, Noël finally took her aside and firmly corrected her with the original line, drily adding, "On a *really* clear day you can see Marlowe and Beaumont and Fletcher."

That wasn't the end of our verbal problems with Edith, until Noël had a brainwave. He went to Edith, who had taken to sulking in her tent, and said gently, "Don't worry, dear, if you feel the part's too much for you.

We've had a rehearsal with Maggie in your part and she's word-perfect. She can always go on." Edith wasn't sure if he was bluffing but, in fact, he *had* rehearsed the entire show with Maggie after the regular performance was over. At the next run-through Edith didn't dry *once*, and Maggie Smith never did get to play the part in that production. That proves the old theatrical adage, there's no substitute for substitution.

A similar phenomenon repeated itself in *High Spirits*. While the show was on the road, Bea just couldn't hold the words, but the moment they hit Philadelphia, something clicked and the words fell into place. Up to that point, Tammy Grimes (as Elvira) owned the show outright because she was the only one who knew what she was doing. Back on form, Bea high-jacked the whole evening. Tammy immediately retired with a mysterious "hairline fracture of the ribs," according to her doctor, but when the understudy proved to be brilliant that hairline fracture miraculously healed overnight. It's probably in *The Guinness Book of Records*.

There was a big dance number in the show, with the dancers dressed up in Arabian costume with masks and veils. Bea would exit and an identically-dressed chorus girl would dash on in her place to be hurled around over the boys' heads. The audience was absolutely fascinated, until one night Bea suddenly stalked on from the wings and shouted, "What's going on?" This, of course, stopped the show cold, and the audience, realising they'd been fooled, was hysterical. Noël was incensed. He'd had quite enough qualms about the adaptation anyway, and now here was this eccentric woman sending it up. But he knew what worked, so raising his eyes to Heaven he said, "Leave it in." And every night the audience loved it.

Beattie was trying, and not simply *being* trying, but her forgetfulness became more serious. In ordinary conversation she'd forget the beginning of a sentence she'd just started. Though she'd always find a droll way round it I'm sure she didn't find it at all comical. It became downright heartbreaking during the filming of *Star!*, the story of Gertie's life. Julie Andrews played Gertie, Daniel Massey (Noël's godson) played Noël. The question was, who should play Beattie, who, after all, had partnered them both? She was in no doubt: "Of course you can use me, darling, I shall play myself!"

She was probably in the early stages of Alzheimer's disease, and she'd certainly had her problems with alcoholism. She never appeared on stage again, and a massive stroke a few years later took her out of public life altogether. The wonder is that the grief of losing her son, Bobby, in the war didn't take its toll sooner, because she certainly never got over it.

How Bea used sheer force of technique to conquer her problems and chalk up one last hit performance is a source of amazement to me. But the clown nursing the private grief never fails, does it?

VIVIEN LEIGH

And then there was Viv. Such ups and downs. Sadly, the downs won out.

I had heard of her long before *Gone With the Wind*, when she opened in a play called *The Mask of Virtue*. In 1936, she didn't have much stage technique. Lilian Braithwaite went to see this rising star, who was absolutely beautiful to behold but had a very high little voice. After the show, in a typical Braithwaite crack, Lilian asked the leading man rather loudly, "Can *you* hear her, dear?"

Vivien and I were friends independent of the "family." Some people

Noël and Viv Putting On the Glitz at the Savoy Hotel for the premiere of Sail Away. *(1962)*

made me welcome only when I was with Noël, but Vivien was not in that category. After the second "house" on Saturday, and our respective shows were over, she'd say, "Why don't we drive down to Notley (the Olivier country house) for the weekend? Noël doesn't have to come. Just us!" So off we'd go. She proudly played the Lady of the Manor in her "stately home." There'd be a formal dinner, not just a light supper on a tray, with the full protocol, until the small hours.

I didn't realise at the time that she was an insomniac, and always wanted to be up as late as possible. Larry, on the other hand, was playing all those strenuous Shakespearean parts and desperately needed his rest. Quite apart from their other problems, Viv was wearing him out, interfering with his career, which truly was his main interest in life. Their asynchronous body clocks must have seriously contributed to their break-up.

Next morning she'd insist on pruning the roses. She'd prick her finger on a thorn and bellow, "Oh, these fucking roses drive me mad!", and in a flash the great lady would be gone! There are many Viviens in my mind but the one I shall always treasure is La Grande Dame of the Fucking Roses.

Noël, though never one to take sides, was more fond of her than of Larry. One of the most moving parts of the *Diaries* are his prayers for her progress. As early as 1953, he records that "poor Viv is in a mental home and has been asleep for a week. She had apparently really gone over the edge....I am desperately sorry for her...and I must help her in any way I can." "Vivien looked papery and rather frail...." His sympathy over the years was tempered by frustration as Vivien's erratic behaviour affected Noël's own productions in which she appeared, or promised to appear.

By 1956: "I sadly fear the trouble has gone too deep." His patience has just about worn out: "Personally I think that if Larry had turned sharply on Vivien years ago and given her a clip in the chops, he would have been spared a mint of trouble. The seat of all this misery is our old friend, feminine ego!"

In the way he invariably behaved towards those he cared for, Noël was still trying to help her when many, including Larry, had given up. Larry put on an agonizing performance of withdrawal for the rest of his life, but essentially he'd handed over the "problem" to someone else. Noël wanted her to work because that was what Viv wanted. She felt work was a lifeline. If she was out there on stage in front of an adoring audience, things couldn't be that bad, could they?

Noël would praise her in a classical role whenever possible, but there were times when his compliments were double-edged. After seeing Viv and Larry at Stratford in *Titus Andronicus*, Noël had this assessment of Viv's performance as Lavinia: "Considering the somewhat restrictive stage directions ('Enter Lavinia - her hands cut off, her tongue cut out and ravished'), I think her performance was all that could be expected."

For a time, *South Sea Bubble* and *Look After Lulu* kept her busy, but the problems went deeper. There was a string of other men which became less and less of a secret. Peter Finch joined the entourage on their Australian tour. We would hear about the new "friends" but we tried to stay out of it, not wanting to take sides.

Much as her erratic behaviour frustrated him, Noël would always rally round in a real crisis. When Larry went to the States, leaving Viv alone one Christmas, we bundled her off to Switzerland with us. Getting wind of the situation, the *paparazzi* turned up on the doorstep. Instead of huddling inside, Noël emerged and held an impromptu press conference, pretending it was *him* they'd come to see. Yes, he was writing a new play. No, he probably wouldn't do any more cabaret for a while. It was a masterly performance from The Master. The journalists made their retreat looking slightly bemused.

It was sad beyond belief. She was a beautiful, talented, amazing woman, but you just never knew what to expect from her. One evening we got a frantic phone call from Jack Merivale, with whom she was living at the time, begging us to come over right away. We arrived to the appalling spectacle of Vivien standing naked on a balcony over a flight of stairs, convinced that she could fly. It took all of Noël's considerable love and skill to talk her back to safety. It was a long way from Scarlett O'Hara.

vicky

Coley, Noël and Little Lad. The tan says we must have just come back from Jamaica!

CHAPTER THIRTEEN

"GOODNIGHT, MY DARLINGS..." THE 1970's

Come the wild, wild weather,
Come the wind and the rain,
Come the little white flakes of snow,
Come the joy, come the pain,
We shall still be together
When our life's journey ends,
For wherever we chance to go
We shall always be friends.
We may find
While we're travelling through the years
Moments of joy and love and happiness,
Reason for grief, reason for tears.
Come the wild, wild weather,
If we've lost or we've won,
We'll remember these words we say
Till our story is done.

(*Waiting in the Wings*)

A Song at Twilight was more than just the title of Noël's 1966 play; it was one last walk around the garden, his chance to say farewell to the many people who'd remained faithful to him in those difficult post-war years.

Though it came at great physical cost, nothing would stand in the way of his fulfilling this particular engagement. If necessary, he'd have rewritten his parts to play them sitting down.

Health problems had come to dominate Noël's life, which was rapidly becoming an obstacle course. His greatest concern was his failing memory. He'd hoped to take a version of *Suite in Three Keys* as an envoi to Broadway, but that was clearly out of the question, and *Suite* didn't reach Broadway until after Noël's death, in the truncated form of *Noël Coward in Two Keys* (1974). (*Shadows of the Evening*, which Noël had always considered "too sad," was dropped.) He'd hoped to play it at last with Maggie Leighton, for whom it was originally written; in the end, the Broadway cast at the Ethel Barrymore Theatre consisted of Hume Cronyn, Jessica Tandy and Anne Baxter.

As his mainspring wound down, Noël would only commit himself to projects which wouldn't tax his resources and which would bring in the money. He played Cæsar in Richard Rodgers' musical version of *Androcles and the Lion* (1967) for American television, with Joe Layton directing and Norman Wisdom starring: "Everyone was extremely nice but I didn't enjoy any of it. I hate television anyway. It has all the nervous pressures of a first night with none of the response." He couldn't resist adding: "However, I was apparently very good."

He appeared in a cameo rôle as the Witch of Capri in Joe Losey's film, *Boom*, with Liz Taylor and Richard Burton; and his final cinematic appearance was with Michael Caine in *The Italian Job* (1968). Noël played a crime lord who ran his evil empire from a deluxe prison cell. In a scene which celebrated the successful conclusion of the "job," Noël took a triumphant walk through the prison corridors. As the scene was about to be shot, it was decided he should be accompanied by an aide, so I was "drafted," kitted out, and found myself acting as film counterpart to my real-life rôle. My final film performance may have been brief, but it was packed with motivation and nuance, and my one line, "Yes, Mr. Bridger," was truly poignant!

I'd virtually retired and now devoted myself to helping Coley run Noël's affairs. Coley took care of the secretarial duties, while I arranged the social calendar. Retiring from the stage wasn't a hard decision for me; I'd been losing my enthusiasm and my confidence for some time. *Waiting in the Wings* (1960) was the turning point. Although I had a strong supporting rôle and a charming song to sing, "Come the Wild, Wild Weather," I couldn't wait for it to be over. I expressed the sincere wish to Noël that I'd never have to sing on stage again. He couldn't understand it. How could anyone not want to be on stage? "You can do it," he encouraged. "Stop being so nervous." He *longed* for me to be a success.

I'd always been so sure of myself, ready to bounce on and reach out to an audience. Now, to quote the song I'd almost sung in *Sigh No More*, it couldn't matter less. Perhaps there'd been just too many near misses. Perhaps I just couldn't bear to see Noël summon up all that energy only to see it fail one more time. Whatever the reason, I was stage shy and, funnily enough, it mattered more to Noël than it did to me.

His own fires were burning lower, too. Dad's Renaissance was preparing a satisfying, if not particularly dramatic, last act for him. What started with the revivals of *Private Lives* and *Hay Fever* had now escalated

Sir Noël Coward, just after the investiture, with Gladys, Joycie and me. (1970)

to the point where he felt his career was finally vindicated. With nothing left to prove, he could sit back and let others do his work for him. This wasn't the Noël we'd always known, but who could blame him?

Suite in Three Keys had proved to him in the only way that meant a damn, up there on stage, that he was not immortal. He couldn't bear to risk any more critical rejection. The years had finally taken their toll, so he was wisely leaving the table while he was still ahead of the game.

When his knighthood was finally granted in January, 1970, it seemed to settle matters once and for all. Noël even gave up writing his *Diaries*. This was one honour that couldn't be topped, even in a Noël Coward show. The accolade meant so much to him, though he was almost the last of his generation to become a theatrical knight. Olivier, Richardson, Gielgud, Redgrave, Guinness (the latter two much younger) had all preceded him, so when the news was made public, it was Alec who expressed the slightly embarrassed relief felt by his peers: "We have been like a row of teeth with a front tooth missing. Now we can smile again." All that mattered to Noël was the Royal Family's personal gift to him, and it made all the waiting worthwhile.

The physical deterioration continued. When he knelt to receive that coveted knighthood, there was no question of going down on one knee. It was *both* or nothing! The Queen looked distinctly worried until she saw him leave the room shakily but safely.

He was diagnosed as having a form of arterio-sclerosis, but the exercise to improve his circulation was too much trouble, and giving up his beloved cigarettes was out of the question. He knew he was living on borrowed time, but he was determined to dictate exactly how that time was to be spent.

In Switzerland, he'd stay in bed most of the time. Coley, Joan, Gladys and I would go up to Noël's bedroom to sit with a drink, laughing and joking. That much didn't change, although visitors were kept to a minimum. Lunch or dinner would be brought in on a tray, but Noël would always eat in private. We'd go downstairs to whatever Jean-René had prepared, before going back up again later. In those last few months we were a supporting cast waiting in our dressing rooms for the next cue.

Living with someone every day, you pretend not to notice the process of change, but I realise now that Noël went downhill very fast around that time. The experience of *A Song at Twilight* was the first clue he had that his Rolls-Royce mind was not as reliable a vehicle as it had always been. He could joke about physical infirmity, but mental deterioration was insupportable to him and most definitely not to be shared with a watching world.

"I have been increasingly worried lately about my memory," he wrote in 1967. "Not my far-away memory. I can still remember accurately plays and events of 1909. But my immediate memory, which has been behaving in a disconcerting manner. A sort of curtain descends in my mind veiling what happened last week! If I concentrate for a minute, all is well, but it is rather alarming to be pulled up by a blank."

The *Diaries* abruptly stopped at the end of 1969, so we'll never know for sure if this was when he gave up. The show seemed to be over, time for whatever curtain call the Great Producer had in mind. Noël had no intention of sitting around playing the part of a vegetable!

On his occasional public outings, stooped and fragile, Coley and I would be there to support him. In the last twelve months, he took to a wheelchair and joked that he wished he'd thought of it years ago. This was Noël determinedly "buggering on" and rising above it. For a man with his vanity, the physical infirmity was a betrayal; for his friends, a personal sadness. Hermione Gingold, seeing Noël after a long absence, summed it up when she wrote, "It's always sad to see very beautiful people getting old."

The tributes poured in from both sides of the pond. Noël was, it seemed, interviewed incessantly on television, and it gave him great pleasure to stare sphinx-like at the camera before delivering the line he had intended to deliver all along. He toyed with the intolerant English-speaking media as they had once toyed with him. They apparently had determined that there were amends to be made while there was still time, and Noël didn't mind in the slightest.

Two compilation shows, Bernard Miles's *Cowardy Custard* at The Mermaid and Roderick Cook's *Oh Coward!* in the US, adopted the song-and-anecdote approach of *Side By Side By Sondheim*, prompting a great deal of renewed interest in Noël's material. He found it all immensely gratifying, and would dredge up enough energy to put on a show of the Noël Coward that fans expected to see.

In November, 1972, there was an evening of famous faces at Claridge's to honour Noël, with literati and glitterati *en masse*. In the middle of it, Noël was the most controlled person present, calmly smoking his cigarettes and putting on a performance worthy of a proscenium setting. The inevitable piano was played by Burt Bacharach, Alan Jay Lerner and Frederick Loewe.

A hush fell on the room as Noël started to rise. Coley and I reached to help him but he was determined to manage on his own. Everyone in that room took each faltering step with him until he reached the piano stool and, with Larry's help, sat down. There was no doubt in my mind he'd manage, that nothing would prevent this final show. Everyone there instinctively knew that this was the last time they'd ever see him perform.

He looked down at his hands on the keys. What thoughts were going through his mind? The child actor holding his mother's hand and listening to the sound of the curtain going up? The glory years when the words and music used him like a conduit? Gertie? Las Vegas? After all the ups and downs, it had ended in a way that he'd never have dared to write!

He picked out a few tentative chords and the whole room breathed again. In that thin little voice, now almost a whisper, Noël took them back forty-three years with a song which seemed to sum up an entire lifetime:

> *...I think if only...*
> *Somebody splendid really needed me,*
> *Someone affectionate and dear,*
> *Cares would be ended if I knew that she*
> *Wanted to have me near.*
> *But I believe that since my life began*
> *The most I've had is just*
> *A talent to amuse.*
> *Heigho, if love were all!*

A small smile playing about his lips, Noël made to get up. Emotion flowed through the room, embracing us all. Twenty years later I can still feel that frail body trembling as he allowed us to take him back to his table.

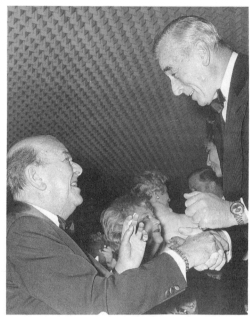

Noël with Larry (left) and Mountbatten (right) at the party to honor his 70th birthday — the celebration of what Noël referred to as "Holy Week."

Noël with Robert Stephens and Maggie Smith.

But that smile was the smile of the boy actor, hearing his first applause.

Larry recalled Noël smiling and waving to him from the rear window of the limousine leaving Claridge's. Everyone who was there that evening had their own tale to tell, except Binkie, who was last seen crawling to his car on all fours. The evening *did* have its lighter moments.

*   *   *   *

A few weeks later we were back in Jamaica, having stopped off in New York to see a few remaining old friends and to catch a performance of *Oh Coward!* How fitting that the last show he saw should be his own.

Coley and I were unwilling to accept the fact of Noël's rapid deterioration, so at Firefly and Blue Harbour we soon slipped back into the old routine: messing around during the day, evening drinks up at Firefly, waiting for the white owl to signal the arrival of dusk as might the formal lowering of a flag at some colonial outpost. Then the fireflies...

The only unfinished business which required attention was the third volume of memoirs, to be called *Past Conditional* (finally published in 1986). Noël had been talking about it for several years, and chastising himself for not having kept notes or a journal during the important period from 1931 to 1939.

He spent most of those last few days reading. He particularly enjoyed Anne Morrow Lindbergh's diary, *Hour of Gold, Hour of Lead*, which he enthusiastically urged us to read. His intellectual curiosity, at least, remained undiminished.

His last evening was like any other, with drinks and chat and lots of laughs, until, like Mrs. Wentworth-Brewster, we'd "totter down the hill." Noël had always enjoyed privacy but lately it had become a necessity which Coley and I respected. As we took our leave that evening, Noël called out, "Goodnight, my darlings. See you in the morning!" We left him sitting in his chair on the terrace, his wire-rimmed glasses perched on the end of his nose and a copy of E. Nesbit's *The Enchanted Castle* propped up in front of him, with *The Would-Be-Goods* close by.

Early next morning Imogen, Miguel's wife, came rushing down to Blue Harbour to inform us breathlessly that "Master" was "not well." We immediately rang for the doctor and raced up the hill.

What happened is perhaps most vividly recounted by Miguel, who ran the house for us:

> "My wife, Imogen, passing by around six a.m. and she hear moaning from the bathroom. It was unusual, since Master like to sleep in. She came get me. First I don't want to go

'cause he get very mad if he disturbed but she say, 'Something wrong there.' I go to the door and say, 'Master, Master, let me in. It's me, Miguel,' but he don't answer, so I get a ladder and climb to the window. I hear more moaning, so I break the shutter and see Master lying on the bathroom floor. I tell my wife, 'Go quick to Blue Harbour and fetch Mr. Payn and Mr. Lesley.' I pick Master up and take him to the bed. He was rubbing at his chest. He open his eyes and say, 'Miguel, where's Mr. Payn and Mr. Lesley?' I say, 'They coming, sir,' then he reach up and pat me twice on the shoulder and say, 'Never mind, Miguel, never mind.' I know he's gone. His teeth came out, so I put them back, then I came to the balcony. The car arrive with Mr. Payn and Mr. Lesley. Mr. Lesley jump out but I call and say, 'Master gone, sir.' Mr. Lesley say, 'Stop it, Miguel. Don't say that.' I say, 'It's true, sir; Master gone, sir.' Mr. Lesley put his hands on top of his head and he go spinning around on the lawn with tears streaming down."

In true Jamaican fashion, Miguel continued to embroider his narrative over time. Sometimes Noël's last words were changed to: "No, it's too early. They'll be asleep," but the truth will never be known, since Miguel is now dead, murdered in some local disagreement.

The only consolation that Coley and I could take was in the fact that Noël died with dignity in his own bed, and not lying on the bathroom floor. That would have been an impossible memory to erase, quite out of proportion to what it represented. It shouldn't matter, but, for Noël, how death would find him was a cause for concern: "I would prefer Fate to allow me to go to sleep when it's my proper bedtime," he wrote in 1967. "I never have been one for staying up too late." On another occasion he claimed, "I don't mind whether the final curtain falls in Jamaica, Japan or Fiji." Had he been allowed to choose, he would certainly have opted for the way it turned out.

His last poem, "When I Have Fears," was a genuine expression of his most heartfelt emotion, as was a remark in a 1972 interview: "I was born alone. I have lived my life more or less alone. And I expect I shall die alone." Thank goodness, for once he was wrong. We could remember him as he had been on that last evening, laughing and joking.

That's the way I shall always remember him...

Eventually we buckled down to sorting everything out. The local people were wonderfully kind. They felt they'd lost a dear friend who had been an important part of Jamaica for over twenty-five years.

There was speculation in the British press that Noël would be buried next to his mother in Teddington, but he'd always wanted to avoid unnecessary fuss, and told Coley and me that he should be buried where he died. His final resting place was on the spot where we would sit with our drinks in days gone by, gazing down upon the Spanish Main.

There was one final incident which sounds like an episode from *Blithe Spirit*. Each day, Coley and I would sit by the grave for a little while, as if maintaining the habit would give us something to hang on to. One day, we quite suddenly looked at each other and said together: "He's gone!" Strange as it may sound, the vibrations that we both felt so strongly abruptly vanished.

My thought was that he'd gone back to Europe or...I don't know where. I don't think we're *supposed* to know. Sure enough, when we got back to Switzerland, the vibrations were there. You may say that's what we *wanted* to think, but friends who came to the house confirmed our feelings by remarking on the happy atmosphere. Even today, though I live there alone, that feeling of Noël's presence is as strong as ever. That's why I'm never lonely.

"I do believe we've risen above it." I revisit Noël's grave at the opening of the restored Firefly. (December 1993)

*   *   *   *

The tributes poured in, many of them written long before in anticipation of the moment. The ones I treasure most are the ones that came later, after people had had an opportunity to consider Noël's lifetime contribution. There are two particularly perceptive observations which stand out.

The first was from Peter Hall, who wrote, "...during the difficult years, [Noël's] talent did in some sense become disconnected from reality...You can't live off the theatre. It's imitation. There has to be some life to imitate in your work." Noël was trying too hard in those later years to re-create the alchemy that had once come to him so effortlessly. Whether he acknowledged it or not, that created a lot of the jealousy that became such a problem.

The second observation was Ken Tynan's: "Coward invented the concept of cool and may have had emotional reasons for doing so. In any event, he made camp elegant and wore a mask of amused indifference ('Go and rise above it') to disguise any emotions he preferred not to reveal."

When the stormy marriage of one famous couple reached its predictable demise, Noël pithily commented on the agonizingly protracted nature of the proceedings: "It really isn't surprising that homosexuality is becoming as normal as blueberry pie." That was the kind of cloaked remark Tynan had in mind.

In public, discretion was paramount, as Noël advised Cecil Beaton: "It's important not to let the public have a loophole to lampoon you...You should appraise yourself...Your sleeves are too tight, your voice is too high and too precise. You mustn't do it. It closes so many doors. It limits you unnecessarily..."

In a late interview with *The New York Times*, he confided: "One's real inside self is a private place and should always stay like that...I have taken a lot of trouble with my public face." That takes us straight back to the plays. In *Design for Living* Leo says: "It's all a question of masks...Brittle, painted masks. We all wear them as a form of protection; modern life forces us to."

He was a simple man, a kind and gentle creature, whose sophisticated image was generated to defend the private person. His "family" knew that and fought to protect his privacy at every turn. He was easily hurt, and though he was consistent in loving his friends, he wrote, "I am no good at love."

It was his honesty, even at the expense of his personal emotions, that was so attractive. It was not his fame or reputation, it was simply that, gauche as it sounds, he was a nice person.

His *Diaries* and conversations were studded with references to the prodigal sons and daughters he was determined to see return to a state of grace. He was always looking for signs of "the old Jack" or that "Viv was really her old self again."

He knew that the temperaments of his "highly-strung" friends would constantly fall short of his hopes, which was why the constant and unquestioning devotion of the "family" was so important to him. He could retreat and be restored among the pet names, the private language, the games.

In what rôle did Noël cast me, the youngest, the latest arrival in this domestic "play"? Our professional and personal relationship really began at the end of the war. At forty-five, Noël was ready to pick up the threads and move on, but he needed an *alter ego*, so he began writing for me the parts he'd like to have played himself, the songs he'd liked to have sung, to relive some of his pre-war glory.

There was, however, one significant problem: I was no Noël Coward! I was certainly ambitious, but I wasn't *driven*, as Noël was. He was driven enough for both of us, though I wasn't conscious of the depth of his frustration on "our" behalf until I read the *Diaries*. He didn't confide in me at the time, perhaps wishing to spare not only my feelings, but his own too.

He wrote of *Ace of Clubs* that "Graham became, before the first act was quite over, a star." He sincerely needed to believe that, but in reality, it never *quite* happened, for the simple reason that "star quality" was an essential element missing from my talent. In the early years I would agonize to myself, "You've been in all these wonderful shows, you've had all these marvellous songs and dances. Why aren't you box office?" Fortunately, I had the temperament to face reality without destroying myself. I was efficient, I was talented, audiences enjoyed watching me, but they didn't *need* to come and see me, that's all there was to it.

I realised this long before Noël did, and I didn't feel badly about it. Star quality is innate, and even though many stars can't act very well, they can walk on stage and captivate the audience with sheer personality.

I was very lucky. I had a lot of fun and some very good parts, many written specially for me. In the early years I relied entirely on Noël, and he treated me like a son, teaching me how to profit by some of his mistakes. He took pride in me, though I never possessed the dedication *he* brought to everything he did. Little Lad, that "idle little sod," used to drive him mad!

Above all, Noël was my friend. I'm well aware that I've said very little about our personal relationship. We said little about it to each other. We never felt that it was a requirement to parade every tiny domestic detail before the world. It was true then, and it remains true today.

Noël was under no illusion about what would happen after his death. In 1955, he speculated in the *Diaries* that "There will be books proving conclusively that I was homosexual and books proving equally conclusively that I was not." Today it's no secret that Noël was homosexual, and he was neither proud nor ashamed of the fact. He firmly believed that his private business was not for public discussion. Flamboyant as he could often be in public, he was fiercely protective of his privacy and considered "*any* sexual activities when over-advertised" to be tasteless. The modern media-hyped self-indulgence would have appalled him.

The brittle facade, the flippant dismissal with a well-turned phrase, were part of his defence against being considered naïve or sentimental, when he was quite capable of being both. Behind his public mask was an extremely vulnerable emotional simplicity. When he gave his love, whether to his mother, to the "family," to Jack or to me, he lowered all his defences against the object of that love. When someone let him down, as Jack had done, all his intelligence couldn't protect him against the eruption of his emotions. But always the excuses would be found, small improvements detected. That person had to be what Noël needed him to be. In love, he never ceased to travel hopefully.

I loved the man totally. At first meeting, and during our early professional collaborations, I saw only the public Noël, fascinating but distant. But I grew to love him as I got to know him, saw the compassion behind the wit, sensed the vulnerability, the need to confide in those precious friends for whom he could let the mask slip. I was lucky enough to become one of those friends. I realised that I wanted nothing more than to share my life with this remarkable man, to help and protect him as best I could.

Like any public figure, he was vulnerable to the temptations of a brief infatuation, but his pleasure was always outweighed by the irritation he felt at losing control of his emotions. Being "in love" bothered him: "How idiotic people are when they are in love. What an age-old devastating disease....To me, passionate love has always been like a tight shoe rubbing blisters on my Achilles heel." He was particularly sensitive about being loved as a celebrity, not as a person. At times like that, a quick drink and a shared laugh at life's stupidities would redress the balance.

It didn't happen often, and it made no difference to our relationship; that's really all there is to say.

I've often tried to analyze the complex chemistry of ingredients that constituted that paradox-in-an-enigma called Noël Coward.

He was a self-made man. Not in the simple sense of pulling himself up by his boot straps, though he certainly did that, but in the sense that he decided early on precisely who he wanted to be and how he wanted to be perceived. (Noël is talking about himself when he has Garry Essendine admit, "I'm always acting - watching myself go by.") He took the tone and the trappings of the 1920's and mixed them with touches of irony and ambiguity. He then served this delicious cocktail to his delighted audiences. Glitter and snobbery were permissible, as long as you knew they were superficial. By the same token, a truth was no less fundamental because it was couched in language that was witty or trivial. After all, wasn't that clever Mr. Coward a commentary on himself? Noël would never stand perfectly still and let himself be counted. "Clever?" Undoubtedly, but in an intuitive rather than an intellectual way, and his antennae were sensitive beyond belief.

With time, the original image lost some of its lustre. There wasn't much to laugh about in post-war England, and Noël was either unwilling or incapable of adapting to the new mood. His intelligence was at odds with the times, until one more turn of the spiral left him perfectly placed above the fray.

He was a simple man. In company of any kind, he was always "on," watching his performance, careful of the way he dressed, never disappointing even the smallest audience that had come expecting to see "Noël Coward." At home with the "family" there was no need for all that. In private, he needed to be ordinary. Nobody can be continually "on" and Noël spent too much of his time wound up to perform.

If he wasn't working on something, he wasn't a particularly early riser. Breakfast in bed, invariably tea and toast, would be followed by the morning-mail ritual with Lornie, if he was in London, or a session with the daily papers. *The Times*, then the *Daily Mail*. Never the *Daily Express;* you never knew what fresh hell Beaverbrook had dreamed up! Later in the day he might have a quick flip through the *Evening Standard.*

Left to his own devices, he'd read for a while, then play the piano. It was usually other people's music, played from memory: Berlin, Kern, Gershwin, Novello, operetta, old music hall songs, whatever came into his head. The Coward material was for only the deserving few. For those in favour, he'd play "I'll See You Again" as they left. If he didn't, it might be some time before they received a return invitation.

A cigarette was never far from his hand, usually a Player's tipped. He got through a couple of packs a day, though he'd take only a few theatrical puffs before stubbing them out. Before lunch there'd be a gin and tonic, before dinner a dry martini. In later years, he would nurse a diluted brandy-and-ginger. He was literally a meat and potatoes man, so meals were nothing elaborate. Bangers-and-mash was a perennial favourite for lunch, and in the evening a light snack before an early night and a book in bed.

Sometimes, even the presence of the "family" was more than he could tolerate, and it was not unusual for him to seek out his private space: "I dined alone... steak and onions and sweet potatoes in a purée whipped up by me. I gave myself a gin and tonic and a Spanish lesson, retired to bed at 9:30 and read an extremely good biography of James I and slept like a top."

He patronised the restaurants where he was known: The Savoy Grill, The Ivy (when Mario Gallati was *maître d'*) and The Caprice, when Mario moved there. Mario always remembered that Noël "loves French cooking...but usually eats very little when he is working on a play! When it's in production he becomes a different man and eats like a true gourmet." Bouillabaisse with aioli was such a favourite of Noël's that Mario threatened to name the dish "Bouillabaisse Noël Coward."

In company, Noël was always immaculately attired, but around the house he'd dress casually: Sports shirt and slacks, a sweater draped around the shoulders if there was a chill in the air. White was the colour of choice.

Sorry if I'm undermining the image, but the long cigarette-holder and the Sulka dressing gowns were merely props. His standard wardrobe was modest and off the peg. The dressing gown he is seen wearing in those last pictures in Jamaica was made by a local lady, as were many of his sports shirts. Noël valued comfort above all, and his casual clothes persuaded him he was off-duty and off-stage.

He was a witty man, and the soul of Noël's wit was brevity. Words fascinated him and he used them precisely and sparingly. Most tellers of Coward stories get them wrong because they embellish, ignoring the golden rule that he applied to all writing and speaking: *simplify!* "Wit," he once said, "is like caviar. It should be served in small, elegant portions and not splodged around like marmalade!"

When you have a reputation as a wit, every epithet is attached to you. Oscar Wilde apparently experienced it first. When he commented to James Whistler that he wished he'd thought of a particular turn of phrase, Whistler replied: "You will, Oscar, you will..." Noël formulated his own response: "If they're really good, I acknowledge them. I generally work myself into the belief that I really said them."

It is usually the legend, rather than the fact, that gets repeated. William Fairchild, the script writer for *Star!* (1968), nervously showed Noël the part of the script that portrayed him and asked for his opinion. Noël dead-panned, "Too many 'Dear Boys,' dear boy."

There are many approaches to humour. The New York Jewish humour of Neil Simon or Woody Allen is based on social self-deprecation, the hero as victim. Much of Noël's humour was based on inversion, or the substitution of an unexpected word in an expected context: "There is less in this than meets the eye" ... "Let me be the eighth to congratulate you" ... writing to T. E. Lawrence in the R.A.F.: "Dear 338171 (may I call you 338?)" ... on Randolph Churchill: "Dear Randolph, utterly unspoiled by failure" ... on a child star in a boring play: "Two things should be cut: the second act and the child's throat" ... "Work is much more fun than fun!". It was the humour of surprise, a device with which his comedies abounded.

His was also the humour of *faux naïveté*. Looking around a chapel decorated by Jean Cocteau, Noël observed: "I had no idea that all the apostles looked so much like Jean Marais." Leaving a turgid play about Queen Victoria: "I had no idea Albert married beneath him."

Edith Evans, who had frequently been on the receiving end, said this of Noël: "He can get into two or three little words, just dripped out, such a witty comment on the situation. He doesn't waste words. It's a style of his own."

Harold Hobson, a critic who had studied Noël's work for many years, concluded that his comedy "lay in carefully-calculated, well-based, discourteous retort, in chic and cultivated bad manners." Ken Tynan, in comparing him with earlier wits like Wilde, noted that "while their best things need to be delivered slowly, even lazily," Noël's wit had the "staccato, blind impulsiveness of a machine gun." He "doses his sentences with pauses as you dose epileptics with drugs."

He could make it look so easy. Alan Bennett tells how Johnny G., playing the headmaster in *Forty Years On* (1968), asked him to write a parody for the second act. "You know the sort of thing, lots of little epigrams, smart, witty remarks. It wouldn't be at all difficult." Alan assured him that it *would* be difficult, to which Gielgud remarked in a rather puzzled tone, "Noël does it all the time."

Noël's curiously clipped delivery implied there was something comical about the everyday world. There is nothing inherently funny about Budleigh Salterton, but the way it was used in *Blithe Spirit* meant many people could never take it seriously again. Uckfield elicits the same response in *Present Laughter*. Even if Norfolk were to sprout mountains overnight, the verdict will forever remain: "Very flat, Norfolk." With a twinkle of the eye and a slight baring of the teeth, Noël could make you look at life anew.

He was a surprisingly prudish man. He wasn't religious, but he envied anyone who clearly did have faith. He was always concerned that his comedy would inadvertently give offence. When Bill Paley of CBS turned down *Present Laughter* for television on the grounds that it would upset America's "Bible Belt," Noël didn't argue. He simply said, "Well, I suppose he knows about these things," and left it at that. It was the only matter of judgement on which he ever trusted Paley, and I happen to think he was wrong.

In a late television interview with David Frost, Noël was asked about his attitude to God. "We've never been intimate," he conceded, "but maybe we have a few things in common." When Frost pressed him on whether he had a particular vision of Hell, Noël replied that he had, and that "They're all to do with over-acting!" In a more serious moment, Noël admitted, "I have no religion, but I believe in courage!" When asked how he'd like to be remembered, he replied: "By my charm."

He was not particularly persuaded by psychiatrists either ("How can anyone else know more about me than I know about myself?"), which is probably why he was unconvincing when he played one in *The Astonished Heart.* "What possible good can it do me to be told that all my problems can be traced to the fact that I was frightened by my rocking horse at the age of four?" After a thoughtful pause he added, "Actually, I'm not at all sure that I *had* a rocking horse at the age of four."

He had a powerful aversion to the way drink and drugs sapped people's energies and intellect. Of Clifton Webb: "He really does display a very bitchy, unpleasant character when fried." Of Edward Molyneux: "He's not exactly tolerant or kind when he gets a few drinks inside him." For someone really close, like Binkie, he said less but felt more.

It's ironic that Noël was attacked for making Nicky, the protagonist of *The Vortex,* a drug addict, triggering speculation that he was writing about dissolution from personal experience. Had the times permitted, he would almost certainly have made Nicky homosexual, which would have made more dramatic and emotional sense. As it was, the substitution gave him enough trouble. The Lord Chamberlain banned the original production, until Noël managed to personally persuade him that the play was *against* drugs, not *about* them.

Noël enjoyed a drink, but strictly as a social lubricant, an excuse for conviviality while the jokes flowed. He would get merry, but never drunk, for the simple reason that he hated losing control. That was why drugs never appealed to him. He valued his sharpness of mind too much. I remember the distressed look on his face when Gertie interrupted him in the middle of an anecdote. "But you've already told us that," she said. Noël had completely forgotten, and he hated repetition. He never made that mistake again.

He was, above all, a kind man. Birthdays were never forgotten, personal events would be recognized by a note or a phone call. He was President of the Actors' Orphanage for twenty years, and the proceeds from the posthumous sale of his paintings, as I have said, went to the Actors Charitable Trust.

Noël took his duties for the Orphanage very seriously and would turn out for all the events, dragging show business friends firmly in his wake. He was marvellous with children, and was always passionate about what interested them. He never patronised them, and always treated them as adults. They repaid his compliment with the warmth of their response. Noël's experiences as a child actor in an adult world undoubtedly helped him to understand them, another example of Peter Pan coming out. Lynn Redgrave, who always called him "Dad," fondly remembers: "He really loved young people. They made him laugh!"

Tynan speculated that this childlike quality was the key to Noël's whole personality and success: "The pipeline to infancy, and all the mischief and imaginative exuberance that go with it, is always open. He was a creature of impulse, who was tough-minded enough to resist the temptation to become what passes, in our society, for a 'grown-up'..."

Although he hated hospitals, he was an unfailing visitor. When Lornie was dying, Noël always found time to visit, to make jokes and talk about better days. He valued his relationships with his "dear ones" as more than precious. I still find it moving to read of his concern in the *Diaries:* "I hate Graham going as I always do....He arrived back safely, thank God. I am never really relaxed when he is between the sea and the sky." The *Diaries* are full of his "fears" for his "family," but the tone is caring, not neurotic.

Why were the post-war years so difficult? It would be naïve to pretend that he was always right and that those who opposed him were always misguided or malicious. It would be equally amiss to explain the relative failure of his later work as the unfocused efforts of an anachronistic talent, since some of his biggest successes were achieved in totally new media.

Therein lies a clue. Unless he was forced to behave otherwise, he clung too tightly to the pre-war world he admired, demanding instead that the modern world change to suit *his* direction. Noël was one of the earliest examples of a "media victim." Today that's a commonplace spectacle, people well-known for being famous and famous for being well-known. Few of them are heroes for longer than Andy Warhol's statutory fifteen minutes.

Noël had a much better run than that, and he had the wherewithal to sustain it. He had to permit his natural talent to have its head, as in his lighter work. In America, he proved he could adapt, but back home it was a different story. A few petty critics were determined to prove that Noël Coward was a dinosaur. He would constantly claim to have taken Milton's advice to "twitch his mantle blue" and rise above it, though he never really did.

The closest analogy I can come to is this: Noël was a Rolls-Royce. Everything about him was constructed to convey the effortless elegance of the pre-war era. Not surprisingly, to many people he looked out of place and elitist cruising down the mean streets of proletarian Britain, where everyone else was riding a bike or waiting for their bus. (America, of course, didn't see him that way.) Then, as the world continued to turn and hair shirts began to be exchanged for something a little more comfortable, more and more people began to appreciate that style, *per se*, wasn't necessarily bad, particularly when it was used to express basic truths about the human condition. A Rolls-Royce, come to think of it, is a pefectly good way to get from A to B. In any case, what had started out as bright and shiny was now well-polished and vintage, well worth another look. After all, we *did* invent it, and it was one of the those things the Yanks couldn't do half as well.

Dad's Renaissance, when it came, was a deserved blessing that soothed his final years, but the tribute was strictly retrospective. What might we have seen him do in those last thirty years, if the ghost of his past had not been peering over his shoulder?

In the dismal days immediately after Noël's death, Coley and I went through the arrangements we somehow thought we'd never have to make. A snatch of that last song Noël had written for me kept repeating in my mind. Did he know it was his last song when he wrote in "Come the Wild, Wild Weather":

> *We shall still be together*
> *When our life's journey ends,*
> *For wherever we chance to go*
> *We shall always be friends.*

If he'd had to write his own epitaph, Noël claimed it would read: "He was much loved because he made people laugh and cry." If mine were to read: "Friend of Noël Coward," that would suit me fine!

Just as a new decade was dawning, there was to be one last twist in the plot.

The Party's Almost Over...Noël contemplates his lifetime's run.

Westminster Abbey. *I lay a wreath on Noël's memorial in the presence of the Queen Mother and the Dean of Westminster, Edward Carpenter.* (March 28, 1984)

CHAPTER FOURTEEN

"VERY 'NOËL COWARD'"
KEEPING A LEGEND ALIVE

*"Someday, I suspect, when Jesus has definitely got me for
a sunbeam, my works may be adequately assessed."*
(Diaries - 1956)

*"I do not think he will ever quite fulfil his promise if
he does not curb his versatility."*
(Marie Tempest)

*"When that which is loosely termed my soul
Goes whizzing off through the infinite
By means of some vague remote control
I'd like to think I was missed a bit."*
(1973)

*"Pertaining to the Thirties. Very rarely used to describe epigrams or
situations, but frequently to describe blazers, white flannels, cigarette-
holders, cocktail shakers, etc., usually in the slightly mocking formula
'Oh, very Noël Coward.'"*
...from an article in Cosmopolitan (1985)

I awoke on the morning of January 3rd, 1980, to the sound of running
footsteps. Jean-René was obviously in a tremendous hurry. It was his habit
to serve Coley and me our breakfast in our rooms. I was jolted from my
drowsy state, and I remember thinking he'd forgotten the orange juice or
the sugar or something.

Then I heard Jean-René frantically calling, *"Monsieur Payn! Monsieur
Lesley est très malade!"* Grabbing my dressing gown, I rushed after him to
Coley's room to find Coley collapsed across the bed. According to his
unvarying routine, he'd got up, showered and shaved, and was on his way
back to bed for breakfast, when the heart attack had struck. He was sixty-
nine.

It was a terrible shock because his health had appeared perfect. Only the previous day, Coley had been full of plans for his forthcoming trip to the University of Southern California to deliver a lecture. Since the successful publication of his biography of Noël, *Remembered Laughter* (1976), he'd been much in demand as a pundit on the Coward era.

Seven short years after Noël's death, the keeper of the keys, the man who had made everything work without apparent effort, was dead. The only person left to run the Noël Coward Estate and all it entailed was the one person who'd never considered such a prospect in his wildest imaginings. Little Lad was no longer waiting in the wings; it was time to play the part.

A few days later, to my astonishment, I found myself in front of several hundred eager-eyed Californian students. They were kind and receptive and I found myself enjoying our common interest in the remarkable man called Noël Coward. It was the best possible baptism for what was to follow.

*   *   *   *

"Dad's Renaissance" blossomed into a still-growing "Dad's Restoration." Somewhere in the world, there are currently dozens of productions of Coward plays on stage or in preparation, roughly twice as many as on the day he died. They have assumed a pecking order: 1. *Blithe Spirit;* 2. *Private Lives;* 3. *Fallen Angels...* and then the field. Noël's personal favourite was *Design for Living,* and on his last trip to London he was still talking to Binkie about casting a revival. The plays have a life of their own which dictates what can and cannot be done with them. For instance, you can't send up *Private Lives.* There's a tendency for modern actors to feel uncomfortable with "period" pieces, so they feel they must show their superiority to this old-fashioned material. Inevitably they overplay, or put on what they think is a "Noël Coward" impersonation, managing only to look affected and silly. However badly it's played, the observation of character and the quality of writing shines through. Only the performer is trivialised.

The advice I give is precisely what Noël gave to me: "The play is strong, the words are good. Play the part for what it's worth but *be yourself.* Do *not* try and copy Noël!"

I had my own bitter experience to support that theory! During the run of *Sigh No More,* I was lunching at The Ivy with Winifred, who surprised me by saying, "You mustn't imitate Noël, you know." I couldn't believe what I was hearing. I said, "I don't imitate Noël at all." When she persisted I thought, "The old girl's lost it!" I mentioned this conversation to Noël.

"She's raving mad," he said, and promptly phoned Winifred to correct her. They had quite a row about it, though it was soon over and forgotten.

Years later, I was listening to the records of the show and, to my horror, I sounded exactly like Noël. It must have stemmed from being around him when the songs were being written and having his original intonations in my head. Winifred was perfectly right, and I deeply regret that I never had the chance to apologise to her.

*   *   *   *

I never saw Gertie as Amanda, so the best I've seen is Maggie Smith. She played the part first with Robert Stephens, when they were married to each other, and later with John Standing. Maggie has Gertie's qualities of natural and visible intelligence coupled with an impudent irreverence. (I can imagine her saying, "Oh, *do* tell me, is my visible intelligence showing?")

It would have rocked the foundations of the Coward Church had it been known that Noël believed Maggie was a better Amanda than Gertie, and told her so at that last revival. "Amanda is common," he said, "and Miss Smith understands that."

Lynn Redgrave tells a story of the National Theatre production of *Hay Fever* in which she and Maggie appeared with Edith Evans. Edith was clearly thrown by the younger women in the cast. She was having trouble piecing her performance together while they were apparently larking about. She quavered to Noël, "Oh, Noëlie, it's all so *difficult*. I mean, what's that young Redgrave gal going to do with that feather... and what's that young Smith gal going to do with that cigarette holder?"

As young as she was, Lynn knew *precisely* what she was going to do with the feather. She was going to hang onto it for dear life! She'd already read the steely glint in Edith's eye and rushed down to Noël. "Dad," she muttered breathlessly, "how do you like my feather?" Dad gave his verdict. It was perfect. When Edith's inevitable query came, it received the shortest of shrifts. When Maggie heard of the cigarette holder contretemps, she threw back her head, struck an impossibly theatrical pose and croaked, "Ooh, I haven't *decided*."

Maggie could be quite wicked. On that same production, she had had enough of the Dame's quaverings. Judith Bliss is a fading beauty, but with enough glow remaining to bedazzle a series of young suitors. Edith had lost the first flush of youth and, at seventy-six, was having trouble remembering the second. Looking at her speculatively one day, Maggie mused to Lynn, "If this was a film, they'd have to shoot her through a pair of lace knickers." Filtered or not, Noël believed Edith was timelessly talented: "She could play Juliet."

Lynn Redgrave retains particularly vivid impressions of working with Noël on that production. Although only twenty at the time, she was a founder member of Larry's remarkable repertory company. To the younger members of the team, Noël Coward was a legend, but icons are there to be tarnished:

> "Before I met him - being young and arrogant - I thought he'd be very old school and maybe a bit - *cross*. Like, 'No,' I said, 'Put your right foot in front of your left foot as you come through the door... no, no, no, do it *again!*' And I thought I'd be quite stymied....I was a little afraid that it would be very dull and I'd find it very difficult.... But that was prejudice, really, based on my generation's *attitude*. It was the image..."

When she was actually directed, she was pleasantly surprised, as so many before her, to find that Noël was one part martinet, nine parts psychologist:

> "Yes, he *did* block it out in a fairly traditional manner but he was open to instinct from anyone who had 'funny bones'....You remember the scene where the guests come down to breakfast one at a time? They each have their own little 'moment'? Well, when you read it on the page that scene takes about fifteen minutes, so it's mostly performance....Sometime in the second or third week of rehearsal Dad - I always called him 'Dad' - took me aside and said: 'You've got precisely two minutes from the time you appear at the top of the stairs until you get to the table and burst into tears. Now, go away and *think* of something for that two minutes. If you can come up with something that makes me laugh, it stays in'....Well, I came up with some bits of business and he liked it and I was thrilled.

> "Then he said - and thinking about it now, this was very clever of him - 'Do one thing for me....' Then he told me something terribly technical on a particular line - I forget which one it was - 'Pick up the spoon, then look to the right, count two and put it down and I guarantee it will get a laugh.' Which, of course, it *did.*

> "You see, the clever thing was that he knew I hadn't learned

that kind of technique at this stage of my career. He could easily have intimidated me with too many instructions - but he didn't. But he knew the scene needed a certain precision on top of the other stuff I'd dreamed up and could handle. He let *me* invent, then *added* something. He didn't edit what *I* did. And it was the only time he ever *told* me what to do. He coaxed the rest of it out of me...out of *all* of us."

Noël had obviously mellowed as a director, and Lynn crossed his path at precisely the right time!

At the other end of the scale was the Burtons' 1983 revival of *Private Lives* in New York. I have only myself to blame for this, since I gave permission for it as part of a season of plays. The result was disastrous because the production was essentially a gimmick.

The Burtons "live" on stage were guaranteed to pull in the crowds. They had, after all, publicly fallen in love during the making of *Cleopatra*, married, messily divorced, then noisily remarried, though they were not in wedlock at the time of this production. It was the stuff of a successful soap. It wasn't, however, the stuff of a serious Broadway play. Richard was a fine actor but no comedian, and he seemed to feel he was "slumming" in the part. Elizabeth tried very hard, but her stage technique was so rudimentary that she seemed to be constantly looking for the camera to record her close-up.

When Richard (with his bad back) had to help her off the sofa in Act 2, it didn't help that Liz was patently overweight. Gertie must have been spinning like a top in her home sweet heaven! The elegance of the original was not enhanced by Richard fondling Liz's left breast. The audience got the point that the Burtons were playing a commercial gig, but Noël and the play deserved better from two such pros.

An interview that Richard gave to *New York* magazine says everything:

"I think there is some fun in it for me, especially when I start inventing my own lines. You remember the bit in the third act when I scream at Elizabeth, 'Slattern!' Well, I've enlarged that. So each night, I hurl a string of invectives at her: 'Slattern, yes, and vermin too, and fishwife, nightmare, horror' - and then Elizabeth will scream them all back at me. That gives me a great deal of amusement, although Noël must be spinning in his grave....Yes, I'm playing to the lines, going for the laughs, the double entendres...."

3 Variations on a Timeless Theme: *Elizabeth Taylor and Richard Burton (1983); Maggie Smith and John Standing (1975); Brian Bedford and Tammy Grimes (1969).*

The Burtons felt that all that was required of them was that they turn up. The paying public felt otherwise. The revival was a flop and never made the planned London trip. But *Private Lives* survived their public lives.

One of the most unusually successful recent revivals was in Sweden, where Liv Ullmann, an actress associated with the dark night of Ingmar Bergman's soul, has broken all box office records. What must "Strange how potent cheap music is" sound like in Swedish?

Hay Fever has had its share of problems, too. Judith Bliss was modelled on the domestic ménage of American actress, Laurette Taylor. Created by Marie Tempest, an actress who could pour tea and arrange flowers to perfection, the rôle has been played by a remarkable series of leading ladies, none of whom has ever managed to diminish the part. Edith approximated it without ever quite speaking the words as written. Celia Johnson played it with charm but little impact. Later performances by Rosemary Harris, Penelope Keith and Maria Aitken have all done the character justice, but I hope these elegant ladies will forgive me if I say that the definitive performance remains to be given by the "Smith gal," who was word-perfect thirty years ago.

Titles of plays or books are funny things the more you come to study them. So many of the titles of Noël's works that we've come to know, underwent several metamorphoses along the way.

Home and Colonial begat *Island Fling*, which begat *South Sea Bubble;*

Scarlet Lady became *Pacific 1860; Present Laughter* was originally *Sweet Sorrow*, which is presumably why the French title is *Joyeux Chagrins; Concerto* was transformed into *Bitter Sweet*. Even dear old *Hay Fever* was not immune. If you're wondering what the title meant, don't bother. It had no meaning. Noël said it was simply a last-minute replacement for his original title, which the producers didn't care for. Never one to throw things away, Noël used that original title a decade later for one of the sections of *Tonight at 8:30*. It was *Still Life*, which, of course, became *Brief Encounter* when David Lean made the film in 1945. Are you still with me?

Fallen Angels (1925), has always been a problem play. It's been revived on several occasions, but its pecuniary success was never matched by Noël's artistic satisfaction. He'd originally written it for Gladys Cooper and Madge Titheradge, but they were never both available at the same time. It was finally cast with Edna Best and Margaret Bannerman, who, after a pre-opening nervous collapse, was succeeded by Tallulah.

The moral thesis of the play has dated badly. It may have been shocking in the 1920's to see two married women drunkenly contemplating capitulation to a French lover, but the social reality of the older woman and her toy-boy makes the premise archaic and potentially vulgar. It can now only be played as farce.

Noël wanted the American production to star Lynn Fontanne and Laurette Taylor, the actress who had largely "sponsored" Lynn's early career. Miss Taylor, however, had become jealous of her "pupil" and refused, telling Noël, "Lynn just clowns around on stage and she'll ruin every scene." She was probably influenced in that judgement by the knowledge that Judith Bliss was based on her. Relations between them remained cool, and the fallen angels were not resurrected on that side of the Atlantic until much later.

Tallulah turned it into a travesty and a big commercial success in 1925. "Disgusting," "Obscene," said the reviews. "Tinkle" went the box-office till.

The two Hermiones, Gingold and Baddeley, vulgarised it and made a comparable hit of it (1949), as did Nancy Walker and Margaret Phillips in an even lower low-comedy Broadway version in 1955.

Noël had long ago come to the conclusion that the play could never be played straight. Henceforth, it would be a vehicle for two ladies *d'une certaine âge* to do with as they thought fit. If the audience found it amusing, Noël didn't want to witness anything except the box-office receipts. If he were here to go through the books, he'd find only *Blithe Spirit* and *Private Lives* are more popular.

Antiques improve with age. They don't decay, they simply acquire

Noël with Hermione Gingold. *He might not have approved of her Fallen Angel but she stayed high in his affections.*

patina. Dear old *Fallen Angels* is firmly in that category. The Mills sisters, Juliet and Hayley, recently put it on for a whole new generation brought up on *Golden Girls*, and they laughed all over again. (Some of them probably thought that Noël had written the play after he'd seen the television series!)

Being forced to run the Coward Estate under tragic circumstances gave my life the focus it had been missing. Noël, Coley, and Lornie all had their assigned parts, but I had no particular skills and was not driven like them. That fateful January morning of Coley's death changed everything. I've since discovered many new skills, like saying "No!", and I've developed into a tough negotiator. One day I shall have to answer to Noël, so I'm not taking any chances!

I immediately had to come to grips with the legal aspects of running of the Estate. I knew about contracts, but dealing with Noël's "intellectual properties," that high-flown legal description for anything he wrote, opened my eyes to a new world. A lot of valuable "real estate" had cheerfully been signed away by Jack Wilson when he was running Noël's affairs in the US. Jack hadn't given a second thought to the small print that said "... and all mechanical rights," when selling the film rights to a particular play. In the 1930's, "mechanical rights" meant gramophone records. Who would have anticipated television and videotape cassettes?

As a result, when he sold the film rights to MGM for *Private Lives* and to Paramount for *Design for Living*, Jack not only assigned those studios (or their successors) control over any subsequent film versions, he also lost the Estate's right to have the plays performed on television or cassette! Anybody wanting to film *Private Lives* today will have to deal with Ted Turner, who bought the MGM film library. (Should he so wish, Mr. Turner can "colourise" Elyot and Amanda until the cows come home.) I dare say Noël has had one or two celestial finger wags with Jack over *that* one...always supposing agents *go* to Heaven.

I really have learned to be firm, even though it's not my natural disposition. Faced with a producer who wanted to wheel and deal (such people *do* exist!), I found myself proclaiming grandly, "Don't bargain with us. We're Cartier, not Berwick Market! We don't need the money!" Noël must have sent that message down, because I'd never have thought of it myself! But I've used it a lot *since*.

A fascinating part of running the Estate is deciding which of the many requests for productions merit approval. How do you judge the fidelity of a Japanese translation? *Blithe Spirit* is enormously popular in Japan, though it's unlikely they understand the first thing about Budleigh Salterton. Current French translations are of inferior quality, as Noël found to his own cost, appearing in *Joyeux Chagrins (Present Laughter)*. They're in the process of "being fixed."

I'm usually quite lenient about "improvisation" if it stays faithful to Noël's original intent. When Joan Collins played in *Private Lives*, I saw no harm in letting her interpolate a brief exchange in which she was asked where she was going. She answered, "Dallas!" The audience loved the reference, it didn't hurt the play and I doubt whether Noël would have minded.

He minded a great deal, however, when Henry Sherek revived the play in 1949 with Margaret Lockwood and Peter Graves:

AMANDA: *Whose yacht is that?*
ELYOT: *The Duke of Westminster's, I expect. It always is.*

Sherek changed Elyot's response to "Stewart Granger and Michael Wilding," who were known to be holidaying together. The topical reference raised a laugh, but not from Noël. He saw the show at Brighton and was backstage, finger wagging, at the first interval. The new line was scuttled and the Duke of Westminster got his boat back.

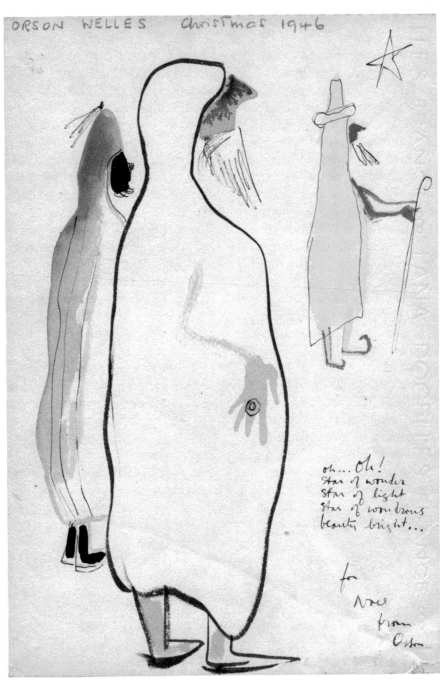

Orson Welles and Noël never worked together, though they often discussed it. The nearest was when Orson played Harry Lime after Noël had turned the part down. This is Orson's personal Christmas card to Noël in 1946 – from one "star of wonder" to another.

The Burtons proved that casting a particular artiste at a particular time adds a shade of extra meaning. It took guts for Joanie Collins to take on the rôle that had been played before her by stage stars like Gertie, Maggie and Maria Aitken. The critics were expected to take cheap shots, though they were ultimately quite fair. The *real* critics she had to please were not dramatic but domestic. Women flocked to the show to see how this "mature" vamp looked in the flesh. The lady, need I add, didn't let them down. The audience became part of the show as, night after night, women turned up, dressed to the nines, and as determined to show *her* as she was to show *them!*

I agreed to let Tom Conti change the ending of *Present Laughter* in the recent London revival. The excuse used by the ladies who "stay over" at Garry Essendine's flat is that they've forgotten their latch key. The play ends with Garry and his reconciled wife, Liz, stealing away from the emotional chaos that the flat has become. Tom had the idea of getting a final curtain laugh by having Garry's secretary, Monica, suddenly return. She has lost her latch key!

It seemed a harmless enough twist and it duly got the laugh. In retrospect, it's clear that the business subtly distorted the meaning of the play in terms of Garry and Monica's relationship. The latch key was the symbol for extra-curricular activity. Did that mean Monica was an occasional member of Garry's gallery, or had she really lost her key? Since Monica was the stage equivalent of Lornie, nothing could have been further from Noël's mind. It wasn't a major issue, but it affected the balance of a carefully crafted play. The "threesome" curtain defeats Noël's typical "Escape-from-Chaos" ending. Conti's interpretation didn't occur to me because I knew what Noël intended, but enough people have taken that other meaning to make me reconsider.

Dallas and latch keys shall pass; the point is to ensure that they do. I've learned to insist that no deviation from the text is put into the "prompt" copies, thus rendering it part of the official Coward text.

One classic example of divergence in *Private Lives*, can be attributed to Gertie herself. I've seen people at dinner parties practically come to blows over whether her famous line about the potency of cheap music begins with "Strange" or "Extraordinary." The answer is both. In the published script the line reads: "Extraordinary how potent cheap music is," but on the gramophone record Noël and Gertie made at the time of the original 1930 London production, Gertie says "Strange..." Extraordinarily strange, isn't it?

One of Noël's lyrics will occasionally pop into my mind with a new significance: *Time will tell / Time will show...*

Like many great writers, Noël had the unique ability to capture the essence of his times. He had many immediate popular successes with the early plays and songs. Occasionally, though, the writer will leap ahead of his time, and it may take a while for someone else to come along and give successful commercial form to the original idea.

There was a strange familiarity about the 1990 Chichester production of *Point Valaine*, a play Noël wrote for the Lunts, which ran for a scant fifty-five performances on Broadway in 1934. I'd never seen the play before, but the tale of a sexually frustrated mature woman, who owns a seedy hotel in the tropics, has a brutal local lover and a mixed bag of guests with assorted problems, sounded suspiciously like Tennessee Williams' *Night of the Iguana* (1962). When I saw the National Theatre's 1992 revival, I thought so again.

Point Valaine was neglected because it wasn't a brittle comedy, an aspect of the Coward perception which dogged him all his days. Neither was *Point Valaine* the vehicle to showcase Lynn and Alfred in the way their fans were accustomed to seeing them. So what was the *point* of *Point Valaine?* Unless it appears on television, the Chichester production was probably the only look we'll get at it. The cast requirements are too big for the West End.

A similar theatrical pre-emptive strike was *Semi-Monde*, written in 1926 and never commercially produced or published. Set in the bar of the Ritz Hotel in Paris, we witness a parade of typical '20's characters, whose groupings form and re-form as the wit flickers. It was considered too daring in its day, with its references to adultery and homosexuality, but, nearly seventy years later, it resembles a series of black-and-white social snapshots that fix a fascinating period in history.

Vicki Baum's *Grand Hotel*, four years later, does bear an uncanny resemblance to it. The publication of *Grand Hotel* sadly put an end to a project to produce *Semi-Monde* in a German translation with Max Reinhardt directing.

They do say there are only so many plots in the world! *Suite in Three Keys*, with its different sets of characters acting out their lives in the same Geneva hotel suite, seems a little like ... what was that Neil Simon play where the different sets of characters act out their lives ...?

Noël's output, though not in the Barbara Cartland dimension, was prolific. He was driven to express himself. Even a postcard was never signed with a simple "Having a lovely time. Wish you were here." There was always a verse or other word play, done as much to amuse the author as the recipient. The cable Noël sent to Gertie when she became Mrs. Richard Aldrich in 1940 has often been quoted:

DEAR MRS. A. HOORAY, HOORAY
AT LAST YOU ARE DEFLOWERED,
ON THIS AS EVERY OTHER DAY
I LOVE YOU, NOËL COWARD.

Here's another example of his obsession with word play from 1957, when Noël was visiting friends in Wyoming. Noël had known his hostess, Mrs. Hope Read, since the 1920's, when, as Hope Williams, she had enjoyed a "brilliant but disappointingly brief stage career." (She had appeared with Noël in *The Scoundrel* in 1935.) He helped her celebrate her sixtieth birthday with:

"THE BIRTH OF HOPE"

(Lines written to commemorate the sixtieth birthday of the eccentric Mrs. Read. Deer Creek Ranch Valley, Wyoming, August 11th, 1957.)

Sixty years ago today
On a radiant August morn
Day of days and date of dates!
In these bright United States
Just imagine who was born
Sixty years ago today!
Sixty years ago today
Weary, flustered, harassed, hot,
Little did they know or heed
That the future Mrs. Read
Lay there dribbling in her cot
Sixty years ago today.

Sixty years ago today
On Wyoming's mountain trails
Moose and bear and stag and steer
Hadn't got the least idea
Who one day, would twist their tails
Sixty years ago today.

Sixty years ago today
(Blow the bugles. Beat the drums.)
Hopie entered upstage centre,
Upside down and bright magenta

Hanging from the doctor's thumbs
Sixty years ago today.

Sixty years ago today
In a stately, shuttered room
Not too far from New Rochelle
Hopie, with a piercing yell
Sprang from the maternal womb
Sixty years ago today.

Here's just one more that Jeffery Amherst, Noël's frequent travelling companion, unearthed. On a 1930 trip to Singapore he stopped off at a city which still enjoyed the protection of the Union Jack. The Consul was Lord —— and the verse addressed his spouse, who clearly did not strike a responsive chord in Noël:

Oh, Lady ——!
You must have read a lot of G. A. Henty
But you've not read Bertrand Russell
And you've not read Dr. Freud.
Which perhaps is the reason
You look so unenjoyed.
You're anti-sex in any form,
Or so I've heard it said
You're just the sort who would prefer
A cup of tea instead
You must have been a riot
In the Matrimonial Bed.
Whoops! Lady ——!

*   *   *   *

Because I knew so many of the characters who peopled Noël's real world, I've enjoyed identifying a phrase or a character description in one of the plays. I'll think, "I know where you got *that* from, chum!"

The most autobiographical example is *Present Laughter*. Garry Essendine is Noël, right down to the last Sulka dressing gown; Monica, his secretary, is Lornie; and the housekeeper, Mrs. Erickson, is a slightly exaggerated version of a Scandinavian lady who used to "do" for us at Gerald Road. The other characters are amalgamations. The business partners, Morris and Douglas, are a sub-divided Jack Wilson. Joanna, who plays fast and extremely loose with Morris, Douglas and Garry, was based

Just back - or poised for flight? Noël at home in Switzerland. (1962)

on Natasha. (Like Joanna, Natasha was not accepted into the "family" until she married. She was considered to be "from a different world altogether.")

Garry and Noël did, however, diverge on one crucial point. Speaking of his celebrity status, Garry remarks: "I enjoy it for what it's worth and fully intend to go on doing so for as long as anybody's interested and when the time comes that they're not, I shall be perfectly content to settle down with an apple and a good book." Noël loved a good book, but would never have risked his expensive dentures on as dicey an enterprise as an apple!

Noël was a literary magpie. If he overheard a particular phrase, or observed a peculiar piece of behaviour, his eyes would light up. It would be only a matter of time before it would turn up in his work: Roland Maule, the neurotic aspiring writer in *Present Laughter*, was a composite of Noël's personal nightmares, both past and future; Peter and Piggie Gilpin, in *Hands Across the Sea*, were based on Dickie and Edwina Mountbatten.

It's virtually impossible to think of Elyot and Amanda as anyone other than Noël and Gertie. Surely these were original creations, sprung fully-grown from Noël's head in that sleepless Tokyo hotel bedroom? In fact, Noël admitted that they were based in part on his aristocratic friends, Lord and Lady Castlerosse, whose domestic spats, often in the Savoy Grill, were well publicised. Of the Lady, Noël observed: "Her wit when she's in a good mood can be devastating, but she doesn't give a twopenny damn about people's feelings." Artistic licence and an inspired actress does the rest:

Enter AMANDA. She comes out onto the terrace. She is quite exquisite with a gay face and a perfect figure.

AMANDA: *I shall catch pneumonia, that's what I shall catch.*

The rest, as they say...

The process could work both ways. Older audiences watching *Upstairs Downstairs* on television may have had a vague sense of *déjà-vu*, particularly if they'd ever seen *Cavalcade*.

Whenever I'm asked to define the essential Coward quality, I resort to one word: *style*. Some heard it in the clipped and precise quality of his speech. He was once referred to as "that young man who talks like a typewriter."

Others saw it in his poised stage presence. Basil Dean, who directed Noël in one of his few non-Coward stage roles, S.N. Behrman's *The Second Man* (1928), wrote of him: "Every effect was sharp and clear as a diamond. By way of minor example, he had already learned - no one more effectively - how to use the cigarette as an instrument of mood, punctuating witticism with a snap of his lighter, and ill-temper with a vicious stabbing-out in a nearby ashtray."

For yet others, it was Noël's consistent attitude that appealed. He was often criticised for not being sufficiently "serious," but many perceived his apparent flippancy in quite a different light. Critic John Lahr felt that his "frivolity acknowledges the futility of life while adding flavour to it...Only when (he) is frivolous does he become in any sense profound."

Noël always knew, to the lift of an eyebrow, precisely what he was doing in public. In a 1955 *Diaries* entry, he makes a rare admission to his own artifice: "I shook hands with hundreds of people, was tirelessly charming, and made cheerful, modest little jokes. Fortunately none of my loved ones was there to witness such a fawning, saccharin display." He couldn't stop teasing, even to his private self.

Noël was once asked to define "Style" in an advertisement for the Gillette Razor Company. His tongue must have been bulging through his cheek when he delivered the following:

"STYLE"

"A candy-striped Jeep; Jane Austen; Cassius Clay; *The Times* before it changed; Danny La Rue; Charleston in South Carolina;

They say *you shouldn't have your tongue in your cheek while shaving. Nobody seems to have told Noël... (1950's)*

'Monsieur' de Givenchy; a zebra (but *not* a zebra crossing); evading boredom; Gertrude Lawrence; the Paris Opera House; white; a seagull; a Brixham trawler; Margot Fonteyn; any Cole Porter song; English pageantry; Marlene's voice... and...Lingfield has a tiny bit."

Whatever style was, no-one could deny Noël had it.

Even when he needed money the most, he was disinclined to go "commercial," though when he learned of the inordinate sum Larry received for his Polaroid spot on American television, there was the merest flicker of an eyebrow. Larry also "leased" his name to a brand of cigarette, eliciting a typical Noël comment: "If Larry and Gerald du Maurier can advertise cigarettes, I can't see why I shouldn't advertise toilet water."

The Gillette ad mildly amused him, but he only did three other commercials. One was for the Jamaican Tourist Board. He parodied his famous record sleeve by posing by the falls, immaculately attired and holding a cup of tea! ("Jamaica. It's no place like home!")

Another was for Phosferine, "the Great *All British* Tonic." For several years after *The Vortex*, Noël could be seen grimly smiling over the declaration that all this writing, rehearsing and acting really took the stuffing out of a chap. His homily was hardly vintage Coward: "I am quite sure that Phosferine helped me to endure this extra mental and physical strain without any ill effects. Whenever more effort is required, or it is necessary to work harder, or longer, I find that Phosferine is an unfailing energiser and preventive of lassitude or brain lag."

Most puzzling was his decision to rent his name to Rheingold Beer, which, as far as I'm aware, never passed his lips. It was during the US tour of *Nude with Violin*. He appears in the ad as his character, Sebastian, presumably because he felt it might help plug his play. I reprint it without further comment!

It's generally assumed that everything Noël ever wrote, down to the last laundry list, has been published. In fact, new material is constantly coming to light, and though much of it is minor, some of the footnotes shed a surprising amount of light.

The greatest disappointment is the absence of the *Letters*. Some people seem to have kept copies of everything they ever wrote, but, while we have numerous letters *to* Noël, we have very few *from* him, unless it was to one of the "family." The surviving correspondence demonstrates the same edge as his other writing, so it's a pity there's such a dearth. If this gives anyone the inspiration to dig out the trunk in the attic, I'd be delighted.

Checking out material that's previously been overlooked can yield some

This remarkable young man

the brilliant author of
"CAVALCADE"
DECLARES

"I HAD a most strenuous time in writing and rehearsing my plays for production, and at the same time learning my own acting parts, and I am quite sure that Phosferine helped me to endure this extra mental and physical strain without any ill-effects. Whenever more effort is required, or it is necessary to work harder or longer, I find that Phosferine is an unfailing energiser and a preventive of lassitude or brain fag."—*Drury Lane Theatre.*

From the very first day you take PHOSFERINE you will gain new confidence, new life, new endurance. It makes you eat better and sleep better, and you will look as fit as you feel. Phosferine is given to the children with equally good results.

PHOSFERINE

THE GREAT ALL BRITISH TONIC FOR

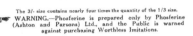

NOEL COWARD
DRAMATIST
COMPOSER
PRODUCER
ACTOR

Influenza	Neuralgia	Lassitude	Nerve Shock
Debility	Maternity Weakness	Neuritis	Malaria
Indigestion	Weak Digestion	Faintness	Rheumatism
Sleeplessness	Mental Exhaustion	Brain Fag	Headache
Exhaustion	Loss of Appetite	Anæmia	Sciatica

From Chemists.   Tablets and Liquid.

The 3/- size contains nearly four times the quantity of the 1/3 size.

☛ WARNING.—Phosferine is prepared only by Phosferine (Ashton and Parsons) Ltd., and the Public is warned against purchasing Worthless Imitations.

Perhaps the strain of writing Cavalcade *(1931) had exhausted him? Certainly the words are not vintage Noël – if he wrote a single one of them! (1930's)*

"*My beer is Rheingold – the Dry beer!*"

says NOËL COWARD

"**When I serve me,**" says writer-director Noël Coward, currently starring as a valet in his comedy, *Nude With Violin*, "the master demands his Rheingold Extra Dry. He insists upon that delicious dryness—never sweet, never bitter. And so do I ...

"**... when I serve my friends**, backstage. We're *all* agreed about the excellence of Rheingold's *real-beer* taste, the taste that's so clean and clear. We're in good company, too—the company of millions who make Rheingold New York's largest-selling beer!"

It's beer as beer should taste!

Always refreshing – never filling

To paraphrase one of Noël's early songs - he never said that to me...

interesting results.   There is at least one example of deficiency in the supposedly complete *Lyrics*. In Noël's last score for *The Girl Who Came to Supper* (1963) there's a waltz in the show-within-the-show, *The Coconut Girl*:

"TIME WILL TELL"
(The Waltz from *The Coconut Girl*)

Time will tell,
Time will show
Whether we shall ever know
Which jealous gods have decided our fate,
What joys and sorrows are lying in wait.
Here we stand,
You and I,
Hand in hand
Beneath the sky
Will the dawn break the spell?
Time alone will tell.

The lyric speaks volumes to me.

Noël's style has long been parodied, often by the best in the business. When Noël "adapted" Cole Porter's "Let's Do It" for his Las Vegas cabaret act, it was by way of repaying a debt. In 1939, Cole had been asked to write a song for the Kaufman and Hart play, *The Man Who Came to Dinner*. Called "What Am I to Do?", it is performed by Beverly Carlton, a Noël clone, for the benefit of the incapacitated hero, Sheridan Whiteside:

"WHAT AM I TO DO?"

Off in the nightfall
I think I might fall
Down from my perilous height;
Deep in the heart of me,
Always a part of me,
Quivering, shivering light.
Run, little lady,
Ere the shady
Shafts of time
Barb you with their winged desire,
Singe you with their sultry fire.

Softly a fluid druid meets me,
Olden and golden the dawn greets me:
Cherishing, perishing,
Up to the stairs I climb.

What am I to do
Toward ending this madness,
This sadness,
That's rending me through?
The flowers of yesteryear
Are haunting me,
Taunting me,
Darling, for wanting you.
What am I to say
To warnings of sorrow
When morning's tomorrow
Greets the dew?
Will I see the cosmic Ritz
Shattered and scattered to bits?
What not am I to do?

In cheeky recognition of his "borrowing," Cole attributed "What Am I to Do?" to "Noël Porter!" (This was not Cole's first Coward pastiche. In his own show, *Jubilee* (1935), a character called Eric Dare has a number called "The Kling-Kling Bird on the Divi-Divi Tree.")

Cole was not the only one. The songwriting team of John Kander and Fred Ebb (*Cabaret, Chicago, Spider Woman*) recently contributed a suitably Cowardesque song to the 1985 Broadway revival of *Hay Fever,* called "No, My Heart":

"NO, MY HEART"

Love and I, you must be told,
Are not a felicitous meld.
So in me you now behold
A lass disinclined to be held
No, my heart!
Not again.
Please don't fall.
Count to ten.
Considering the last time,
How sordid it became,

Remember love's a pastime,
Empty words, just a game.
No, my heart!
No, not now!
Don't be kissed.
Resist
Somehow.
Let other fools be tempted
But no, mon cher, not I
No, my heart!
Once burned, twice shy
I'll soon be a victim,
No matter how I try
Oh, my heart,
Dear heart,
Goodbye.

Every production of any Coward play must be cleared through the Estate, and though I have veto power over the casting of major productions, it would only be wielded in an extreme case. When an all-male version of *Private Lives* was proposed, it didn't take long to reach a decision. No! Ditto with *Fallen Angels*. Remembering the posters which advertised the fact that "*The Boys in the Band* is not a musical!", I shudder to imagine what they'd have done to us!

Occasionally something slips through the net. An Australian production of *Blithe Spirit* featured a male Madame Arcati, until word got back to Switzerland!

A Denver company wanted to "revise" *Sail Away*, which was a troubled book in the first place. The proposed revision did nothing to rectify that situation, but that *is* still the official Coward text. Eventually permission was granted for them to write a *new* book "in the Coward style." The new show was re-christened *Bon Voyage*, with a "Score by Noël Coward." It was an unhappy compromise because audiences don't study the small print. Any mention of the Coward name says to them that Noël wrote it, despite the disclaimer. As we learned in the '60's, collaboration doesn't count. From now on, it's all or nothing!

Some people fill an idle moment mentally selecting their all-time best cricket or football team. I find myself peopling Noël's plays with my version of the ideal cast. What if Rex Harrison had played Garry Essendine? What if Kate Hepburn had played Madame Arcati? (We did discuss it, but she felt she lacked the strength for a stage run.) Though written with Bea Lillie in mind, Beattie played only the "adapted" version,

High Spirits. What if Myrna Loy had played Ruth? It was discussed, but MGM wouldn't release her. And what if Cary Grant had played Charles Condomine? What if Kenneth Branagh and Emma Thompson were to try their hand at *Private Lives? That* might be very interesting.

High on Noël's list of "These We Have Not Loved" was Jeanette MacDonald's portrayal of Sari in the 1940 MGM film of *Bitter Sweet.* "It was when she suddenly decided to dance the can-can, I thought she'd perhaps not got a *full* grasp of the character." He described the film as "an affair between a mad rocking-horse and a rawhide suitcase," the "suitcase" presumably being Mr. Nelson Eddy. Noël believed, wrongly, as it turned out, "Now I can never revive *Bitter Sweet,* a pity, as I was saving it up as an investment for my old age!"

Fifteen years later, Miss MacDonald was still in hot-headed pursuit of the definitive performance. She'd been touring with it and had made a few "small improvements." She'd found a way to work "Mad About the Boy" into Manon's "If Love Were All," and she wanted to take it to Broadway. With all his majestic firmness, Noël said "No!"

There are some projects I positively encourage. We may have no record of Noël in *Present Laughter* (thanks to Bill Paley!), but there's one performance I'm determined not to allow to get away. There is a feature film currently being funded to demonstrate that the perfect Judith Bliss for this generation, without a shadow of a doubt, is "the Smith gal," Dame Maggie.

I'm not a particularly religious person but, before I end this narrative, it would be fitting to bring Him on, even in a non-speaking role. Noël wasn't religious either, but he had great veneration for the principles of religion and their obvious importance to many. He didn't believe it was something to be treated lightly.

He refused to see *Jesus Christ, Superstar* (1972), feeling it was in bad taste to bring the image of Jesus down to that of a "superstar." Andrew Lloyd Webber was not pleased when he heard that, but when reading Noël's plays one doesn't find a lot of superfluous language that "takes the name of the Lord in vain." He simply felt he didn't need it.

When Noël died, I phoned the Dean of Westminster to ask permission for a Memorial Service for Sir Noël in Westminster Abbey. He flatly refused, and when I pressed him for a reason he said: "Because he wasn't a churchgoer." I made the point that Noël would not be there, but that his friends, who wanted to honour him, *were* churchgoers and, in any case, wasn't the House of God open all the time? This failed to make any impression, so I said, "Well, you don't mind if I give the story to the *Evening Standard,* do you?" and hung up.

I had no intention of doing any such thing, but I was extremely upset by the incident. Eventually we held the service in St. Martin's-in-the-Fields. Some years later, I ran into Sir John Tilney, who expressed an idea that many felt: "There should be a stone to Sir Noël in Westminster Abbey." I recounted my previous experience and Sir John offered to deal with it. Sure enough, he obtained permission from the new Dean, Edward Carpenter. Poets' Corner was long since full, but the stone would be right next to it.

This may not be precisely the correct terminology for an event set in the Abbey, but in almost every respect it was exactly like putting on a show. The staff at the Abbey are extraordinarily capable, and everything went like clockwork until a few minutes before our Guest of Honour, the Queen Mother, was due to arrive. I felt a tap on the shoulder from the leader of the orchestra. "There's a camera and a mike up there," he said, pointing up into the arches. "If this is going to be recorded, we're not going to play."

Barely able to control my temper on what was already an emotional day, I said, as calmly as I could, "Oh, that's a strictly private recording for the archives." He believed me and went away, inadvertently doing me a big favour. My anger superseded my emotional turmoil, and I took my place on the receiving line quite under control.

In that packed "house" a little magic took place. Echoing around the vaulted ceiling, the familiar strains of Noël's music took on an ethereal quality I'd never heard before. When Johnny G. read Noël's last poem, "When I Have Fears," I couldn't catch anyone's eye for a moment, but Dickie Attenborough saved my composure, bless him, by over-running outrageously on the Address. It may sound irreverent, but I could imagine a celestial Finger Wag, with Noël admonishing, "Aren't we indulging ourselves a little, Dickie-darling? Let's not forget whose service this is."

The Queen Mother unveiled the memorial stone. After much soul-searching, I'd decided on this inscription: "Sir Noël Coward 1899-1973. Buried in Jamaica. A Talent to Amuse."

On really important occasions, time seems to telescope. I suddenly found myself standing at the West Door of the Abbey saying my goodbyes, my heart bursting with the memories these dear faces have brought back. Larry and Viv holding court at Notley...Joycie's wicked wit in The Game...the music of Johnny G.'s incomparable voice...Anna Neagle standing next to Evelyn "Boo" Laye, senior ladies now, but still recognisable as Sari in *Bitter Sweet*...Johnnie Mills and Dickie Attenborough, looking as boyish as they ever did in *In Which We Serve* forty years ago.

I thought of days in the Jamaican sun with Noël nursing a brandy and ginger ale, laconically eyeing Coley and me as we argued the relative merits of our paintings; or of sledging down the snow-covered hill on the way home in Switzerland.

Like a dazzling movie montage I had a flashback to hands applauding, curtains going up, stars taking bows, Mary, Bea, Gertie, Marlene, Cyril, Leslie, Lornie. Somewhere in the middle of it, a little boy in a white suit sings his heart out.

A gentle nudge brings me back to the present. The Queen Mother is about to take her leave. I hear myself mumbling, "Thank you, Ma'am. We're so pleased you could be here today." With that incomparable smile that makes her a girl again, she says, "I came because he was a friend of mine."

Inside the Abbey, with perfect timing, the orchestra plays:

> *Time may lie heavy between,*
> *But what has been*
> *Is past forgetting...*

Indeed it is.

Coward-san. *Noël's popularity extended to Japan, but he found it hard to visualise Madame Arcati in a kimono... Drawing by Makoto Wada.*

COWARD ON THEATRE

"Speak the speech, I pray you, as I pronounced it to you, trippingly on the tongue..."

(*Hamlet* Act III. Sc.ii)

"You ask my advice about acting? Speak clearly, don't bump into the furniture and if you must have motivation, think of your pay packet on Friday."

(Noël to the Gallery First Nighters' Dinner) (1962)

"The Theatre must be treated with respect. It is a house of strange enchantment, a temple of dreams."

"I will accept anything in the theatre...provided it amuses or moves me. But if it does neither, I want to go home."

Until the war, Noël's romance with the UK critics was marred only by the occasional lovers' tiff. He could do almost no wrong. After the war, however, a new generation of critics determined that he could do little right. Every epithet and gesture in a Coward show was called as witness to prove their case, causing Noël to lament, after more than fifteen years of such treatment, "I really do seem to be without honour in my own country."

That honour arrived shortly thereafter, fortunately, and, by the time Noël reached his seventieth birthday, the critics were busily dusting off all the adjectives they'd been withholding. In 1969, there was a "Holy Week," as Noël rather smugly referred to it. The *Financial Times* critic, B.A. Young, delivered a typical example of the adulation. Referring to Noël as "the Mozart of comedy writers," he even went so far as to compose a Homeric tribute:

"THE NOËLIAD"

Now see where gay Thalia, the comic Muse,
Ascends the stage and for attention sues,
Her smiling mask a little bit awry,
Her ivy-wreath aslant across her eye.
In silvery and not too solemn voice
She lauds the object of her latest choice.

From these same boards (says she) where in his day
Immortal Shakespeare held unchallenged sway,
Where Wycherley and Congreve flashed their wit,
And Sheridan and Goldsmith did their bit,
And Wilde, and Haddon Chambers, and Pinero,
To-day I introduce another hero.
Let all Parnassus with one voice enthuse
For Coward and his "Talent to Amuse."

She ceas'd; and as the air resounds with cheers
From out the wings great Coward now appears,
His face and figure young and lithe again,
And (so indulgent are the gods to men)
Attired as a Rear-Admiral, R.N.
He stands a while to savour his ovation,
Then answers with a courteous oration.

"My dears (quoth he), I would have given odds
'Gainst such a warm reception from the gods.
But, deeply though I'm moved by your affection,
I'd like to make one overdue correction
'A talent to amuse' may seem complete
For this nice character in Bitter Sweet
But it's a bore when people will suggest
That it's the only talent I possess'd.

"T'would not have been at all what I was after
If folk had left The Vortex weak with laughter,
Or if a giggle were the only need
The audience offered to This Happy Breed.
To make the people sing, or laugh, or weep
Was easy. I could do it in my sleep.

"But sometimes when I got beneath their hides
I made the darling creatures think besides.
Not that I've dealt, I own without apology,
With current politics or sociology
Like all that clever intellectual crew
Who throng the Court and Centre 42.

"Yet in my work I hope you can detect
The simple virtues that I judge correct.
Like patriotism, pride and self-respect.
And while I'm up I'd rather like to speak
About some subtle points in my technique."

Here Coward paused: and ere he could resume
A spate of voices echoed round the room.
First. Polyhymnia. Muse of sacred song,
To whom two more accomplishments belong -
One, Mimicry, the other, Eloquence -
Who thus began: "It clearly makes more sense
If Coward's art's so serious and fine
To move him from Thalia's care to mine."

But ere she'd well begun, Melpomene
Called out "Sirocco was a tragedy!"
Calliope's voice now made confusion worse -
"Mad Dogs and Englishmen is epic verse!"
Quick to put in her claim, Terpsichore
Cried "Dance Little Lady must belong to me!"
While, as a final damper on the jollity,
Astronomy's Urania claimed Star Quality.

Dissent among the Muses grew so rife
That soon all nine were lock'd in mortal strife,
And Coward was wisely running for his life.

One brief reproof he flung them from the portal.
"None of you knows what made me an immortal.
It's none of all the ingredients of your schism -
It's my immaculate professionalism."

Noël often threatened a book on theatre, as his conversation and his notes in the *Diaries* attest, but he never did. After his run-ins with Richard

Halliday and Carlos Thompson, he would have had "...a thing or two to say about theatrical spouses - of whatever sex....Marriage in the theatre is not an enviable state." The unsuitable clothes affected by some of the more senior actresses would draw comments of the "*mouton*-dressed-as-*agneau*" variety. And there would undoubtedly have been a pithy piece on the Learning of Lines. In the end, we are left with some few scattered remarks and published articles.

In 1961, at the height of the "Kitchen Sink" controversy, he wrote three pieces for *The Sunday Times* on the state of the English theatre. The heated reaction they caused convinced him that a need really existed for a volume of "Coward on Theatre," but other projects took priority. All we have left are the articles, three chapters of a work in progress, and an edited version of a long BBC-TV interview on "The Art of Acting." All are included in the following pages.

I unearthed a few other rare items. For instance, *Redbook,* an American magazine, interviewed Noël and Judy Garland together, when they were in Boston for the try-out of *Sail Away,* in 1961. A tape recording of that informal conversation recently surfaced, and I've included an abridged version of two very old friends exchanging trade secrets about their craft.

Finally, from dozens of articles, interviews, and personal recollections, I've culled a broad spectrum of opinions that Noël expressed about the profession he loved so much. Let us hope that they fill a small part of the void left by The Book That Never Was.

COLLECTED OBSERVATIONS

On Being a Playwright
On Constructing a Play
On Writing Plays v. *Writing Novels*
On "The Method"
On Actors
On Listening to Your Audience
On Theatre Audiences
On Feeling and "Being"
On Playing Comedy
On Writing Comedy
On Learning One's Lines
On Chekhov
On J.M. Barrie
On Samuel Beckett

On T.S. Eliot
On Dramatic Critics
On Explicit Language
On Taste
On Not Being "Noël Coward"
On Style
On the "Pleasure Principle"
On Confidence
On Film Acting
On Directing
On Revue
On Taking Light Music Seriously
On Writing Lyrics

ON BEING A PLAYWRIGHT

"If you want to be a playwright...go and get yourself a job as a butler in a repertory company, if they'll have you. Learn from the ground up how plays are constructed and what is actable and what is not. Then sit down and write at least twenty plays one after the other, and if you can manage to get the twenty-first produced for a Sunday night performance, you'll be damned lucky!"
                    Garry Essendine to aspiring playwright,
                    Roland Maule, in *Present Laughter* (1939)

"Work hard, do the best you can, don't ever lose faith in yourself and take no notice of what other people say about you."

(1951)

"Wise beginners of playwrights will, of course, after a little while compare their press notices with their royalties and decide that they still have a great deal to learn."

ON CONSTRUCTING A PLAY

"I wish they'd understand," he'd lament, "that writing a play is both a craft and an art." Whenever a "well-made" play, perfected by writers such as Shaw or Maugham, Lonsdale or Rattigan, was rejected in favour of inferior, poorly constructed work, he was genuinely appalled. Noël flirted unsuccessfully with more flexible forms, and he confided to his *Diaries* that, "I will never again embark on so much as a revue sketch that is not carefully and meticulously constructed beforehand." The discipline of structure gave him more, not less, freedom of verbal expression.

"I can see no particular virtue in writing quickly; on the contrary, I am well aware that too great a facility is often dangerous and should be curbed when it shows signs of getting the bit too firmly between its teeth. No reputable writer should permit his talent to bolt with him. I am also aware, though, from past experience, that when the right note is struck, and the structure of the play is carefully built in advance, it is both wise and profitable to start at the beginning and write through to the end in as short a time as possible....*Private Lives* lived in my mind several months before it emerged. *Present Laughter* had waited about, half formulated, for nearly three years before I finally wrote it...Before the first word of the first act is written the last act should be clearly in the author's mind, if not actually written out in the form of a synopsis. Dialogue, for those who have a talent for it, is easy; but construction, with or without talent, is difficult and is of paramount importance. I know this sounds like heresy in this era of highly-praised, half-formulated moods, but no mood, however exquisite, is likely to hold the attention of an audience for two hours and a half unless it is based on a solid structure."

(*Future Indefinite*, 1954)

Once construction was complete, the words became the paramount decoration, and few post-war playwrights ever matched Noël's exacting standards. He came to favour Harold Pinter, although he hated *The Dumb Waiter*, consigning it to "the surrealist school of non-playwriting." From *The Caretaker* onwards, he saw that Pinter was indeed a pioneer of the language. Noël later described Harold's pregnant pauses as equivalent to a "Cockney Ivy Compton-Burnett," a considerable compliment! In Pinter's mature plays, each word served a specific purpose, and was not merely filling space until another significant one came along. Pinter would have sympathised with Noël's complaint about an over-rehearsed but under-directed *Nude with Violin*. "Neither my lyrics nor my dialogue require decoration; all they do require are clarity, diction and intention and the minimum of gesture or business."

"The most important ingredients of a play are life, death, food, sex and money - but not necessarily in that order."

ON WRITING PLAYS v. WRITING NOVELS

Reading the "exquisitely phrased verbosity" of Henry James caused

Noël to reflect on the technical differences between the writing of a play and a novel:

"It is good for me technically because I am inclined to oversimplify my descriptive passages and reduce them to staccato interludes rather than letting them be part of the general structure. This is the natural result of years of dialogue writing. It is only when I have done a couple of pages of - to my mind - elaborate and drawn-out description that, on reading it over, I discover to my astonishment that it is neither elaborate nor drawn-out. On the contrary, it is usually on the skimpy side. This, I suppose, is the reason that so few playwrights write good novels and vice versa. Particularly vice versa. Most novelists overload their plays with masses of words. Personally, I am quite determined to be good at both!"

ON "THE METHOD"

Noël had absolutely no patience with "The Method" school of acting. "Every star I've ever known has had a method. But there can be no one Method." His concern was that the actor's excessive search for "motivation" encouraged too much introspection, and frittered away precious rehearsal time.

"The influence of psycho-analysis on acting is a great bore. Whether the actor is right with himself is not in the least important. It's being right with the part that matters."

Noël was a martinet about studying the script and learning the words. "When you've learned the words, analyse the part. Find out what it's about. When he goes out on that stage, an actor should forget himself and remember the part....Remember the other actors who are sharing the stage with you. Look at them. Not at their foreheads. Not at their ears. But at their eyes. Then learn to laugh and cry - without feeling happy or sad." He parted company with Method actors who felt they should live their parts. ("You cannot 'be' on stage. You can only create the illusion of being.") It was impossible to replicate an emotional state night after night on stage which you might genuinely have felt perhaps once in your life. The actor's business, he felt, was to create a replica that can be delivered to every audience. That delivery required technical control. ("Lose yourself on stage and you lose your audience.")

Only when the intellectual approach to the role had been settled did the technical aspects of the performance come into play: "Take care to project, pushing the words forward in the mouth. The good actor projects without shouting. He must appear intimate and at ease - but every individual word must be heard."

"Do justice to the playwright first and only then to yourself as an actor."

ON ACTORS

"Actors are incredibly silly and leading ladies idiotic." On another occasion he was more optimistic about the profession: "[The actor] is a recollection with a lot of gold dust on it."

"You know you've arrived in the profession when you don't have to read *The Stage* every week."

"She stopped the show, but then, the show wasn't really travelling very fast."

"What fascinates me about acting is that a wonderful, beautiful, talented actress can come on the stage and give a performance that really makes your blood curdle with excitement and pleasure, and she can make such a cracking pig of herself over where her dressing-room is, or some triviality, that you hate her. Intelligent actors never do that, but then they're seldom as good as the unintelligent ones. Acting is an instinct, a gift, and it's often given to people who are very silly. But the moment they come on the stage, up goes the temperature."

"The nicest words I know in the theatre are: 'That's all, sir,' which signify the end of a mass audition. It means that we shan't hear 'Phil the Fluter's Ball' again that morning."

ON LISTENING TO YOUR AUDIENCE

"As an actor your mind must work on several different layers at once. You must think of many things simultaneously. It's like reflexes in driving a car. It becomes so automatic that it isn't even conscious thought.

"You must remember your character, your voice pitch and the other actors. But, most of all, you must listen to the audience... one night they may be cods' heads out there, the next night - marvellous!

"Do not, under any circumstances, let them lead you astray and make you overplay.

"The most dangerous thing that happens to so many actors - and certainly happened to me, too - is if you're playing a high comedy part and you've got a wonderful audience, you begin to enjoy it a little bit too much. And the winks come and the face begins to react and it isn't till later that somebody tells you - and pray God they do! - that you were 'overplaying.' That solitary tell-tale cough may mean you're losing them. Or it may simply mean that somebody in the house has a cough!

"I believe that all acting is a question of control. The control of the actor of himself and, through himself, of the audience."

ON THEATRE AUDIENCES

"...in England the public is more prone to think for itself. In America they have to be told what to enjoy and what to avoid, not only in the theatre but in every phase of life. They are told by television and radio what to eat, drink and smoke, what cars to buy and what laxatives and sanitary towels to use. They are told, in no uncertain terms, what movies to go to and what stars to admire....The power of individual thought has been atrophied in them by the incessant onslaughts of commercialism."

"...I am aware of a tremendous change in the quality of the New York audiences since I played here twenty-one years ago [this was written in 1957]. They used to be quick on comedy, quicker often than London audiences. Now, however, this quickness has gone. They are quite appreciative on the whole, but much dimmer. In fact they have lost the capacity for participation."

ON FEELING AND "BEING"

"Acting is acting - not being. An actor must give the impression of what he's feeling - not feel it. You might feel it truly once but not eight times a week. Somewhere along the line your 'feeling' is going to let you down...If it's real feeling, then you're liable to lose your performance - and your audience."

It was always said of Charles Hawtrey (one of Noël's early mentors) that he was "always the same," that he never "did anything." In other words, he wasn't "acting." Noël, who had watched Hawtrey from the wings hundreds of times, profoundly disagreed: "Every time he went on stage, he'd raise his voice half a tone. He looked perfectly relaxed and natural but he wasn't in the least. One can never be relaxed and natural, if one is a good comedian. There are far too many things to think about.

"Hawtrey was the master of the naturalistic gesture. When I worked for him as a very young actor, I remember him teaching me how to laugh on stage, how to use my hands and body freely, so that I wasn't constantly aware of them and making unnecessary use of them."

It was from Hawtrey that Noël derived the advice he passed along to me in *Words and Music.* Noël was playing a page boy and emoting all over the place, until Hawtrey explained to him that the character was not a junior version of the star, but a "common little boy" who would undoubtedly speak with a Cockney accent.   Suitably motivated, Noël became a common little Cockney.

Years later, Noël was commended by James Agate for his display of "emotional" acting in *The Vortex.* Reflecting on his performance on that opening night, Noël felt he "got away with it."   The problems in getting the play staged made him play too much on his nerve endings.   Two weeks later, he said, he was able to "turn it on at will and not feel it," which may have been wishful thinking, because in a later interview he admitted, "I gave myself a nervous breakdown by playing *The Vortex* for two years.   To cry for twenty-five minutes eight times a week for two years is a terrible strain!"

He had a theory, which he proved to his own satisfaction, about "emotional" acting: "If you're playing a very strong scene, a moving scene, there is a moment at rehearsal, when your words are clear, when you know it very well, and you're really beginning to flow, when you feel it.   This is a very important moment. You cry, you overplay... but you've genuinely felt it.   From then onwards until the opening night you have to begin to eliminate. Because you cannot afford really to feel... it is not 'acting'."

ON PLAYING COMEDY

"The whole of comedy depends on timing - and if you are really on your toes, you play the audience and you control the laughter. You mustn't ever let the audience get out of hand.

"The first rule of comedy is to play quickly.   I don't mean gabble. There's a difference between speed and pace. You throw your laughs away deliberately in the first act, then pull them in the last.   In the first act you have to get the audience's attention - once you have it, they will repay you in the second. Play through the laughs, if you have to.   It will only make the audience believe there are so many of them that they missed a few.

"In all the plays I've been in - with Gertie and with Alfred and Lynn - we'd know by how a certain line went...If it got a laugh, we'd say, 'Ha! We're home! Nice warm audience.' If it got a titter - 'Tricky!' If it got silence, 'Get to work, chaps!'"

Actors who frequently work together develop a form of shorthand. In *Private Lives,* Noël and Gertie had "The Wink." After the opening scene, if he felt the audience was a little slow to respond, he'd give Gertie "The Wink," and she'd speed things up in her inimitable fashion. According to Noël, "By the end of the first act, we'd got 'em!"

"Darling, if you could do it a little more like this*..." Noël demonstrates a point of performance as he rehearses* Relative Values. *(1951)*

In the 1920's and '30's, Noël made regular visits to New York to observe the speed and tempo of American comedy, which was much more sophisticated than the English equivalent. After the war, he found it much less so. English comedy, he felt, lost a great deal of its style because of a dearth of new light comedy playwrights. It was no longer fashionable to deal with the apparently trivial, although it became obvious with revivals that the "trivial" could deal with the fundamentals perfectly well.

He was always realistic about his own shortcomings. At the time of *The Young Idea* (1922), he observed that "I was still forcing points too much and giving knowing grimaces when delivering comedy lines. I had not learned then not to superimpose upon witty dialogue the top-heavy burden of personal mannerisms. In this instance, of course, I was both author and actor, and the former suffered considerably from the antics and over-emphasis of the latter."

Throughout his career he continued to rely on his mentor, Charles Hawtrey: "He taught me everything I know. Every time nowadays when I am playing a comedy scene, and I'm in trouble and it's tricky to do, I think: 'What would the Governor have done?'"

Of his own mature skills as a player of comedy, he observed, "I am probably the best comedian alive but the sort of acting I do wouldn't do at all at Stratford, though I'd probably have been quite good as Malvolio or Iago at one time. I was offered Hamlet five times." The Malvolio ambition died quite early. ("I saw Larry and I stopped wanting to play it.") Hamlet was still-born. ("I just knew that the day I declaimed 'To be or not to be...' in public, it would be the death of me.") In a late interview, he was asked if he would ever now consider playing Shakespeare? Noël thought long and hard: "I think I've left it a bit late. I might play the Nurse in *Romeo and Juliet.*"

One part he always coveted was Madame Arcati: "I think I'd have been rather good!" He wasn't joking, and he probably would have. As it is, we'll all live with our indelible memory of Margaret Rutherford. It's hard to believe, but she originally turned the part down. Margaret respected spiritualism and felt the play was an attack on it. It took Binkie Beaumont's most lavish lunch and silken manner to talk her into it. It was, he claimed, an attack on fraudulent mediums. In that case, the lady persisted, how can Madame Arcati raise two ghosts? "Ah," replied Binkie, "that was a stroke of luck that can happen to even fraudulent mediums!" There was a pause before Miss Rutherford nodded her several chins in agreement. "Very well, but I must warn you that I regard this as a very serious play, almost a tragedy. I don't see it as a comedy at all." Which is precisely the way she played it, and why it was so funny.

ON WRITING COMEDY

"Comedy is nearly always despised in its generation and honoured more latterly, except by the public."

It irritated Noël that comedy was dismissed as being of no consequence. Plays of "social significance" seemed to be springing up wherever he turned in the 1950's and '60's:

"A light comedy, whose sole purpose is to amuse, is dismissed as trivial and insignificant," he said in a filmed introduction to one of his comedies on TV. "Since when has laughter been so insignificant? No merriment, apparently, must scratch the grim set patina of these dire years. We must just sit around and wait for death. Or hurry it on, according to how we feel. To my mind, one of the most efficacious ways of hurrying it on is to sit in a theatre watching a verbose, ill-constructed humourless play, acted with turgid intensity, which has received rave notices and is closing on Saturday."

"To me the essence of good comedy writing is that perfectly ordinary phrases such as 'Just fancy!' should, by virtue of their context, achieve greater laughs than the most literate epigrams. Some of the biggest laughs in *Hay Fever* occur on such lines as 'Go on,' 'No, there isn't, is there?' and 'This haddock's disgusting.' There are many other glittering examples of my sophistication in the same vein."

ON LEARNING ONE'S LINES

A particular *bête noire* to Noël was the word-imperfect actor. He believed it was obligatory to arrive at the first read-through properly prepared. When learning his own lines he would exercise iron self-discipline, putting a postcard over the next line until he'd mastered what preceded it. One mistake, and he'd go right back to the beginning.

"I need three to four weeks rehearsal to decide how to play a part. I can't possibly decide that if I don't know my words....I always call for a reading a fortnight before we go into rehearsal, so that any wrong intonations can be corrected and marked. Then I send them away and say 'Now, learn it!' I can't rehearse people with books in their hands writing down things....You've got to be able to play it anywhere without depending on anything outward....When they have the words, I tell them 'Move where you feel. I'll tell you if you take a wrong turning.'"

During the preparation of *Relative Values*, Noël had heated arguments with Gladys Cooper, who was used to learning her lines at rehearsal. She later recalled him saying: "I did not expect word perfection at the first rehearsal but I had rather hoped for it on the first night."

ON CHEKHOV

Noël was not greatly enamoured of Chekhovian symbolism. Of *The Seagull* he said: "I hate plays that have a stuffed bird sitting on the bookcase screaming - 'I'm the title, I'm the title!'"

That, of course, was a typical Coward crack, but there are clear parallels between Arkadina, the fading actress of *The Seagull*, and *Hay Fever's* Judith Bliss, and even, perhaps, a touch of Florence Lancaster in *The Vortex*. Having said that, I have no idea when Noël first saw Chekhov's play!

On another occasion, having suffered through a version of *The Cherry Orchard* set in the Deep South, he referred to it as "A Month in the Wrong Country."

ON J.M. BARRIE

Noël had a very sentimental streak, to which he was quite prepared to admit: "I'm violently sentimental - I have to be led out of cinemas sobbing when a mother comes back to her son, or something ghastly... I cry like a baby." But the sentiment had to be genuine to have its effect on him. "A deliberately laid-on-with-a-trowel sweetness puts me into exactly the opposite mood. I become very sour. But, for instance, I cannot go to any play by James Barrie without crying before the curtain goes up. There are moments of Barrie's of such tremendous sentiment, like in *Dear Brutus* when the father realises that it has only been a dream. Barrie I love. I thought he was a marvellous playwright. Construction. His plays were made of steel. I played in *Peter Pan* for two years and there were moments that used to fix me. I used to cry. Not on the stage."

ON SAMUEL BECKETT

"He must have read too many of his own plays. It gets him down, I expect."

ON T.S. ELIOT

Eliot once said that Noël hadn't spent one hour of his life in the study of ethics, to which Noël replied, "I do not think it would have helped me, but I think it would have done Mr. Eliot a lot of good to spend some time in the theatre."

ON DRAMATIC CRITICS

"I have always been very fond of them....I think it is so frightfully clever of them to go night after night to the theatre and know so little about it."

"Criticism and Bolshevism have one thing in common. They both seek to pull down that which they could never build."

(1925)

"My feelings about critical attacks have never been very strong because I've been in the theatre too long. Only occasionally could I pick up a hint - but only from a good critic, like Agate. He once or twice said something or other that made me think, but as a general rule, as I only played a three-month season at a time, we were always sold out for the three months before we opened, so it didn't matter what the critics said anyway.

"I'm so terribly, terribly sorry for critics. They have to go to the damned theatre every night, and see all sorts and kinds of nonsense, and I think their senses - if you'll forgive the phrase - get dulled. And I think that they suddenly will spring a surprise on you, and you come out with a rave and a long scream. And then very often the play closes. You can't tell."

Although he pretended to "rise above it," Noël was not invulnerable to the sustained post-war attack: "I have been bitterly hurt inside by the English fusillade of critical abuse." (1956) He frequently compared "the grudging patronage of the English press" with the "whole-hearted pleased generosity" he encountered in the U.S.A.

"Thanks to the vilifications poured upon my head...I now find myself as big a celebrity as Debbie Reynolds."

ON EXPLICIT LANGUAGE

"I'm not passionately interested in the moral aspect but artistically it is very much better to make a suggestion and not a statement. And I don't like a rash of four-letter words - for the simple reason that I use so many myself that I'm bored with them!"

ON TASTE

"It can be vulgar, but it must never be embarrassing."

ON NOT BEING "NOËL COWARD"

"I've been a 'personality' actor all my life. I've established in my early years the sophisticated, urbane type, which is in tune with my own personality. But if I play something which looks like me but isn't like me at all, then I have to reconstruct in my mind at rehearsal my gestures, so that I'm no longer like 'Noël Coward.' Again, you come up against this thing of the image you create in the public mind of yourself.

"I always, when I was a little boy and a young man, longed to be a big star and a great success. In those days I wouldn't have cared to put on too much nose paste. I was too occupied in somebody asking me for an autograph in a bus....

"Luckily, I've become a more experienced and a better actor...Acting a character is far more interesting than anything else and it's lovely to do. To do my own sort of dialogue - flibberty-gibbet, witty, quick, all that - that is another sort of technique. But I loved playing *Fumed Oak*, for instance, with that terrible moustache. I've loved all the little bits of character acting I've done in my life....

"I always forget when playing my own plays that I'm the author. Not at rehearsals, when I'm after the others, but when I'm actually doing it, I can't remember - I never thought that I'd written the play....Of the two I think - possibly - I prefer playing other people's plays to my own."

His advice to actors playing the parts he had created was unequivocal: "Do not try and be me!" He was, as John Osborne said, "his own creation," and unfortunately, too many actors tried to re-create themselves in his image. Hugh Sinclair, Nigel Patrick, Donald Sinden and countless others from West End revival to the humblest provincial repertory company tried to carbon-copy Coward. It only made one realise how original an "original" can be.

One actor who most certainly did not copy Noël was George C. Scott. In the 1982 Broadway revival, he played Garry Essendine as a latter-day John Barrymore, complete with pouting profile and pseudo-Shakespearean rumble. Barrymore's narcissism was a relevant point of reference for a Broadway audience. It also saved George C. from having to attempt an English accent!

ON STYLE

Noël firmly believed that a lot of younger actors had none of the sense of style that he and his contemporaries had.

"In my early days in the theatre, in the actor-manager's time - which is certainly going back a bit - I would never go into a theatre belonging to Charles Hawtrey or Gerald du Maurier or Sir George Alexander or Sir Herbert Tree without being spick and span - whatever I was going to play. If I was going to play a dustman, I would have my suit pressed for rehearsals, out of respect for the theatre itself - the edifice, the building. You couldn't see a lot of people in denim and dirty old sweaters walking about the stage of the St. James's!

"I don't know why I feel like this. I suppose it's old hat and sentimental. It isn't, entirely. It's a question of discipline. I don't believe you can rehearse - easily - a highly articulate comedy, dressed in a slovenly manner. A young creature of twenty-one thinks it's perfectly all right to come slouching in without thinking of his poise, without thinking of his 'line,' his head, his stance. And now, when suddenly he's put into the clothes, he doesn't quite know how to wear them. I don't blame him. I blame the directors. I think a slovenly appearance indicates in some way a slovenly mind.

"I wish I could only explain - and it sounds almost pompous - that with the decline of manners and of elegance, it's much more difficult for young actors to achieve 'range'....It's so easy to play 'natural' when you can scratch yourself - even then it's got to be well done - but it's much easier than being slick, timing every line and very sharp looking.

"There's room for everything in the theatre. I think there's still room for a drama or a comedy or a play about kitchen sinks or tramps or whatever - that's fine, providing they're good enough. But there's still room for a charming upper middle class family, who have hearts and limbs and feel and think, just the same as anybody else does. And even dukes and duchesses. There are still a few extant!"

He returned to the subject frequently: "You must never appear in public looking less than your best.... God, how dismally bored I am with these people who slouch out of the stage door with handkerchiefs over their heads!"

"Comedies of manners swiftly become obsolete when there are no longer any manners."
        Crestwell, the sceptical butler in *Relative Values* (1951)

ON THE "PLEASURE PRINCIPLE"

"You, as a comedian, must enjoy what you're doing. I hate this new 'solemnity' in the theatre. If anybody says to me, 'She's a dedicated actress,' I'd like to strangle her. What's she 'dedicated' about? It sounds wretched. And this means all this gloomy searching for 'motives.' Acting must be a pleasure, even if you're playing something immensely tragic and dramatic - there's that sort of pleasure, too."

ON CONFIDENCE

"When you're writing something, you know, at the time, that it is brilliant beyond belief. Otherwise you wouldn't go on with it. But then rehearsals start and doubts begin to creep in and, even so, a success doesn't necessarily mean that it's all that good a play: It may mean that the leading lady's got a wonderful part and is very good in it. It may mean a lot of things. So may a real rousing failure. I've always done it the big way. After the first night of *Sirocco*, they spat at me in the streets - literally spat all over my tailcoat. And I thought: I must be a good playwright because nobody's going to take all that trouble unless they feel badly disappointed. They needn't have made all that much fuss. It wasn't all that terrible. In fact, there were many worse running triumphantly. But I'd set a standard for myself...."

ON FILM ACTING

"The Czar of all the rushes" was how Alexander Woollcott dubbed Noël, a statement which owed more to Woollcott's predilection for a well-turned phrase than to the facts. Noël never considered himself a major film actor.

Noël's screen debut was in D.W. Griffith's silent film, *Hearts of the World*, in 1917. He had the smallest of bit parts as a youth pushing a wheel barrow, with his back to the camera. He managed to persuade Griffith that his film would be dramatically improved by having Noël push the barrow towards the camera, so that anxious audiences could see his face!

He didn't appear in films again until 1935, when he starred in *The Scoundrel* (*Miracle on 49th Street*). By that time, he was something of an American stage celebrity, having performed in *Private Lives* and *Tonight at 8:30* on Broadway. Famous friends like the Lunts, critic George Jean Nathan, and novelist Edna Ferber would visit the set and be pressed into "extra" service, presumably unpaid.

Noël told an interviewer, "What really induced me to try films was that I wanted the experience." He went on to express his admiration for Ben Hecht and Charles MacArthur, the well-known playwrights who were producing and directing the film. In reality, it's more likely that he felt he had something to prove to himself. When MGM filmed *Private Lives* four years earlier, Noël and Gertie had done a joint screen test and been rejected for the parts they had created themselves! Elyot and Amanda were played by Robert Montgomery and Norma Shearer. It would have been easy to argue that, since Miss Shearer was married to the studio head, Irving Thalberg, the "test" was somewhat biased. Noël did not see it that way. He (and Gertie) had "failed" on film, and he wanted to put that right.

"I learned, when I started doing movies, an enormous amount that helped me as an actor - the meticulousness of having to do a movie. On the stage you can make a little fluff, give a merry laugh and get on with it and nobody notices. In the movies, one wrong word and 'Cut!' And I hate that word 'Cut!'"

Filming appealed to him because he had a tendency to get bored very quickly: "The fascinating thing about filming is that each day you have something different to do. The boring part of the theatre is that you have to do the same thing eight times a week..."

During *In Which We Serve* (1942), his "*Cavalcade* about the Navy," as he put it, he had to play very much against type as a naval officer. He recalled doing it using other people's hands: "I had to be awfully careful. I act a great deal with my hands - and naval officers do not! I was clasping my hands behind my back, doing anything rather than do a 'Noël Coward' gesture."

There is a scene where he says goodbye to the remaining crew members of the sunken *Torin*. He found this very difficult to play due to his technical inexperience. The members of the crew had to part to allow the camera to track through for an enormous close-up. Noël had to emote solely to the camera, a challenge to his "stage-taught" technique. This was not something he was used to, but the hardest part was expressing the emotion itself:

"I found it very, very difficult to adapt myself - and not to use too much emotion. I had to have the emotion inside and do as little with my face as possible. Because, if I'd done it as I did in the first take we did, I looked emotional. And that was the one thing I didn't want to do. A naval officer, you should feel it in his voice and heart but you would not see it in his face.

"I had a great deal on my side. I had, to start with, real sailors....So all the drill was accurate and not a lot of actors putting their lanyards in unorthodox places. All had been in action. They knew what I was talking about and at the end - after that finale - I had to say goodbye, stand still and say goodbye to each one of them. I had written some things in and I tore up my script and said, 'Please, chaps, say what you think you would have said in this situation'. And this I could hardly take. Each one of them said their own line, like 'Good luck, sir!' or 'Chin up, sir' - all these perfectly trite, ordinary phrases, spoken from the heart. Talk about improvisation. It was nothing to do with 'acting.' They were being. But then, it was only a film and only a take. I doubt if they could have got that amount of emotion in, if they'd been playing it eight times a week."

He found working with Carol Reed on *Our Man in Havana* (1959) very helpful. This time, it wasn't his hands, but another part of his anatomy that was the problem:

"I have to remember in a close-up not to use my lips. And I'm not a particularly adroit film actor....I don't pay particular attention to the camera. Carol used to say to me: 'I shouldn't do that, if I were you.' And I'd say, 'What was I doing?' He said, 'Well, your mouth. Your under lip in this shot is a foot wide.' I was pitching to get to the back of the gallery....You don't have to 'sustain' in a picture. You have to sustain a character, if you've got any sense, but you haven't got a long scene to play."

Years later, Noël realised why Carol Reed's advice had sounded so familiar. It was precisely what D.W. Griffith had said to him forty years earlier. From then on he was very careful to give a director less lip.

He also had to adapt his vocal delivery: "I have to relearn once more not to pitch my voice... not to 'put in' expression....I still feel that acting for the 'silver screen' is fairly silly and infinitely difficult, but I expect that is because I am inexperienced and don't do it very well.

Noël rehearses
Blithe Spirit. *(1941)*

"I'll always love the theatre a little better and I know why that is - it's the contact with an audience. I'd rather play a bad matinée at Hull - incidentally, I've never played a good matinée! - than do a movie, even though I enjoy doing movies."

Noël's youthful plays were snapped up for the "silver screen," usually with limited success. *The Vortex* (starring Ivor Novello), and *Easy Virtue* (with Hitchcock directing) both suffered from what now seem obvious shortcomings. A Coward play without the Coward dialogue is little more than a plot that any competent playwright could devise. Realising this, Michael Balcon, in his early days as Czar of Ealing Studios, asked Noël to write an original screen treatment. Noël came up with *Concerto*, a film that was never made, but which Noël later adapted as *Bitter Sweet.*

Noël confided, rather pompously, to *Picturegoer* magazine, "You may take it that I am not interested in writing scenarios at all. I want to write words, not stage directions....As a dramatist, dialogue and its psychology are practically my whole career."

ON DIRECTING

"It is of little help at the first rehearsal to be able to translate Cicero."

Over time, Noël the Director mellowed.   When he directed the National Theatre's revival of *Hay Fever* in 1964, Lynn Redgrave recalls how he coaxed the performance from her and allowed her to improvise.   Had she strayed too far, though, she would have found the path fairly narrow. Nonetheless, her experience was not commensurate with most recollections of Noël as director.

There are two accounts that express the more common view of Noël's working methods.   The first was written by a member of the cast of *Words and Music* and appeared in December, 1932:

MR. COWARD REHEARSES

"'I never lose my temper at rehearsals.   But if I did, this would be my great moment.'   With these words Noël Coward annihilated eight trembling 'Show Girls' who were rehearsing 'Children of the Ritz,' one of the hit numbers in his *Words and Music.*   The words were delivered quite quietly, yet they had a quality behind them that froze the girlish giggles that had hitherto accompanied these beautiful young ladies' inability to cope with the task set them, which happened to be the movement of their heads in time with music.

"Noël Coward is like that.   He never loses his temper, and the only thing that makes him angry is slackness.

"However, it is not so easy to slack with Mr. Coward.   He is consumed with such a terrific smouldering activity that he automatically carries one along with him.

"The sight of him rehearsing is awe-inspiring.   He always rehearses with footlights as well as overhead lighting.   When he stands on the front of the stage with these lights shining onto his working face, striking electric sparks from his already electric eyes, one is tempted to mistake him for some incarnate spirit.

"All the critics in their reports of *Words and Music* seemed to have one thing in common - they all said that this show had a remarkable unity.   This is not only due to the fact that Noël Coward wrote the 'words' and the 'music,' but to the fact that in production he has made everybody do everything in his own way. Every important gesture, and most of the apparently negligible ones, were carefully thought out and demonstrated to the artiste by Noël Coward himself.   He spent hours in getting the actors to play a scene exactly as he had shown them, with every gesture and every movement.

"All the brilliantly timed movements of 'Mad About the Boy,' for instance, are the result of hours of intensive work on his part. The result is that the show has stylisation which is lacking in other shows, where actors are allowed to develop on what lines they please.

"This stylisation may submerge the actors' personality a little, but without exception they are all giving better performances than they have ever given.

"Noël Coward is the 'be-all and end-all' of rehearsals. If he is unavoidably delayed and he is late for rehearsal (he is usually the first person there) the time is entirely wasted until he arrives. Various groups of actors may make a feeble effort to rehearse some scene or other, but the effort invariably peters out and riot reigns triumphant.

"The moment he arrives on the scene, however, there is hush. The ear-splitting rhythm of the 'dancing boys' practising stops, and 'Mr. Cochran's young ladies' stop screaming at the top of their voices. It only needs, 'Quiet, company, please!' from him, and the whole company settles down for a hard day's work.

"And it certainly is a hard day's work. For Mr. Coward has taken his coat off and pulled down the 'zip' fastener of his woollen sports shirt, and has announced that he will do a certain scene. The stage manager and his assistant rush on to the stage with chairs, which they place in position to represent scenery. The actors take a final glance at the parts they are supposed to have learnt and prepare to rehearse in real earnest. This goes on till midnight, with two short intervals for meals, and yet Noël Coward's eyes never stop blazing and his brain never flags from facilely directing his enormous company. Though it may be a hard day's work it is, however, a useful day's work, for Noël Coward never has to 'scrap' a scene and start all over again. He knows exactly what he wants to do, and what effect he is going to get. No time is ever wasted.

"This systematic way of working enables him to indulge a fad of his - that is not to rehearse over week-ends. Most companies when they start in to rehearse for the usual four weeks very rarely leave the theatre except to eat and sleep for the whole of that time. During the first week they may possibly get a night or two off, but they certainly rehearse every day, including Sundays. Noël Coward gives his company not only Sunday, but Saturday as well. An almost unheard of luxury. The result is that he and his company reassemble on Monday fresh and eager for a good week's work.

"System is the keyword of his success as a producer. Even dress rehearsals - which are always a nightmare - are made almost bearable by the orderly way he conducts things. He generally has three or four dress rehearsals. At each one he concentrates on something different. The first one is generally an orchestral rehearsal. Noël Coward has an instinct for finding mistakes, and woe betide any musician who plays a wrong note! The second dress rehearsal is generally taken up with the question of scenery and the preliminary lighting. During the third he puts the final touches to the production, where all mistakes which are left over from the first two are rectified. He generally concludes with one complete 'run-through' a few hours before the first night, after which he gives the company time to have a meal and rest before the show opens."

Norman Marshall, in his 1957 book, *The Producer and the Play*, renders this account of Noël at work:

"Coward is today the only playwright of any note in the English theatre who still produces his own plays. He dictates every inflexion, demonstrates every bit of business in exact detail. He begins by reading the play to the company, portraying every part so vividly that some of the cast are apt to be reduced to a state of gloom because they doubt their ability to give a performance anything like as good as the author's own reading of their part. During rehearsals the actor never has that encouraging moment when he makes the rest of the cast laugh by neatly timing a line or a bit of business: Coward has got all the laughs in advance during that first reading. He insists on the cast reproducing exactly his own inflexions. Most actors and actresses willingly submit to this because they realise that Coward knows better than anyone else how to time his own laughs, how to point his own lines with absolute precision. His sense of audience is so unerring that he is quite confident that lines and bits of business which do not seem amusing during rehearsals will never the less get their laughs. He will say to an actor: 'On the first night you will find your part is full of laughs where you didn't think there were any' - and the first night will prove Coward to have been right.

"Coward's rehearsals are virtually a series of dictation lessons. In theory this should result in an atmosphere of dullness at a rehearsal because the actors feel they are being deprived of all initiative, but Coward is so electric a personality that he keeps his actors alert and eager. One of his cast told me that when Coward arrives for rehearsal in a chilly, dimly lit theatre on a dreary, wet morning, 'you feel as if all the lights have suddenly been turned on and a glass of champagne put into your hand.'

"A peculiarity of Coward as a producer is that he insists on the cast knowing their lines at the first rehearsal. Engaging an actress for a part he will end the interview by handing her the script and saying: 'Now, go home and learn your lines, duckie; that makes practising a pleasure' - advice that is usually followed up by a note from H.M. Tennent Ltd., politely intimating that 'Mr. Coward would be very pleased if you would know your lines by the first rehearsal.' Of course no actor can really be word-perfect until he has become accustomed to hearing the other actors and actresses speaking his cues, so for the first two or three days of Coward's rehearsals the cast are so busy trying to remember strings of words that they have no time for interpretation or characterisation. Presumably this is Coward's intention. All he requires from the actors is that they should present him with the skeletons of their parts to which he himself adds the flesh and blood."

ON REVUE

"The art of Revue writing is acknowledged by those unfortunates who have had anything to do with it as being a very tricky and technical business. Everything has to be condensed to appalling brevity. The biggest laugh must be on the last line before the black out. No scene or number should play for more than a few minutes at most, and, above all, the Audience must never be kept waiting. The moment their last splendid laugh at the end of a sketch has subsided into a general chuckle, their attention must immediately be distracted by a line of vivacious chorus girls (preferably with bare legs) or a treble-jointed acrobatic dancer with no bones at all; in fact, anything arrestingly visual that will relax their strained mind and lull them into a gentle apathy while the next onslaught upon their risibilities is being prepared behind the scenes.

"The lessons which have to be learned by aspiring Revue writers are many and bitter. The bitterest really being the eternal bugbear of 'Running Order.' Running Order is the sequence in which the various items in the show follow one another, and, however carefully the Author may have planned it originally, this sequence is generally completely changed by the time the show reaches dress rehearsal, and frequently drastically reorganised after the first night. For instance, the leading lady upon perceiving that the pretty blonde danseuse will undoubtedly make a tremendous success,

Don't *Put Your Daughter On the Stage, Mrs. Worthington... Noël in cabaret at the Café de Paris. (1951)*

resolutely refuses to follow immediately afterwards with her Powder-puff number with the girls, whereupon everything is changed round, and the low-comedy lodging house scene is substituted in place of the Powder-puff number. Then, after a suitable interval, it is discovered that with this rearrangement it is impossible for the chorus to make their change from 'The Jungle Scene' to the 'Tower of London in 1586' because, according to the original lay-out, the six-minute lodging house scene came in between, whereas now they only have half a minute's reprise of the Theme song to enable them to get in and out of their wimples. At this point the Author is usually dragged, protesting miserably, into a cold office behind the dress circle and commanded to write then and there a brief but incredibly witty interlude to be played in front of black velvet curtains by no more than four minor members of the Cast (the Principals all being occupied with quick changes), without furniture, as there is no time to get it on and off, and finishing with such a gloriously funny climax that the Audience remain gaily hysterical for at least a minute and a half in pitch darkness.

"Another problem which the writer has to face is the successful handling of Danger Spots. The principal danger spots in Revue are (1) The opening of the whole show, which must be original and extremely snappy. (2) The sketch immediately following it, which must so convulse the Audience that they are warmed up enough to overlook a few slightly weaker items. (3) The Finale of the first half. This should essentially be the high spot of the evening, so that on the first night the bulk of the Audience and the critics can retire to the bars (if not already there) and, glowing with enthusiasm, drink themselves into an alcoholic stupor for the second half. The fourth danger spot is the strong low-comedy scene, which should be placed as near as possible to the second-half finale and should be strong, low, and very comic indeed.

"If, upon reading the notices in the newspapers after that first night, it is found that different critics take exception to different scenes, you can safely predict a successful run. If all the critics unanimously take exception to one particular scene, it is advisable to move that scene to a more conspicuous place in the programme. If, on the other hand, no particular critic dislikes any particular scene and they all unite in praising the whole production, it either means that you have such a good show that they haven't the face to attack it, or such a bad show that they like it. In either case it will probably be a failure."

ON TAKING LIGHT MUSIC SERIOUSLY

"I was born into a generation that still took light music seriously. The lyrics and melodies of Gilbert and Sullivan were hummed and strummed into my consciousness at an early age. My father sang them, my mother played them, my nurse, Emma, breathed them through her teeth while she was washing me, dressing me and undressing me and putting me to bed. My aunts and uncles, who were legion, sang them singly and in unison at the slightest provocation. By the time I was four years old 'Take a Pair of Sparkling Eyes,' 'Tit Willow,' 'We're Very Wide Awake, the Moon and I' and 'I Have a Song to Sing-O' had been fairly inculcated into my bloodstream.

"The whole Edwardian era was saturated with operetta and musical comedy: in addition to popular foreign importations by Franz Lehar, Leo Fall, André Messager, etc., our own native composers were writing musical scores of a quality that has never been equalled in this country since the 1914-18 war. Lionel Monckton, Paul Rubens, Ivan Caryll and Leslie Stuart were flourishing. *The Quaker Girl, Our Miss Gibbs, Miss Hook of Holland, Floradora, The Arcadians* and *The Country Girl*, to name only a few, were all fine musical achievements; and over and above the artists who performed them, the librettists who wrote them and the impresarios who presented them, their music was the basis of their success. Their famous and easily remembered melodies can still be heard on the radio and elsewhere, but it was in the completeness of their scores that their real strength lay: opening choruses, finales, trios, quartettes and concerted numbers, all musicianly, all well balanced and all beautifully constructed.

"There was no song-plugging in those days beyond an occasional reprise in the last act; there was no assaulting of the ear by monstrous repetition, no unmannerly nagging. A little while ago I went to an American 'musical' in which the hit number was reprised no less than five times during the performance by different members of the cast, as well as being used in the overture, the entr'acte and as a 'play-out' while the audience was leaving the theatre. The other numbers in the show, several of which were charming, were left to fend for themselves and only three of them were ever published. In earlier days the complete vocal score of a musical comedy was published as a matter of course, in addition to which a booklet of the lyrics could be bought in the theatre with the programme. These little paper-bound books were well worth the sixpence charged because they helped those with a musical ear to recapture more easily the tunes they wanted to remember and to set them in their minds.

"In the years immediately preceding the first world war the American Invasion began innocuously with a few isolated song hits until Irving Berlin established a beach-head with 'Alexander's Ragtime Band.' English composers, taken by surprise and startled by vital Negro-Jewish rhythms from the New World, fell back in some disorder; conservative musical opinion was shocked and horrified by such alien noises and, instead of saluting the new order and welcoming the new vitality, turned up its patrician nose and retired disgruntled from the arena.

"At this moment war began, and there was no longer any time. It is reasonable to suppose that a large number of potential young composers were wiped out in those sad years and that had they not been, the annihilation of English light music would not have been so complete. As it was, when finally the surviving boys came home, it was to an occupied country; the American victory was a *fait accompli*. This obviously was the moment for British talent to rally, to profit by defeat, to absorb and utilize the new, exciting rhythms from over the water and to modify and adapt them to its own service, but apparently this was either beyond our capacity or we were too tired to attempt it. At all events, from the nineteen-twenties until today, there have been few English composers of light music capable of creating an integrated score.

"One outstanding exception was the late Ivor Novello. His primary talent throughout his whole life was music, and *Glamorous Night, Arc de Triomphe, The Dancing Years, Perchance to Dream* and *King's Rhapsody* were rich in melody and technically expert. For years he upheld, almost alone, our old traditions of Musical Comedy. His principal tunes were designed, quite deliberately, to catch the ear of the public and, being simple, sentimental, occasionally conventional but always melodic, they invariably achieved their object. The rest of his scores, the openings, finales, choral interludes and incidental themes he wrote to please himself and in these, I believe, lay his true quality; a much finer quality than most people realized. The fact that his music never received the critical acclaim that it deserved was irritating but unimportant. One does not expect present-day dramatic critics to know much about music; as a matter of fact one no longer expects them to know much about drama. Vivian Ellis has also proved over the years that he can handle a complete score with grace and finesse. *Bless the Bride* was much more than a few attractive songs strung together and so from the musical standpoint, was *Tough at the Top*, although the show on the whole was a commercial failure.

"Harold Fraser-Simson, who composed *The Maid of the Mountains*, and Frederic Norton, who composed *Chu Chin Chow*, are remembered only for these two outstanding scores. Their other music, later or earlier, is forgotten except by a minority."

"Proceeding on the assumption that the reader...is interested in the development of my musical talent, I will try to explain, as concisely as I can, how, in this respect, my personal wheels go round. To begin with, I have only had two music lessons in my life. These were the first steps of what was to have been a full course at the Guildhall School of Music, and they faltered and stopped when I was told by my instructor that I could not use consecutive fifths. He went on to explain that a gentleman called Ebenezer Prout had announced many years ago that consecutive fifths were wrong and must in no circumstances be employed. At that time Ebenezer Prout was merely a name to me (as a matter of fact he still is, and a very funny one at that) and I was unimpressed by his Victorian dicta. I argued back that Debussy and Ravel used consecutive fifths like mad. My instructor waved aside this triviality with a pudgy hand, and I left his presence for ever with the parting shot that what was good enough for Debussy and Ravel was good enough for me. This outburst of rugged individualism deprived me of much valuable knowledge, and I have never deeply regretted it for a moment. Had I intended at the outset of my career to devote all my energies to music I would have endured the necessary training cheerfully enough, but in those days I was passionately involved in the theatre; acting and writing and singing and dancing seemed of more value to my immediate progress than counterpoint and harmony. I was willing to allow the musical side of my creative talent to take care of itself. On looking back, I think that on the whole I was right. I have often been irritated in later years by my inability to write music down effectively and by my complete lack of knowledge of orchestration except by ear, but being talented from the very beginning in several different media, I was forced by common sense to make a decision. The decision I made was to try to become a good writer and actor, and to compose tunes and harmonies whenever the urge to do so became too powerful to resist.

"I have never been unduly depressed by the fact that all my music has to be dictated. Many famous light composers never put so much as a crotchet on paper. To be born with a natural ear for music is a great and glorious gift. It is no occasion for pride and it has nothing to do with will-power, concentration or industry. It is either there or it isn't. What is so curious is that it cannot, in any circumstances, be wrong where one's own harmonies are concerned. Last year in New York, when I was recording *Conversation Piece* with Lily Pons, I detected a false note in the orchestration. It happened to be in a very fully scored passage and the mistake was consequently difficult to trace. The orchestrator, the conductor and the musical producer insisted that I was wrong; only Lily Pons, who has perfect pitch, backed me up. Finally, after much argument and fiddle-faddle it was discovered that the oboe was playing an A flat instead of an A natural. The greatness and gloriousness of this gift, however, can frequently be offset by excruciating discomfort. On many occasions in my life I have had to sit smiling graciously while some well-meaning but inadequate orchestra obliges with a selection from my works. Cascades of wrong notes lacerate my nerves, a flat wind instrument pierces my ear-drums, and though I continue to smile appreciatively, the smile, after a little while, becomes tortured and looks as if my mouth were filled with lemon juice.

"I could not help composing tunes even if I wished to. Ever since I was a little boy they have dropped into my mind unbidden and often in the most unlikely circumstances. The *Bitter Sweet* waltz, 'I'll See You Again,' came to me whole and complete in a taxi when I was appearing in New York in *This Year of Grace.* I was on my way home to my apartment after a matinée and had planned, as usual, to have an hour's rest and a light dinner before the evening performance. My taxi got stuck in a traffic block on the intersection of Broadway and Seventh Avenue, klaxons were honking, cops were shouting and suddenly in the general din there was the melody, clear and unmistakable. By the time I got home the words of the first phrase had emerged. I played it over and over again on the piano (key of E flat as usual) and tried to rest, but I was too excited to sleep."

"There is, to me, strange magic in such occurrences. I am willing and delighted to accept praise for my application, for my self-discipline and for my grim determination to finish a thing once I have started it.   My acquired knowledge is praiseworthy, too, for I have worked hard all my life to perfect the material at my disposal.   But these qualities, admirable as they undoubtedly are, are merely accessories.   The essential talent is what matters and essential talent is unexplainable.   My mother and father were both musical in a light, amateur sense, but their gift was in no way remarkable.   My father, although he could improvise agreeably at the piano, never composed a set piece of music in his life I have known many people who were tone-deaf whose parents were far more actively musical than mine.   I had no piano lessons when I was a little boy except occasionally from my mother who tried once or twice, with singular lack of success, to teach me my notes.   I could, however, from the age of about seven onwards, play any tune I had heard on the piano in the pitch dark.   To this day my piano-playing is limited to three keys: E flat, B flat and A flat.   The sight of two sharps frightens me to death.   When I am in the process of composing anything in the least complicated I can play it in any key on the keyboard, but I can seldom if ever repeat these changes afterwards unless I practise them assiduously every day.   In E flat I can give the impression of playing well.   A flat and B flat I can get away with, but if I have to play anything for the first time it is always to my beloved E flat that my fingers move automatically.   Oddly enough, C major, the key most favoured by the inept, leaves me cold.   It is supposed to be easier to play in than any of the others because it has no black notes, but I have always found it dull. Another of my serious piano-playing defects is my left hand.   Dear George Gershwin used to moan at me in genuine distress and try to force my fingers on to the right notes.   As a matter of fact he showed me a few tricks that I can still do, but they are few and dreadfully far between.   I can firmly but not boastfully claim that I am a better pianist than Irving Berlin, but as that superlative genius of light music is well known not to be able to play at all except in C major, I will not press the point.   Jerome D. Kern, to my mind one of the most inspired romantic composers of all, played woodenly as a rule and without much mobility.   Dick Rodgers plays his own music best when he is accompanying himself or someone else, but he is far from outstanding.   Vincent Youmans was a marvellous pianist, almost as brilliant as Gershwin, but these are the only two I can think of who, apart from their creative talent, could really play.

"At the very beginning of this introduction I said that I was born into a generation that took light music seriously.   It was fortunate for me that I was, because by the time I had emerged from my teens the taste of the era had changed.   In my early twenties and thirties it was from America that I gained my greatest impetus.   In New York they have always taken light music seriously. There, it is, as it should be, saluted as a specialized form of creative art, and is secure in its own right."

From the Introduction to *The Noël Coward Song Book* (Methuen)

ON WRITING LYRICS

"I can only assume that the compulsion to make rhymes was born in me. There is no time I can remember when I was not fascinated by words 'going together.' Lewis Carroll, Edward Lear, Beatrix Potter, all fed my childish passion, in addition to all the usual nursery rhymes that the flesh is heir to....I can still distinctly recall being exasperated when any of those whimsical effusions were slipshod in rhyming or scansion."

"Oscar Hammerstein wrote wisely and accurately that the perfect lyric for a musical should be inspired directly by the story and the characters contained in it. In fact, ideally, a song in a musical should carry on where the dialogue leaves off. Apart from one or two very rare occasions I concur with him entirely. Revue writing is, of course, different because there is no definite storyline on which to hang the numbers. But any young potential lyric writer should learn that if he wishes to write a successful 'book' show he must eschew irrelevance and stick to the script."

Noël with Alec Guinness in Our Man in Havana.

THE UNPUBLISHED PLAYS

A Personal Commentary

There are five full-length Coward plays that have never been published. These are: *Semi-Monde* (1926), *Time Remembered* (1941), *Long Island Sound* (1947), *Volcano* (1957) and *Star Quality* (1967). There was also an incomplete play, *Age Cannot Wither* (1967), of which only the first act was written before being abandoned for unknown reasons.

Semi-Monde and *Volcano* were given one evening "concert" performances under the evangelical production eye of the late, and much-missed, Martin Tickner, one of the leading Coward academics, if that isn't too grand a description.

Sadly, there seems little likelihood that Mander and Mitchenson's invaluable *Theatrical Companion to Coward* (1957) will ever be brought up to date, so, for anyone interested in the details: *Volcano* was given a "rehearsed reading" on June 26th, 1989, at The Mill at Sonning. The cast included Judi Dench, Adam Faith, Hannah Gordon, Michael Williams, Jennifer Hilary and Sally Hughes.

Star Quality was written in 1967. Based on a short story of the same name, it was later dramatised by Stanley Price as the opening play in a 1985 television series, for which several of Noël's stories were adapted. Susannah York played Lorraine Barrie, the kind of bittersweet "mature" actress that plagued Noël's later professional life:

> *"She is an exceedingly attractive woman in her forties but, of course, looks a good deal younger than she really is. She is obviously and unmistakably a 'star' which means that over and above her natural good looks she has enormous vitality and an air of assurance acquired from years of indiscriminate praise and adulation. She is wearing grey linen slacks, a lime coloured sports shirt and enormous dark glasses. In her left hand she carries a blue-covered type-script; in her right, a small Pekinese called Bothwell."*

None of the unpublished works could be considered a major Coward work, but they all have their points of interest. There is a variety of reasons why they were never commercially produced.

Semi-Monde was written shortly after *The Vortex* and suffered something of a backlash from the controversial success of that play. Noël had great trouble persuading the Lord Chamberlain to allow it to be performed at all. That custodian of public morality was probably not convinced by the play's success that he had been correct in setting aside his original concerns. *Semi-Monde*, as its title suggests, existed in the half of the world that was whining, rather than roaring, in the '20's. Relationships criss-cross and emotionally double-cross, and homosexuality is clearly *à la carte*.

The action ebbs and flows through the bar of the Ritz Hotel in Paris, and was deemed too decadent for the audiences of its time. Today, it would be considered too dated. Nonetheless, it remains a significant period piece, brightly enamelled and with a distinct whiff of de Reske cigarettes.

Because it depends on the interplay of so many disparate characters, the size of the cast would make a revival impractical today, except on television. There are thirty-nine characters, including waiters, lift-boys, hotel guests, and so on.

Time Remembered was written in 1941 and later re-christened *Salute to the Brave*. In the 1950's, the title was used for the English-language version of Jean Anouilh's *Léocadia*.

1941 was the strange interim period when the European war was at its worst and America was still hoping to hang on to its neutrality. Pearl Harbor finally settled that in December. The artificiality of the international atmosphere strained more than one transatlantic relationship.

Beneath the surface, the propaganda machine was creaking into action. Several Hollywood studios were turning out thrillers in which the Bad Guys just *happened* to bear a passing resemblance to Germans. Popular films like *Casablanca* (1942) were scrutinised for coded calls to join the fight. It was even said that Casablanca was a synonym for the White House (the Spanish translation means just that) and the film a plea for Presidential commitment.

This was also the time when Noël was asked to visit the US to try and drum up support for the Allied cause. It was a move which, once again, upset sections of the British press. "Mr. Coward is not the man for the job," trumpeted the *Sunday Express*. "His flippant England has gone.... As a representative of democracy, he's like a plate of caviar in a carman's pull up."

Noël was never sure how much, if anything, he'd been able to contribute, and perhaps the orientation of the play is a reflection of this confusion of purpose. The propaganda is probably too overt. American producers presumably felt it was an inappropriate message for a "Noël Coward" vehicle. At any rate, it went unproduced in the US, and the piece obviously had no relevance for a West End audience, who hardly needed to be reminded there was a war on. Today, the subject matter is irrelevant, except as a historical footnote.

The action of *Time Remembered* is set in Connecticut at a weekend house-party. An assortment of guests is engaged in the usual psycho-drama when they are surprised by the arrival of Lelia Heseldyne. Formerly a leading light in their social circle, she had returned to her native Britain at the outbreak of the war, along with her husband and two small sons.

> *"LELIA is a woman of great personal charm; attractive, chic and typical of what is known as 'The International Set.' She is witty and articulate and has more intelligence than most of her kind. Her age is about forty. For the past so many years she has accepted the values of those with whom she has mixed but not quite unquestioningly, because her own innate personal honesty with herself, at moments, causes her, most uncomfortably, to see through the whole business. Instead of utilising this intuition and really getting down to brass tacks, she has allowed herself to drift with the tide, with the result that she is strung high; the strain in her manner is almost imperceptible."*

London is under siege from the Luftwaffe, and Lelia, at her husband Tony's insistence, has reluctantly left him and brought their children to the "safety" of the U.S.A.

The play takes place in the living room of Norma Ryerson's house in late September, 1940. Life goes determinedly on as usual for Norma's friends, a pre-war life that Lelia, too, was used to but, when she returns, she brings a different perspective. She has seen what none of them apparently wants to see.

By Act Three Lelia, sickened by the triviality of her old friends, tells them precisely what she thinks of their see-no-evil attitude and decides to return to an embattled Britain to take her chances in the "real" world. Significantly, her arguments inspire at least one of her contemporaries to make the same decision, and give the others something to think about.

The sentiments are meaningless to anyone who didn't live through that strange period. America, after all, was only going through the same process of appeasement that had seemed perfectly acceptable to many high-minded

Brits only a few years earlier. A year later, the whole argument was academic.

Nonetheless, as a piece for its time, *Time Remembered* had a number of distinctively patriotic Noël touches and tells us a lot about what was on his mind (other than singing "Mad Dogs" in the cannon's roar) during these critical years.

It also contains some vintage Coward speeches. Lelia's criticism of her American friends' selfish myopia compares favourably with the toast to the future in *Cavalcade*, or Frank Gibbons' speech to his new-born grandson at the end of *This Happy Breed* (a play written in 1939, but performed in 1942, at the height of the war):

> *"You belong to a race that's been bossy for years and the reason it's held on as long as it has is that nine times out of ten it's behaved decently and treated people right. Just lately, I'll admit, we've been giving at the knees a bit and letting people down who trusted us and allowing noisy little men to bully us with a lot of guns and bombs and aeroplanes. But don't worry - that won't last - the people themselves, the ordinary people like you and me, know something better than all the fussy old politicians put together - we know what we belong to, where we come from, and where we're going. We may not know it in our brains, but we know it in our roots. And we know another thing, too, and it's this. We 'aven't lived and died and struggled all these hundreds of years to get decency and justice and freedom for ourselves without being prepared to fight fifty wars if need be - to keep 'em."*

*   *   *   *

Long Island Sound (1947), based on a short story called "What Mad Pursuit," suffers from the principal problem that Noël had done the same thing better in *Hay Fever* more than twenty years earlier. He may also have been recording personal history too closely to obtain the objectivity that comedy requires.

A famous British writer (Noël, thinly disguised) visits a Long Island estate, where his encounter with a stereotypical cross-section of unsympathetic Americans reduces him to a catatonic state. He ultimately escapes from the unbearable chaos through a window, and makes his chastened way back to town.

The stealthy "Escape from Chaos" exit is a Coward trademark. Events build to an impossible crescendo until there seems to be no possible resolution. Then the central figure literally walks away. (A song lyric says it best: "Let's steal away from the day.")

Noël used this device in *Private Lives* when Elyot and Amanda leave Victor and Sybil squabbling exactly as *they* used to; in *Hay Fever*, the guests quietly tiptoe out of the madhouse they've been trapped in; and in *Long Island Sound*, Noël's alter ego does it all over again.

It should also be noted that Garry Essendine is the male mirror-image of Judith Bliss; he creates and feeds the chaos, only to walk out when he can't take it any more. Judith at least stays to continue feeding the chaos!

Noël struggled with the basic construction of *Long Island Sound*, even though he said he had "great fun writing in the American idiom." It somehow escaped his ear. He claimed at the time of *Come Into the Garden, Maud*, that it was "easy to play Americans. All you do is say 'Hi, folks!' very loudly and then do the rest in English." Which, frankly, was about all Noël could do. He admitted later that the character was funny solely on the strength of a distinctly non-American called Coward who was clearly "playing it": "If a genuine American did it, it wouldn't be nearly so effective."

Long Island Sound suffers from its unsympathetic characters and its single joke, which was too drawn out. Even Noël's description of the leading character is ambiguously stated:

> *"An Englishman of about fifty is in a dinner jacket. He is a quiet, intellectual man; a writer of some distinction, both in appearance and in behaviour, a model of what an Englishman of letters should be. His hair is greying slightly at the temples, he has a small neat moustache and an urbane smile. Perhaps there is a certain dryness about him. Perhaps every now and then he might incline towards pomposity but these defects, if true, could only be perceived by the hypercritical."*

Most of the characters spend too much of their time putting in their drinks orders, and there is a distinct air of *Alice Through the Looking Glass*, a weakly Americanised version of *Hay Fever*, but without the charm. Unsurprisingly, there are many classic Coward touches in the dialogue.

A few readings to close associates like Jack and Binkie convinced Noël of the correctness of his verdict, and he laid it aside with few regrets. Of all the unpublished plays, *Long Island Sound* is the least likely to be produced.

If *Long Island Sound* was *Hay Fever* revisited, then *Volcano* has elements of *Point Valaine*. Set in a hotel in Samolo, we have another strong lady in

Adela Shelley ("A handsome woman in her middle forties"). Widowed shortly after the war, she has decided to "stay on" and live alone in the family home on the slopes of the mountain which gives the play its name. A motley crew of guests visits just before the volcano erupts.

Noël rarely allowed outside influences to determine the course of the action, preferring the drama to emerge from the characters. Aside from the symbolic volcano, plenty of heat is generated by the guests themselves. Adela has had an affair, which she regrets, with the island's resident Lothario, Guy. His desire to rekindle the relationship is thwarted by the arrival of his embittered wife, Melissa, who is anxious to confront her latest rival.

Filling in the background are other, younger couples who are trying, with mixed results, to uncomplicate their own emotional lives. Everyone is forced to re-evaluate their positions in the face of the impending natural cataclysm which threatens to destroy them.

Tropical islands, especially Samolo, were a pitfall for Noël, and tended to dominate the action of the plays on which they were set. *Volcano* never quite resolves the atmospheric problems that bedeviled *Point Valaine*, but the midday sun does generate enough steamy heat to trigger off some effective scenes.

Melissa and Adela sniffing around each other is worthy of a better play, as is the scene in which Melissa goads her philandering husband into a discussion of what it's like to fall *out* of love. Guy and Melissa represent the dark side of Elyot and Amanda, a cautionary tale of what *might* have been.

Now we come to "The Case of the Missing Tenth Play." It is popularly supposed that Noël wrote nine one-act plays during 1935 for the production of *Tonight at 8:30*. Gertie and he appeared at the Phoenix Theatre in early 1936, playing three a night in repertory, starting with *Hands Across the Sea, The Astonished Heart,* and *Red Peppers.*

In fact, Noël wrote a tenth play for the cycle, but it was dropped after only a couple of out-of-town performances. The play was called *Star Chamber*, and was set in an empty theatre during the board meeting of a theatrical charity. Assembled for this thankless task of good work are, among others, a crusty Dame (à la Sybil Thorndike), a fading ingenue, a pretentious producer, and a Hollywood-bound leading man. These self-obsessed thespians constantly interrupt the proceedings with their gossip and petty concerns.

Gertie was to have played Xenia James, a larger-than-life star not entirely unlike Gertrude Lawrence. Noël was to be Johnny Bolton, a stand-up comedian ("The Man Who Made Kitchener Laugh!") in the Max Miller style. A pre-emptive Archie Rice, he is never allowed to deliver the punch line to any of his appalling gags. Noël confessed that the character contained more than a *soupçon* of Leslie Henson, a comedian whose relentless off-stage patter had always bored him.

Lacking the form of *Still Life* or *Fumed Oak*, it is, nevertheless, a pleasantly sustained comedy routine. Noël had dealt with similar subject matter more pointedly in *Red Peppers*, but *Star Chamber* still reads well. Audiences of the time would have found it amusing to match the stage characters with their historical counterparts.

Noël explained that he had written the part of the bore for himself and had simply bored the hell out of the audience, which may be hard to believe, but in *Tonight* he certainly had an embarrassment of riches to choose from.

Noël loved to incorporate everyday events from his own life into his plays. Just before he wrote *Star Chamber*, he had been persuaded to take over as President of the Actors' Orphanage from Sir Gerald du Maurier. Presumably his new post gave him some insights into the workings of charitable institutions. Part of his dissatisfaction with the piece undoubtedly stemmed from the realisation that he had inadvertently satirised people who, whatever their personal affectations, were doing very valuable work. Noël took his own charitable duties seriously, and he truly appreciated others who did the same.

The idea of a home for "destitute actresses," called Garrick Haven in *Star Chamber*, was later developed into The Wings in *Waiting in the Wings* (1960). The home, by the way, was named for Noël's favourite club, the Garrick.

In his introduction to the published version of the plays that were performed, Noël wrote of the form:

> "A short play, having a great advantage over a long one in that it can sustain a mood without technical creaking or over-padding, deserves a better fate, and if, by careful writing, acting and producing I can do a little towards reinstating it in its rightful place, I shall have achieved one of my more sentimental ambitions."

I believe he more than fulfilled that ambition. In a recent public session at Lincoln Center in New York, all nine plays were read over a two-day period. One is struck by the sheer versatility of Noël's talent, as he varies mood, form and social setting. The Coward wit is a constant ("She was wearing a hat that looked like it was in a great hurry and couldn't stay around for long") but in every other regard they could be plays by nine different people.

The technical daring is particularly impressive. The use of fractured time in *Shadow Play*, for instance, makes *Follies* look flat and Priestley pedestrian. Ayckbourn students would do well to start their studies right here.

Seymour Chwast's elegant poster for the TV dramatisation of Noël's short stories, sponsored by Mobil. Noël also turned Star Quality into a full length play but it was never produced. (1987)

"CONSIDER THE PUBLIC":

The Sunday Times Trilogy

January, 1961, was enlivened for readers of *The Sunday Times* (and subsequently a wider audience, as the debate caught fire) by the publication on successive Sundays of Noël's series of three articles on the shortcomings, as he perceived them, of the "New Movement" in the English theatre.

Under the general heading of "Consider the Public" he wrote "A Warning to Pioneers" (published on January 15th as "These Old-Fashioned Revolutionaries"). On January 22nd, "A Warning to Actors" appeared as "The Scratch-and-Mumble School," while January 29th concluded the series with "A Warning to Dramatic Critics" (from which, the sub-editors facetiously deleted the word "Dramatic" from the title).

Reaction was immediate and intense. How dare this pre-war dramatic relic have the audacity to express opinions on post-Coward theatre? The fact that most of the correspondence from the general public was supportive of Noël's views enraged many of the "new" playwrights even more. *The Sunday Times'* "Letters to the Editor" column was so over-subscribed that letters had to be abbreviated.

"Nobody else, since the death of Shaw, could have evoked such an angry banging of dustbin lids nor have so violently stirred the dramatic garbage which there lies concealed," said Beverly Nichols, himself a person from the literary past. Nonetheless, he had expressed what many felt.

CONSIDER THE PUBLIC

A Warning to Pioneers

In the last decade I have been a fairly detached spectator of what is described as "The New Movement In The Theatre," and I feel that now, after fifty years of activity in the profession as an actor, playwright and director, my age and experience entitle me to offer a little gentle advice to the young revolutionaries of today and also to those of our dramatic critics who have hailed their efforts with such hyperboles of praise.

My advice, in essence, is simple and can be stated in three words: Consider the Public. This I know may appear to be senile heresy to those who are diligently occupied in sweeping away, or attempting to sweep away, all the conventions and traditions which, with certain inevitable and gradual mutations, have kept the drama alive and kicking for several hundred years; but it would be unwise to dismiss it too contemptuously. If you intend to be a successful actor, playwright or director (and to embark on any of these three careers *without* intending to be successful would be plain silly), you must remember that it is the support of the public and only the support of the public that will earn you your living.

The Public! Exacting, careless, discerning, undiscriminating, capricious, loyal and unpredictable, is that goose that lays your golden eggs. To batter it with propaganda, bewilder it with political ideologies, bore it with class prejudice and, above all, irritate it with wilful technical inefficiency, is a policy that can only end in dismal frustration and certain failure.

Here I would like to quote my colleague Terence Rattigan, who writes in the preface to his second volume of plays: 'A play can neither be great, nor a masterpiece, nor a work of genius, nor talented, nor untalented, nor indeed anything at all unless it has an audience to see it. For without an audience it simply does not exist. No audience means no performance and no performance means no play. This fact, sadly lamented though it may have been over the centuries by aspiring, talented but unperformed dramatists, is hard, I admit, but utterly inescapable...plays, though they may give incidental pleasure in the library are first intended for the stage. If they are not, they are not plays, but novels, poems or philosophies in dialogue form, and their author, writer of genius though he may well be, has no right to use the title of dramatist.' Obviously I would not have quoted the above sensible statement if I were not entirely in agreement with it.

To my mind one of the principal faults of the 'New Movement' writers is their supercilious attitude to the requirements of an average audience. Presumably this is accounted for by the fact that the majority of any average audience is usually composed of the despised 'bourgeoisie.' Another of their grave defects is what I will describe as 'inverse snobbery.' Their plays, to date, have dealt exclusively with the lower strata of society from which one concludes that, in their opinion, the people of these strata are the only people worth writing about. This is both didactic and inaccurate for it is absurd to imply that the problems, emotions, dramas and comedies of one class are intrinsically superior to those of another, particularly as the lower strata today represent merely a small minority of the population as a whole.

I am a staunch upholder of the theory that a beginner should first write about the class he knows best, but I also believe that, having done so, once or twice or even three times, his allegiance to his own creative talent should compel him to start learning about other classes as soon as he possibly can. It is as dull to write incessantly about tramps and prostitutes as it is to write incessantly about dukes and duchesses or even suburban maters and paters, and it is bigoted and stupid to believe that tramps and prostitutes and underprivileged housewives frying onions and using ironing boards are automatically the salt of the earth and that nobody else is worth bothering about. Equally bigoted is the assumption that reasonably educated people who behave with restraint in emotional crises are necessarily 'clipped,' 'arid,' 'bloodless' and 'unreal.'

It is true that a writer should try to hold the mirror up to nature, although there are certain aspects of nature which would be better unreflected. In some of the recent 'New Movement' plays I have noted several examples of trivial and entirely unnecessary vulgarity. In *A Taste of Honey*, for instance, the heroine parodies the labour pains of her imminent childbirth. In Samuel Beckett's *Endgame* one of the characters, a tramp I think, urinates in his trousers. In *Roots* an alcoholic farmer defecates, off stage, in his trousers and has to be hosed down. In *Chicken Soup with Barley* one of the characters also defecates in his trousers, this time on stage and has to be led off to the toilet. Whether or not this preoccupation with excreta is Freudian symbolism, psychopathic compulsion or merely a desire on the part of the authors to shock the susceptibilities of the audience I neither know nor care, but I do know that it has no more genuine humour nor dramatic significance than four-letter words scribbled on the walls of a public lavatory.

Now in my experience an audience is quite prepared to have its susceptibilities shocked from time to time and frequently enjoys it but, and it is a very big but, only up to a point. Once that point is reached and passed, the audience, who has paid its money into the box-office in order to be entertained, stimulated or moved, rebels. Its rebellion is passive and unsensational. It just stays away.

It is interesting to note that at the moment of writing there is only one 'New Movement' straight play playing to good business in a London theatre - *The Caretaker* by Harold Pinter. This, to me, is in no way a strange phenomenon. Mr. Pinter is neither pretentious, pseudo-intellectual nor self-consciously propagandist. True, the play has no apparent plot, much of it is repetitious and obscure and it is certainly placed in the lowest possible social stratum but it is written with an original and unmistakable sense of theatre and is impeccably acted and directed. Above all, its basic premise is victory rather than defeat. I am surprised that the critics thought so well of it. Doubtless, they were misled by the comfortingly familiar squalor of its locale and the fact that one of the principal characters is a tramp.

A few weeks ago Mr. Kenneth Tynan, that most articulate of *avant-garde* torchbearers, slithered gracefully backwards off the barricades and announced plaintively: 'The present state of the English theatre is one of deadlock. Its audience is still predominantly conservative, wedded by age and habit to the old standards; its younger playwrights, meanwhile are predominantly anti-conservative, irretrievably divorced from the ideological status quo. Obviously they need a new audience; but in order to attract it they will have to define and dramatise the new values for which they severally stand. We know what they are *against* - the human consequences of class privilege, the profit motive, organized religion and so forth - but what are they *for?*'

In spite of Mr. Tynan's disillusional *cri du cœur* I cannot feel that this is really a very difficult question to answer. Having in the first place decided to become professional playwrights they must obviously be 'for' the proven success of their plays. Not necessarily success in the *Chu Chin Chow / Mousetrap* sense, but at least success enough to relieve them of financial anxiety and bring them some of the material satisfactions that reward their, perhaps less earnest, but certainly more commercially popular, colleagues. I suspect, possibly unworthily, that their anti-class privilege, anti-profit theories might suffer a sea-change could they manage to achieve an eighteen months run in a largish West End theatre on a ten per cent of the gross contract.

It is well known that there are all sorts of audiences for all sorts of plays. The public that packs the theatre nightly for *Simple Spymen* or *Watch It, Sailor* is entirely different from that which queues up for *Ross* or Shakespeare seasons at Stratford or the Old Vic. Somehow or other there always seem to be enough to go round. I disagree with Mr. Tynan when he says that the younger playwrights need a 'new' audience. What they need is just an audience, new or old it doesn't matter which; and this, with one or two exceptions, they have so far been unable to get. They have received tumultuous acclaim from the critics (always a sinister omen). They have gained awards and won prizes and, in most cases, had their plays extremely well acted. But in spite of this and in spite of the fact that the plays themselves cost little in costume, decor and overhead expenses, they have failed to run. And their managements, who perhaps still retain a tiny interest in the 'profit motive,' have been forced to withdraw them.

Without wishing to be unkind, I must honestly admit, having read or seen most of the 'New Movement' works under discussion, that I am not in the least surprised at the public's lack of response. In none of them to date, with a very few exceptions, have I observed any sign of genuine theatrical effectiveness. I have seen excellent acting, adroit direction and, once or twice, even good lighting, but nowhere among the torrents of words, propaganda, self-pity, vituperation, pretentiousness and self-conscious realism have I heard an original idea movingly expressed or a problem concisely stated.

I am aware that most of the young writers of today are obsessed by left-wing socialism and the grievances of the underprivileged, and that many of them, possibly owing to their own personal circumstances, are prejudiced against any form of what the Americans are pleased to call 'Gracious Living.' But the fact must be faced that a very large proportion of English people, even in our tax-ridden Welfare State, contrive to live, if not graciously, at least comfortably. The men manage to earn reasonable salaries in offices, banks, shops and factories; the women manage to run houses or flats, have children, bring them up and educate them and on the whole live fairly contented lives. For all the eager young talent of our day to be encouraged to dwell exclusively on the limited and monotonous problems of a fast diminishing proletariat seems to me to be not only foolish but very definitely old-fashioned.

In the early Twenties the *avant-garde* Piscator theatre in Berlin was presenting, to a bored and apathetic public, very similar plays to those which are being presented at the Royal Court Theatre today. There was the same 'Down With The Rich - Up With The Poor' propaganda, there were the same sinks and dustbins and washtubs and onion frying; the same composite 'imaginative' sets with different levels, and windows and doors opening onto nothing, and the same naïf conviction on the part of authors, actors and directors that they were pioneers sweeping away forever the moribund, fustian conventions and traditions of the commercial theatre.

As I saw all this nearly forty years ago it is natural enough that I should not be deeply impressed with the 'new values for which our present-day young authors severally stand.' To me these 'new' values are as familiar as a maid and butler opening a first act with a brisk exposition of the characters about to appear. What neither the critics nor the contemporary pioneers take into consideration is that political or social propaganda in the theatre, as a general rule, is a cracking bore. In spite of much intellectual wishful thinking to the contrary, the theatre is now, always has been and, I devoutly hope, always will be primarily a place for entertainment.

If a young writer is burning with social injustice and quiveringly intolerant of 'the ideological status quo,' he would be well advised to choose some other medium in which to express his views. He can address crowds at Marble Arch, write pamphlets, novels or free verse, stand on soap boxes and incite factory workers and dock-hands to strike, or go into politics. He can even march up and down the main thoroughfares of

London (protectively escorted by the long-suffering Metropolitan Police Force) waving banners and shouting at the top of his lungs that he is against this or that, or the other thing, but in fairness to himself and his future hopes, he had better keep away from the theatre; for theatre, after perhaps a brief start of surprise, will in a comparatively short space of time disown him, ignore him and ultimately forget him entirely.

The first allegiance of a young playwright should be, not to his political convictions, nor to his moral or social conscience, but to his talent. And what is more, over and above this initial talent, it is his duty as an artist to impose upon himself and his work, industry, lucidity, economy of phrase, self-criticism, taste, selectivity and enough technical ability to convey whatever he wishes to convey to a large audience. (I say 'large' audience advisedly because it is palpably a waste of time to appeal merely to a minority of the already converted.) This cannot be achieved only by hatred of established conditions and the impulse to destroy. It can be achieved occasionally, however, by the forms of self-discipline I have outlined above, coupled with a certain humility, humour and an intelligent and respectful attitude to the public.

Consider the public. Treat it with tact and courtesy. It will accept much from you if you are clever enough to win it to your side. Never fear it nor despise it. Coax it, charm it, interest it, stimulate it, shock it now and then if you must, make it laugh, make it cry and make it think, but above all, dear pioneers, in spite of indiscriminate and largely ignorant critical acclaim, in spite of awards and prizes and other dubious accolades, never never never bore the living hell out of it.

CONSIDER THE PUBLIC

A Warning to Actors

Having, in a previous article, delivered a measure of warning and advice to our pioneer playwrights, I should like, in this essay, to give a few pointers to our young actors and actresses. Before I begin laying about me however I must say in all fairness that the standard of acting among the youth of our New Movement in the theatre is, within its limits, remarkably high. Nevertheless, 'within its limits' is the operative phrase, for these limits, imposed principally by left-wing socialism, are dangerously narrow.

To perform small grey plays in small grey theatres with the maximum of realism and the minimum of make-up is a great deal easier than to play classic drama or modern comedy with enough style and technical assurance to convince an audience of fifteen hundred to two thousand people.

The fact that wit, charm and elegance have been forced into temporary eclipse by our present day directors and critics, many of whom would be incapable of recognizing these qualities if they saw them, does not mean that they will not return. The wind and the weather will change: it always does, and, when this happens, some of our young scratch-and-mumble-school players will find that their hitherto circumscribed training and experience have ill equipped them to perform in *milieux* to which they are totally unaccustomed.

This is largely the fault of contemporary playwrights and directors but not entirely. It is also the fault of the actors themselves for they should realise that *one* approach to the mastery of their medium, however intelligent that approach may be, is not enough. The duty of every young actor, regardless of what political beliefs he may hold, or what particular class he comes from, is to widen his views and his scope as much as possible.

Many of our greatest and most distinguished actors and actresses have come from humble beginnings and one of the principal contributory causes of their later greatness and distinction was the fact that they were not content to stay as they were. With determination, hard work and concentration they strove during their early years to improve themselves. They studied dancing, fencing and elocution; they banished from their speech, both on the stage and off it, the tell-tale accents of their early environments; they trained their ears and their tongues to master alien dialects, and to many of them the most alien of these was the speech of the educated. In fact they rigorously disciplined themselves to a point where they could play Kings and Queens, north country farmers, foreign diplomats, Cockney cab drivers, Irish colleens, Welsh miners and average middle-class business men, without strain and with equal authenticity. I have noticed few signs of this deliberately and painstakingly acquired versatility to-day. It can be argued, of course, that there is no longer any demand for it, and this up to a point is true, but it must be remembered that when the pendulum begins to swing back again, there will be.

Theatrically, one of the more depressing aspects of the present transition phase through which the civilized world is passing, is the monotonous emphasis on the lot of the Common Man; for the Common Man, unless written and portrayed with genius, is not dramatically nearly so interesting as he is claimed to be. A glance at the list of currently successful plays in London will show that the public, on the whole, prefer to see extraordinary people on the stage rather than ordinary ones; fantastic situations rather than familiar, commonplace ones, and actors of outsize personality and talent rather than accurately competent mediocrities.

I am quite prepared to admit that during my fifty odd years of theatre going, I have on many occasions been profoundly moved by plays about the Common Man, as in my fifty odd years of restaurant going I have frequently enjoyed tripe and onions, but I am not prepared to admit that an exclusive diet of either would be entirely satisfying. In this I am fully convinced that the general public is in complete agreement with me.

From the acting point of view, of course, the Common Man is the easiest and most immediately rewarding assignment in the theatre, particularly in straight, down-to-earth plays where no comedy values are involved. For any experienced actor who has mastered the poetic nuances of Shakespearean verse and the intricate subtleties of modern high comedy, 'Dear Old Dad' in a kitchen sink drama is the equivalent of a couple of aspirin and a nice lie-down. Some years ago when I was giving alternate performances of *Present Laughter* and *This Happy Breed* at the Haymarket Theatre I can remember to this day the relief I used to feel when, after a matinée of the former with its tension and tempo and concentrated timing, I returned in the evening to play Frank Gibbons in *This Happy Breed*. To wander about in shirt-sleeves, take off my boots, pick my nose and drink cups of tea was so infinitely less demanding than dashing about at high speed in coloured dressing gowns and delivering comedy lines accurately enough to reach the back of the gallery.

I am well aware that this confession will probably bring forth howls of derision from my younger, more dedicated colleagues, but the fact remains that it always has been and it always will be easier to play realistic drama than artificial comedy. That this is not generally accepted by our modern pseudo-intellectual groups, merely proves that they don't know nearly so much about the theatre as they think they do.

This brings me, with a slight yawn, to what is colloquially known as The Method.

A number of years ago Vladimir Ilitch Lenin was conveyed, in a sealed compartment, across Europe to Russia. This furtive adventure resulted in a great deal of trouble for a great many people. A few years later, whether in a sealed compartment or not I have no idea, a book by Constantine Stanislavski found its way to America where it, in its turn, caused a great deal of trouble to a great many actors, actresses, directors and, ultimately, to the unfortunate public. The only ones who benefited from it being a few performers who, having proved themselves dismally inadequate on the stage, decided to set themselves up as teachers.

Actually there were two books, *My Life In Art* and *An Actor Prepares*, in both of which Mr. Stanislavski states his views on the art of acting. In the former, which is autobiographical, he explains without humour but in merciless detail, his psychological, spiritual and technical approach to every part he played in the course of his distinguished career. These esoteric soul-searchings are accompanied by a series of photographs which prove at least that he was a great one for the nose-paste and crepe hair and not above a comical posture or two when the role demanded it.

In *An Actor Prepares* he is more objective and, under the thin disguise of a director called Tortsov, he sets out to explain his theories to a group of embarrassingly earnest young drama students. That this book should become a sort of theatrical bible in Russia is quite understandable. It is written by a Russian for Russians with, naturally enough, a proper appreciation of the Russian temperament, but that it should be regarded as holy writ to the theatrical youth of the Western world is less understandable and to my mind excessively tiresome.

It would be foolish to deny that among Mr. Stanislavski's analyses of acting there are not a few simple and basic truths concealed beneath his laboured and tortuous verbiage, but these truths are so simple and so basic that I doubt if they would have called forth more than a casual grunt of agreement from the late Sarah Siddons.

There is quite a lot to be said in favour of certain aspects of The Method. It stresses a few essential 'musts' such as the necessity of finding the correct psychological values of the part to be played and concentrating first on the interior truth of a character before attempting the exterior projection of it. As this however is what every experienced actor I have ever met does automatically, I cannot entirely welcome it as a dazzling revelation. In my opinion The Method places too much emphasis on actual realism and too little on simulated realism. To Be, up to a point, and Not To Be, over and above that point, is the whole art and craft of acting. Every intelligent actor realises the impossibility of *genuinely* feeling the emotions necessary to his part for eight performances a week over a period of months or even years. His art lies in his ability to recreate nightly an accurate simulation of the emotions he originally felt when he was first studying and rehearsing it. If acting were actually a state of 'Being,' anybody playing a heavy dramatic role in a smash success would be in a mental home after a few weeks. In any event, emotion on the stage without the technique to project it and the ability to control it merely results in mistiming and untidiness and has nothing whatsoever to do with acting.

Technique, although a much despised word nowadays, is, beyond a shadow of doubt, indispensable. It is impossible to give a consistent and continued performance without it. However progressive and revolutionary a young actor's theories may be and however many rules, conventions and traditions he may hold in contempt as being 'ham' and old fashioned, he would be well advised to learn these rules, conventions and traditions before attempting to break them. It is as palpably foolish for an actor to try to play a major role, or even a minor one for that matter, without first learning to move about the stage and speak audibly, as it would be for a budding pianist or violinist to embark on a concerto without first having mastered his scales. And it is here that I feel that The Method, as a method, breaks down. I myself have heard a famous Method teacher in New York inform a student that audibility was unimportant compared with 'the moment of truth!' This lofty statement of course evaporates immediately when even cursorily examined, for how can fifty moments of truth be of the faintest significance on the stage if no one in the auditorium can hear what the actors are talking about?

In addition to a large number of grimy, introspective, megalomaniacs, The Method has undoubtedly produced a small number of brilliant actors. But then so has the Royal Academy of Dramatic Art, The Old Vic Drama School and every other sort of acting school down to 'Miss Weatherby's Shakespeare In Twelve Easy Lessons, 36, Station Approach, Sidcup.'

Genuine talent can profit from or survive any given system of instruction, although unquestionably the best training of all is acting to paying audiences either in touring companies or repertory companies. Audience reaction is of paramount importance to learning the job, for without it, the acting, however brilliant, has no point. To perform to a handful of fellow students and relatives in a small fit-up studio theatre is a waste of time and not even good practice; in fact it is very often bad practice because the reaction, both from teachers and prejudiced spectators, can be misleading. The aim of every budding actor should be to get himself in front of a paying audience, no matter where, as soon as he possibly can.

This salutary experience might conceivably rub off a little of the solemn, dedicated gloom that Mr. Stanislavski and his disciples have imposed on our hitherto cheerful and fairly ramshackle profession. The Theatre may be regarded as an Art with a capital letter, a craft, a means of earning a living or even a showcase for personal exhibitionism, but it is not and should not be a religion. I am all in favour of actors taking their work seriously, in fact on many occasions I have been accused of being a martinet in this respect. But I am definitely not in favour of every member of the company embarking on endless, ego-feeding, quasi-theological discussions of the possible reactions and motivations of the parts they have to play. If they have studied the play intelligently and learnt the words they should *know* the necessary reactions and motivations already and not waste my time and their own in gabbing about them. All this tedious argument, recapitulation and verbose questing after 'Truth,' apart from giving the individual actor an overblown opinion of his own intellectual prowess, is pretentious nonsense and not to be tolerated for a moment by a director of integrity. The director of a play is analogous to the Captain of a ship, and few ships' Captains in moment of crisis lend a benign and tolerant ear to the suggestions of every minor member of the crew.

Another, to my mind, dangerous assumption on the part of the Method teachers is that actors are cerebral and can be relied upon to approach the playing of a part intellectually. In my experience, the really fine actors whom I have known and admired and often worked with have been, in varying degrees, intelligent, shrewd, egotistical, temperamental, emotional and, above all, intuitive, but never either logical or intellectual. Their approach to their work, according to their respective characters and techniques, is guided almost mystically by their talent.

It is this that has propelled them up from the ranks of small part players into the position of loved and envied stardom. It is this, combined with every trick and technical device they have acquired on the way, which enables them on a nerve-strained, agonized opening night to rise supremely to the challenge and sweep the play into success. And it is this, curiously enough, in which most of them have the least confidence and for which they require the most reassurance. However much self-confidence they may appear to have, this basic uncertainty is their most valuable and endearing asset. It is also the hallmark of the genuine article. I have encountered few fine actors and few real stars in the true meaning of the word who, beneath God knows how much egotism, temperament and outward flamboyance do not possess a fundamental humility.

Alas and alack, I have encountered quite a number of our young actors and actresses of to-day who, sodden with pretentious theories and trained to concentrate solely on their own reactions and motivations to the exclusion of their fellow actors and the audience, have not even a bowing acquaintance with humility. They apparently despise the far past as thoroughly as they despise the immediate past. They arrogantly condemn the 'commercial' theatre, which in essence means the public that they must hope ultimately to please, thereby, it seems to me, spitting in the eye of the golden goose before it has even met the gander.

It is this innate contempt for the values of other days which accounts, I presume, for their physical slovenliness on the stage. I have watched, with Edwardian dismay, these talented young creatures arriving at a rehearsal. The boys, unshaven, wearing grubby open-necked sweaters and stained leather coats, and with dark finger nails. The girls, in strained jeans, equally grubby sweaters, with their hair unwashed and unbrushed or twisted into unalluring pony-tails. Admittedly this very young sartorial defiance is perfectly consistent with most of the parts they are called upon to play, but my point is that if they are really to succeed over the years they will be called upon to play all sorts and kinds of parts and that all this initial grubbiness will suddenly turn out to be a severe handicap. There is, after all, no theatrical law decreeing that an actor should identify himself off stage with whatever he is going to play on stage. In point of fact it is a dangerous and confusing premise. Slovenliness of appearance all too often indicates slovenliness of mind and no actor can afford to have that.

I do not wish to imply by the above that I am so advanced in my dotage as to be entirely out of sympathy with the facile defiance of the young. I was young myself once; defiant, pushing and self-confident - outwardly at least - and, like most intelligent, ambitious youngsters, I imagined I knew a great deal more than I actually did. But never, in all my youthful arrogance, was I idiotic enough to allow myself to be influenced by any current political creed, nor conceited enough to curl my lip contemptuously at the 'great' of the theatre because they happened to be commercially successful.

On the contrary, I was deeply in awe of them and blushed with pride whenever one of them deigned to speak to me. I had only two presentable suits, but these were daily pressed within an inch of their lives. I would never have dreamed of attending even an understudy rehearsal, and in those days I attended many, without going to immense pains to look my very best.

The theatre should be treated with respect. The theatre is a wonderful place, a house of strange enchantment, a temple of illusion. What it most emphatically is not and never will be is a scruffy, ill-lit, fumed-oak drill-hall serving as a temporary soap-box for political propaganda.

The theatre still spells magic for many millions of people and that magic should be a source of deep pride to all those who are privileged to serve in it.

CONSIDER THE PUBLIC

A Warning to Dramatic Critics

In the long history of the arts there have been almost as many harsh things said by artists about critics as there have been by critics about artists. Byron, Pope, Dryden, Coleridge, Hazlitt, to name only a few, have all, in their time, lashed out when driven to exasperation by the carping of those they considered, rightly, to be their inferiors.

Like the cobra and the mongoose, the artist and the critic have always been and will always be Nature's irreconcilables. Occasionally a temporary truce may be established, based insecurely on a sudden burst of enthusiasm from the latter for the work of the former, but these halcyon interludes are seldom of long duration. Sooner or later a dissonant note is sure to be sounded and back we tumble again into the dear old basic status quo.

"For never can true reconcilement grow,
When wounds of deadly hate have pierced so deep."

My personal attitude to the dramatic critics, after fifty years of varying emotions, has finally solidified into an unyielding core of bored resignation. Every now and them the outer edge of this fossilized area in my mind can be twitched into brief sensitivity by an unexpected word of praise or a stab of more than usually vicious abuse, but these occasions are becoming rarer and rarer and the core remains, hardening imperceptibly with the passing of time until, presumably, it will achieve absolute invulnerability.

However before this state of Nirvana finally sets in, I feel an impulse to rise up, gird my loins and have just one valedictory bash at my natural enemies. Not, I hasten to say, on my own account; I have never been attracted to lost causes - but on behalf of the love of my life which is the theatre.

The Theatre, in all its diverse aspects, fascinates and enchants me today as much as it did when I first became a professional actor at the age of ten. A fine play impeccably acted or a good musical well sung and danced can still send me out into the street in a state of ecstatic euphoria, just as a mediocre play indifferently acted can depress me utterly and rob me, temporarily, of all hope and ambitions.

Naturally, I do not expect dramatic critics to scale such heights of enjoyment or plumb such depths of despair, for in order to do so they would have to know a great deal more than they do about playwriting and acting. And if they did know a great deal more about playwriting and acting, it is highly probable that they would be playwrights or actors themselves and not critics at all, for either of the above occupations are more attractive and financially remunerative, when successful, than journalism.

A dramatic critic is frequently detested, feared, despised, and occasionally tolerated, but he is seldom loved or envied. The awareness of this must, in course of time, lower his morale and corrode his spirit, either consciously or subconsciously. Some of them, of course, seek compensation by making small names for themselves, usually by the use of sensational vituperation, but alas, both the vituperation and the names are soon forgotten.

The well worn cliché that most critics are frustrated artists has, like most clichés, a certain basis of truth: and this truth, from time to time, has been fairly dismally proved when one of other of them, rendered mad by the monotony of his nightly calvary, has attempted to free himself from his bondage and write a play. With a few notable exceptions, these sporadic bids for freedom have been painfully abortive. Unfortunately, I cannot recall any occasion in England when a dramatic critic decided to become an actor, but there is still hope in my heart and my fingers are crossed. Mr. Kenneth Tynan, we know, started as an actor, but was soon forced, by managerial and public apathy, to desist.

In earlier years it was customary for critics, after they had given their opinions of the play and the leading actors, to mention some of the lesser members of the cast. This provided a certain encouragement to supporting players, if only to the extent of bringing their names to the attention of the public and to other managements. That this custom, of late, seems to be gradually dying out is perhaps regrettable, but only up to a point, for the critic is yet to be born who is capable of distinguishing between the actor and the part. A minor actor playing a brief showy role, however ineptly, can always be sure of good notices, whereas a popular favourite, using all the subtle resources of long experience to bring life to a long, unrewarding part, is dismissed with a caution.

In the course of an interview some months ago with Mr. Robert Muller, whose Teutonic earnestness is finely matched by his lack of humour, I was horrified to learn of the circumstances in which the critics of today have to work, particularly those who write for the daily newspapers. These poor beasts are apparently allowed only a brief half an hour and sometimes even less, in which to collect and correlate their views of an opening performance and get them down on their typewriters. Now this would be a formidable assignment even for men of lightning perceptiveness, and none of our present crop could honestly be credited with that.

Apart from this cruel time limitation, it appears that they are also crushed into a position of cowed subservience by an omniscient being called a Sub-Editor. This Sub-Editor, whose knowledge of the Theatre is probably limited to his local Odeon, holds all these fearsome oracles in deadly thrall. It is he who has the power to slash their columns to pieces and he who is responsible for those sensational headlines which are so often entirely irrelevant to the reviews they preface. Thousands of members of the public I believe seldom read further than these headlines and so when they are confronted by large black-lettered phrases such as 'Not This Time, Sir Laurence!' or 'Noël Flops Again!' they automatically follow their own instincts and go out to book seats.

In consideration of these circumstances, therefore, it is perhaps unfair to blame critics too much for their lack of selectiveness. They have to sit night after night in different theatres, staring glumly at what is put before them, haunted by the spectre of the Sub-Editor waiting for them, and aware that Time's Wingèd Chariot is goosing them along towards their deadline. All they can do really is to scribble a few hurried notes onto their programmes and run like stags to their desks as the final curtain touches the stage.

For most Theatre people, however, both the Sub-Editor's headline and the criticisms beneath them have an importance far out of proportion to their actual significance. Most playwrights, stars, actors, directors and managers devour avidly every review from *The Times* down to the *Express*, and allow themselves to be either depressed or elated, according to what they read. What few of them seem to realise is that an average member of an average audience seldom takes more than one or, at most, two newspapers, and even then he is more than likely to turn to the latest crime or the sporting page before casting his eye over the theatrical news.

There is no doubt, however, that a unanimously unfavourable press can sometimes do considerable damage to a production, particularly if the play in question happens to have no famous name on the bill, either author or star, to attract the public. Just as a unanimously enthusiastic press can ensure good business for two or three weeks. If the play is good and worthy of the praise it has received, it will run. If not, the public, within a comparatively short space of time will discover that it has been duped and stay away.

This has occurred with increasing frequency of late because the public has become wise to the fact that most of our contemporary critics tend to favour 'dustbin drama' to the exclusion of everything else. The prevalent assumption that any successful play presented by a commercial management in the West End is automatically inferior in quality to anything produced on a shoe string in the East End or Sloane Square is both inaccurate and silly. It also betrays an attitude of old-fashioned class consciousness and inverted snobbism which has now become obvious even to the ordinary playgoer, who gives little thought to 'movements' or 'trends' and merely goes to the theatre expecting to be entertained.

It is quite apparent that 'The New Movement in the Theatre' with all its potential talent and genuine belief in its own significance, is failing. And it is failing because it has been so shrilly over-sold, not only to the public but to itself. For young, aspiring playwrights and actors to be consistently over-praised because what they write and act happens to coincide with the racial, political and social prejudices of a handful of journalists, can only have a disastrous effect on their creative impulse. Very few beginners, however talented, can be expected to survive indiscriminate acclaim without becoming complacent and over-sure of themselves. The wise ones among them will, of course, after a little while, compare their notices with their royalties and decide that they still have a great deal to learn. But alas, such wisdom is usually the fruit of experience and in this the majority of them are, naturally enough, lacking.

To state that the dramatic critics of today are doing a grave disservice to the Theatre and to the public is a sweeping generalization that needs qualifying, although in my, far from humble, opinion it is very largely true. However I will qualify it to the extent of saying that those who write for the more respectable newspapers such as *The Times, The Daily Telegraph, The Sunday Times* and *The Observer,* can at least be relied upon to treat an author or an actor with courtesy. But then, being men of reasonable integrity, they presumably do not allow themselves to be bedevilled either by ignorant sub-editors or the dubious policies of overlords.

The critics of the *Daily Mail,* the *Daily Express,* the evening papers and the picture papers, however, have, of late years, flung all thought of courtesy to the winds and devoted themselves, with increasing virulence, to witless and indiscriminate abuse. Being myself one of the principal victims of this vulgarity, I feel perfectly justified in pointing out that they are making cracking idiots of themselves and proving nothing beyond the fact that they are entirely out of touch with the public they are supposed to be writing for.

It surely cannot be good for the reputation of a popular newspaper for its dramatic critic to be proved dead wrong over and over again. I am aware of course that the Lords Beaverbrook and Rothermere are not particularly interested in the Theatre, but even so it must dawn on them that quite a number of their readers are. And that these readers should be continually misled and misinformed about even so trivial a matter as a new play, cannot in the long run redound to the credit of the paper they represent.

In conclusion, I would like to suggest that our contemporary critics, if they wish to retain an atom of respect from their readers and the theatrical profession, should rid themselves of their more obvious personal prejudices, endeavour to be more objective and, if possible, more constructive.

In any event they should mend their manners.

THEATRE ESSAYS

The reception the "Consider the Public" pieces received greatly gratified Noël. An element of reasoned debate, at least, had been brought in to balance the unquestioning critical approval the "New Drama" had been receiving.

Noël decided that he really must write the book, *Coward on Theatre*, although, as far as I know, he never determined an actual title. No doubt it would have been something far more provocative. In the end, the book was never completed.

After "Dad's Renaissance" took off, Noël was much in demand for television, radio and press interviews in which his views on theatre were widely canvased. Many of the quotations I've collected are drawn from those interviews.

All that he left were four more chapters, which are published here for the first time. It's a pity there isn't more of this elegant, ironic prose, elaborating the theatrical philosophy that created his plays, but Shakespeare left even less, and we haven't done too badly piecing *him* together!

STAGE FRIGHT

Stage fright is an occupational disease which attacks the middle-aged and elderly more than the young and grows with increasing malignancy over the years until it can become, in certain acute cases, a serious theatrical hazard. I have seen actors and actresses of established reputation, proven talent and technical brilliance acquired by decades of experience, sitting in their dressing-rooms on an opening night in a state of neurotic hysteria, staring at themselves in the mirror and quivering with fear to such an extent that they are almost incapable of coherent speech and frequently have to retire to the lavatory to be sick. To my mind such sensitivity to nervous tension is not only excessive but self-indulgent.

Nearly all actors who have achieved positions of responsibility suffer from first-night nerves to a certain degree. It is only natural that they should. To act in a play for the first time before an audience after weeks of rehearsing it without one is inevitably an ordeal, but it is an ordeal that one has been trained to endure, and any professional performer who permits herself to be so terrified of enduring it would be well advised to seek other employment.

One of the most irritating aspects of this particular malaise is that it is contagious and, to a large extent, self-induced. Not consciously, of course; no actress in her senses would consciously encourage herself to suffer the tortures of the damned before doing a job for which she is not only well equipped but extremely well paid. It is a subtle process which usually begins after a certain amount of success has been achieved. Before that, during the early struggles and ambitions, when the longing for personal recognition outweighs all other considerations, excesses of first night nerves are not so much in evidence; also small part actors are less burdened with responsibility and indeed less pampered than established stars.

Children, of course, have no nerves at all. When I was a child in the Theatre the idea of being scared on an opening night never occurred to me nor can I remember it affecting any of my pert and bouncing contemporaries. To us theatre children a first performance was an occasion of excitement and delight, a consummation devoutly to be wished, a red-letter day to which we had all been looking forward with the same degree of thrilled anticipation that civilian children look forward to birthdays and Christmases. Speaking for myself it was not until I had been a professional actor for ten years and had reached my twenty-first birthday that I began to view an imminent first night with less exuberance and more apprehension. Later still, at the hoary age of twenty-four, when I first experienced authentic stardom in *The Vortex*, the rot began to set in. Not to any alarming degree at first, but as the years went on and rehearsals and try-outs and opening nights followed each other in fairly rapid succession, I became more and more aware of my responsibilities to the public, the management and indeed to myself. I had sniffed much of the sweet smell of success and fear of this heady fragrance evaporating began to haunt me.

Happily for my ultimate sense of balance I didn't have to wait long for it to be blown away by a hurricane of critical and public abuse. I attained the curious distinction of being booed off the stage twice in the course of two months in 1927. Although this was as a playwright and not as an actor, it proved to me once and for all that disaster in the theatre, however unhappy and discouraging it may be at the time, is neither final nor irrevocable. It is indeed surprising how swiftly the pain passes and is forgotten, or if not quite forgotten, at least relegated to its proper perspective. At all events, I have never, since that singular experience, suffered more than the normal nervous reactions on opening nights. It must not be imagined that I recommend being shrieked at by a hostile audience as a specific cure for stage fright.

So far as I know, no specific cure has yet been discovered. Different actors have developed different methods of combatting it. Some of the more misguided ones find that a stiff drink before going onto the stage can allay the pangs. This, however, is dangerous because a stiff drink is liable not only to allay the pangs but to annihilate that extra sense of timing which is essential to all actors, especially comedians. Others, in later years, have taken to swallowing tranquillizing tablets with the object of inducing a state of euphoria in which they don't care if the play goes well or ill and whether or not they themselves are good, bad or indifferent. This course, quite obviously, has so many disadvantages that it would be a waste of time to enumerate them. Another method is the adoption of a "Christian Science-God-is-Love-there-is-no-pain" attitude. This, although comforting to the actress or actor who can believe in it, is apt to create a certain bland, arid serenity which is baffling to the other members of the cast and sometimes irritating to the audiences. It can also be carried too far.

Many years ago I remember a famous actress explaining to me with perfect seriousness that before making an entrance she always stood aside to allow God to go on first. I can also remember that on that particular occasion He gave a singularly uninspired performance.

There is one way, however, to mitigate first-night nerves if not entirely to banish them, and this is to see to it that you are absolutely sure of your lines, for the dread of drying up is for every actor the worst nightmare of all. Personally, I have always considered that the first essential in approaching a new part is to learn the words thoroughly and accurately before even beginning to rehearse. To me, the rehearsal period of a play is exacting, exciting and, above all, exhausting. At the end of a long day's rehearsal I am in no condition to go home and concentrate on cramming words into my brain for the simple reason that by that time my brain is too tired to register them. I much prefer to dine quietly with friends or go to a movie and not think of the play again until the next morning's rehearsal.

This theory of learning the words before rehearsal is viewed with disfavour by actors and actresses of my acquaintance. They argue hotly that the only way to create a vital and integrated performance is to allow the characterization to grow naturally during the rehearsal period; to co-ordinate the dialogue with the movements dictated by the director and to acquire, as they go along, a true understanding of the motivations and mood changes of the part until suddenly, just before the opening night or perhaps even *on* the opening night, the expected revelation occurs and the performance emerges shining and complete. This, on the surface, appears to be a perfectly valid method, if perhaps a little inconsiderate to the author, the director and the other members of the cast; and there is no denying that it has resulted in many fine and impressive performances. It can also result in a great waste of time, emotion and nervous energy. In fact on closer analysis it isn't nearly so valid as it looks. In the first place all star performers receive the script they have agreed to play a long while in advance so therefore they have ample time to discuss before-hand with the author and the director any psychological problems in the text that they find difficult to understand. To leave these vital discussions until rehearsals begin is, in my opinion, both arrogant and lazy.

The actor's first allegiance should be not to himself, but to the author and if, on his initial readings of the play, he considers it good enough to appear in, his first duty is to learn it accurately, to study it with a post-card over the cues for two or three hours a day, if necessary for weeks, so that he can utilise rehearsals as they should be utilised, to experiment with feeling, movement and implication, without embarrassing his colleagues and director by fluffing and insulting the author by paraphrasing.

I am aware that this regime that I have outlined is not easy. It is hard work, it is lonely, and for most of the time it is sheer drudgery, but it pays off in the end. I know that, within my limits, I am an accomplished actor. I also know that I am not so conceited as to imagine that I can build a good performance *and* learn the words in a brief four weeks. As a director I have for years resolutely refused to rehearse actors with books in their hands. I am willing to sit round a table with the cast and read the play through with them but the moment they get onto their feet they must know their words well enough to give me some idea of what they are going to do with them.

There are certain great stars with whom I have worked who fight me on this and, occasionally, *because* they are great stars I have allowed myself to be over-ruled, always with disastrous results. I have seen these great stars of glittering effulgence and with years of triumphant success behind them, stumbling through a final dress-rehearsal, fluffing their lines, muddling their effects, massacreing my dialogue, casting agonized looks in the direction of the prompter and finally dissolving in panic-stricken tears in their dressing rooms afterwards. On the following night, after God knows what private hells they have gone through, I have seen these same talented, exasperating creatures sail onto the stage as though they hadn't a nerve in their bodies and play the whole play through with technical assurance and apparently a complete command of their dialogue (not always the author's) that is little short of miraculous. I have also on certain occasions seen them play the play straight down the drain. As a general rule however they manage to come through.

The audience, watching the play unfold for the first time, accepts this brilliant virtuosity with no surprise. They laugh and applaud and cheer, sublimely unaware of panic and strain and also happily ignorant that utter chaos is constantly being averted by a hair's breadth before their innocent eyes. To the author and director (in my case usually the dual capacity) sitting out in front, the whole evening is a nightmare. It is also a nightmare for the stage management and the supporting actors who, although they dutifully recognize the talent and reputation of their leading lady, know only too well that at any moment she may dry up dead, throw them inaccurate cues and very possibly cut several pages of plot. If the star in question happens to get away with this tour de force, she is acclaimed as usual, or even more than usual. One more histrionic victory is chalked up on her scroll of honour. The company crowd round her after the final curtain and overwhelm her with relieved congratulations; the author and director and management burst through the pass door and embrace her ardently, followed eagerly by hordes of enthusiastic first-nighters who belabour her with facile superlatives. She herself, benign and relaxed now that the ordeal is over, receives the plaudits with well trained graciousness, forgives, with weary magnanimity, the author and director and anyone else who has happened to irritate her during rehearsals and if she is a fool, which she usually is, accepts her very hazardous triumph as her natural due. It obviously does not occur to her that the frenzied nerve-strain she has undergone, the almost super-human effort of will and concentration she has forced herself to make and the frustrated anxiety she has inflicted on her fellow workers, were largely unnecessary. For if she had employed one quarter of that will power and concentration on doggedly learning the words by heart before rehearsals started, she could have stepped onto the stage for the first performance without her natural nervousness being exacerbated by the ghastly fear of drying up, ruining the play and making a cracking ass of herself.

To conclude: I have yet to discover a final and definitive cure for stage fright but the elimination of conceit and self-indulgence and a certain amount of disciplined homework and humility can help considerably to assuage the dreadful fears.

"HOW I WONDER WHAT YOU ARE"

Throughout all the years that the living theatre has existed the "Star System" has been decried and abused by devotees of the drama who are dedicated to the idealistic theory that "The play's the thing" and should rank first in importance in any theatrical enterprise. This theory is entirely admirable and, if only it were as realistic as it is admirable, the "Gay mad world of powder and paint" would be a great deal more comfortable than it is.

Every now and then a gleam of hope is discernible on the Utopian horizon. Somebody puts on a play with a cast of virtually unknown actors and is a "smash." A repertory company appears from some alien land devoid of any outstanding personalities and is crowned with laurels, but also, these shining auguries, unlike Mr. Christopher Fry's Phoenix, are *not* too frequent. The "Star System" - like some brash, bejewelled courtesan, remains triumphantly in power, smiling contemptuously at all abortive efforts to dislodge her.

The grim fact must be faced: that the majority of the theatre-going public would rather pay their money to see an extraordinary creature than an ordinary one. An extraordinary actress playing a relatively ordinary part may indeed lay waste the author's original intentions, but she will bring to that part a certain quality, a composite of her own personal magnetism, her reputation and her acquired technique which will hypnotize the audience into loving her. An ordinary, possibly better actress, playing the same part honestly and with loyal adherence to the author's text, will usually succeed in being little more than accurate. She will of course be effusively thanked by the author, director and the management and, if she happens to be an understudy, cheered to the echo by the gallery, but the business will drop steadily until the star returns to the cast. From the point of view of the dedicated drama enthusiasts this is indeed a desperate injustice, but then the theatre world is as packed with desperate injustice as is the world outside it.

Now we come to the burning question. "What is it that stars have that others haven't?" Is it an earthy quality or a spiritual quality? Is it concrete, abstract, animal, vegetable or mineral? There will obviously never be a satisfactory answer. A young girl decides to go on the stage. She is strikingly beautiful and by no means untalented. She is adequately taught at an acting school or by the better method of playing small parts in a repertory company. After a year or so she procures a job in London for which she receives honourable mention in *The Sunday Times* and an "Among others" in *The Daily Telegraph*. She at once acquires an agent, or has one thrust upon her, and her future is shining with promise. Twenty years later, having played two leading parts, one on tour and one in the West End in a play that ran only a fortnight, bits in movies, snippets on the radio and an endless succession of heroine's friends, she one day looks at herself in the mirror, and, if she is wise, notes that she is not quite so strikingly beautiful as she was, marries a well disposed dentist in Kettering and is heard of no more. If she is not wise she sticks doggedly to the Theatre and finally has to be assisted to the grave by the Actors' Benevolent Fund.

This, I admit, is a gloomy picture but it is not an unusual one. It is astonishing how often it has been proved in the Theatre that good looks, even when bolstered with talent, are not enough. Something extra is required and what that extra something is has never been satisfactorily explained. Of course, there are thousands and thousands of actors and actresses in the theatre who earn reasonable salaries and manage to live useful and happy lives. In fact, without these the Theatre would cease to exist. But surely at the very beginning of all their careers "To be a great star" must have been the ultimate goal? And surely, somewhere along the line there must have been a dismal moment when they realise that they hadn't made it and were never likely to?

Then, on the other side of the coin you take another young girl who decides that she wants to be an actress. She may not be outstandingly pretty and her talent may be negligible but these defects are mercifully veiled from her by the possession of a strong ego and a plentiful supply of ruthless determination. She will endure, possibly only briefly, the routine early struggles. Somebody will spot her either in a leading role in a repertory company or in a small part in a London production. It may not be because she is particularly gifted that they spot her, it is because she possesses an extra "something" that demands attention.

This extra "something" is an amalgam of various elements: vitality, sex-appeal, an intriguing voice (nearly all big stars have distinctive voices), an individual style of movement and some sort of chemical emanation, of which she may or may not be conscious, which places her on a different plane from her possibly more talented colleagues. The balanced mixture of all these ingredients is recognized as "personality" or, in other words, "Star Quality." Very very occasionally this "Star Quality" may be acquired by years of experience, determination and the assurance of polished technique, but as a general rule it is something that people either have or have not and when they have, it is unmistakable.

In any event this fortunately endowed creature, whoever she may be, is hailed, within a relatively short space of time, as a Star, and it is in this glorious moment that the rot usually starts to set in. Her hitherto unblemished character begins, subtly at first, to suffer that "sea change - into something rich and strange." The name in lights, tumultuous applause, hosts of admirers, acres of first-night flowers and extravagant publicity all contribute their insidious magic until, a few years later, we see, bowing graciously to us on an opening night, a triumphant, assured, fascinating, adored, rip-snorting megalomaniac. During the few weeks immediately preceding that glamorous moment, Heaven alone knows what hair-raising scenes and dramas have taken place.

At least, it isn't Heaven alone that knows, everybody backstage from the director to the assistant stage manager knows only too well. From the first reading of the play until about the end of the second week of rehearsal all goes smoothly. The star behaves like an angel - who, oh who, invented those unjust rumours about her being "difficult" in the theatre? She is modest, unassuming, almost over-considerate to the minor members of the cast. She lunches daily with the director and returns radiant to be both comradely and coquettish with the leading man. She is easily adored by everyone but the stage manager who has worked with her before and is inclined to be cynical. She is sometimes late for the morning rehearsal but so enchantingly apologetic that she is immediately forgiven. She is not quite happy about the second act scene with Hubert, because she has to sit still for such a long time without doing anything so she cajoles the besotted author to write in a few extra lines. This upsets the balance of the scene and also the leading man who has to be comforted. This tiny warning of the shape of things to come however is swiftly glossed over and rehearsals proceed, perhaps without quite the enthusiasm with which they started, but smoothly enough.

Then suddenly, like a thunderbolt falling from a cloudless sky, the first major row occurs. Any number of trivial reasons may spark this off; a bit of direction of which she doesn't approve, a headache from having been up too late the night before, an onset of panic, because she isn't sure enough of her lines or an inadvertent prompt from the assistant stage manager when she is experimenting with a pregnant pause. Anyhow, the battle is joined and the angel is transformed into a fiend. The company is stunned, the director enraged and the author in despair. The fiend, after getting a great deal more off her chest than should ever have been on it, either stamps out of the theatre vowing never to return, or bursts into floods of tears and has to be led to a dressing-room and cosseted. In either event the day's rehearsal is ruined and the One-big-happy-family atmosphere completely disrupted.

From then on the climate changes, the barometer plummets down and grey clouds gather. A week or so later the real trouble starts with the first dress-rehearsal. Everything is in the wrong place, the colour of the set is entirely different from the one she passed in the original sketch. The scene designer takes exception to her favourite dress and the director suggests, with quivering tact, that she must either wear a wig or do her hair differently. After a series of blistering exchanges her agent is sent for and all hell breaks loose, while the company wander about looking mournful and munching thick sandwiches.

The opening performance of the try-out is sheer misery. The fiend-angel has refused to rehearse on the Sunday evening, because she has lost her voice. On the opening night she finds it, but loses a lot of laughs, the blame for which she places squarely on the shoulders of the author, the director and her fellow actors. She is, of course, rapturously received by the audience, but this in no way mollifies her. By this time the director and she are not on speaking terms and the author is locked in a hotel room cutting his favourite lines and rewriting his favourite scenes. There are dreadful conferences after each night's performance in the managerial suite at which everyone talks a great deal, nothing much is achieved and wild suggestions are put forward of other actresses for the part who may or may not be available. These suggestions are patiently dismissed by the producing manager who is aware that, good, bad or indifferent, the fiend-angel is a big box-office draw and has a run-of-the-play contract.

At long last, after several weeks of arduous re-rehearsing, foot stampings, incessant scenes and oceans of tears, the long dreaded moment arrives when the star steps onto the stage on the opening night in a West End theatre. The atmosphere backstage is crackling with tension, nerves are lacerated and everyone is exhausted. She, the angel-fiend, receives an ovation on her first entrance from which moment on she plays the part as she has never played it before. Her timing is flawless, her charm devastating and in the new dresses, which have cost the management fourteen hundred pounds, she looks utterly ravishing. At the supper party after the performance she publicly kisses the leading man, the author and the director, while her dresser is left to engage two taxis to take her floral tributes back to her flat. The next morning she reads five ecstatic notices about herself and one not so good, upon which she bursts into tears and telephones her agent immediately to start legal proceedings. The play may be a success or a failure but, whichever way it goes, she is all right and she knows it, but what she doesn't know, what she never for an instant realises is that, without the author's lines, the director's skill, the talented support of her fellow players and, above all the indefinable gift of personality bestowed on her by benevolent destiny, she might be playing a muted revival of *The Last of Mrs. Cheyney* in Norwich.

It is obviously unnecessary to state that the rather florid example of megalomania I have described does not apply to *all* star actresses. There are many who are intelligent enough to employ their precious, indefinable quality with grace and humility, but these, regrettably, are far far rarer than they should be. Megalomania in the theatre is an insidious disease and there are, like Mr. Heinz's pickles, at least fifty-seven varieties. It is liable to attack females more than males as a general rule, possibly because it is in the nature of things for women to attract more of the outward attentions and trappings of success than men, although I must admit to having encountered a few male stars who were not entirely displeased with themselves. The original cause of infection is a combination of adulatory press notices, over-flattery and the heady sound of personal applause.

Certain egos expand under these stimuli with lightning rapidity; others, more controlled, accept them calmly and concentrate on more lasting values. The angel-fiend type I have just sketched so affectionately swiftly grows to accept the praise and the cheering as her natural right and, if she is fortunate or unfortunate enough to go on receiving it night after night for a number of years, her megalomania becomes chronic and she is as near barmy as makes no matter. Her exigence increases with every play she plays, her demands for various privileges outstrip all sanity and yet - and yet - without her the Theatre would lose much of its fascination.

In most adventurous vocations there are unexpected hazards to be dealt with and vanquished. The captain of a ship scans the heavens for evil portents; the air pilot braces himself to combat fog, sudden electric storms and any form of what is comprehensively described as "engine trouble." The Big Game hunter dreads the stampeding elephant and the sly, irrelevant cobra, and I can only conclude by saying that in all my long years of directing straight plays and musicals, I would rather face any of the above-mentioned perils than be forced to cope with a glamorous female star on the rampage about her dresses or her hair.

THE DECLINE OF THE WEST END

In these stirring days of astronautical adventure, nuclear fission, social equality, sexual abandon, the Common Market, the very Common Man, Apartheid, Centre 42, the Beatles and the Royal Court Theatre; when the winds of change are whistling through the thinning hair of our elder actors and tangling intolerably the very long hair of our younger ones, I feel that the moment has come for someone to step forward authoritatively and say a few kindly words in defence of what is now contemptuously described as "The Commercial Theatre."

Today the "Commercial Theatre" has become, in the eyes of everyone but the public, a shameful and sordid business. From the viewpoint of our modern theatrical intellectuals, Shaftesbury Avenue, Charing Cross Road, St. Martin's Lane and the Strand have become almost unmentionable areas. No Victorian missionary could have regarded the red light district of an alien city with more lofty disdain. The playgoers in search of cultural refreshment may travel East and South, possibly North, but never never West. He may bumble along in a tube or a taxi to Stratford Atte Bowe, he may be jerked through the English countryside in a dusty nationalised British railway carriage to sit in draughty converted aeroplane hangars or inadequately transformed country chapels for his entertainment and pleasure, but for him to book two stalls at Keith Prowse and proceed in a comfortable manner to the Globe Theatre, Wyndham's Theatre or the Savoy Theatre stamps him ineradicably as a reactionary clot. He may even find, as the merry years go marching on, that Sloane Square is a tiny bit too near.

I am perfectly prepared to admit that the West End of London has of late acquired a certain shoddy, red-light-district atmosphere compared with its glamour of earlier days, but in those squalid thoroughfares it is still possible to find pleasantly upholstered theatres in which a playgoer can sit at ease and enjoy the age-old pleasure of seeing the lights go down and an actual curtain go up. He may even, when it has gone up, have quite a good time. At least, if he doesn't have a good time, he can go out and return home without beating his way through muddy fields.

There has been a lot of talk during the past few years about "The Theatre of Ideas" as opposed to the "Theatre of Entertainment." And a lot of very silly talk at that. In the first place it is arbitrary to assume that the "Theatre of Ideas" must necessarily be opposed to the "Theatre of Entertainment." A play of "Ideas" can be just as entertaining as a play of "Pure Entertainment" can be boring. Everything depends, as always, on how it is written, directed and acted. But the basic error in all the argument is the assumption that a commercial enterprise is a bad thing and a non-commercial enterprise, a good thing. In the old days, when the critics were happily presumed to be Philistines, the theatrical skies were clearer.

Now, when the critics have become pseudo-intellectuals and range themselves firmly on the side of the experimenters to the virtual exclusion of every other form of production, the values have become badly muddled. In any case, while we're on the subject, what exactly *is* a play of ideas? I have read and seen a number of the *avant-garde* plays of the last few years, some of which interested me and some of which did not. *Look Back in Anger*, for instance, which rightly caused a tremendous sensation, cannot be described as a play of ideas. It is a brilliant essay in invective and psychology and provides a super-star part for an intelligent actor. Is *The Caretaker* a play of ideas? If so, where and what are they? To me it was a theatrical tour de force of intricate interplay of character upon character and a fascinating experiment in photostatic dialogue impeccably acted and directed. Mr. Pinter's idea in writing it was certainly excellent but so, in a slightly different way, was Baroness Orczy's idea of writing *The Scarlet Pimpernel*.

However much the "Theatre of Ideas" may be considered to be opposed to the "Theatre of Entertainment," I am personally very vigorously opposed to the assumption, prevalent among some of our *avant-garde* pioneers, that what the large public enjoys must inevitably be bad and what the critics enjoy must be good. This is a perilous point of view for those who wish their talents to be generally recognized, and I have yet to meet an actor, writer or director who, in the depths of his base and secret heart, would not prefer success to failure.

I am perfectly aware, of course, that there are varying degrees of success just as there are varying degrees of failure. A highly intelligent serious play at the Royal Court Theatre cannot expect to achieve so long a run as a popular West End farce or musical but if it is good enough it will attract a large enough public to pay its production and probably make a little profit. If it is not good enough, it won't. If it is so boring, abstruse, esoteric and pretentious that it fails to satisfy even the conditioned public who are accustomed to enjoying the theatre the hard way, it will close because nobody will go, and a play to which nobody will go, however worthy, idealistic, experimental and intellectual the motives that inspired it, is a flop. No paeans of articulate praise will revive its failing pulse, no indignant letters to *The Times* or impassioned pleas on the radio will save it. It's a goner, and, without the slightest apology for my flippancy, I say serve it bloody well right.

There have been far too many plays of this calibre presented to us during the last few years, several of which I have been trapped into seeing, either by my own curiosity or by the misguided advice of other people. I have invariably left the quarter-full theatre irritated and depressed and sadly bewildered by the conceit and silliness of some of my hitherto respected colleagues. Naturally, I have often been equally disillusioned by productions in the commercial theatre but in those cases the irritation and boredom were less painful, principally I suspect because the productions, however badly written and acted, were at least untainted by false reverence.

I do not wish to give the impression that I am unsympathetic to those who are trying to inject fresh blood and new techniques into the Theatre and I am the first to acknowledge it when they produce something of genuine value, but I must admit I become a little fractious when I hear it suggested that certain of our experimental drama groups should be subsidised by a government department such as the Arts Council, which in effect means that they would be subsidised by the British tax payer.

Playwriting, directing and acting are surely professional jobs and should be recognized as such. In England, as in many continental countries, a National Theatre and an Opera house are subsidised, to my mind, very sensibly, because they both present in the best manner possible classics that are too well known to attract the public for a straight run. Occasionally these establishments allow themselves a little experimental flutter or two, but their main *raison d'être* is the keeping alive of tried and true masterpieces. If Government subsidies were to be granted to every producing company that asked for them, the Theatre would inevitably cease to be a profession at all. Nobody up to date has suggested seriously that the Government subsidise fishmongers, grocers, stock-brokers or truck drivers during the early years of their apprenticeship and I see no reason why any theatrical groups, however high-minded and well intentioned, should be given public funds to fiddle about with when they should, in fact, be earning their living in a profession which after all they themselves have chosen. If a certain Management of a certain Theatre voluntarily decides to present a series of different plays to the public, all good luck to them, but it must be remembered that nobody asked them to.

As far as I can recall no subsidies were granted to Sir Henry Irving, Sir Herbert Tree, Sir Charles Cochran, Vedrenne and Eadie, Granville-Barker, Jack Hylton or Emile Littler. I cannot believe that at any moment of their careers Shaw, Maugham, Barrie, Ibsen, Pinero or Galsworthy sat back comfortably in their stalls during rehearsals reflecting that, whatever might happen to their plays, the financial side of the business was generously taken care of. And I am quite quite sure that I have never found myself in such a cosy situation.

If a commercial manager produces a play that fails to attract the public, he closes it and endeavours to recoup his losses by producing something else. Whatever wailing and gnashing of teeth this entails is generally confined to the cast and the backers and others immediately concerned. There are never protests in the public Press by critics or anyone else. But it seems that the commercial theatre nowadays is deserving of neither pity nor praise. Whatever good it may inadvertently do for the reputation of the British drama by presenting a play with taste and elegance, this good is automatically negated by the fact that it happens to be a financial success. The basic truth that the theatre is and should be a money-making business is no longer regarded as valid. This new snobbism that has grown lately about the theatre only being good when it is *not* a money-making business is both pretentious and unrealistic.

Success in the theatre, as in every other trade, is an essential goal to strive for. "To fail gloriously" is a vapid, defensive cliché. There is little glory in failure. "To succeed triumphantly" has a happier ring to it and it is much rarer and more difficult to achieve. Speaking for myself I have never had a "glorious" failure in my life. I've just had failures, and the inescapable reason for these failures was that the plays in question were just not quite good enough. Whenever a "flop" occurs in the theatre there is always a number of the faithful, a group of fervent loyalists to affirm that the play is far and away the best thing one has ever done, that the theatre was too big or too small, that the leading lady was miscast and that the critics are pigs. These facile alibis must be dismissed and the injured author must waste no time in wound-licking but sit down and write something else as soon as possible.

I am prepared cheerfully to admit that I have never once achieved an intellectual success, or an intellectual failure for that matter, which is not surprising because I am not, never have been and never could be described as an Intellectual.   I am, however, talented, observant, technically proficient, emotional, intelligent and industrious, and the sensible application of these qualities has brought me many comforting rewards. Not the least of these is the knowledge and experience I have gained in a profession that I have loved and respected for fifty-five years.   It is because of this knowledge and experience that I felt myself entitled to express my profound gratitude to The Commercial Theatre and to the cheerful, entertainment-loving public who so stubbornly supports it.

THE ART OF ACTING

(Adapted from a radio interview "Talking of Theatre" {BBC Network Three} with Walter Harris and first published in the October 12th, 1961 issue of *The Listener*)

You do not feel a comedy part to the extent that you feel a serious part. But, if you have an emotional scene to play, it is essential to feel it as early as possible in rehearsal and then set your feeling so that you can reproduce it without strain and in almost any adverse circumstances afterwards. I very much disapprove of the adage that you have to feel the performance completely every night on the stage. This is technically an impossibility, and really is the negation of the art of acting. The art of acting, after all, is not actual feeling but simulation of feeling, and it is impossible to feel a strong emotional part eight performances a week, including two matinées.

But if you are a good actor and an experienced actor, you can give the audience the semblance of the feeling you originally felt of the character and of the part, and this is to my mind what is great acting. I have seen many very, very great actors in my day, and I have never found one of them who comes off and says that they felt every minute of their performance that night. They know perfectly well I wouldn't believe them if they did. It is an impossibility. There is an old theatrical saying, "Lose yourself, lose your audience," and, even in an emotional part, you have to be aware with one part of your mind that the audience is there and that they are attentive; you have got, with a little extra sense, to listen for those coughs that might start, which may mean that you have either got to play more softly or hurry the scene a little bit or something; you have, in fact, to regulate your audience as well as be the character, as well as consider the other people on the stage with you. This is a very important aspect of acting: no really good acting is achieved without the complete co-operation of your fellow artists. You cannot play the scene by yourself unless you are alone on the stage. And if you are with somebody else on the stage you have to consider them and their reactions, help them to get their reactions, in return for which they will help you to get yours, and this is what makes fine acting.

This, of course, applies most particularly in comedy, when the getting of a laugh depends on a hairline of sensitivity and also must not always be considered the ultimate goal. It is not only getting laughs in comedy that is important; it is stopping them. There are certain laughs that have to be quelled in order to get a bigger one later. If you have a sentence, for instance, in which there is a titter in the first part of the sentence and probably a big laugh at the end of it, a technical comedian will see to it that he hurries the first part so that they hear it but have no time to laugh, so that he can get the full laugh at the end. Many inexperienced comedians will get the first laugh and lose the rest of the sentence in the laugh.

The whole of comedy depends on timing, and if you are really on your toes you play the audience and you control the laughter; you must never let the audience get out of hand - Rex Harrison today is a great exemplar of this exquisite timing - and this is achieved first of all, I suppose, by natural talent for comedy playing, but certainly by acquired technique. It is something that I am sad to see is not very prevalent in the theatre today, principally I think because there are not many comedies of wit and quick timing written.

This is all highly technical, but was drummed into my head as a small boy and as a young man by one of the greatest comedians of our stage, the late Charles Hawtrey. He taught me all I know about comedy acting, and I am grateful to him to this day. But then comedy is nearly always, in its time, treated as something trivial, whereas it is far and away the most complicated and the most difficult aspect of acting. Nearly all good comedians can play tragedy but very few tragedians can play comedy. Of course the great actors, such as Laurence Olivier, can play any part with the utmost ease. Larry, whose Macbeth at Stratford I think was one of the greatest performances I ever saw on the stage, also played Mr. Puff in *The Critic*, and it was one of the most brilliant, light, soufflé comedy performances that I have seen - incomparable technique. He can play anything. Edith Evans can play comedy as well as she can play tragedy. Nearly all the great ones can.

But I think that the nonsense that is talked today about the motivation of character and all these jargons that have developed is really a considerable waste of time. If a young actor comes up to me and I am directing a play, and says: "What is the motivation of this scene?" - well, there are one or two answers to that. One is: "Your salary cheque next Friday," and the other is: "If you haven't learned the motivation of the scene when you read the play, then you'd better not attempt to play it, because you must know that much by now." In fact a great deal of time is wasted in these dear, democratic days in the theatre with everybody giving their opinions. But it would be unwise for the captain of a ship when faced with a sudden storm to call all his crew together and ask their various opinions as to what to do about it, by which time I should think that the ship would have foundered. This, I feel, is rather the same for the director of a play. If he listens to all the actors giving their opinions about what they think their characteristics should be, the play is liable to founder. In fact, I have seen several submerge in the last few years for that very reason.

The last time I was directed by a director was when I did Bernard Shaw's *The Apple Cart*, and I was directed by Michael MacOwan. I explained to him that I always arranged to be word-perfect at the beginning of rehearsal, and when I was directing myself I always insisted that my actors should be word-perfect at the first rehearsal. This causes great rage and conflict among many actors, because they say that they like the part to grow with the movements they are given, and so on; and there might be cuts and they would have learnt a whole lot of stuff that was unnecessary. But actually it makes it much easier for an actor if only he has the sense to learn his part, not absolutely perfectly but well enough to be able to rehearse without a book, very early on; so many actors increase their own opening-night nervousness because they have not troubled to learn their parts accurately, and suddenly in the last week of rehearsal they realize this, and go home after a long day's rehearsal, which is very exhausting anyway, cut out all friends, all dinner parties, and everything, and try and cram the words into their tired brains. Whereas I always learn the part well in advance, so that at the end of a long day's rehearsal I go to another theatre or to a movie, or have a little quiet dinner or talk to my friends, and I wipe the play from my mind till the next morning rehearsal - because I know it, and this does eliminate the terrible fear of drying up on an opening night. You cannot, to my mind, rehearse too much.

It takes me a good three weeks' rehearsal, knowing the part, to give an adequate performance, and several weeks of performance with audiences to give a good performance, leaving aside a possible nervous *tour de force* on an opening night, when I might be very good indeed without quite knowing why. But with *The Apple Cart*, for instance, Michael MacOwan was courteous, wise, and sensible, and came up after each scene we had rehearsed with notes which we listened to, all of which were intelligent and sensible, and he did say one thing to me which completely made my conception of the part, and I am deeply grateful to him. He said: "I want you to understand that King Magnus is essentially a sad man." This, curiously enough, though I had studied the part, I had not thought of; it gave me the balance to play the part right, and I think I did play it right.

I don't think that a part possesses many actors outside the theatre, but there is a moment when you are playing an emotional part when the part gets hold of you. This occurs usually about the end of the first week of rehearsal. And a curious thing happened to me very many years ago. When I was in Singapore I gave three special performances of *Journey's End* with a touring theatrical company, including John Mills. I had always wanted to play Stanhope, and I thought it would be an interesting and exciting experiment. I had only two days to learn the part and I learned it, word-perfect. But I had no time to rehearse it and settle the emotions in their right balance. So I came on to the stage for the first of my three performances and gave, I suppose, one of the worst performances ever given in the theatre; because the part of Stanhope is immensely emotional underneath, and on the surface hard and ungiving. The emotion, which I had not had time to experiment with, took charge of me and I gave a sort of lachrymose, sobbing performance, in fact entirely the wrong performance for the play. One of the Singapore critics was smart enough to see it. The others, of course, were excited that I was playing it anyway, and so just gave me very polite notices. But I knew I was terrible; and that was because the emotion took charge of me instead of my taking charge of the emotion. This is what I would like to point out to many of the modern young actors who believe in the theory that you have to feel everything completely all the time. It is a mistake; it is not the art of acting, it is something entirely different, and the art of acting is really what they are trying to achieve.

Overacting is my pet loathing. There are several other things I hate about the theatre, but that, I think, is what I hate most. I don't entirely blame actors for this always; it depends on the circumstances. If an actor has been playing a part for months and months he is liable, even without knowing it, to come out and do much more than he was doing originally. I have often seen a subtle and beautiful performance on an opening night, and gone to see the play again a few months later and found that all the little nuances are over-emphasized. That is because when you play a play for a long run the quality - not the quantity but the quality - of the audience is liable to deteriorate; it is an actor's instinct to come out to the audience, and unless he is a very great actor indeed he often comes out too much without realizing it. The great ones seldom transgress in this way. Lynn Fontanne, for instance, will give as great a performance on the last night of a play as she did on the first, possibly a greater because she develops all the time.

From the actor's point of view, repertory is the answer to the long-run business; for to play three or four plays instead of one gives you a fresh edge on each one and does not allow monotony to creep in. I do not like long runs because my interests are so divided. I am a playwright and a composer, and when I am playing as an actor only it is a whole-time job. If I am playing eight performances a week of a star part, I can think of nothing else but that, and I have no time to write, to compose, or to do any of the other things I have to do. That is why, over so many years, I have limited my runs to three months, because to go on playing the same thing for a year, however successful it was, would turn out eventually to be a waste of time, because in the long run my writing is more important to me, much as I love acting.

Writing and composing are the two most creative of my talents. I think that directing is very interesting and obviously fascinating, both theatrically and psychologically, but on the theatre side I really prefer acting; I love performing, because I was, I suppose, brought up to it and I have been doing it since I was ten years old, on and off. But I do get slightly frustrated if I have to play for too long, for the reasons I've given. If I hadn't got the other talents to look after, I think I would be only too grateful to have a long run.

The prime purpose of the theatre is entertainment. I have always held that. Of course, I am far from infallible and I may be quite, quite wrong: the prime purpose of the theatre may be to show people how miserable life is, and how there is no hope for the human race. That may, indeed, be the prime purpose of the theatre, but I have never been brought up to view it that way. But at my age I can safely be called old-fashioned. I, personally, am still stage-struck after fifty-one years in the theatre, and it always gives me pleasure to go to a theatre and be entertained in it. It does not always give me pleasure to go to a theatre and be bored stiff in it, and therefore I hold grimly to my original training, which was that the theatre is primarily a place of entertainment.

If by any chance a playwright wishes to express a political opinion or a moral opinion or a philosophy, he must be a good enough craftsman to do it with so much spice of entertainment in it that the public get the message without being aware of it. The moment the public sniffs propaganda they stay away, and curiously enough, I am all in favour of the public coming to the theatre, paying for their seats at the box office, and enjoying themselves. If they enjoy themselves it means they come again, and if they come again it means so much more in the pockets of the playwright, the actors, and even the dear managements.

Noël with Judy Campbell in Present Laughter. *(1942)*

ACTING WITH NOËL

Judy Campbell Remembers...

Judy Campbell was one of Noël's favourite actresses.

During the war, she toured with him as Joanna in *Present Laughter*, and as Elsie in *This Happy Breed.* She also joined Noël in his many troop concerts, getting to know him off stage as well as on. After the war, she played in one more Coward production, *Relative Values* (1951), with Gladys Cooper, in which she created the part of Miranda Frayle, the extraordinarily superficial Hollywood "star."

Here are some of Judy's recollections of what it was like to work with Noël:

"I first met him in a 1940 revue called *New Faces.* Or rather, he came to see *me* in *New Faces*... I was singing 'A Nightingale Sang in Berkeley Square.' I was a straight actress, not a singer, so I *acted* it for all I was worth. I made it into a monologue, almost. Afterwards there was a tap on my dressing room door and a voice said: 'I'm Noël Coward. May I come in?'

"So he came in and said: 'It takes great talent to put over a number when you don't have a *voice.* Some day you must come and act with me.' And off he went. I didn't say a thing. Well, there's no answer to that, is there?

"Later we were both having supper in the Savoy Grill - at different tables and it was a very gloomy night. The doorman on the Embankment side had been killed in an air raid - one of the many bad raids around the Adelphi and along the river. There were just a handful of depressed diners sitting around, and Carroll Gibbons - whose band couldn't play downstairs because of the raids - had a piano, and he was playing to keep people's spirits up. He asked Noël to sing and in those days Noël hadn't yet done cabaret but he obliged. He sang 'Mad Dogs' and 'I'll Follow My Secret Heart' and then suddenly, to my horror, he turned round and said: 'Well, I'll take a rest but I see a new friend here - Judy Campbell with a song about a nightingale...' He came over to my table and I said: 'I can't do it. I've never sung it outside a theatre. I don't even know what key I *sing* it in.'

"I sensed immediately he was one of those who fling down little challenges and, if you can't take it up - well, it's too boring for words. It was like a female version of Kipling's 'If' ... 'If you can sing when asked without excuse or stammer...!' So I got to my feet and went over to Carroll Gibbons who said: 'Don't worry. You just start singing and I'll follow you.' And I said: 'That's just the trouble. I start *talking!*' Anyway, I got through.

"The next time I met him was with Winifred (Clemence Dane). Noël used to spend a great deal of time with her in her flat in Covent Garden during those war years. One day Winifred said: 'Let's go and have a picnic.' So I helped her pack up all these imitation things you had in wartime, and off we went. And Winifred said: 'It's a pity we're not going in the country. We could have baked hedgehogs!' And I thought: 'I'm glad we're only going to Hyde Park!'

"Noël was there waiting for us and we started eating our ersatz sausage rolls or whatever. At that point a sailor came by who was on injury leave - he'd been on a destroyer that was sunk - and Noël asked him to join us. At that time he and Winifred were writing what was to become *In Which We Serve.* And I still remember all of us sitting there on the grass in Hyde Park with the sailor telling us what had happened and Noël and Winifred taking it all in... and wondering later, when I saw the film: 'I wonder if he gave them the idea for *that* bit?' They were stories of a war you couldn't possibly invent.

"Then later, when I was in Lillian Hellman's *Watch on the Rhine*, I got a call from Binkie saying : 'Noël wants you to go into his new plays - *Present Laughter* and *This Happy Breed.*' I was enjoying what I was doing and couldn't help wishing the call had come a few months later. But you don't say 'No' to Noël!

"It was a very strange period that's hard to describe now. The other day I came across my appointments book for late 1942. It was full of very ordinary things like - 'Fitting - Molyneux!' You'd never know there was a war on. Despite all the horrors, you all tried to carry on as normal. 'Rehearsal: 2:30.'

"Rehearsal was at Noël's flat in Gerald Road. We read the plays through in two days, including the third play, *Blithe Spirit.* Noël put it in, in case we got bored! It was still running at the Piccadilly and Noël said: 'Will you all go and see it, in order to get an idea of the ghostly make-up and the moves? It will save time, because we only have four weeks to rehearse all the plays.' We were going to do a six-month tour and then six weeks at the Haymarket - in the end we did three months. Noël's whole point was that, since the provinces can't come to the theatre, the West End must go to the provinces. So we went *everywhere...*

"Rehearsing, we had a week for each play - which is like weekly rep. And *two* of these plays, don't forget, were brand new. Noël's need to have us word-perfect came - in this case, at least - from the experiences of limited rehearsal time. Binkie helped out wonderfully by having the sets designed and put up in the Scala, so that when we came to dress rehearsals in that last week, there was no excuse for anyone saying, 'Oh, I didn't know that door opened *this* way,' or 'Nobody told me the stairs started *here...*'

"So, in this case, learning the words first made practical sense. Later it became something of a 'thing' with Noël. I remember doing *Relative Values* about ten years later with dear Gladys Cooper (whom Heaven preserve); tremendous star quality and panache. She was a *great* friend of Noël's and everything he liked, but she could not or would not learn the lines. She used to say - and this is a line she *did* remember - 'I never had the book out of my hand before the dress rehearsal for *Gerald* (du Maurier) and I'm *damned* if I'm going to start for Noël!' I forget what word she actually used in those days but it was a lot stronger than 'damned.' It was hard to tell whether it was bravado or whether she really *was* having trouble with her memory. She *was* sixty. I think it was a mixture of the two.

"With these earlier plays it was quite difficult. In many ways it was *harder* than rep. In weekly rep you usually walked the play through on Tuesday to plot the moves; Wednesday you start work on Act One and so on, so that by Friday you knew it. To go to first rehearsal with no book was bizarre to say the least of it. Personally, I'd rather rehearse with the book, so that you make notes for yourself and write in your moves but that wasn't what Noël wanted. Mind you, from what I heard, he never asked this from the original cast of *Blithe Spirit*. They had a proper rehearsal time of three to four weeks.

"When it came to the two *new* plays - again to save time - Noël said at the very beginning: 'Look, when there are three or more people on the stage, I've blocked out the moves. When there are just two of us, I'll leave us to work it out and see what happens. And he was very good at letting me improvise. He was the one who would adapt. For instance, if we found we were both sitting down at the same time, he'd say later: 'Tomorrow, why don't you go to the mantelpiece and *I'll* go to the sofa. Let's see how *that* works.' It was all very constructive and helpful. That period of working with him was so enriching, so smooth. You learned something every day. He never criticised; only suggested. He built up your confidence by letting you *try* things; he left it to you. When you were with him on the stage, you were two *actors*. He was not, until you needed it, the author and director. When you did, he'd be there to explain a line or suggest a move. And, of course, that *also* saved time. Normally, when you're rehearsing and you come across a line you don't understand, the Director will say: 'I'll have a word with Charlie on the phone this evening and see if you can cut or change that line.' You might have to wait a day or two to find out the answer. With Noël the decision was made there and then.

"I don't remember ever changing one of his *lines* but you could certainly alter a *move*. We were *always* improvising. Even after we'd opened, he'd say: 'Keep that in,' or 'That didn't work - let's lose it tomorrow,' either in an aside while you were on or afterwards privately. He never called a rehearsal. And no 'notes' after the show. If you wanted a note, he'd give it to you while you waited in the wings... It was all practice, not precept.

"I can only remember one exception and that was *Blithe Spirit*. Noël had always said: 'Play it your own way. Don't try and copy Kay Hammond (the original Elvira) or Margaret Rutherford.' So there we were, playing it - and I *adored* it. I loved drifting around being this ghost. Then one night in the wings Noël said: 'I've got one teeny-weeny criticism. You're *dancing* too much. One less twirl on the way to the piano would make the scene much funnier.' I took it very badly; I wasn't aware of the twirling. I said sniffily, 'Oh, very well.' And Noël said: 'I know you're a tall girl and you study to be graceful.' That was my Achilles heel. I *am* a tall girl and I *did* want to be graceful - but I didn't want anybody to *know* it. I said: 'I don't know what you mean - it just comes naturally.' So Noël said: 'For what it's worth, I'm telling you - what's funny about Elvira is that she behaves *normally*, like any ex-wife. Stomps about when she's angry, as though she's wearing gumboots, but she does *not* drift ghost-like. All that is in your make-up and the green follow spot. Let the light do it for you. Don't do it yourself. Don't be 'ghostly.' Fling yourself into armchairs - that's the trick of it.' My eyes filling with tears of humiliation, I said I'd try. Well, the next night, going on, I tripped over a rug and fell flat on my face. From behind his hand Noël said: 'Better, but perhaps a *little* too much, dear!' After that I did a lot of stomping around and it *was* twice as funny. As usual, he was dead right....

"We talked about it a lot later and Noël said that in the original rehearsals they had lots of clever production ideas and had actually called in Maskelyne and Devant (the famous illusionists) to try things with mirrors, so that Elvira could appear and disappear. When Charles wasn't seeing her, she'd disappear and then appear again when Charles said, 'You *must* see her....' They'd had a lot more tricks like that, Noël said - by 'they' he meant Binkie, Gladys Calthrop and himself. They'd gone into it all but decided it distracted from the *comedy*. People were going to be thinking: 'Oh, where's she gone now? Is it done with *mirrors?*' And in the meantime - because people are always attracted to the visual before the verbal - the joke's gone, the funny line won't be heard.

"I also remember Noël being tetchy one night and having a drink with us in the bar after the play, when we were somewhere up in Scotland. He had a semi-row with Beryl Measor, who was playing Madame Arcati - and playing her wonderfully, I should add. Noël said she looked like John Barrymore.   There was something about her profile that was quite wonderful when she came in and said that line: 'I've leaned my bike up against that little bush. It will be perfectly all right if no one touches it.' The whole thing was so incongruous! Noël was her great admirer, but in her cups she was a bit aggressive. In the bar they began having a spat and Measor said: 'Oh, you make me so mad, I could *throw* something at you!' And Noël said: 'You might start with my *cues*.'

"Unlike a lot of people who worked with him, I did sometimes see him on his own, because of the troop concerts. Everywhere we went on this tour Noël had agreed that after the play he would entertain any unit in the vicinity that wanted to be entertained. The whole thing lapsed when we got into the factory areas, where we had to compete with the sound of the lathes. As Noël said, the factory workers were deeply disappointed, hoping it was Vera Lynn and finding it was only Noël Coward and Judy Campbell. So we stopped until we got back into towns near the camps.

"With the troop concerts, it meant assembling in Noël's room, and anybody from the Coward 'family' who was available would come up: Coley (if he was on leave), Gladys, Winifred...There'd be a piano, because he wanted to work while he was on tour. (One of the things I remember him composing was a rumba - 'Nina.') I had to sing something else besides 'Nightingale' to fill out seven or eight minutes and give him a rest, although he took me *because* I sang 'Nightingale.' He was an awful tease, which scared the life out of me. I'd change and go to his room and there would be Robb Stewart, his accompanist, as well as the 'family' and any guests who happened to drop in - the Duchess of Buccleuch, the Mountbattens, whoever. And, if he was in the mood, Noël would say peremptorily: 'The cars aren't here. We'll have a song,' - and look at me.

Well, not being a singer, the only way I could perform on stage was to create an empathy with the audience, so that you know they're listening to what you're telling them. And when you've got that pin-drop attention, you know you're all right. But to stand up in a room with all the lights on and people standing around drinking is not for me. It was my idea of hell. I never said this to Noël, because I knew he was doing it for my own good, in a way.

"I can't say he talked a lot about his beliefs or his philosophy of life, and I never met anyone else outside the 'family' who would claim to know him well. The nearest I suppose I got was on the way to the troop concerts. Almost always we'd travel alone in the same car and anyone else in the car behind. I'd be nervous - not in a theatrical first night sense of nervous but in an almost physical way. I just knew every time this was going to be a terrible failure. I wouldn't be able to make them listen.

"Sometimes in the car we'd have a little nip of gin. Now, Noël was very strict about drinking in the theatre. He said he'd seen so many careers wrecked - Henry Ainley, Wilfred Lawson and others - that he made it a rule never to drink himself. But I remember him producing a hip flask and saying: 'This isn't like a professional engagement. If we want to give ourselves a little Dutch courage, why not?' And while we relaxed, he taught me what to do.

"He said: 'When you get there, you walk out and look round at the assembled company, as though you were giving a party and you were delighted so many of your friends and acquaintances had managed to make it. Then you smile and Robb will play *ad infinitum*. Don't think you've got to come in on cue. Just look at them and say what you're going to sing. And when you have hush, nod to Robb and then start. If you're going to make a gesture, make it above the waist - never, never *below*. And remember - *panache, panache, toujours panache*. If *you* believe you can do it, you'll make *them* listen. And that's the whole trick.' They're the only precepts he ever gave that were formulated; the rest followed.

"There was one thing about those concerts and visits I never forgot. Noël got jaundice and missed a week towards the end of the tour, and we just did *Blithe Spirit* for a week with Dennis Price standing in. It meant that we missed Plymouth, so, after the Haymarket run, we went back and played Plymouth. Noël and I did the troop concerts that went with Plymouth, of which there were many, being the naval area it was. Noël's feeling for the Navy and those who go down to the sea in ships was very real. We went to many places with Gladys Calthrop driving and one day turned up at a place that was a mental hospital taken over by the Navy for the treatment of naval personnel who were in shock. We did a concert to an audience in wheel chairs, then - as with all these concerts - we'd go round the wards afterwards. Noël would go up one side and I'd go up the other, talking to everybody. Then we'd cross over at the top and go down the other side. Well, he'd taught himself to remember names. When I came down the side where he'd already been, not once but several times people would say: 'He *remembered*. He said: "Well, Cooper, what are you doing *here?*"' And they'd been in *In Which We Serve*; they'd been seconded. And he remembered their names and there must have been a *hundred* of them! Some of them called him 'Captain Coward,' because they really thought he *was* a naval captain. And it made me realise how good he was; he had a well of goodness in him. He wasn't being 'Noël Coward'; he was a man radiating warmth and help to people in need of it. People talk about him being shallow and snobbish and doing anything for a laugh - but *that* was real.

"When we'd been performing the plays for a bit, he would start *not* coming in on a broken sentence, so that you were left in the air. This was to test whether you could go on. I remember most vividly his doing it in *This Happy Breed*, when we were waiting for the taxi: I had a line like: 'I wonder where Reg has got to?' And he was meant to interrupt and say, 'Don't fuss, Ethel' but he didn't, I should think on purpose, because he *never* forgot. So I had to go on - 'Perhaps he's gone round to...' - thinking wildly, where *could* Reg have got to? 'Perhaps he's gone round to see where the taxi's got to. I certainly hope so... I hope he'll be coming back soon...' Labouring away and Noël smiling to himself and giving me no help at all.

"Or sometimes he'd do the reverse and refuse to be interrupted. In *Present Laughter* it happened to Beryl Measor as Monica. When she said: 'Don't be a fool, Garry, I'm going' and sweeping off, he'd just go on talking, until she had to manhandle him out of the way and say: 'I refuse to stay here a moment longer.'

"They weren't things you kept in; they were just for a night. He never, never did anything that would spoil a laugh or a cue that was pertinent to the play. It was simply to keep you on your toes, to prevent you from playing on automatic pilot.

"Noël didn't approve of my hair style in *Present Laughter*. I had a 'fall' added, so that I could have that long page-boy bob on to the shoulder: It was rather film-starry at the time and I felt it was right for Joanna. He wanted me to have my hair piled up. I thought that was too like Joycie Carey playing the wife; it was also very fashionable and very chic. I thought Joanna should be more sexy and he didn't like that, which distressed me. Then Cecil Beaton came down to take the photographs and said: 'I'm mad about that hair!' So, it stayed in, because Noël was inclined to take Cecil's side in things like that. But I didn't get away with it entirely. He used to do an awful thing. There was a point when I leaned back against the sofa and one night he came and put his *elbow* on it, leaning on the back of the sofa. I couldn't *move*. My false bit would have come off. He made me play several lines, if not a page or two! Muttering between the lines: 'Gotcha *now!*'

"Another example of the kind of thing that happened on that tour. We were playing in *This Happy Breed* - in which Noël told people he always preferred my performance - and one night I rubbed my shoulder. Noël immediately broke off from what he was saying and told the girl who was playing my daughter: 'Go and give your mother's back a rub,' which she did. It was charming, because we were all so relaxed with one another. And it was in *character*. The plays *grew*.

"And, of course, in *Present Laughter* there's *nothing* he wouldn't do. There's his big histrionic scene, that great collapse at the end. For a few performances he was learning *Cyrano* for something to do in his spare time. One night when he says: 'Go away, all of you. I hate you all...!' he wouldn't be silenced. Other people are coming in with *their* lines: 'Well, it's time we went to supper...' or 'Oh, come off it, Garry...' - and he suddenly launched into one of the *tirades* from *Cyrano* and nobody could stop him. He went on and on and on in this fluent French, pouring out these hexameters or whatever they were. Everybody gave up. In the end he fell face down on the floor. Roars of laughter. So they all said: 'Well, goodnight, Garry' and stepped over him on their way out.

"But the wickedest thing he ever did to me was when we were up in Scotland somewhere. It was bloody cold, as it always seemed to be in Scotland, and worse for me, because I was wearing this flimsy chiffon dress. I couldn't even wear a bra with it, because it was completely backless. There's a point where Noël comes up to me and runs his hand up my arm before resting it on my shoulder. This particular evening, when he gets to my shoulder, his hand continues inside my dress until he's firmly clutching my bosom. I remember thinking to myself - without really believing it! - 'Hello, is this the breakthrough?' But I was soon put in my place. As soon as the curtain came down, Noël grinned at me and said: 'Thank you for that. It's the warmest I've been all day!'

"He was a devil for building you up and then letting you down. He once said to me: 'You know, you really look like a fascinating bitch...' - Ah well, I thought - then he went on, with a wicked gleam in his eye, 'But you're really an old lavender bag!' *One* day I'll think up a suitable answer.

"Another thing he used to do when we were playing out of town on Saturday night. Being wartime, it was going to be a blacked-out slow train, quite likely to be diverted via Norfolk or somewhere. We'd all be going for it and Saturday night was always *This Happy Breed*, the longest of them, close on three hours. So, sometime around Act One he'd start jumping lines and it was up to you to pick it up from where he'd jumped to. Just a few lines, a little snip here and there. He would jump to: 'It's time Frank got here' instead of whatever it was.

"Despite this, acting with him was very easy. It was like ballroom dancing in that you had to concentrate on what you were doing, otherwise you'd trip yourself over. He anticipated your move the way somebody you danced well with could do - a slight pressure on the shoulder, or a squeeze of the hand and you knew they were going to do something dashing. Well, acting with Noël was a bit like that.

"Later on, in *Relative Values*, not at all like that. A bit cruel. He was a kind man but he'd *stopped* being kind then... I think he was bitter at the constant criticism he'd been getting since the war. Not that he ever said anything. It was Binkie who came down and did the great interpretation. Rehearsals had been miserable. Although, I must say, he was kind to me. He'd called *evening* rehearsals, because Gladys couldn't learn her lines and he said to all of us: 'I *know* what's going to happen. The first night will be brilliant and not *one* word will be mine! And the dull crack you hear from the back of the circle will be me shooting myself. So, we are going to have evening rehearsals.'

"It was a nightmare for me, having three children under six and living sixty miles outside London, which is outside the contractual limit. But the problem was outside my control. I was desperate and went to Noël, who looked at me coolly and then said: 'All right, but I shall say that you're ill.'

"That was kind but that was about the last time. After that it was back to the 'study-to-be-graceful' thing but this time it was said in front of other people. I had flat-heeled shoes made to match my dress, because of my complex about being tall. I don't know why - Margaret Leighton was taller and nobody minded. I'd worn the same sort of shoes in *Present Laughter,* but at the dress rehearsal Noël said, 'Why don't you take off those bloody ballet shoes and wear high heels like everybody else? Go away and put some heels on!' I thought it was unnecessary in front of the assembled company but I went off, found some heels and came back. There was no comment. It was said in a way he wouldn't have said a few years earlier. The only comfort was, it wasn't just me - it was everybody. He was at daggers-drawn with Gladys; he wasn't getting on too well with Angela Baddeley. Everyone was getting the rough edge of his tongue.

"We did a pre-West End tour, usually a seaside town, and it was Eastbourne, I think, where I was contemplating throwing myself off the end of the pier, because Noël used to appear once a week, on a Wednesday or a Thursday, and one knew one was in for stick again. Then one day out of the train stepped Binkie, who invited Gladys out to supper and Angie out to lunch and me out to lunch the next day and then called a rehearsal. He explained over lunch: 'The idea came to me while I was pruning the roses. Noël isn't in the best of moods and he's also having tooth trouble. He's not at his best, so I thought *I'd* come instead and I told Noël, "You stay here and have a nice rest."' It was Binkie at his greatest, he was the perfect diplomat. He called this rehearsal and we all thought: 'What's going to happen? Binkie's never taken a rehearsal in his life. He's never directed, he's never interfered.'

"What happened was that he was given a prompt copy, which he immediately handed over to Gladys and said: 'Gladys, you're better at this than I am.' And *Gladys* took the rehearsal. Everything was cut that she wanted cut - and rightly. Even an armchair we all used to fall over was done away with. She took charge in a brisk, salutary way. We opened in London and it was a dazzling success for Noël as well as for her. I don't think she did anything that he wouldn't have done, if he hadn't been so uptight and so edgy. They were little cuts that he probably would have made.

"He still went on after we'd opened in London, I have to say. He came round after we'd been running a bit with notes - which was reasonable enough - and was nice to me for, I felt, the first time. And I said: 'Is that *all?*' - because I was quite surprised. And he said: 'Yes, that's all. I'm very pleased with you. You're in my *good* books. But pity poor So-and-So. I'm sharpening my knife!' And went off along the passage and was perfectly bloody to somebody else....Because we'd had that good first night and those excellent notices, he was jolly well determined we were going to *keep* it that way. Actually, I don't think it's a very good part, the film star, Miranda. People laugh *at* her, not *with* her....Nobody minds playing a villainess or Hedda Gabler, but when you're simply set up as an Aunt Sally... *and* you're a silly bitch...

"I remember rehearsing a scene I had with Gladys when we were on tour. I was being hectored by Gladys and someone said - I think Gladys - 'Put in something so that I can cut in.' So that evening I said: 'Fiddlesticks!' and it got a laugh. It was quickly squashed with a note from Noël saying: 'We do not require *you* to get a laugh here. The scene is Gladys's.'

"I never worked with Noël again. Of course, we met and talked and he came round to see me and was sweet. I was told later that, if I'd phoned when he was in town, he'd have been pleased to see me. But I never did. Not because I felt there was anything wrong but because I felt there wasn't anything particular going for me. Because of the travelling episode, I didn't work for Tennent's for years, and when I *was* finally welcomed back into the fold, it was too late for Noël....

"In those later years it seemed to me he was indrawn and very much happy with his own world and I didn't want to intrude. The last time I saw him remotely privately was with Michael Denison and Dulcie Gray. They'd asked Noël to lunch. Noël (for once) was late and I remember he arrived and said: 'Darling, you look *twelve!*' and we had a jolly theatre lunch about who was doing what. It was like having been - married, of course, is far too exaggerated - but we had had a long period of being close. It had been a very special time, like in a time capsule."

Judy and Noël as Ethel and Frank Gibbons in This Happy Breed. *(1942)*

Judy Garland and Betty Bacall backstage with Noël at The Desert Inn. (Las Vegas, 1955)

NOËL AND JUDY GARLAND

A Conversation

In August, 1961, the out-of-town tryout of *Sail Away* reached the Colonial Theatre, Boston. The audience glittered. The show did not and Noël knew he had a lot of work to do before it reached Broadway.

He would not be allowed to get on with it uninterrupted. One of the chores that faces a playwright who is in the creative throes of revision is confronting the media. Once the cry of "Author sighted!" goes up, the interviews begin and it's a brave author indeed who steadfastly says "No." Noël knew only too well he needed all the good publicity he could get for his first original Broadway musical.

When the reporter arrived, Judy Garland and Kay Thompson were present. The reporter asked if he could use his tape recorder to help him later with the accuracy of quotes. Noël agreed, and as the conversation took off in free-wheeling style, he forgot its presence. What ensued was a discussion, largely between Judy and himself, two child prodigies who had managed in their respective ways to adapt their precocious talents to a changing world. In what follows they exchange a few trade secrets:

NOËL Judy and I are very old friends. In moments of crisis in my life, Judy appears - at my last opening night in Las Vegas and my closing night in London... She's a beloved friend of mine. She is probably the greatest singer of songs alive. (I'm not so bad myself when I do my comedy numbers!) And we know a great deal about our jobs, because we're *very* professional. Perhaps we should talk about that - the way to handle audiences, the way to make 'em laugh when you want 'em and to stop them laughing when you don't want them to.

When you're professional, you have to fall back on every trick in the book. You have to take the notes you know you can't hit with such a radiant smile that they think it's wonderful.

JUDY And also *act* - cheap acting?

NOËL 'Cheap acting' and also immense calm with your heart pounding.

JUDY When you know you're *coming* to that particular note and you know it's there and you know you can't avoid it and you know you can't take it an octave down and you know that it's going to sound *ghastly*. You know twenty-eight bars before and you get there and it *is* lousy...

NOËL ...and you do a gesture you've *never* done before - of *radiant* charm!
  The first night I opened in the Café de Paris in London with the whole of London waiting to see how lousy I was going to be - I lost my voice completely and for an hour before the show my throat doctor took my vocal cords and threw them up in the air like ping-pong balls and then said, 'You're not to say one word or even whisper until you're on.' And I said, 'Yes, but what happens if I go on and still no sound comes out?' And he said, '*Something* will come out.' And I said, 'But what?' I went down those stairs - and I'm not, as you know, over-nervous, because I can't *afford* to be - but I was good and nervous then because I didn't know what sound was going to come out. And as I opened my mouth a very curious voice was heard that I couldn't recognise at all. But it went all right. It was terrible! Then I quickly got into some comedy numbers and saved myself.
JUDY It's good that you can rely on comedy numbers - I think we've managed to save ourselves from many years in this kind of act. I think we started at about the same age, didn't we?
NOËL How old were you?
JUDY I was two.
NOËL Oh well you've beaten me. I started at the age of ten in the *theatre*. Before that I was at ballet school.
JUDY Did you want to be a dancer?
NOËL Yes, I *was* a dancer for quite a while. Fred Astaire did two dances for me in 1923. He choreographed one for Gertie Lawrence and me and one for me alone. And I was in the *Charlot Revue*. I don't think he was very proud of the dances, because I don't think they were very well executed.
JUDY Were they well choreographed?
NOËL Oh, brilliant. But there was a lot of that cane-whacking and tum-te-tum...
JUDY Was there anybody else in your family involved in the theatre?
NOËL Nobody. Except my father. He was in the piano business - he used to *sell* pianos. But otherwise they didn't know anything about it. I was taken to the theatre when I was five years old and it was my birthday treat. Every 16th of December I used to be taken to a theatre. I was given a toy theatre for Christmas by my mother. She loved the theatre, you see, and I was *wildly* enthusiastic about it and so that's how it all started.
  But the reason that I went on to the stage was that I was set to go into the Chapel Royal choir, because I had a perfectly beautiful voice. I suppose the inherent acting in me headed its ugly rear, because I did Gounod's 'There is a Green Hill Far Away' - and I tore myself to shreds. I made Callas look like an amateur! And the poor man, the organist

fell back in horror. I gave it the expression. I did the whole crucifixion bit. And they turned me down because I was over-dramatic. And I was only nine and a half with an Eton collar, going 'There was no other good enough to pay the price of sin...' I did the whole lot. So then Mother was very very cross and said the man was common and stupid anyway. Then we saw an ad in the papers for a 'handsome, talented boy' and she looked at me and said, 'Well, you're talented and *maybe* you can get by on looks.' So off I went and gave an audition. And that's how I got on the stage.

JUDY My older girl (Liza) is in summer stock now. I think it's rather stupid to be involved in the theatre or in movies and just leave your children every night or every morning and say, 'I'm going away and you mustn't know where I'm going, because I don't want you exposed.'

NOËL Very sensible.

JUDY So I've taken them along. They've been on stage with me, they've been in the wings, and I don't know if they'll become entertainers. I think my oldest girl is fairly talented.

NOËL If she's *really* talented, she ought to do it.

JUDY Yes, she's really quite amazing. I think actresses who say 'Mother's going out tonight' and 'Don't photograph my children' have children who will end up thinking that maybe Ma doesn't want any attention taken away from *her*.

NOËL And also the children might *adore* being exposed. Why not enjoy themselves?

JUDY I think it's fun for children to go to the theatre, if you have a good steady relationship with them and if your home life with them is a good one...

NOËL If you are the daughter of an actress, you've got to take it on the jaw - then you've got to *understand* that you *are* the daughter of an actress and you grow up in the atmosphere.

JUDY And, you know, it isn't a *bad* atmosphere - I wouldn't have traded it in for anything in the world. Liza has been exposed to all of the best of theatre. I wasn't. I was in vaudeville - not *good* vaudeville. I came in *after* the Orpheum time and before television. So there was nothing very inspiring about that. But *she* has grown up with the *best*. Her father (Vincente Minnelli), who is a very talented man, has exposed her to the best of it. She does have taste. She started to dance when she was five.

NOËL And you encouraged her?

JUDY Yes, I did. She's a brilliant dancer. I have a second daughter (Lorna) who is eight and who really is the Gertrude Lawrence of Hyannisport. She's just impossible and the most beautiful creature that has ever lived, I think. She's so shocking and so bright and so cunning and clever and hip and she's such a great actress that we don't know what we're going to do with her. I just know that she's going to turn into something rather important. I don't know what it will be but it will be something rather startling and flamboyant.

NOËL She'll be a *waitress*, probably!

JUDY Now, Liza has *my* kind of cow-like, going-along quality.

NOËL Is this an *accurate* description? This 'cow-like going-along' at Carnegie Hall? This 'cow-like going-along' at the Palladium?

JUDY Between working times I just *sit.*..

NOËL Chewing the cud? Crying a little from time to time?

JUDY Oh, weeping *all* the time. Terribly important...

NOËL Judy started the other morning in floods of tears, because the weather was so bad and she finished in floods of tears because the party was so hot.

JUDY I'm surprised you didn't go along with me in floods of tears.

NOËL Wait a minute - I *finished* in floods of tears.

JUDY Did you, darling? After we left you?

NOËL Oh yes, I was so exhausted - I think it was all those *Shriners*, really. I thought it was a very enjoyable party but there were far too many people. And I was slightly proud that the enormous picture of George Washington had been taken off the wall and one of mine substituted. They had a picture of me looking like a very old bull moose blown up in place of George Washington. In Boston - considering the Boston Tea Party - it was really very kind of them. So they've obviously forgiven us for that now...!

(The conversation moves on to Child Stars)

NOËL When I saw Judy when she was a little girl - although she talks about the vaudeville - but *that* is the way to learn theatre and *not* acting school. Playing to audiences, however badly, however corny...

JUDY Trial and error, trial and error...

NOËL And you see, when I see her appearing with the authority of a great star now - as long as she's not in one of her 'cow-like' moods - I know that every single heartbreak she had when she was a little girl, every number that was taken away from her, every disappointment she had, went to make this authority.

JUDY Exactly. It truly is worth it when you can walk out and handle hundreds of people and *make* them enjoy themselves. And it's only something you can learn through heartbreak...

NOËL Nobody can teach you, no correspondence courses, no rehearsals in the studios. I assure you I would never have been a success at the Café de Paris or at Las Vegas if it hadn't been for three years singing to troops. Because very often the troops didn't wish to see me at all. They would have loved to have seen Marlene, they would have loved to have seen a glamorous lady or a comic who could drop his pants and get a laugh. They didn't want to see me coming on and being sophisticated. But I also knew that if I played down to them and altered my material, they would see through it. So I had to make them like what I was *doing*. And on the whole I succeeded. Not always. I had a *few* bad moments. Sometimes it would take me about twenty minutes to get them.

JUDY Have you ever *cheated* an audience? I bet you never have.

NOËL How do you mean?

JUDY I mean, when you are terribly successful, when you are going well and you're working very hard and you have a difficult programme - like you had in Las Vegas. And two a night. If you had a bad throat, did you ever think to yourself - 'Oh, I'll just go out and cut the show.' *I'm* unable to do it.

NOËL Can't do it - any more than at a rehearsal I can 'walk through.'

JUDY I really use my voice so stupidly because I cannot walk through the rehearsal.

NOËL But do you know why? Do you know the psychological reason for this is that if you walk through a rehearsal 'marking,' you are not giving what you're *going* to give and this affects *you*. We can all understand that you're just walking through but you are not really *rehearsing*. Because it pulls you down. You might just as well not *be* there. If you come out and *do* the part you're rehearsing - full out - wrong, maybe, but full out - you learn your mistakes. But if you're only marking it, you haven't come out and you haven't shown yourself what's wrong and what's right.

JUDY I'm asking this because I've never done an acting part on the stage. I've only *sung* on the stage. I've acted in the movies, so I've never had a chance to go through a rehearsal, an *acting* rehearsal on stage. And I hope someday...

NOËL Oh, wouldn't that be wonderful?

JUDY Don't give me that 'Wouldn't that be wonderful!' You've promised me for years!

NOËL The race is to the swift. In our profession the thing that counts is *survival*. It's comparatively easy if you have talent - comparatively easy to have a success. But what is *really* difficult is to hold it over a period of years, to keep up there, to maintain what you've established. You see, nowadays, when everything is promotion and the smallest understudy has a personal manager and an agent rooting for her and a seven-year contract with somebody, they don't have time to learn their job...If they allow that to interfere with their public performance, they're *bores!*

JUDY   They receive so much approval and love (and for God's sake, that's what we're all looking for in life). And they receive it every night, if they're good, they receive love and applause and if they insist on leaving the stage - I *did* this for many years, I was the most awful *bore* - I went off the stage and I'd go into my own little shell and remember all the miserable things and how tragic - and it wasn't tragic at all. I was just a damn bore. And I think that anyone who clings to this is a poseur. I think they're acting for themselves, I think it's self-pity and there's nothing more boring than self-pity.

NOËL   And it's a very great temptation when you're a great star and you know you have an enormous amount of responsibility, you are liable to fall into the trap of self-pity. Somebody else doesn't please you or something, you've been made such a fuss of that you make a scene that is quite unnecessary. If you're an ordinary human being working in an office every day, you wouldn't be like that. It's only that you've got to watch your own legend and see that you stay clear and simple.

JUDY   But you've always done this. Now, I've known you for many years and you've always done it. You are a terribly wise man who, in spite of many talents and brilliance and so forth, you have kept your mind in complete order and your *emotions* in order. You have great style and great taste. Were you ever inclined to fall into self-pity?

NOËL   Oh, yes.

JUDY   Oh good, that makes me feel much better!

NOËL   Judy, I'm much older than you and all my early years were spent understudying, touring round the country in touring companies and gradually... I certainly had my success early enough for anybody. I was only in my early *twenties.*

JUDY   How old were you when you did *The Vortex?*

NOËL   Twenty-four. It opened in London on my twenty-fifth birthday. It opened in Hampstead when I was still twenty-four. And then I went through a dangerous stage after *The Vortex* when suddenly *everything* became a success. Then I was in great danger. And I learned some lessons, because I wrote one or two things that weren't so good.

JUDY   But, darling, you wrote things that were completely successful -

NOËL   Booed off the stage and spat at in the streets at the age of twenty-seven. Booed off the stage by the public on an opening night and spat at outside the stage door. Three years later.

JUDY   For what reason?

NOËL   Because I'd made this meteoric rise. I had had five plays running at once and I was the belle of the ball and they got *sick* of it. And *I* got careless. I thought it was easy. And it's *never* easy. But that was a shock. It didn't *hurt* me. Well, when you're told - well say, for instance, if I was handed a list of the compliments I was paid last night over this show, I would now get into a nice car and drive to Martha's Vineyard and have a lovely holiday with Kit Cornell and lie in the sun. But, as *I* know that last night had a wonderful audience, receptive and kindly and warm, the show, considering it was an out of town opening, was remarkably slick. But *now* is when I start work... Because what was seen on that stage last night was not a *quarter* of what I'm going to *get* out of this by the time it gets to New York. And even *then* I'll be in trouble with the critics... I never said I was grateful to the critics in my life - because I'm not. Only occasionally - once or twice - I've had what is called a constructive criticism. Generally they miss the point, poor beasts. They really *don't* know much about it and if they *did* know much about it they'd be doing it. They're all writing plays like mad and all their plays are failures, so, therefore, I know that I know more than they do. But, in fairness to them, they judge what they *see* and it's up to me to see that they see what I *want* them to see. The critics come into that theatre and get a first impression.

Now, for instance, last night, which is a very good case in point, I had everything on my side. I had an extremely good cast, a very good orchestra, wonderful choreographer and a lot of very good material - which I'm very proud of. What was *wrong* with it from my point of view - and I know this - there are certain moments when it needs tightening. There are certain numbers that occur here, when they should occur *there*. The first part of the play goes too long without an 'up' number and it's merely a question of transposing. There are a whole lot of lines that might have been hilariously funny but didn't get over. I've seen it now with two good audiences and now those lines will be cut. That's what.

JUDY I don't remember a good line that anybody missed...

NOËL There wasn't a *good* line that anybody missed. It was the *bad* lines!

In those tourist scenes, which went terribly well last night, there are interpolations from the other people, which I thought were fairly funny - not a *smile*. And after all, if it doesn't get a laugh with this audience, it won't get a laugh with *any* audience. Out with it. And let's tighten up so that we highlight the good spots. But this is entirely and completely *technical*. Tonight I shall sit in the theatre with my secretary and make a note of every line I'm going to cut and I should think there'll be over fifty....

Noël and Rex Harrison. (New York, 1950)

"MERELY PLAYERS..."

Acting Contemporaries

REX HARRISON

In the ranks of light comedy stage actors, the top three would almost certainly include Noël and Rex Harrison. (Don't ask me who the *third* would be; do some work for yourself!)

Noël greatly admired Rex's tremendous ability to appear effortless, a trait he shared himself. Indeed, Noël is supposed to have said that "Rex Harrison is the best light comedian in the business - after me!" Rex always preferred a slightly different version: "If Rex Harrison wasn't the best light comedian in the business after me, he'd be a car salesman!"

The professional admiration was mutual; the personal affection definitely fluctuated. They both agreed that David Lean's film version of *Blithe Spirit* (1945) was disappointing, a filmed stage-play. Rex was particularly irritated on two counts: one, he'd never liked the play, and two, he was taken out of the RAF to play Charles Condomine because, he claims, Noël was "so insistent and Mountbatten intervened."

Whether the latter statement was true, I don't know, but the former presumably was, because throughout his autobiography, *A Damned Serious Business* (1991), Rex insists on referring to the film as *Blythe Spirit!*

After Noël's death, Rex could be less than charitable. In an interview, he described Noël's acting as "mannered and unmanly." Later, in the same interview, he complained that, while contemporaries of a certain sexual persuasion had been honoured (referring to Noël's knighthood in 1970 and Terence Rattigan's a year later), he hadn't been given a "bloody thing." Leaving the mean-spiritedness aside, I do believe he had a legitimate grievance. Eventually, "Sir Rex Harrison" *did* have an appropriate ring to it.

Like many eminent actors, he left his charm on stage, and could be a tiresome man. He visited us frequently wherever we were, and entertained us in Portofino with whomever he was married to at the time. He seemed compelled to score points off his spouse in even the most trivial ways. He'd look at our roses, turn to his wife and say, "Look at *their* roses. They're fine. Much better than *our* roses. Don't you ever do our bloody roses?"

Rex was a far cry from the man who talked to the animals and taught the English how to speak, but when that curtain went up, it was a pleasure to even watch him *listen*. The man was stage magic.

There was one notable instance when he literally forgot to be himself: When Kay Kendall was terminally ill, nobody could have been more caring or compassionate than Rex.

JOHN GIELGUD

John Gielgud followed in Noël's footsteps for much of his early career, though his mature range far exceeded Noël's.

Gentle soul that he was (and is), he was the ideal replacement for Noël as the agonized Nicky in *The Vortex,* and as the rumpled academic, Lewis Dodd, in *The Constant Nymph* (1926). Noël often found him "...a little false in his performance... but very effective."

Their professional paths crossed many times, and it was Johnny G. who memorably created Sebastian in *Nude with Violin*. Just how he came to do that is worthy of one of his own *faux pas* stories.

Noël couldn't play it himself. Nor could Noël's first choice, Rex Harrison. Nor could Alec Guinness, Laurence Olivier or Robert Morley. Binkie had the idea of changing the sex of the character and casting Yvonne Arnaud, the great French comic actress. This was seriously considered until, eventually, John was granted the honour. Had John told the story, it would undoubtedly have ended with the line, "Oh, you know, for quite a long time I was under Yvonne."

John suffered through Noël's theories on directing, though with his great experience he differed completely from Noël on the question of coming to rehearsal word-perfect:

> "In my view, it is much easier to learn the words when you have the movements and the business. It is important to know how the other actor is going to speak his lines, so that both of you can react properly. If you start absolutely word-perfect, like a parrot, I think it makes everything flat and dull."

The difference, perhaps, between the pure actor and the actor/writer.

Deep down, Noël was always a little nervous of Johnny G.'s acting style, much as he admired it in the classical roles. He felt that John suffered from a fault he'd criticised in me: an obsession with the *sound* of the words

John Gielgud. (1938)

rather than the *meaning*. (At that point, I hasten to add, any comparison between us ends.)

Johnny was very proud of possessing the "Terry voice," a musical instrument in its own right. Noël frequently referred to him as being "verbally beautiful," which was qualified praise. That underlying concern was best expressed by Harley Granville-Barker's comment on Gielgud's Lear. "Lear should be an oak, you're an ash."

The great thing about Johnny G., Noël used to say, is that "...he has never been afraid to fail. As a result, he has the greatest range of all of them."

To my mind he was, and thankfully remains, the *nicest* of all of them. I remember him as the amateur pianist, sitting down at the second piano in Switzerland to play duets with Noël. These two geniuses could play only in one key each, however, so the twain very rarely met! It must have been one of the few times either of them failed to make beautiful music. I have a shining picture of Johnny at Firefly having the time of his life, giggling like a teenager, words tumbling over themselves, jokes, usually at his own expense, pouring out. The ideal house guest.

LAURENCE OLIVIER

I don't suppose anyone would seriously oppose the argument that Larry Olivier was the greatest actor of his generation. His range and passion were unequalled, though he had some remarkable competition for most of the time. (I always liked the comparison someone made between him and Donald Wolfit: Larry was a *tour de force*, Wolfit was "forced to tour.")

Larry's professional path first crossed Noël's when he was cast as Victor opposite Adrianne Allen in the original 1930 production of *Private Lives*. On the page, Victor and Sybil look nothing more than foils for Elyot and Amanda. Noël knew, though, that the parts must be strongly played if the play is to maintain its balance.

Larry was poised to take off as a romantic lead. Hollywood was in the wings. He was ideal casting for Victor, except that his experience in light comedy was not great, and he suffered from the one problem no comedy actor can afford: he "corpsed." If he found the lines funny (as he often did), he couldn't stop himself from breaking up with laughter. He'd already been fired from several plays for the theatrical form of premature ejaculation.

Some actors do this deliberately, usually in an attempt to persuade an audience that an unfunny script is, in fact, so hilarious they can hardly get the words out. Once, as a young actor with the Lena Ashwell Players (!), Larry was playing the small part of Flavius in *Julius Caesar*. At one point, he had to tear down a couple of tatty-looking wreaths, and by a twist of the wrist, he found he could grab them and tear the black velvet backdrop at the same time. Fellow cast members were treated to a tantalising glimpse of the bare bottoms of certain ladies who were changing costume behind it. When Miss Ashwell "caught the act," Larry found himself looking for another job. The tendency to create unscripted laughs was by no means curtailed by the experience.

What Larry was doing in *Private Lives* did not amuse Noël at all, because he was interrupting the rhythm of a carefully constructed play. Noël cured him in draconian fashion. He warned Larry that every night, when least expected, he would throw in a line or piece of business to *make* him laugh. This threat, carried out to the letter, so re-focused Larry that it cured him completely, something for which he was forever grateful to Noël.

Some of the diversions were indeed dire. Noël would pretend to detect a little bit of mouse-shit on the brioche Gertie had just handed him; or he would address remarks to his non-existent dog, Roger, finally commanding the dog to bite Larry. God knows what the audience made of *that* night's performance!

On another evening, when Amanda was supposed to choke over something, Victor has to pat her on the back. Larry was a little heavy-handed, and Gertie, now *really* choking, couldn't get the words out. What finally emerged was, "You great clob!" Noël couldn't resist elaborating. "*Clob?*" "Yes," said Gertie, entering into the spirit of the thing, "clob." "Ah," said Noël, enlightened at last. "The man with the clob foot!" Larry couldn't deliver his next line.

Larry's natural talent and personal charm had made his professional progress relatively painless, and he'd been able to coast. Working with a taskmaster as strict as Noël pulled him up short at a critical stage of his career and made him more self-analytical, a characteristic that became a very visible aspect of the mature Larry. He was the first to admit that he was no intellectual, and always insisted that it was Noël who made him use his "silly little brain."

Noël was also among the first to spot Larry's characteristic obsession with changing his physical appearance. Noël wrote: "I cannot think of another living actor who has used such quantities of spirit-gum with such gleeful abandon. I believe that this rather excessive determination to be old before his time was the result of an integral shyness in his character. He has never had the smallest inclination to look or be himself on the stage."

Noël and Larry never acted together again on stage in the more than forty years that remained. The stage got too small to hold both of them. They each made a point of seeing just about everything the other did, however, and appeared briefly on film together in Otto Preminger's *Bunny*

Lake is Missing (1965), in which Noël played a rather effete landlord to Larry's stolid policeman. There was talk in the mid-1940's of Larry starring in a film version of *Present Laughter*, but it never came to anything.

Their personal friendship was occasionally complicated in later years by Vivien's mental and physical state, but Larry did play one last supporting role. At the "farewell" party at Claridge's, when Noël finally managed to make his way to the piano, it was Larry who was on hand to push the chair beneath him. If he hadn't, Noël would have found himself sitting on thin air!

ALFRED LUNT AND LYNN FONTANNE

Noël's friendship with the Lunts, or Alfred Lunt and Lynn Fontanne as the playbills had it, went back to their apprentice days. He knew Lynn first, in England at about the time of the Great War: "...a scraggy, friendly girl with intelligent brown eyes and a raucous laugh." There must have been a mesmerising quality about her, because Ivor Novello claimed the sight of her leaning against a tree in blossom had inspired him to write "We'll Gather Lilacs."

Noël met them as a couple during his first US visit in 1921, when his pressing lack of funds made him a grateful and frequent guest at their theatrical "digs," and from that time on their lives were intertwined. The Lunts were frequent visitors to White Cliffs and Goldenhurst, since they played both sides of the Atlantic with equal ease, though they remained first and foremost Broadway stars. Noël admired their thorough professionalism. More than anyone else he ever worked with, they shared his own attitude: "The Lunts and I are dedicated and meticulous but we do not turn the theatre into a cathedral or lecture hall."

During a run of *Design for Living* Noël suffered a throat infection. The doctor told him to take four performances off, but Alfred, even when Noël took his own temperature and showed him the thermometer reading of 103°, wouldn't hear of it. So Noël appeared, though no-one more than three feet away could possibly hear him. The next night, Alfred was so concerned about Noël's condition that he forgot his *own* lines.

In *Design for Living*, the three old friends had such instinctive stage rapport that they would "experiment" without telling each other.

Lynn might deliver a speech from next to the window instead of against the fireplace. Alfred would then enter to find an entirely different configuration from what he'd expected, but could pick it up without missing a beat. They found this kind of thing kept their performances fresh.

Noël was notoriously concerned about getting bored in a sustained

Alfred, Lynn and Noël in a parody of a Boucher painting. A mural from Billy Rose's 95th Street town house in New York City.

Noël with Lynn and Alfred at the Pyrenees restaurant after receiving his "Tony" award. (April 1970)

run, and made it a rule that he would never appear in a West End or Broadway production for more than three months. Irrespective of the box-office, he stuck to this for the whole of his career.

One evening, Noël and Alfred found themselves playing a verbal version of Russian roulette. In the scene, both men are supposed to be drunk. Alfred accidentally delivered one of Noël's lines, so Noël replied by giving Alfred's next line. The scene continued with both men playing the other's part without a fluff.

The scene had to end with Noël giving a burp ("And that we *couldn't* swap because Alfred couldn't burp"), so he snatched back "his" final line, burped and they got off. Because the characters were supposed to be drunk, no-one spotted the role reversal!

Lynn was most definitely *not* amused. "Nothing," she sniffed, "that either of you did in that scene was even remotely amusing." She would not have taken such a disciplinarian point of view if she'd been in on the game!

During a stay at Goldenhurst, Lynn and Alfred tried to persuade Noël to appear in a London production of S.N. Behrman's *The Second Man* (1928). To demonstrate how wonderful the play was, they enacted the entire thing in Noël's living room, playing all four parts. Lynn was so carried away that she began to criticise Alfred for forgetting one of the most important scenes. He promptly burst into tears. To prevent a divorce, Noël agreed to secure the British rights and appeared in the play. It was, as they'd predicted, a great success for him.

When asked if this display had surprised him, Noël replied, "If the subject had come up, they could have taken all the parts in *War and Peace*."

Lynn once came to Noël with the news that she'd finally worked out how to do a particular piece of business, which involved a complicated spring device in her purse. "I'm afraid you're a little late, darling," said Noël. "We're closing the show tonight." But she still got to do it once, and got a laugh she'd been missing all along.

Lynn was not alone in her perfectionism; Alfred, too, was known to agonise.

He was playing Professor Higgins in *Pygmalion*, and somehow the part wouldn't come together to his satisfaction. One night he sat bolt upright in bed, grabbed Lynn and said, "I know, I'm going to have a green umbrella!" As soon as he acquired this mystical prop, his performance took off.

Noël was a firm believer in the Green Umbrella psychology. Every actor needs a mannerism, an accent, a walk, that he's invented for himself.

The Lunts' professional perfectionism spilled over into their domestic lives. Alfred was obsessed with cooking and his state-of-the-art kitchen at their home in Genesee Depot, Wisconsin. He saw it as his alternative stage, and he didn't have to share the billing. Noël could gauge the degree of welcome by whether or not Alfred had baked a cake.

Lynn's concerns started with her personal appearance. As a girl, she was rather skinny, and she felt that her looks were costing her parts. She resolved to become a beautiful woman, not by resorting to cosmetics and plastic surgery, but by thinking of herself as beautiful, and then following a strict regimen to achieve her aim. In her senior years, she secretly enjoyed the surreptitious glances of other women who tried to see the "cracks." She happily shared her beauty tips with anyone who asked, but a lengthy explanation of her half-hour teeth-cleaning activity with a dozen different brushes, both morning and night, and a description of how to lie on the bed with your head hanging down, tended to pall after a while. Lynn once delivered a lecture on keeping the throat muscles taut to a bemused Joan Hirst, who had come to Lynn's hotel for the sole purpose of delivering a parcel!

Though the trio never appeared on stage together after *Design For Living*, Noël wrote two plays, *Point Valaine* and *Quadrille*, specifically for Alfred and Lynn. (He also persuaded them to appear briefly in a crowd scene in his film, *The Scoundrel*.) There was talk in the early 1960's of a reunion play in which Noël and Alfred were to play a pair of retired actors appearing for one last performance. It was first entitled *Rehearsal Period*, and then *Swan Song*, but, like the plan for a similar reunion with Gertie, it came to naught. Noël probably felt it would be billed as "The Lunts (with Noël Coward)." The ambiguous ending of *Design For Living*, with the *ménage à trois* rolling around on the floor in laughter, their future unresolved but their relationship insoluble, was symbolic of the erratic intimacy they enjoyed throughout their lives.

Point Valaine (1934) briefly starred them on Broadway. The Lunts were supposed to play the Lunts, without the laughs; Lynn was not a neurotic lady hotelier on a tropical island, any more than Alfred was her lugubrious Russian lover. The play was written off after a few dozen performances, and was never commercially produced in England until its inclusion in the 1991 Chichester repertory season. It was assuredly a curate's egg of a play, but definitely good in parts.

A moderate success was made of *Quadrille* (1952), an elegant period piece, beautifully designed by Cecil Beaton. This was much more what the punters wanted and, though it was no great dramatic shakes, the design pleased the eye, the Lunts pleased the ear, and the customers were pleased to come. Over three hundred performances in London were followed by a respectable run in New York a year later (1954).

Lynn Fontanne and Joyce Carey in Quadrille *(1952). Gowns (and photograph) by Cecil Beaton.*

The Lunts' main influence, though, was not as interpreters of Noël's material, as much as being friends and touchstones.

Inevitably they became, like any couple whose existence is planned entirely round the well-being of each other, somewhat introverted. Though they were not aware of it, this tendency became more marked as they got older. To the end they projected a quality of selfish innocence. Noël summed up his affectionate ambivalence about them as early as this 1953 *Diaries* entry:

> "They really are the most extraordinary couple. They are gay and sweet and warm and friendly; Lynn is mentally slow with flashes of brilliant swiftness; Alfred quick as a

knife with flashes of dreadful obtuseness. They are deeply concerned with only three things - themselves, the theatre (in so far as it concerns themselves), and food... Lynn has a strong character and is to be trusted. Alfred is frightened of everybody's shadow except, unfortunately, his own. He is weak, hysterical and not to be trusted on stage. On the other hand he has tremendous charm, great humour and is, or can be, an actor of genius...It is very confusing and exceedingly irritating, especially because I love and admire them both so much."

Fortunately, their mutual love and admiration lasted for the entire run of their personal play. After Noël's death, the first invitation for Coley and me to come and stay was extended by ... you've guessed it. The Folks who lived at Genesee Depot, Wisconsin.

NOËL COWARD

When referring to his appearance in *The Astonished Heart*, Noël mockingly described himself as "that splendid old Chinese character actress." He'd obviously never recovered from the notion of being the "heavily-doped Chinese illusionist" of a 1920's photograph taken after *The Vortex* success.

It was a typical Noël witticism, no truer than Garry Essendine's histrionic claim that "complete naturalness on the stage is my strong suit." The ironic audacity of such a claim raises the smile and diverts attention from serious debate.

The typical Coward role shone with a polished veneer which retained not a single speck of dust. His early mentors, like Hawtrey and du Maurier, had perfected the art of "naturalistic" playing, and yet here was Noël deliberately dealing in an ironic persona that was essentially artificial and certainly stylised. The "Noël Coward" style was based on recognisable social models, but the satire with which Noël infused his versions made them not only acceptable, but positively glamorous. Although his technique was essentially created in his formative period, the 1920's, it survived as an artefact of a more desirable era. Like P.G. Wodehouse, Noël created an emotional universe of such consistency that it never really dates because it never truly existed in the first place. "Noël Coward" and the world he created was strictly his own invention, a stage on which he gave an "eternal performance."

Even among his loyal supporters he attracted an admirable ambivalence of attitude. Michael Arlen, a friend and writer, sounded quite

Cowardesque when he wrote in *Portrait of a Lady in Park Avenue:* "Emotionally she was unimportant, like a play by Noël Coward; but her construction was faultless, like a play by Noël Coward."

Noël's acting range was quite narrow and he rarely, if ever, attempted to extend it. His French aristocrat in *Conversation Piece* was an unintentional parody with an awkward accent, even though he could speak French tolerably well. (He once played a season in Paris of *Present Laughter* / *Joyeux Chagrins* to reviews that commended his use of the language, even if the reviewers understood little else of what was going on.) In the case of *Conversation Piece*, Noël could, and did, plead the excuse that he'd taken over the part at short notice from Romney Brent.

Although he enjoyed working-class parts, like Frank in *This Happy Breed* and the hen-pecked husband who finally bites back in *Fumed Oak,* he wasn't as authentic as he liked to think. His interpretations were affectionately intended, but an element of pastiche always remained. Technically effective, he ended up by playing down in these roles. The irony was that the social class he was depicting was closer to his own origins than the majority of his more famous roles.

Ken Tynan summed it up when he said:

> "Theatrically speaking, it was Coward who took sophistication out of the refrigerator and put it on the hob....His stage expression of boredom is vivacious; he is mask-like and supercilious, but raffishly eager, so he never less than glows; there are no ashes in his work....

> "Listening, it struck me that he had done what no other actor or playwright of our time had done; invented, not only a new acting style, but a new life. Not merely a new character, the result of grease and skill, but the instant projection of a new kind of human being, which had never before existed in print or paint...."

He concluded:

> "Even the youngest of us will know, in fifty years' time, precisely what is meant by 'a very Noël Coward sort of person.'"

ENVOI

So many of Noël's lines sum him up. He made a game of concocting new exit lines for himself. However ironically he intended it, I think this one comes closest:

> "Summing myself up, I would say that I have a talent to amuse, that I write very good dialogue, and that I have a strong and noble character as well."

My own summary of the way I feel borrows these words:

> *I'll see you again,*
> *I live each moment through again.*
> *Time has lain heavy between,*
> *But what has been*
> *Can leave me never;*
> *Your dear memory*
> *Throughout my life has guided me.*
> *Though my world has gone awry,*
> *Though the years my tears may dry,*
> *I shall love you till I die,*
> *Goodbye!*

BIBLIOGRAPHY

Beaton, Cecil
    Self Portrait with Friends: Selected Diaries
    (Ed. Richard Buckle)
    Pimlico 1991
Beaton, Cecil
    The Face of the World 1957
Bordman, Gerald
    Jerome Kern: his life and music
    Oxford 1980
Briers, Richard
    Coward and Company: a light-hearted and affectionate
    evocation of Noël Coward and his world
    Robson Books 1987
Brown, Jared
    The Fabulous Lunts
    Atheneum 1986
Castle, Charles
    Noël
    W.H. Allen 1972
Citron, Stephen
    Noël and Cole: the Sophisticates
    Sinclair-Stevenson 1992
Coward, Noël
    Present Indicative
    Heinemann 1937

    Future Indefinite
    Heinemann 1954

    The Lyrics of Noël Coward
    Heinemann 1965

    The Noël Coward Diaries
    (Edited by Graham Payn and Sheridan Morley)
    Weidenfeld & Nicolson 1982

The Noël Coward Song Book
Simon and Shuster 1980

Dean, Basil
   The Theatre at War: the story of ENSA
   Harrap 1956
Dean, Basil
   Mind's Eye: an autobiography 1927-72
   Hutchinson 1973
Dietz, Howard
   Dancing in the Dark: Words by Howard Dietz
   Quadrangle/N.Y.Times Book Co. 1974
Ellis, Mary
   Those Dancing Years: an autobiography
   John Murray 1982
Fleming, Ann
   Letters
   Edited by Mark Amory
   Collins Harvill 1985
Freedland, Michael
   Jerome Kern: a biography
   Robson Books 1978
Gallati, Mario
   Mario of The Caprice
   Hutchinson 1960
Gielgud, John
   An Actor and his Time
   Sidgwick & Jackson 1976
Gielgud, John
   Backward Glance: Times for Reflection and
   Distinguished Company
   Hodder & Stoughton 1989
Gill, Brendan
   Tallulah
   Holt Rinehart Winston 1972
Gingold, Hermione
   How to Grow Old Disgracefully
   Victor Gollancz 1987
Green, Benny
   Let's Face the Music: the Golden Age of popular song
   Pavilion 1989

Grenfell, Joyce
>Darling Ma: Letters to Her Mother 1932 - 44
>(Ed. James Roose-Evans)
>Coronet 1988

Grenfell, Joyce
>The Time of My Life: Entertaining the Troops -
>Her Wartime Journals
>(Ed. James Roose-Evans)
>Coronet 1989

Hall, Peter
>Diaries: The Story of a Dramatic Battle
>(Ed. by John Goodwin)
>Harper & Row 1984

Harding, James
>Ivor Novello
>W.H. Allen 1987

Harrison, Rex
>A Damned Serious Business: My Life in Comedy
>Bantam 1991

Harwood, Ronald (Ed.)
>The Ages of Gielgud: An Actor at Eighty
>Hodder & Stoughton 1984

Huggett, Richard
>Binkie Beaumont: Eminence Grise of the
>West End Theatre 1933-1973
>Hodder & Stoughton 1989

Kiernan, Robert
>Noël Coward
>Ungar, New York 1986

Kimball, Robert (ed.)
>The Complete Lyrics of Cole Porter
>Knopf 1983

Lahr, John
>Coward: the Playwright
>Methuen 1982

Lesley, Cole
>Remembered Laughter: the Life of Noël Coward
>Knopf 1976

Lesley, Cole, Payn, Graham & Morley, Sheridan
>Noël Coward and His Friends
>Weidenfeld & Nicolson 1979

Lewis, Milton
      Noël Coward
      Twayne Publishers, Boston 1989
Lillie, Beatrice
      Every Other Inch a Lady: an autobiography
      Doubleday 1972
Loy, Myrna (with James Kotsibilas-Davis)
      Being and Becoming
      Knopf 1987
Mander and Mitchenson
      Revue
      Taplinger, N.Y. 1971
Mills, John
      Up in the Clouds, Gentlemen Please
      Penguin 1981
Morley, Sheridan
      A Talent to Amuse: a biography of Noël Coward
      Pavilion Books 1985
Noble, Peter
      Ivor Novello: Man of the Theatre
      The Falcon Press 1951
Olivier, Laurence
      Confessions of an Actor
      Weidenfeld & Nicolson 1982
Olivier, Laurence
      On Acting
      Simon & Schuster 1986
Olivier, Tarquin
      My Father, Laurence Olivier
      Headline 1993
Palmer, Lilli
      Change Lobsters and Dance: an autobiography
      1976
Pope, W. MacQueen
      Ivor: the Story of an Achievement
      W.H. Allen 1951
Schwartz, Charles
      Cole Porter: a biography
      The Dial Press 1977
Spoto, Donald
      Laurence Olivier
      Fontana 1992

Stokes, Sewell
      Without Veils: the intimate biography of Gladys Cooper
      Peter Davies 1950
Tynan, Kathleen
      The Life of Kenneth Tynan
      Weidenfeld & Nicolson 1987
Tynan, Kenneth
      The Sound of Two Hands Clapping
      Holt Rinehart Winston 1975
Tynan, Kenneth
      Profiles
      Nick Hern Books 1989
Vickers, Hugo
      Cecil Beaton
      Primus 1985
Webster, Margaret
      Don't Put Your Daughter on the Stage
      Knopf 1972
Zolotow, Maurice
      Stagestruck: the Romance of Alfred Lunt and Lynn Fontanne
      Harcourt, Brace & World 1965

INDEX

Ace of Clubs, 60-63, 115, 145, 164-165, 189, 247
Actor Prepares, An, 329-330
Addinsell, Richard, 27, 171
After the Ball, 71-72, 76-77, 147, 164, 172, 215
Agate, James, 44, 292, 296
Age Cannot Wither, 314
Ainley, Sir Henry, 362
Aitken, Maria, 262, 267
Alexander, Sir George, 298
"Alexander's Ragtime Band," 309
Alice in Wonderland, 27-28
"Alice Is At It Again," 41, 96
"All I Do the Whole Day Through is Dream of You," 66
Allegro, 105
Allen, Adrianne, 187, 197, 380
Allen, Woody, 250
"Always," 99
Amherst, Jeffery, 270
And On We Go, 19
Andrews, Julie, 232
Androcles and the Lion, 238
Anna and the King of Siam, 105
"Annabel," 96
Annie Get Your Gun, 99
Anouilh, Jean, 315
Apple Cart, The, 91, 179, 203, 353
April, Elsie, 99
Arc de Triomphe, 309
Arcadians, The, 308
Architectural Digest, 198
Arlen, Michael, 201, 387
Arnaud, Yvonne, 378
Arnold, Tom, 27
Around the World in Eighty Days, 110
As You Like It, 152, 219
Ashton, Winifred - see Dane, Clemence
Astaire, Fred, 23, 28, 66, 116, 370
Astonished Heart, The, 63, 179, 252, 319, 387
Attenborough, Richard (later Lord), 280
Aumont, Jean-Pierre, 215
Auntie Mame, 176

Awful Truth, The, 39
Ayckbourn, Alan, 321

Bacall, Lauren, 124-125, 368
Bacharach, Burt, 241
"Bad Times Are Just Around the Corner," 59, 66-67
Baddeley, Angela, 69, 365
Balcon, Michael (later Sir), 302
Bankhead, Tallulah, 59, 225, 228-230, 263
Bannerman, Margaret, 263
Barbara Walters Show, The, 204
Barber, John, 80
Barbour, Joyce, 2, 6
Barrie, Sir James M., 12-13, 96, 286, 295-296, 350
Baxter, Anne, 238
Baxter, Sir Beverley, 77
Beaton, Cecil (later Sir), 79, 89, 155-157, 201, 214, 222, 246, 363, 385-386
Beaumont, Hugh "Binkie," 45, 80, 110-111, 126, 143-147, 162, 179, 201, 211, 222, 231, 243, 252, 258, 294, 318, 358-360, 365, 378
"Beautiful Soup," 27
Beaverbrook, Lord Max, 136, 147-150, 154, 200-202, 249, 337
Beckett, Samuel, 286, 296, 324
Beerbohm, Sir Max, 21, 139, 179
Behrman, S.N., 272, 384
Bennett, Alan, 251
Bergman, Ingmar, 262
Berlin, Irving, 28, 99, 102, 249, 309, 312
Bernstein, Leonard, 61, 173
Best, Edna, 125, 140, 263
Bill of Divorcement, A, 220
"Bird Songs at Eventide," 9
Bitter Sweet, 2, 5, 21, 23, 52, 71, 77-78, 141, 164, 263, 279-280, 284, 302, 311
Black Pirate, The, 8
Black, Conrad, 148
Blackwell, Blanche, 137, 145, 200-201, 206

Blackwell, Chris, 206
Bless the Bride, 310
Blithe Spirit, 54, 56, 88-89, 99, 116, 124, 126, 144, 153, 173-174, 178, 203, 215, 219, 221, 245, 251, 258, 263, 265, 278, 302, 358-360, 362, 377
Bogart, Humphrey, 124-125
Bon Voyage, 278
Bonynge, Richard, 205
Boom, 238
Box, Sydney, 62
Boys from Syracuse, The, 26, 105
Boys in Brown, 63
Boys in the Band, The, 278
Bradley, Buddy, 14, 19
Braithwaite, Dame Lilian, 140-141, 219, 233
Breadwinner, The, 138
Brecht, Bertholt, 78
Brent, Romney, 2, 388
Brice, Fanny, 59
Bridge On the River Kwai, The, 106
Brief Encounter, 173, 218, 263
"Bright Young People," 5
Broome Stages, 220
Brouhaha, 82
Browne, Irene, 77
Bryan, Dora, 64, 67, 81
Bryden, Ronald, 161
Brynner, Yul, 56, 106, 164
Buccleuch, Duchess of, 361
Buchanan, Jack, 28
Bunny Lake is Missing, 381-382
Burke, Patricia, 25-26
Burton, Richard, 238, 261-262, 267
Byng, Douglas, 22, 25

Cabaret, 277
Caine, Michael, 238
Call Me Madam, 99
Calthrop, Gladys, 23, 28, 30-31, 40-41, 45, 69, 98, 125, 140, 146, 157, 162, 183, 188, 190, 194, 202, 212-214, 223, 231, 239-240, 263, 295, 357, 359-362, 365-366
Campbell, Judy, 69, 356-367

Campbell, Mrs. Patrick, 26
Careless Rapture, 71
Caretaker, The, 288, 324,
    348
Carey, Joyce ("Joycie"), 26,
    88, 140-141, 146, 183,
    188, 208, 218-221, 223,
    239, 280, 363, 386
Carmichael, Ian, 64, 67
Carpenter, Edward, Dean of
    Westminster, 256, 280
Carroll, Lewis, 28, 313
Cartland, Barbara, 142, 268
Caryll, Ivan, 308
Casablanca, 167, 315
Casino Royale, 200
Casson, Sir Lewis, 163
Castlerosse, Lord and Lady,
    271
Cavalcade, 14, 23, 42, 44,
    78, 89, 126, 128, 142,
    183, 272, 275, 300, 317
Cecil, Lord David, 179
Chamberlain, Neville, 187
Champion, Gower, 174
Chanel, Coco, 150
Change Lobsters and Dance,
    179
Chaplin, Sir Charles, 26,
    115, 122, 194-195
Charlot Revue, 370
Charlot, André, 22, 24-25,
    94
Cherry Orchard, The, 295
Chevalier, Albert, 205
Chicago, 203, 228-229, 277
Chicken Soup with Barley,
    324
"Children of the Ritz," 303
Chu Chin Chow, 310, 325
Churchill, Randolph, 251
Churchill, Sir Winston, 107,
    111, 130-132, 134-135,
    148-149, 153-155, 186
Circle, The, 59
Claire, Ina, 213
Clare, Mary, 162
Cleopatra, 261
Coates, Eric, 9
Cochran's 1931 Revue, 5
Cochran, Sir Charles B.
    ("C.B." or "Cockie"), 1,
    5, 7, 20-25, 53, 57, 304,
    350

Coconut Girl, The, 276
Cocteau, Jean, 251
Colbert, Claudette, 81, 125
Collier, Constance, 179
Collins, Joan, 265, 267
Colman, Ronald, 3, 115
Come Into the Garden,
    Maud, 160, 318
"Come the Wild, Wild
    Weather," 163-164, 237-
    238, 254
Concerto, 263, 302, 331
Congreve, William, 89, 284
Connolly, Cyril, 220
Constant Nymph, The, 378
Conti, Miss Italia, 12
Conti, Tom, 267
Conversation Piece, 23, 39,
    71, 89, 311, 388
Cook, Roderick, 241
Cooper, Lady Diana, 81
Cooper, Dame Gladys, 31,
    69, 125, 140, 146, 162,
    231, 263, 295, 357, 359
Cornell, Katharine ('Kit'),
    59-60, 196, 375
Cosmopolitan, 257
Cottens, Joseph, 188
"Could You Please Oblige
    Us With a Bren Gun?",
    18, 66
Country Girl, The, 308
Courtneidge, Dame Cicely,
    153, 177-178
Coward, Arthur (Noël's
    father), 13
Coward, Violet (Noël's
    mother), 97, 113, 163,
    183, 188, 190, 241, 245,
    248, 308, 312, 370-371
Cowardy Custard, 241
Crawford, Joan, 115
Cree, Patricia, 77
Crisham, Walter, 28
Critic, The, 352
Cronyn, Hume, 238
Cukor, George, 202
Cummins, Peggy, 28
Cyrano, 364

Dad's Army, 18
Daily Express, The, 80-81,
    148, 154, 164, 181, 249,
    336-337
Daily Herald, The, 164

Daily Mail, The, 62, 81,
    164, 249, 337
Daily Telegraph, The, 164,
    181, 193, 337, 343
Daladier, 187
Damned Serious Business, A,
    377
Dancing Years, The, 71, 309
Dane, Clemence (Winifred
    Ashton), 27, 111-112,
    188, 218-223, 258-259,
    358, 361
Darewski, Herman, 93
Darewski, Max, 93
Darlington, W.A., 181
Davies, Hunter, 85
Davis, Bette, 115
Davis, Joan, 19
Davis, Sammy, Jr., 120
"Day War Broke Out, The,"
    18
Dean, Basil, 141, 272
Dear Brutus, 296
Dear Sir, 103
Dear, Peggie, 33
Dench, Dame Judi, 314
Denis, Eileen, 69
Denison, Michael, 366
Dent, Alan, 44, 77
Design for Living, 79, 246,
    258, 265, 382, 385
Devine, George, 79
Dexter, John, 176
Diaries (The Coward
    Diaries), 45, 76, 78, 82,
    91, 107, 110, 125, 135,
    138, 142, 146, 148, 150,
    155, 158, 164, 170, 180,
    191, 209, 2 14, 216-217,
    225, 234, 239-240, 247-
    248, 253, 257, 272, 285,
    287, 386
Dietrich, Marlene, 118, 155,
    165, 192, 224-228, 274,
    281, 373
Dietz, Howard, 103
Dixon, Alfred, 118
Dr. No, 200
"Don't Let's Be Beastly to
    the Germans," 66, 134
"Don't Put Your Daughter
    On the Stage, Mrs.
    Worthington," 6, 221
Douglas, Alfred, 5

Drake, Betsy, 165
du Maurier, Daphne, 188
du Maurier, Sir Gerald, 78,
    231, 274, 298, 320, 359,
    387
Dumb Waiter, The, 288
Dunne, Irene, 39, 105-106,
    115

Easy Virtue, 302
Eddy, Nelson, 279
Eden, Anthony (Lord Avon),
    191
Edward VIII, King (later
    Duke of Windsor) - see
    Windsor, Edward
Eliot, T.S., 161, 287, 296
Elliott, Madge, 34-35, 37
Ellis, Mary, 26, 71-72, 77
Ellis, Vivian, 310
Enchanted Castle, The, 91,
    243
Endgame, 324
Evans, Dame Edith, 146,
    162, 176, 178, 231-232,
    251, 259, 262, 352
Evening News, The, 44, 164
Evening Standard, The, 63,
    79, 164, 249, 279
Evening with Beatrice Lillie,
    An, 174, 176
Everyone Comes to Rick's, 167

Face of the World, The, 159
Fairbanks, Douglas, Jr., 115
Fairchild, William, 250
Faith, Adam, 314
Fall, Leo, 308
Fallen Angels, 156, 229, 258,
    263-264, 278
"Falling In Love With Love,"
    26
Faster Than Sound, 174
Fenn, Jean, 167
Ferber, Edna, 105, 159, 300
Ferrer, José, 172-173, 175
Feydeau, Georges, 81, 171,
    216
Fielding, Fenella, 177
Fielding, Harold, 171
Financial Times, The, 283
Finch, Peter, 235
Findlater, Richard, 81
Fitzgerald, F. Scott, 159

Fleming, Ann - see
    Rothermere, Lady Ann
Fleming, Ian, 157, 188, 197-
    198, 206
Floradora, 308
Flower Girls, The, 220
Fontanne, Lynn, 80, 137,
    157, 194, 196, 204, 228,
    263, 268, 292, 354, 382-
    387
Forbes-Robertson, Jean, 12
Ford Star Jubilee, 125
Formby, George, 135, 153
Forty Years On, 251
Fosse, Bob, 174
Fraser-Simson, Harold, 310
Friml, Rudolf, 71
Frost, David, 252
Fry, Christopher, 343
Fumed Oak, 297, 320, 388
"Fumfumbolo," 40
Funny Face, 66
Funny Girl, 172
Future Indefinite, 45, 86, 88,
    186, 196, 288

Gabor, Eva, 218
Gaieties (Henson's), 28
Gallati, Mario, 250
Galsworthy, John, 350
Garbo, Greta, 192, 220
Garland, Judy, 66, 115, 286,
    368-375
Gay's the Word, 5
Gaynor, Mitzi, 164
Gershwins, George and Ira,
    103
Gershwin, George, 249, 312
Ghost of a Chance, 215
Gibbons, Carroll, 35, 357-
    358
Gielgud, Sir John, 80-82,
    146, 221-222, 239, 251,
    280, 378-380
Gilbert and Sullivan, 205,
    308
Gingold, Hermione, 240,
    263-264
Girl Who Came to Supper,
    The, 172, 174-175, 276
Glamorous Night, 26, 71,
    309
Glaser, Joe, 117
Globe Revue, The, 59, 66-67
Golden Girls, 264

Goldfinger, 200
Gone With the Wind, 233
Gordon, Hannah, 314
Gould, Jack, 124
Grand Hotel, 220, 268
Granger, Stewart, 265
Grant, Cary, 39, 279
Granville-Barker, Harley,
    350, 380
Graves, Peter, 71, 265
Gray, Dulcie, 366
Gray, Timothy, 173, 177
Great Victor Herbert, The, 39
"Green Carnation," 5-6
"Green Eye of the Little
    Yellow God, The," 28
Greene, Graham, 106, 201,
    203
Gregg, Hubert, 28
Grenfell, Joyce, 34, 36-37
Griffith, D.W., 141, 300-
    301
Grimes, Tammy, 174, 232,
    262
Guide to Samolo, A, 39
Guinness Book of Records,
    The, 232
Guinness, Alec (later Sir),
    106, 165, 203, 239, 313,
    378
Guinness, Loel and Gloria,
    136
Guys and Dolls, 61

Hackforth, Norman, 32, 58,
    65, 99-100, 118
Hale, Binnie, 25-26
Hale, Sonnie, 25
Hall, Peter (later Sir), 83,
    144, 246
Halliday, Richard, 41, 180
Hamlet, 91, 283, 294
Hammerstein, Oscar, II, 57,
    103, 105, 313
Handley, Tommy, 10
Hands Across the Sea, 50,
    151, 271, 319
Hare, Doris, 2
Harriman, Averill, 154
Harris, Radie, 60
Harris, Rosemary, 262
Harrison, Rex (later Sir),
    105, 172, 278, 352, 376-
    378

Hart, Lorenz ("Larry"), 101, 105
Hawtrey, Sir Charles, 291-293, 298, 352, 387
Haxton, Gerald, 139
Hay Fever, 89, *174-176, 178, 190, 219-220, 231, 238, 259, 262-263, 277, 295, 303, 317-318*
Heal, Joan, 64, 66-67
Hearts of the World, 300
Hecht, Ben and MacArthur, Charles, 300
Hello, Dolly, 172
Helpmann, Robert, 73, 76-77, 82, 172
Henderson, Florence, 172, 175
Henson, Leslie, 25, 28-29, 132, 320
Hepburn, Audrey, 195
Hepburn, Katharine, 115, 118, 192, 195, 203, 227, 278
High Spirits, 173-178, 230, *232, 279*
Hilary, Jennifer, 314
Hirst, Joan, 183, 213, 385
Hitchcock, Alfred, 302
Hobson, Harold, 138, 251
Holliday, Judy, 165
Holloway, Stanley, 25, 28
Holtzmann, Fanny, 49, 52, 216
Home and Colonial, 81, 262
Home, William Douglas, 63
Horne, Lena, 66
Hour of Gold, Hour of Lead, 243
Hughes, Sally, 314
Hulbert, Jack, 153
Hylton, Jack, 27, 350

"I Am No Good At Love," 168, 246
"I Have a Song to Sing-O," 308
"I Hear You Calling Me," 2, 9
"I Like America," 60-61, 115
"I Never Realized," 101
"I Remember Her," 172

"I'll Follow My Secret Heart," 89, 99, 189, 357
I'll Leave It To You, 102
"I'll See You Again," 1, 205, 249, 311, 389
"I've Been to a Marvellous Party," 156, 230
Ibsen, Henrik, 350
"If Love Were All," 52, 241, 279
"If We Could Lead a Merry Mormon Life," 103
"If You Will Be My Morganatic Wife," 103-105
L'Ile Heureuse, 215
"In An Old Fashioned Town," 9
In Which We Serve, 152-153, 156, 222, 280, 300, 358, 362
"Indian Love Call," 119
Irving, Sir Henry, 350
Island Fling, 81, 125, 262
"It Couldn't Matter Less," 31, 238
Italian Job, The, 238

Jacobi, Derek (later Sir), 176
James, Henry, 288
Jean-René, 194, 240, 257
Jesus Christ, Superstar, 279
Joel, Doris, 94
John, Augustus, 229
Johnson, Celia (later Dame), 63, 178, 262
Johnson, Geoffrey, 213, 218, 220
Johnson, Van, 165
Journey's End, 223, 354
Joyeux Chagrins (Present Laughter), 263, 265, 388
Jubilee, 102, 277
Julius Caesar, 380

Kander, John and Ebb, Fred, 277
Kaufman, George and Hart, Moss, 209, 276
"Keep the Home Fires Burning," 93, 95, 140, 153
Keith, Penelope, 262
Kelly, Gene, 115
Kendall, Kay, 378

Kern, Jerome, 103, 187, 249, 312
King's Rhapsody, 26, 71, 142, 309
Kirby's Flying Ballet, 12, 28
Kirkwood, Pat, 60, 62
Kiss Me, Kate, 5, 101
Kiss of the Spider Woman, 277
Kitchen, The, 79
"Kling-Kling Bird on the Divi-Divi Tree, The," 277
Korda, Sir Alexander, 106
Kretzmer, Herbert, 181
Kurnitz, Harry, 171

Lady Windermere's Fan, 71, 215
Lahr, John, 272
Last of Mrs. Cheyney, The, 346
"Last Time I Saw Paris, The," 187
Later Than Spring, 165
Laura, 116
Lawrence, Gertrude, 12, 23, 41, 46-57, 78, 81, 106, 165, 169, 188, 203, 228, 230, 232, 241, 252, 259, 261, 267-268, 271, 274, 281, 292, 300, 319, 370-371, 381, 385
Lawson, Wilfred, 362
Laye, Evelyn "Boo," 280
Layton, Joe, 171, 193, 238
Lean, David, 126, 153, 263, 377
Lear, Edward, 313
Leave It To Me, 102
Lee, Vanessa, 71-72, 142
Lehar, Franz, 71, 308
Leigh, Vivien, 81-82, 145-146, 171, 191, 225, 227, 233-235, 247, 280, 382
Leighton, Frank, 25
Leighton, Margaret, 63, 179-180, 238, 365
Léocadia, 315
Lerner, Alan Jay, 101, 241
Lesley, Cole ("Coley"), 5, 38, 45, 53-54, 64, 80, 87, 89, 99-102, 107, 110-111, 119, 147, 183-185, 188-189, 193, 196, 208, 211, 214-216, 223, 227, 236,

238, 240-241, 243-245,
254, 257-258, 264, 274,
276-277, 280, 361, 387
"Let's Do It," 101-102, 276
Levin, Bernard, 81
Levin, Herman, 171
Lewis, C.S., 12
Lewis, Jerry, 63
Lilac Domino, The, 27
Lillie, Beatrice, 22, 25, 174,
176-177, 225, 230-232,
278, 281
Lindbergh, Anne Morrow,
243
Listener, The, 351
Little Lord Fauntleroy, 10
Littler, Emile, 350
Littler, Prince, 145-146
Lockwood, Margaret, 220,
265
Loesser, Frank, 61
Loewe, Frederick, 241
Lohr, Marie, 162
Lolita, 106
London Calling, 23
"London Pride," 26, 35,
140, 153
Long Island Sound, 314, 317-
318
"Long Live the King (If He
Can)!", 173
Lonsdale, Frederick, 287
Look After Lulu, 36, 81, *158,*
216, 235
Look Back in Anger, 78, 348
Looking Back, 138, 310
Loraine, Lorn ("Lornie"),
27, 45, 183, 188, 210-
214, 216, 222-223, 249,
253, 264, 267, 270, 281
Losey, Joe, 238
Loss, Joe, 10
Lough, Master Ernest, 9
Love Letter, The, 59
Lowry, L.S., 109
Loy, Myrna, 4, 279
"Lucky Day," 64, 66
Luft, Lorna, 371
Lunts, The (Alfred Lunt and
Lynn Fontanne), 47, 60,
79-80, 155, 157-158,
188, 191, 194, 196, 204,
228, 268, 292, 300, 382-
386

Lunt, Alfred, 80, 137, 194,
196, 228, 268, 292, 382-
387
Lynn, Vera, 94-95, 361
Lyric Revue, The, 64, 66-67,
215
Lyrics (Collected Lyrics of Noël
Coward), 132, 276

Macbeth, 89, 352
McClintic, Guthrie, 60
MacCarthy, Desmond, 138
MacDonald, Jeanette, 279
MacOwan, Michael, 353
Macqueen-Pope, W., 142
Macrae, Arthur, 64
"Mad About the Boy," 2-4,
6, 33, 230, 279, 304
"Mad Dogs and
Englishmen," 2, 93, 118,
131-134, 204, 285, 317,
357
Maid of the Mountains, The,
310
Man Who Came to Dinner,
The, 102, 276
Manchester Mail, The, 164
Mander and Mitchenson,
314
Mantovani, 33-34
Marais, Jean, 251
Margaret, Princess, 150
Mark of Zorro, The, 8
Marshall, Norman, 305
Martin, Hugh, 173-174
Martin, Mary, 39-44, 50,
62, 71, 106, 118, 120-
124, 213, 216, 281
Mask of Virtue, The, 233
Massey, Daniel, 232
Matalon, Vivian, 180
"Matelot," 32-33, 105, 189
Matthews, Jessie, 153
Matz, Peter, 62, 118, 121
Maugham, W. Somerset, 59,
87, 92, 138-139, 179,
190, 287, 350
Measor, Beryl, 361, 363
Melville, Alan, 67
Merivale, Jack, 235
Merman, Ethel, 165, 169
Merrick, David, 143
Messager, André, 308
Michell, Keith, 172, 174
Might Have Been, 60

Miles, Bernard, 241
Miles, Sarah, 176
Millar, Ronnie, 115
Miller, Gilbert, 90
Miller, Marilyn, 59
Miller, Max, 319
Mills, Hayley, 264
Mills, John (later Sir), 2, 6,
222, 280, 354
Mills, Juliet, 264
Minnelli, Liza, 371
Minnelli, Vincente, 371
Miss Hook of Holland, 308
Molyneux, Edward, 165,
187, 202, 252, 358
Monckton, Lionel, 308
Monroe, Marilyn, 172
Montez, Maria, 215
Montgomery, Robert, 300
Morley, Robert, 378
Morley, Sheridan, 46
Mountbatten, Lady Edwina,
81, 151-152, 155, 271,
361
Mountbatten, Lord Louis
(later Earl), 148, 150-155,
194, 242, 271, 361, 377
Mouse That Roared, The, 82
Mousetrap, The, 325
Munshin, Jules, 82
Murdoch, Rupert, 148
My Fair Lady, 106, 145,
171-172, 214
"My Heart Belongs to
Daddy," 39, 41
My Life In Art, 329
Myerson, Joel, 7

Nathan, George Jean, 300
Neagle, Dame Anna, 280
"Nearer My God to Thee," 1
Nesbit, E., 12, 91, 243
Nesbitt, Robert, 19
Neutral Territory, 178
New Faces, 357
New Statesman, The, 161
New York Journal-American,
The, 124
New York Magazine, 261
New York Post, The, 123
New York Times, The, 124,
165, 246
News Chronicle, The, 44, 77,
79-80
Nice People, 59

Nichols, Beverley, 322
"Night and Day," 89
Night of the Iguana, The, 268
"Nightingale Sang in
    Berkeley Square, A," 357,
    361
"Nina (From Argentina),"
    35-36, 102, 124, 361
"Ninety Minutes is a Long,
    Long Time," 120, 123
"Ninety Years On," 134
Nivens, David, 195
"No, My Heart," 277-278
Noël Coward in Two Keys,
    237
Noël Coward Song Book, The,
    313
Norton, Frederic, 310
Norton, Kay, 188
Novello, Ivor, 5, 13-14, 26-
    28, 44, 57, 71, 77, 93,
    95, 139-143, 141, 153,
    185, 202. 249, 302, 309,
    382
Nude with Violin, 80, 82, 91,
    110-111, 127, 145, 217,
    219, 274, 288, 378

"O, For the Wings of a
    Dove," 9-10
Observer, The, 63, 337
Occupe-toi d'Amélie, 81, 216
Oh Coward!, 241, 243
Oklahoma!, 145, 172
Olivier, Laurence (later
    Lord), 82, 105, 146, 172,
    175, 191, 234-235, 239,
    241-243, 260, 274, 280,
    294, 335, 352, 378, 380-
    382
On With the Dance, 23
One Touch of Venus, 39
Operette, 17, 39, 71, 131,
    143
Osborne, John, 78-79, 298
Our Man in Havana, 164,
    200, 203, 301, 313
Our Miss Gibbs, 308
Oxford Dictionary, The, 138

P and O 1930, 107
Pacific 1860, 30-31, 35, 38,
    40, 43-45, 49, 60, 62, 71,
    120-122, 145, 157, 168,

189, 213, 215-216, 263
Paley, William (Bill), 55,
    121, 126, 216, 251-252,
    279
Palmer, Lilli, 160, 179, 181,
    227
Palmucci, Carlo, 180
Passing Fancy, 172
Past Conditional, 45, 243
Patrick, Nigel, 298
Payn, Philip Francis "Frank,"
    7
Payn, Sybil, 1, 7-15, 17, 22,
    26, 33, 45, 163, 189
Peace in Our Time, 60
Perchance to Dream, 71, 309
Perry, John, 146, 222
Peter Pan, 12-13, 28, 296
"Phil the Fluter's Ball," 290
Phillips, Margaret, 263
Picturegoer, 302
Pinero, Sir Arthur Wing,
    284, 350
Pinter, Harold, 78, 288, 324
Plummer, Christopher, 172
Point Valaine, 268, 318-319,
    385
Pomp and Circumstance, 38,
    81, 165
Pons, Lily, 311
Porter, Cole, 5, 53-54, 89,
    99-100, 102-103, 274,
    276-277
Portrait of a Lady in Park
    Avenue, 388
Potter, Beatrix, 313
Powell, Michael and
    Pressburger, Emeric, 76
Preminger, Otto 381
Present Indicative, 45, 47,
    86, 93, 140, 190, 210
Present Laughter, 49, 116,
    126, 128, 147, 210, 216,
    251, 263, 265, 267, 270-
    271, 279, 287-288, 329,
    356-358, 363-365, 382,
    388
Pretty Polly Barlow, 107
Pretty Polly, 107
Price, Dennis, 362
Price, Stanley, 314
Priestley, J.B., 321
Prince and the Showgirl, The,
    172

Prisoner, The, 219
Private Lives, 23, 26, 47, 49-
    50, 53, 79, 89, 101, 138,
    150, 165, 173, 175, 187,
    202-203, 228-230, 238,
    258, 261-263, 265, 267,
    278-279, 288, 292, 300,
    318, 380-381
Producer and the Play, The,
    305
Prout, Ebenezer, 310
Punch, 63, 174
Pygmalion, 106, 384

Quadrille, 79, 157-158, 214,
    385-386
Quaker Girl, The, 308
Queen Mother, Elizabeth
    (formerly Duchess of
    York), 136-138, 154, 204,
    213, 239, 256, 280-281
Queen Mother, Mary, 136
Quilley, Denis, 177

Rank, J. Arthur, 62
Rattigan, Terence (later Sir),
    134, 171, 222, 287, 323,
    377
Read, Hope, 269
Red Peppers, 50, 55, 319-320
Red Shoes, The, 76
Redgrave, Lynn, 176, 253,
    259-261, 303
Redgrave, Michael (later
    Sir), 63, 106, 162, 239
Reed, Carol, 301
Rehearsal Period, 385
Reinhardt, Max, 268
Reith, Lord, 134
Relative Values, 31, 69, 79,
    146, 231, 293, 295, 299,
    357, 359, 364
Remembered Laughter, 216,
    258
Richardson, Ralph (later
    Sir), 239
Ritchard, Cyril, 25, 28-29,
    34-37, 281
Ritz Bar, 5
Rodgers and Hammerstein,
    57, 105, 167, 215
Rodgers and Hart, 26
Rodgers, Richard, 57, 102,
    105, 238, 312
Romberg, Sigmund, 71

Romeo and Juliet, 173, 294
Roose-Evans, James, 173
Roosevelt, President Franklin
    D., 131-132, 187
Roots, 324
Rose Marie, 71, 119
Rothermere, Lady Ann (later
    Fleming), 157, 188, 200-
    201
Rothermere, Lord, 200, 337
Rubens, Paul, 308
Runyon, Damon, 61
Russell, Rosalind, 165
Rutherford, Margaret, 28,
    221, 294, 360

"Sail Away," 62
Sail Away, 165, 167-169,
    171, 174, 218, 233, 278,
    286, 369
Sally, 59
Salute to the Brave, 315
Scarlet Lady, 39, 106, 263
Scarlet Pimpernel, The, 348
Scott, George C., 298
*Scoundrel, The (Miracle on
    49th Street)*, 225, 269,
    300, 385
Seagull, The, 295
Searle, Alan, 138
Second Man, The, 272, 384
Sellers, Peter, 82-83
Selznick, Irene, 146, 203
Semi-Monde, 5, 268, 314-
    315
Set to Music, 4, 92-93, 96,
    230-231
Shadow Play, 46, 50, 57, 78,
    321
Shadows of the Evening, 237
Shakespeare, William, 12,
    89, 91, 220-221, 284,
    294, 325, 331, 338
Shaw, George Bernard, 91,
    203, 287, 322, 350, 353
Shaw, Glen Byam, 180
Shearer, Norma, 300
Shephard's Pie, 25
Shephard, Firth, 18-20, 25-
    26
Sherek, Henry, 265
Sheriff, R.C., 222-223
Show Boat, 39
Shuberts, The, 22, 143
Shuffle Along, 59

Shulman, Milton, 63
Side By Side By Sondheim,
    241
"Sigh No More," 105, 225
Sigh No More, 24, 29, 31,
    33-37, 45, 188-189, 214,
    222, 225, 238, 258
Simenon, Georges, 89
Simon, Neil, 250, 268
Simple Spymen, 325
Simpson, Mrs. Wallis, 134
Sinatra, Frank, 119-120
Sinclair, Hugh, 298
Sinden, Donald, 298
Sirocco, 140-141, 285, 299
Sitting Pretty, 18, 116
Sleeping Prince, The, 171-
    172
Smith, Maggie (later Dame),
    176, 178, 203, 232, 242,
    259, 262, 279
Snowdon, Lord, 150
"Somewhere A Voice Is
    Calling," 10
Sondheim, Stephen, 61, 101
Song at Twilight, A, 139,
    179, 237, 240
South Pacific, 44, 167
South Sea Bubble, 38, 81,
    125, 145, 235, 262
Spencer, Marian, 158
St. Helier, Ivy, 2, 52
Stage, The, 290
Standing, John, 203, 259,
    262
Stanislavski, Constantine,
    329-331
Star Chamber, 319-320
Star Quality, 314
Star!, 250
Stephens, Robert, 176, 242,
    259
Stevens, Marti, 165, 177
Stewart, Robb, 99, 361
Still Life, 50, 263, 320
Stop Flirting, 23
"Story of Peter Pan, The,"
    94-96
Stritch, Elaine, 167, 169,
    171
Stuart, Leslie, 308
Suite in Three Keys, 139,
    146, 160, 179-180, 237,
    239, 268

Sunday Dispatch, The, 81
Sunday Express, The, 77, 315
Sunday Graphic, The, 62
Sunday Times, The, 44, 79,
    286, 322, 337, 343
Sunset Boulevard, 225
Surprise Package, 164
Susan and God, 49
Sutherland, Dame Joan,
    195-196, 205
Swan Song, 385
Sweet Aloes, 219
Sweet Sorrow, 263

Tabori, George, 82
Tails Up, 94
"Take a Pair of Sparkling
    Eyes," 308
Tales of Hoffman, 76
Tales of the South Pacific, 167
"Tamarind," 103
Tandy, Jessica, 238
Taste of Honey, A, 324
Tatler, The, 29, 80
Taylor, Laurette, 262-263
Taylor, Elizabeth, 196, 238,
    261-262, 267
Taylor, Pat, 27
Tempest, Dame Marie, 257,
    262
Terry-Thomas, 68
Thalberg, Irving, 300
"That Is The End Of The
    News," 36
Thatcher, Margaret, 115
*Theatrical Companion to
    Coward, The*, 314
"There Have Been Songs in
    England," 85
"There is a Green Hill Far
    Away," 370
"There Will Always Be," 100
"Think Pink," 66
Third Man, The, 106
"This Can't Be Love," 25-26,
    105
This Happy Breed, 125-126,
    128, 222, 284, 317, 329,
    357-358, 363-364, 367,
    388
"This Is A Changing
    World," 31, 168
"This Is A Night For
    Lovers," 168

"This Seems To Be The Moment," 215
This Year of Grace, 23, 183, 230, 311
Thompson, Carlos, 180-181, 286
Thompson, Kay, 64-66, 167, 174, 191, 369
Thomson, Lord Roy, 145, 148
Thorndike, Dame Sybil, 28, 162, 319
Tickner, Martin, 314
Tilney, Sir John, 280
Time Remembered, 314-317
Times, The, 47, 139, 164, 249, 272, 336-337, 349
"Tit Willow," 308
Titheradge, Madge, 12, 263
Titus Andronicus, 234
Toad of Toad Hall, 28
Todd, Mike, 110
Together with Music, 44, 120-121
Tonight at 8:30, 24, 46, 48-51, 53-55, 63, 179, 197, 216-217, 226-227, 263, 300, 319-320
Topper, 24, 215
Tough at the Top, 310
Tree, Sir Herbert, 298, 350
Tree, Viola, 140
Tribune, 77, 81
Trinder, Tommy, 50
Trollope, Anthony, 90
Turner, Ted, 265
Twelfth Night, 89
Tynan, Kenneth, 12, 70, 78-79, 175, 183, 246, 251, 253, 325, 335, 388

Ullmann, Liv, 262
Unsinkable Molly Brown, The, 174
Up and Doing, 25-26, 28-29
Upstairs Downstairs, 272

Variety, 120
Vedrenne and Eadie, 350
Verdon, Gwen, 174
Volcano, 314, 318-319
Vortex, The, 5, 40, 53, 78, 87, 157, 219, 252, 274, 284, 292, 295, 302, 315, 339, 374, 378, 387

"Wait a Bit, Joe," 33, 37, 189
Waiting in the Wings, 146, 161-164, 237-238, 320
Walker, Nancy, 263
Walston, Catherine, 201, 203
War and Peace, 384
Warhol, Andy, 253
Washington, Dinah, 3
Watch It, Sailor, 325
Watch on the Rhine, 358
Waters, Elsie and Doris, 10
Waters, Jan, 177
Waugh, Evelyn, 150
We Were Dancing, 38
"We'll Gather Lilacs," 382
"We're Very Wide Awake, the Moon and I," 308
Webb, Clifton, 5, 116, 216, 252
Webb, Mabelle, 117
Webber, Andrew Lloyd, 279
Webster, Margaret, 162
Welles, Orson, 266
"Weren't We Fools?", 102
Wesker, Arnold, 79
West Side Story, 61, 172
West, Dame Rebecca, 188
Western Brothers, The, 10
Westminster, Loelia, Duchess of, 150
"What Am I to Do?", 276-277
"What Mad Pursuit," 317
"What's Going to Happen to the Children (When There Aren't Any More Grown-Ups?)", 66
"When I Have Fears," 49, 209, 244, 280
"When You Come Home on Leave," 93-94
Where the Rainbow Ends, 13, 28
Whistler, James, 250
"White Christmas," 99
White Ensign, 153
"White Tie and Tails," 28
Who's Who, 190
Wilde, Oscar, 5, 71, 76-77, 89, 171, 250-251, 284
Wilding, Michael, 82, 179-180, 219, 265

Williams, Michael, 314
Williams, Tennessee, 268
Wilson, John C. (Jack), 50, 53-56, 81, 144, 146-147, 189-191, 202, 214, 216-218, 247-248, 264-265, 270, 318
Wilson, Natasha, 55, 157, 199, 202, 216-217, 271
Wilson, Sandy, 142
Wilton, Robb, 18
Wind in the Willows, The, 28
Windsor, Edward, Duke of Windsor (formerly King Edward VIII), 134-136, 150
Winwood, Estelle, 59, 228
Wisdom, Norman, 238
Wiseman, Joseph, 200
Withered Nosegay, A, 212
Wodehouse, P.G., 138, 387
Wolfit, Sir Donald, 180, 380
Woodward, Edward, 175
Woollcott, Alexander, 159, 300
Words and Music, 1-2, 4, 6, 12, 14, 23-24, 31, 222, 230-231, 292, 303
Worth, Irene, 179
Would-Be-Goods, The, 243

York, Duchess of - see Queen Mother, Elizabeth
York, Susannah, 314
Yorks, The, 136, 162
"You Were Meant For Me," 23
Youmans, Vincent, 312
Young Idea, The, 293
Young, B.A., 283

Ziegfeld Follies, 59, 321
Ziegfeld, Florenz, 22, 59